The Liberal Consensus Reconsidered

UNIVERSITY PRESS OF FLORIDA

Florida A&M University, Tallahassee
Florida Atlantic University, Boca Raton
Florida Gulf Coast University, Ft. Myers
Florida International University, Miami
Florida State University, Tallahassee
New College of Florida, Sarasota
University of Central Florida, Orlando
University of Florida, Gainesville
University of North Florida, Jacksonville
University of South Florida, Tampa
University of West Florida, Pensacola

The Liberal Consensus Reconsidered

American Politics and Society in the Postwar Era

Edited by Robert Mason and Iwan Morgan

University Press of Florida
Gainesville · Tallahassee · Tampa · Boca Raton
Pensacola · Orlando · Miami · Jacksonville · Ft. Myers · Sarasota

Published in the United States of America

This book may be available in an electronic edition.

First cloth printing, 2017
First paperback printing, 2019

24 23 22 21 20 19 6 5 4 3 2 1

Library of Congress Cataloging-in-Publication Data
Names: Mason, Robert, 1970– editor. | Morgan, Iwan W., editor.
Title: The liberal consensus reconsidered : American politics and society in the postwar era / edited by Robert Mason and Iwan Morgan.
Description: Gainesville : University Press of Florida, 2017. | Includes bibliographical references and index.
Identifiers: LCCN 2016055640 | ISBN 9780813054261 (cloth)
ISBN 9780813064444 (pbk.)
Subjects: LCSH: United States—Politics and government—1945–1953. | United States—Politics and government—1953–1961. | United States—Politics and government—1961–1963. | Liberalism—United States—History—20th century.
Classification: LCC E813 .L53 2017 | DDC 320.510973—dc23
LC record available at https://lccn.loc.gov/2016055640

The University Press of Florida is the scholarly publishing agency for the State University System of Florida, comprising Florida A&M University, Florida Atlantic University, Florida Gulf Coast University, Florida International University, Florida State University, New College of Florida, University of Central Florida, University of Florida, University of North Florida, University of South Florida, and University of West Florida.

University Press of Florida
2046 NE Waldo Road
Suite 2100
Gainesville, FL 32609
http://upress.ufl.edu

Contents

Acknowledgments

The editors are happy to acknowledge the financial assistance that this project received from University College London's Commonwealth Fund, as well as the help of colleagues in London and in Edinburgh. We are grateful, too, to all the contributors for the generosity of their engagement in the project. It has been our good fortune to have the chance to work with the University Press of Florida, and we are eager to express our thanks, too, to Meredith Babb, Sian Hunter, and their colleagues for their assistance and support, together with the press's anonymous reviewers for their thoughtful and thought-provoking comments.

Introduction

Reconsidering the Liberal Consensus

ROBERT MASON AND IWAN MORGAN

Journalist-scholar Godfrey Hodgson's book *America in Our Time* won immediate recognition from scholars and other analysts as a major interpretive study of the postwar era when published in 1976. Though intended for a wider readership than the academy, it found a particularly warm reception from historians seeking to understand what made the political characteristics of this period distinctively different from those of the Depression era and the post-liberal era taking shape in the 1970s. Hodgson's greatest contribution to historiography lay in positing the existence of a "liberal consensus" that gave cohesion and direction to public policy, party politics, and political debate. "Confident to the verge of complacency about the perfectibility of American society, anxious to the point of paranoia about the threat of communism—those were the two faces of the consensus mood," he commented.[1] That thesis served as a reference point for much ensuing historical scholarship on the 1950s and early 1960s in particular. It also informed the work of many scholars seeking to explain the roots of the social and political turbulence that the United States experienced in the later part of the 1960s. As testimony to its importance, Hodgson's book was reissued by Princeton University Press in 2005 and has continued to influence a new generation of scholars in the early twenty-first century.[2]

Although the term "liberal consensus," or its approximation, had received some previous expression, Hodgson was responsible for its entry into the lexicon of American history. No one else had defined it with such precision for application by many survey texts of postwar history and a goodly number of specialist studies of the period. "Significantly," historian

Willian Chafe later observed, "each axiom of the liberal consensus that Hodgson described had far-reaching import for what could or could not be considered an option within American political discourse; moreover, each axiom so thoroughly informed the others that none could be isolated or considered separately from the others."[3]

For Hodgson, the liberal consensus was a substantive phenomenon rather than a mere mood or reaction to events. He summarized the interrelated assumptions that gave it reality, intellectual vitality, and cohesion:

1. The American free-enterprise system is different from the old capitalism. It is democratic. It creates abundance. It has a revolutionary potential for social justice.
2. The key to this potential is production: specifically, increased production or economic growth. This makes it possible to meet people's needs out of incremental resources. Social conflict over resources between classes (which Marx called "the locomotive of history") therefore becomes obsolete and unnecessary.
3. Thus there is a natural harmony of interests in society. American society is getting more equal. It is in process of abolishing, may even have abolished, social class. Capitalists are being superseded by managers. The workers are becoming members of the middle class.
4. Social problems can be solved like industrial problems: The problem is first identified; programs are designed to solve it, by government enlightened by social science; money and other resources—such as trained people—are then applied to the problem as "inputs"; the outputs are predictable: the problem will be solved.
5. The main threat to this beneficent system comes from the deluded adherents of Marxism. The United States and its allies, the Free World, must therefore expect a prolonged struggle against communism.
6. Quite apart from the threat of communism, it is the duty and destiny of the United States to bring the good tidings of the free-enterprise system to the rest of the world.[4]

According to Hodgson, the impact of these shared assumptions was significant. "For some seven years after 1955," he wrote, "few fundamental disagreements, foreign or domestic, were aired in either presidential or Congressional politics." Differences involved detail, not America's larger goals.[5]

Despite widespread scholarly reference to the "liberal consensus," as defined above, there has been no significant effort to reconsider Hodgson's paradigm in light of the huge quantity of new scholarship that has appeared since its initial publication. This volume, published four decades after the original issue of *America in Our Time*, brings together fresh insights by historians about American society and politics in the period examined by Hodgson's classic work.

The book that appeared in 1976 was inescapably a product of its time in its assumptions. As a number of contributors to this volume indicate, the notion of the "liberal consensus" was very much the preserve of a white, male, straight elite. As such it did not conform to the bottom-up history then gaining ascendancy in the academy in the wake of the upheavals of the 1960s. This new approach emphasized class, gender, ethnicity, and race as sources of division in every epoch of American political history, including the postwar period. *America in Our Time* also appeared some twenty years before the scholarly discovery of conservatism as an ascendant tradition in America history rather than the paranoid and peripheral aberration it appeared to the political and intellectual actors caught up in the shaping of a supposed "liberal consensus."[6] The massive outpouring of literature that has found evidence of a significant conservative presence at the grassroots level from the 1930s to the 1960s—not only among activists but also in the corridors of political and economic power at state and local levels—might appear to call into question the existence of a liberal ascendancy, let alone a liberal consensus, in the heyday of the New Deal–influenced political order.

Inevitably, therefore, the "liberal consensus" paradigm has been controversial as well as influential over time, but it cannot be ignored. It has certainly not gone the way of ideas that once constituted scholarly orthodoxy but were discarded as new knowledge and research revealed their limitations. In his essay for this volume, Godfrey Hodgson acknowledges that, even at the time of writing, "I was well aware that this was a schematic and over-simplified idea. Forty years' experience and reflection have taught me how much more complicated the historical process was." In particular, he recognizes how the African American freedom struggle necessarily challenged the parameters of the liberal consensus and ultimately contributed to its decline. Nevertheless, the contributions to this volume underline the ongoing utility of the "liberal consensus." Even the authors who question its validity recognize it as a concept that requires robust engagement to justify their dissenting position. While there may be no agreement among our group as to its existence, it is still possible to discern some important themes that emerge from this volume about the characteristics of postwar American history in regard to Hodgson's original statement of the "liberal consensus."

It must be recognized that Hodgson never regarded the "liberal consensus" as a catchall descriptor of the American polity in the postwar era. True, he conceptualized it as "the operational creed of a great nation at the height of its power," but it was evident that "nation" in this context was predominantly synonymous with the corporate, political, and academic-intellectual establishment of the Northeast.[7] The outlook of this elite was shaped by the spectacular recovery of America's economy and the triumph of its military power in World War II. The roots of this "dominant American ideology" lay in "a simple yet startling empirical discovery," according to Hodgson: "Capitalism, after all, seemed to work."[8] In contrast to the crisis years of the Great Depression, it now appeared that American business enterprise had entered a golden era of success that could bring abundance to all strata of society. The emergence of the United States from global war at the historic peak of its relative international preeminence also fueled optimism about the country's limitless future. The establishment identified by Hodgson consequently had unbounded confidence about what America's government could achieve at home and abroad through the application of its resources of prosperity, power, and knowledge to solve all problems.

In this context, the "liberal consensus" paradigm was never intended to signify the absence of political dispute—whether on specific policy details at the elite level or, more broadly, criticism of its fundamental precepts by dissenting groups outside the establishment. Moreover, Hodgson was careful to emphasize that the "liberal consensus" was basically centrist rather than avowedly liberal: "It was born of a fusion of certain elements from both liberal and conservative tradition. Specifically, it came into existence . . . when most conservatives came to accept some of the economic and domestic polices of Rooseveltian liberalism, while many liberals adopted a foreign policy whose major premise was the kind of anticommunism that had once been the mark of conservatives."[9] Fully aware of the limitations of the elite-based liberal consensus as a progressive force, he commented: "A strange hybrid, liberal conservatism blanketed the scene and muffled debate."[10]

The contributions to this volume by Iwan Morgan on economic policy, David Stebenne on welfare policy, and Andrew Preston on foreign policy—in essence the trio of domains that constituted the core of consensus—further support that proposition and its inherently limited notion of consensus. The variety of Keynesianism that emerged after World War II was a business-friendly doctrine that acknowledged the need for government to prevent another depression and facilitate expansion of prosperity without engaging in excessive statism and redistribution of wealth. The social welfare consensus envisaged a very limited welfare state in comparison to those of Western Europe and was far from being universally accepted by groups outside the establishment. There was consensus that the Soviet Union represented a threat to American security and the values of the "Free World"—but there was no "Cold War consensus" in the 1950s and 1960s over how the United States should deal with this menace.

More broadly, Gary Gerstle argues that acceptance of a strong federal state defined the reach and boundaries of the liberal consensus. In his assessment, there was political agreement in the postwar era about its need with regard to political economy and national security, but not to matters of race, religion, and sexuality. In essence, most Democrats, Republicans, and business leaders accepted the necessity for a dynamic national government capable of waging the Cold War, resolving economic and socioeconomic problems, and financing its extensive operations through preservation of the World War II system of taxation. However, there was never consensus over federal efforts to nationalize the Bill of Rights at the expense of the traditional powers of the state over police matters pertaining to equality, morality, and standards for a good life within their own borders.

Hodgson's thesis also raised questions about the duration of the liberal consensus. He was precise in locating its peak years as extending from 1955 to 1963, essentially from the downfall of Senator Joseph McCarthy to the assassination of John F. Kennedy. Many of the contributors to this volume offer a more diverse chronological framework for engaging with it. For Wendy Wall, establishment promotion of consensus was very much a product of Depression-era experience. According to Iwan Morgan, the Keynesian consensus that underpinned the liberal consensus stretched from the passage of the Employment Act of 1946 to the Vietnam-era inflation two decades later. In Andrew Preston's assessment, the Cold War consensus (which he distinguishes from the liberal consensus) was a short-lived phenomenon stretching just from 1946 to 1949, in effect from initial recognition that the wartime alliance with the Soviet Union was dead to the Chinese Revolution that signaled the extension of the struggle with communism to Asia. None of this necessarily discredits Hodgson's peak-era thesis, but it does widen the terms of debate over his paradigm beyond a consideration of the extent to which consensus existed. In particular, the divergent notions of the historical takeoff of consensus point to the importance of its origins for understanding of this phenomenon. As Wendy Wall notes in her essay, "historians and others should ask why so many American elites [in the postwar era] chose to emphasize political agreement and to what ends they deployed the rhetoric of consensus." This consideration raises larger questions about the utility and robustness of periodization in informing historical analysis.

Of course, some contributors to this volume dispute the fundamental existence of the liberal consensus. From the first, Hodgson's thesis faced criticism for its exclusion of the concerns of African Americans and women.[11] What is surprising, therefore, is that the two chapters in this volume dealing with these particular groups offer a distinctly nuanced assessment of their relationship to it. George Lewis contrasts the 1963 March on Washington with its 1983 commemoration event held in the anti-statist Reagan era. In the former, a succession of civil rights activists decried the assumptions of the liberal consensus about the resolution of racial problems; in the latter, African American leaders and their supporters called on government to reengage with the postwar commitment to expanding employment opportunities and improving living standards for all Americans. Helen Laville begins her chapter with an understatement: "It would be fair to say that gender is not a central concern of Godfrey Hodgson's account of the era of liberal consensus." Yet her review of how middle-class women sought to modify gender roles within its framework concludes that their effort was intended not as a critique of its operating principles but as a way of supporting and strengthening them.

Other contributors suggest that the principal challenges to the liberal consensus occurred at the intersection of ideology, class, and region. Elizabeth Tandy Shermer's study of the parallel rise of Barry Goldwater and Lyndon Johnson reveals that the emergent and development-hungry Sunbelt of the Southwest and South stood outside the liberal consensus framed by the northeastern establishment. Indeed, her chapter signifies that the corporate elite of the so-called Steelbelt was less than unified in support of its core principles, as manifested by the efforts of some business leaders to employ inward investment and political contributions as a means to ensure that the Sunbelt remained an oasis of anti–New Dealism from the 1930s to the 1960s. In contrast, Jonathan Bell's study of California Democrats suggests that welfare liberalism in the Golden State in the 1950s reframed social assumptions of citizenship rights in opposition to the corporate-led notions of economic citizenship inherent in the liberal consensus.

Both Shermer and Bell identify labor-capital conflict, notably over right-to-work issues, as a fundamental antithesis to the notion that these two groups were engaged in a prosperity-induced accord throughout the nation.[12] For Robert Mason, too, at the heart of Eisenhower's "middle way" politics was a project to promote labor-management consensus in place of the strife that was so perturbing to contemporary Republicanism. According to Shermer, in the Sunbelt, at least, there was no harmony of interests tying labor and business into the consensual framework identified by Hodgson. Alex Goodall similarly questions the existence of a liberal consensus in the domain of internal security in the wake of Joseph McCarthy's eclipse. In his assessment, domestic anticommunism remained a force in national politics that would fuel the eventual emergence of the conservative movement. Significantly, he also demonstrates how court-curbing campaigns against judicial liberalism in this field united southern elites and segments of the corporate community in defense of states' rights that preserved Jim Crow and right-to-work laws.

Even the Cold War's contribution to the liberal consensus appears to have been more complex than suggested in Hodgson's original construct. As Goodall demonstrates, it did not involve a simple dichotomy of anticommunism abroad and anti-McCarthyism at home. Andrew Preston similarly challenges any assumption of a "Cold War consensus" beyond the 1946–49 period. Certainly, there was almost universal recognition that communism as represented by the Soviet Union and its allies constituted an existential threat to the American-led Free World. That said, there was hardly consensus over the means to deal with it, particularly with regard to the use of force. Bipartisanship in foreign policy also became a fragile entity after 1949. Republican accusations that the Democrats had lost China and by implication Asia in that "year of shocks" found their echo in the wake of *Sputnik* in Democratic charges that Eisenhower's parsimony was undermining America's security—reproaches also voiced, albeit in different ways, by the president's critics on the conservative and liberal wings of his own party. The rhetoric of consensus was wholly absent, for example, from Senator John F. Kennedy's missile-gap allegations that defined the issue facing America as being "which gamble . . . we take, our money or our survival."[13]

Even those contributors who identify the existence of a liberal consensus of sorts follow Hodgson in adjudging that it contained the seeds of its own destruction—most notably in the misguided belief that America's problems could be resolved on its own terms. For Hodgson, the assumptions that underpinned the liberal consensus "happened to be diametrically wrong."[14] These errors eventually resulted in military failure abroad and dissensus at home. However, the eclipse of the liberal consensus cannot simply be explained in three words: *Vietnam*, *stagflation*, and *backlash*. There were broader forces at work that gave rise to a newly confident conservatism promoted by corporate leaders, Sunbelt boosters, and religious activists. With regard to the last, Uta Balbier demonstrates how Billy Graham and like-minded clerics did much to move conservative evangelicalism into the political and religious mainstream through their appropriation of core elements of the liberal consensus, notably, anticommunism, patriotism, and consumerism. This enabled them to lay the conservative ecumenical groundwork for the rise of the Religious Right in the 1970s.

It is something of a historical orthodoxy—albeit not a universal one—that America turned right in the late 1960s and has continued in this direction ever since. What is less open to dispute is that political conflict became more evident and overt than it had been in the era of liberal consensus identified by Hodgson. Viewed from the early twenty-first century, which is likely to be seen by future historians as an era of considerable polarization, the politics of this early period appears very different in tenor to those of America in our time. If dissensus were hardly in abeyance, it was sufficiently contained to avoid the excesses of gridlock that characterized Washington, DC, during Barack Obama's presidency.

Of course, it should be borne in mind that contemporaries did not usually speak of a liberal consensus—or indeed any other kind—during the period that Hodgson wrote about, even if sociologist Daniel Bell declared the "end of ideology" in 1960. What can appear as consensus (or conflict) to a later generation was seen by some at the time as a lowest-common-denominator approach to domestic policy in a political system dominated by electoral coalitions. In 1950 the American Political Science Association issued a report calling for a "more responsible" two-party system that offered genuinely different public-policy alternatives for the electorate to decide upon. A decade and a half later, the eminent scholar James MacGregor Burns lamented "the deadlock of democracy" created by what he termed a four-party system composed of change-oriented "presidential" Democrats and "presidential" Republicans in control of the White House and status-quo-oriented "congressional" Democrats and "congressional" Republicans in control of the legislature. While Burns employed the idea of consensus to describe the political process, he used the term quite differently from Hodgson's "ideology of the liberal consensus" to observe that the imperative for "government by consensus and coalition" within his four-party system was an impediment to the action-oriented agenda he saw as necessary.[15]

It is doubtful that these earlier analysts would have recognized the liberal consensus as the "operational creed" driving postwar politics. Nevertheless, it is equally possible when looking back at this period to perceive a historically unique phenomenon that merits scholarly attention. Though fully aware of the complacency, delusions, and arrogance of the elitist assumptions underpinning the liberal consensus concerning the U.S. government's capacity to solve all its problems at home and abroad, Hodgson sees some cause for regret at its passing. With this, "there disappeared that sense of a common project: that a democratic society could use the power of government to correct its own failings and to make life better." Disputes and divisions there may have been within the broad American polity, but this was still a time when important elements of the corporate community and both political parties were in agreement that government should proactively and constructively address public-policy issues of national significance. If this was not an era of liberal consensus in the absolute sense, it was arguably so within the constrained terms outlined by Hodgson.

The contributors to this volume seek to explain why this was the case, what were the limits of agreement on the role of the state and what were the areas of disagreement over it, and why the liberal consensus, however defined, eventually fell apart. The first four chapters provide an overview of the liberal consensus. Godfrey Hodgson reevaluates his paradigmatic idea forty years on; Michael Heale assesses its historiographical influence in the intervening years; Gary Gerstle considers the role and boundaries of the strong federal state as key to understanding the liberal consensus; and Wendy Wall traces the roots of this phenomenon to the Depression era through examination of leading proponents of the postwar ideal of national purpose.

The next five chapters consider the liberal consensus idea in relation to key policy areas. Iwan Morgan explores its connection with the Keynesian ascendancy; David Stebenne examines the extent to which there was consensus on social welfare; Alex Goodall demonstrates the continuation of McCarthy-era political disputes over internal security during the supposed heyday of the liberal consensus; Andrew Preston reviews the "liberal consensus"/"Cold War consensus" dichotomy in arguing for the need to look beyond the near-universal agreement that Soviet communism was a menace; and Elizabeth Tandy Shermer disputes the applicability of Hodgson's concept to the emerging Sunbelt that was fundamentally anti-statist in outlook after World War II.

Two chapters then consider the partisan dimensions of the liberal consensus. Robert Mason demonstrates that the Republican right was constantly at odds with Dwight Eisenhower's "middle way" politics that aimed to promote social harmony in place of the tumult of the New Deal era; and Jonathan Bell shows the challenge of the Democratic left to consensus in the 1950s through a case study of California. The final essays reveal how different groups in American society related to the liberal consensus. Uta Balbier explores how Billy Graham appropriated conservative elements of the liberal consensus to mobilize evangelicals despite the opposition of other evangelical leaders to such adaptation; Helen Laville assesses how women campaigned to ensure that the conceptual masculinization of the public sphere of politics did not result in their exclusion from political life in the era of consensus; and lastly, George Lewis explores the positive historical memory that African Americans constructed of the liberal consensus from the vantage of Reagan's America.

Lewis's chapter raises important issues of historical remembrance about an era now far more distant than when Hodgson wrote about it in 1976. Those who read this volume will have the opportunity to decide whether they agree with Hodgson's ultimate assessment of postwar America in the era of the liberal consensus: "It was a time of false complacency and of hubristic and dangerous illusions. The promise was flawed from the beginning. America has paid a price, but she has done well to be rid of the assumptions of 1960."[16]

Notes

1. Godfrey Hodgson, *America in Our Time* (Garden City, NY: Doubleday, 1976), 75. All references are to this issue of the volume, which was published under a somewhat different title in the United Kingdom, namely, *In Our Time: America from World War II to Nixon* (London: Macmillan, 1977).

2. Godfrey Hodgson, *America in Our Time: From World War II to Nixon—What Happened and Why* (Princeton: Princeton University Press, 2005).

3. William Chafe, introduction, in Chafe, ed., *The Achievements of American Liberalism: The New Deal and Its Legacies* (New York: Columbia University Press, 2003), xi.

4. Hodgson, *America in Our Time*, 76.

5. Ibid., 72.

6. Arguably, the seminal influence on this development, which also drew inspiration from the revitalization of political history in the wake of the Reagan era, was Alan Brinkley's essay "The Problem of American Conservatism," *American Historical Review* 99 (1994): 409–29. For a discussion of its significance, see Julian Zelizer, "Rethinking the History of American Conservatism," *Reviews in American History* 38 (2010): 367–92.

7. Hodgson, *America in Our Time*, 492.

8. Ibid., 76.

9. Ibid., 491.

10. Ibid., 73.

11. Hodgson also faced criticism for implying "the absence in this country of a strong, vigorous left that could have offered an alternative to the consensus policies." See Richard R. Lingeman, "The End of Consensus," *New York Times*, February 5, 1977, 10. Other reviewers finding similar fault were Webster Schott, "The Star-Tangled Banner," *Washington Post*, November 7, 1976, 75; James T. Patterson in *New York History* 59 (1978): 91–92; and Alonzo L. Hamby in *American Historical Review* 82 (1977): 774–75. Rather more sympathetically, Garry Wills commented: "[Hodgson] sees the end of liberalism; and he knows this is not a failure *of* the left, but a failure to *have* a left." See "Carter and the End of Liberalism," *New York Review of Books*, May 12, 1977.

12. For a discussion of the labor-management entente in the traditional manufacturing heartland, see Robert Collins, *More: The Politics of Economic Growth in Postwar America* (New York: Oxford University Press, 2000), 23–24.

13. Quoted in *New York Times*, March 1, 1960, 4.

14. Hodgson, *America in Our Time*, 97.

15. Daniel Bell, *The End of Ideology: On the Exhaustion of Political Ideas in the Fifties* (1960; Cambridge: Harvard University Press, 2000); "Toward a More Responsible Two-Party System: A Report of the Committee on Political Parties," *American Political Science Review* 44 (September 1950), part 2 (supplement); James MacGregor Burns, *The Deadlock of Democracy: Four-Party Politics in America* (Englewood Cliffs, NJ: Prentice Hall, 1963) (quotation on 7). Writing recently to challenge the "deadlock of democracy" perspective on "the long 1950s," political scientist David R. Mayhew instead characterizes the period as "enormously busy and consequential in policy terms"—featuring "a family of interrelated policy goals involving the economy, aiming for growth, development, efficiency, and productivity." Mayhew, "The Long 1950s as a Policy Era," in Jeffery A. Jenkins and Sidney M. Milkis, eds., *The Politics of Major Policy Reform in Postwar America* (New York: Cambridge University Press, 2014), 28.

16. Hodgson, *America in Our Time*, 16.

1

Revisiting the Liberal Consensus

GODFREY HODGSON

Forty years ago, in my book *America in Our Time*, I suggested that for a certain period after the coming of the Cold War and the domestic anticommunism of the immediate postwar years, the prevailing public philosophy in the United States was what I called the "liberal consensus." Other writers had used this phrase before.[1] I used it to describe what I conceived as a gigantic, unspoken deal between liberals and conservatives. Liberals, in part because of "McCarthyism" and because of a genuine fear of international communism, accepted an essentially conservative anticommunist foreign policy. Conservatives, in part because of the general perception that conservative Republicans in general and Herbert Hoover in particular bore much of the responsibility for the Depression, accepted, albeit grudgingly, important elements of the "liberal" New Deal domestic philosophy.

Even in the mid-1970s, of course, I was well aware that this was a schematic and oversimplified idea. Forty years' experience and reflection have taught me how much more complicated the historical process was. Still, I believe the idea helps us to understand important aspects of American history in that critical period. I think it will be useful, first, to restate the original thesis, and then to ask two questions: Why did the idea of a liberal consensus fade away? And does it matter today that the liberal consensus is no more?

Two qualifications. First, the word *liberal* is notoriously treacherous. Its use has been confused by the fact that it originally described ideas and individuals that rejected traditional monarchical, aristocratic, and hierarchical values and institutions. So, in Europe liberals were those (many of them members of a new class of capitalist entrepreneurs and their admirers) who emphasized freedom from these traditional constraints.[2] In the United

States, where monarchy had been abolished, aristocrats had no political privileges, and religion was specifically excluded from political discourse by the Constitution, liberalism of that kind had no place. So in Europe liberalism lived in a middle position, between traditional Tory conservatism and the evolving forms of socialism. It was natural for it to be nicknamed "Manchester liberalism," after the nineteenth-century British politicians who opposed Toryism but feared socialism. To this day, of course, in every Western European language, the equivalent of "liberal" describes a position distinctly to the right of the left. In America, that kind of liberalism was not so necessary. So the word came to be used as a kind of euphemism for "left," or as a less alarming synonym for social democracy.[3] In the early twentieth century the word *progressive* was used by many people who would later have been called liberals. The Liberal Party of New York was founded in 1944 as an explicitly anticommunist party by a group that included the religious philosopher Reinhold Niebuhr. For many years it endorsed liberal Republicans, such as John Lindsay (U.S. congressman and later mayor of New York) and Charles Goodell (U.S. congressman and, briefly, U.S. senator), as well as Democrats.

I should also dispose of a second misunderstanding. The liberal consensus was not in itself a "liberal" idea. Certainly numerous liberal intellectuals, most notably Arthur Schlesinger Jr. in *The Vital Center*, stressed that liberal domestic policies were by no means incompatible with anticommunism.[4] In like fashion, Daniel Bell perceived an intellectual consensus in the 1950s whose dual foundations were the fear of the communist threat from abroad and the conviction that America's problems at home were all capable of resolution without provoking the kind of animosities faced by previous reform movements.[5] On the other side of the ideological divide, however, two archconservatives of that generation accepted consensus, if perhaps for tactical reasons. After Barry Goldwater's landslide defeat in the 1964 presidential election, Frank Meyer, chief ideologist of William F. Buckley's *National Review*, argued that conservatives could no longer openly seek to repeal the New Deal, as they had done since the 1930s. Most Americans, he wrote, would now interpret a move to abolish programs like Social Security as "a radical tearing down of established institutions . . . it has to be made very clear that conservatives by their nature proceed in all changes with caution."[6] And Richard Nixon's conservative economic mentor, Arthur Burns, wrote, "It is no longer a matter of serious controversy whether the government shall play a positive role in helping to maintain a high level of economic activity."[7]

In the mid-1950s it became fashionable to say that the age of ideology was over. I was by no means the only one to point out that this idea was in itself a new, American ideology, none other than the ideology of the liberal consensus. It was, I went on to say, "[c]onfident to the verge of complacency about the perfectibility of American society, anxious to the point of paranoia about the threat of communism."[8] I then promulgated six interrelated assumptions underlying the consensus, which can be summarized as follows (see the Introduction for the full text): postwar American capitalism can generate abundance for all; its capacity to do so derives from the endless potential for economic growth; this creates a natural harmony of interests by promoting a more equal society; it also furnishes the resources for government to resolve social problems; the main threat to this beneficent system comes from communism, against which America and its allies must engage in prolonged struggle; America's destiny is to spread the message of the benefits of capitalism to the rest of the world.

"A state of sociological hygiene," I wrote of the 1950s American consensus, "could be attained as directly, as *technologically*, as the U.S. Army public-health people, in war-time Naples, had abolished typhus and malaria. The poor could be sprayed with money, and the enemy sprayed with lead, it was assumed, just as efficiently as the Italians had been sprayed with DDT. . . . Poverty and communism would become extinct, like typhus."[9] Pushing the same analogy, I went on to point out that, just as DDT turned out to be a carcinogen, so over the next decade or so many of the assumptions of the liberal consensus turned out to be wrong, or superseded, or dangerous; they were challenged, and they disappeared, or at least went underground into a limbo of those popular delusions that influence politics, even after the elite that formulated them no longer believes in them.

Quite separately, at about the same time I was pursuing the idea of an American foreign-policy establishment. Its instinct, I wrote, was for the center, "steering the middle course between the ignorant yahoos of the Right and the impractical sentimentality of the Left."[10] Later I realized that, if the focus of the liberal consensus was wider than that of the foreign-policy establishment, their core membership overlapped, close to the point of identity. Both were disproportionately recruited from white people living in the Northeast, educated at Harvard, Yale, or Princeton; many were occupied as bankers, lawyers, academics, or foundation officials, or as politicians, journalists, or publicists of one sort or another.

Although one of the characteristics of the new free-enterprise society was supposed to be growing equality and the obsolescence of class divisions, the liberal consensus does not seem to have grown spontaneously from popular emotions. It was in fact closely identified with an elite. Specifically, it was formulated and fostered by the new, or newly ambitious, foundations, themselves in the most important cases literally the heirs of the great industrial fortunes of the late nineteenth and early twentieth centuries, Rockefeller, Ford, and Carnegie.[11] With a generosity and a high-mindedness that put the attitudes of most of the European super-rich to shame, but also with a shrewd eye to their own higher self-interest, scions of these families and an elite recruited from their friends and peers promoted a public philosophy. They were disproportionately educated at the aforementioned Ivy League universities, and indeed at a handful of New England boarding schools. The foundations poured money into studies of the state of the nation and the world. Subsequently, the utility of such institutions for disseminating ideas was recognized by the antagonists of the liberal consensus. A different stamp of wealthy individuals founded conservative institutions like the Heritage Foundation or the American Enterprise Institute. But the early great foundations, in spite of their historical association with capitalism, were predominantly, if moderately, liberal.

Nelson Rockefeller was almost an embodiment of the liberal consensus.[12] He contributed to thinking about both foreign and domestic policy. He worked first for Franklin Roosevelt's New Deal, then for the Eisenhower administration, before becoming the philosopher-king of a kind as governor of the Empire State. He combined firm and unquestioning anticommunism with liberal attitudes to domestic policy. He presided over the Eisenhower administration's Special Studies Project, set up in 1956 and published as the *Prospect for America* in November 1960, the very month John Kennedy was elected president. Among those who labored in that vineyard were future Kennedy-Johnson secretary of state Dean Rusk, formerly head of the Rockefeller Foundation; Rockefeller protégé Henry Kissinger, later national security adviser to President Richard Nixon and secretary of state under both Nixon and Gerald R. Ford; Edward Teller, the father of the hydrogen bomb; Roswell Gilpatric, soon to become Robert McNamara's deputy at the Pentagon; not to mention Henry Luce, proprietor of *Time*, *Life*, and *Fortune*.[13]

Those with a taste for prosopography can have a field day tracing the interconnections among the philanthropic elite.[14] Ben Whitaker, for example, pointed out that "over half of the trustees of the thirteen largest American foundations attended Harvard, Yale or Princeton. The most salient characteristics of this group were that they were white Episcopalian or Presbyterian males, who were between 55 and 65 years of age and who served on the boards of several foundations concurrently." They constituted, said Whitaker (a British Labour member of Parliament for Hampstead, a London suburb long associated with affluent radicalism), "a wholly unrepresentative influence and one which supports the established traditions of the power elite."[15]

The philanthropic elite was intimately entwined with the political and business elites. Of the top officials of the Rockefeller Foundation, for example, John Foster Dulles, Dean Rusk, and Cyrus Vance became secretaries of state. John J. McCloy was assistant secretary of war in World War II, the first American high commissioner in Germany thereafter, president of the World Bank, chairman of the (Rockefeller-influenced) Chase Manhattan Bank, and a trustee of the Rockefeller Foundation. McGeorge Bundy was dean of Harvard College, national security adviser to Presidents Kennedy and Johnson, and president of the Ford Foundation. Robert S. McNamara, secretary of defense under Presidents Kennedy and Johnson, was president of the Ford Motor Company before going into government and president of the World Bank afterward. I could go on; indeed, many people have done so.

Nelson Rockefeller was not alone. His brother David Rockefeller, whose main career was as chair of the Chase Manhattan Bank, was also the president of the Carnegie Endowment for World Peace. The Rockefeller brothers (who had their own foundation, the Rockefeller Brothers Fund, one of the ten biggest) were only the wealthiest of a whole elite who sat on the boards of foundations.

The foundations were intimately bound up with a wide range of "citizen committees," characteristic of the age of the liberal consensus, which studied and proposed remedies for various aspects of American society. They were especially concerned with the Cold War itself, and with aspects of the military contest with the Soviet Union, and only secondarily with how such matters as education, scientific research, and "leadership" (a favorite topic for a group who saw themselves as natural leaders) affected the competitive performance of the United States in the context of the Cold War. Indeed, it is striking how much the Kennedy administration, largely recruited from the establishment, at first saw the civil rights problem as a foreign-policy issue: it was embarrassing, and an opportunity for Soviet propaganda, if non-white diplomats of newly emergent nations could not stay at motels in Maryland en route from New York to Washington.

The influence of the foreign-policy establishment and of the interconnected elite of international bankers, international lawyers, relatively liberal business executives, and centrist academics was older than the liberal consensus. Its origins can be traced back to the progressive movement of the last years of the nineteenth century and the early years of the twentieth. Its influence was potent in the Inquiry, the collection of scholars brought together by Colonel House to advise Woodrow Wilson before the peace negotiations in Paris, and specifically in the origins of the Council on Foreign Relations, whose membership largely coincides with that of the foreign-policy establishment.[16] Indeed, before World War II the foreign-policy elite saw its task as being to resist isolationism, and its victory in that dispute was sealed by the Japanese attack at Pearl Harbor. The foreign-policy elite was overwhelmingly recruited from the East, with the exception of a few midwestern industrialists like Paul Hoffman of Studebaker and the Marshall Plan, Charles Percy of Bell and Howell and later Illinois GOP senator, and J. Irwin Miller of Cummins Inc., makers of diesel engines.[17]

The earliest of these citizen committee reports was the "War-Peace Project," funded from 1939 onward by a series of munificent grants to the Council on Foreign Relations to plan for the peace. The recommendations of this project were, first, that the United State must guarantee access to raw materials and markets to safeguard the expansion of the American economy and national security; second, that America's prosperity depended on corporate expansion, which in turn depended on raising living standards in Europe and the rest of the world; and, third, that these goals could only be assured in a stable, non-communist world.[18]

This was followed by the Report of the Study for the Ford Foundation on Policy and Programs, chaired by H. Rowan Gaither, delivered to Henry Ford in November 1949; the Special Studies Project set up by Nelson Rockefeller and paid for by the Rockefeller Brothers Fund in 1956, in which the young Henry Kissinger played a key role; and the second "Gaither report," on survival in the nuclear age, given to the Department of Defense in November 1957 and later published as *Deterrence and Survival.*

This was not the only way in which the big foundations influenced foreign policy. The Harvard seminar, for example, which made Henry Kissinger's reputation, was founded under the influence of William Yancey Elliott and with the help of a grant of $15,000 from the CIA. It became the forum at which a number of men who were to become influential foreign statesmen were recruited to follow the main lines of American policy. They included Denis Healey, often said to have been the ablest politician never to be prime minister of Great Britain; Helmut Schmidt, later chancellor of West Germany; Valéry Giscard d'Estaing, future president of France; and many others. The Salzburg seminar, founded by Klemens Heller and two other Harvard graduate students, and also supported by the Ford Foundation and by CIA, was another outgrowth of the foundation system.

The ability of wealthy men to pay for research projects, the institutional support of permanent foundations devoted to policy formulation, and the bringing together in various committees of like-minded individuals to promote their recommendations all helped to disseminate the ideas and values of a particular elite. Those values were the essential principles of the liberal consensus. In his scholarly analysis of the Carnegie, Ford, and Rockefeller foundations, Edward Berman categorized them as "class institutions." While the beneficial effects of their programs "must be applauded," he concluded that "the foundations are clearly part of the American ruling class"—part of that class division which the liberal consensus claimed to have been abolished. "Their vast wealth," he went on, "enables them to articulate programs, set certain agendas, and shape the world order in a manner consistent with the interests of the few associated with them. Much of their work is carried out by carefully chosen and subsidized individuals, who elaborate ideologies supportive of the existing social, economic and political order."[19]

One does not have to share all Berman's negative conclusions to agree that, insofar as it was fashioned and promoted by the foundations, the liberal consensus was indeed the working ideology of enlightened American capitalism. It reflected the American upper class's fear of extremism of both left and right, its optimism, and its instinct for nonconfrontational, and therefore nonpolitical, solutions to the problems of America and the world: indeed, one might add, its reservations about electoral politics.

A second potent force in spreading the assumptions and ideals of the liberal consensus was the new, national press of the time. I am not aware of any formal academic study of this phenomenon, but as one who worked as a journalist in the United States in the 1960s and 1970s, including a period of several years in the newsroom of the *Washington Post*, I am convinced that this is so.[20] The journalists of that generation, and especially the editorial page writers, shared many of the attitudes of the liberal consensus. Many of them worshipped John F. Kennedy, whose own policy positions often echoed those of the consensus.

For the greater part of the nineteenth century, the main medium disseminating news about politics and (often in the same breath) commenting on politics was the newspaper press. In all sizable cities, two or more managements, often clearly identified with the Republican or Democratic Party, then competed. Readers received plural, often highly partisan views of what was happening. Even the "muckraker" episode in the late nineteenth century was essentially nonpartisan, as it was supported by progressives from both major parties.[21] After the midpoint of the twentieth century, most major newspaper groups were becoming monopolies. They had a vested interested in appearing centrist. They rejected communism, but they also kept their pages clean of any contamination from the far right, such as the John Birch Society, provoking conservatives to accuse them of bias in favor of the center. Regardless of rightist denunciations, the *New York Times*, *Washington Post*, and *Los Angeles Times* actually followed the centrist line of the liberal consensus and in those days sedulously eschewed any hint of left-wing bias. So on the whole did the then influential news magazines.[22]

The television networks, whose influence grew rapidly in this period, were theoretically bound to party neutrality by the regulator, and in practice, from their own commercial interest in maximizing audiences, strove not to be seen as *parti pris*.[23] Before the coming of CNN, based in Atlanta, and Fox News, part of a corporation based in Los Angeles, American television news reflected the ethos of the New York liberal capitalism of its neighbors in midtown Manhattan. All three networks, ABC, CBS, and NBC, had their head offices within a few blocks of each other on Sixth Avenue, close to the headquarters of the Rockefeller empire in the West Fifties, Time-Life Inc., the great foundations, and such pillars of consensual thought as the Council on Foreign Relations, the *New York Times*, and major publishers—and indeed to the various places of refreshment where upper-middle-class New Yorkers liked to forgather and those who labored downtown would meet them in the evening. In a word, the liberal consensus projected the values and the interests of an elite based in New York, Boston, and Washington that emphasized anticommunism abroad and an optimistic, melioristic version of capitalism at home.

A third and equally potent force was the great universities themselves. They had become used to receiving very substantial subsidies from the federal government not only for research into scientific and engineering problems relevant to the defense and space industries but also for research and publication in social science, humanities, and politics. While independence of mind flourished and was proudly defended in most great universities, the pressures to conform to the extent of following a centrist path and avoiding extremism and speculative flights were strong enough to favor the consensus.

Why Did the Liberal Consensus Come to an End?

One obvious reason for the relative decline of the liberal consensus was the *relative* decline of the eastern establishment, of the universities that nourished it, the cities where it nested, and the industries that supplied its wealth. The rise of California and Texas, in particular, of new universities, new schools of thought, new industries, new media, did not destroy the influence of Harvard, the wealth of Wall Street, or the power of the networks and the *New York Times*: but old centers of power and influence encountered new competition from Stanford and Chicago, from CNN and Fox, and from Texas oil and Silicon Valley that diluted traditional monopolies.

More important, the persuasiveness of the liberal consensus waned because of flaws in its own assumptions, flaws that were exposed by many of the social and political changes of the new age, not least by the two cataclysmic events of that period, the Vietnam War and the civil rights movement.

The liberal consensus was essentially the product of American primacy as a result of World War I, and even more of American domination after World War II. In the Cold War the United States remained dominant, challenged only by the Soviet Union, but it was no longer invulnerable. This explains a strange combination of self-confidence and self-doubt. The first allowed bold acts of wisdom, such as the Marshall Plan. The second explained the anticommunist paranoia of red-baiting and McCarthyism. Very gradually it became plain that the Soviet challenge was more apparent than real. The idea of a missile gap, derived in part from the lucubrations of the deterrence and survival committees, and used by John F. Kennedy, with more than a dash of cynicism, to win the presidential election of 1960,was exposed as a myth. Ironically, it was Kennedy himself who exploded it, through the mouth of his Pentagon official Roswell Gilpatric, when it became necessary to call Nikita Khrushchev's bluff at the height of the 1961 Berlin crisis. Nevertheless, it was not until Mikhail Gorbachev's time in the 1980s that the weakness of the Soviet economy and the limitations of Soviet military power were generally acknowledged. Before that, the Vietnam War had exposed the limitations of American power. To be sure, the

U.S. defense budget approximated and eventually exceeded the military expenditure of all the other nations on Earth put together. But in terms of effective power, much of this crippling burden of spending was wasted.

The United States, for example, once paid for fifteen and even sixteen carrier battle groups, at fabulous expense: at time of writing they have been renamed carrier strike groups and reduced in number to eleven. No more than at most two or three of these at a time were used in war: their function has been to project political and imperial power. Nuclear and thermonuclear bombs, again, have consumed vast sums, year by year, for well over half a century, though the evolving calculus of deterrence means that the value of those expenditures could be measured only in terms of the value gained by not using them.

No doubt it can be argued that these prodigious expenditures brought the world peace. No doubt, too, their almost unlimited cost has contributed to the ending of the effortless domination the United States had enjoyed in the few years after World War II. One consequence of the ruinous nuclear standoff was that the Soviet leadership abandoned any project it might have had of invading Western Europe and set out to strangle the capitalist world by supporting local struggles in the developing world, which Moscow called "wars of national liberation." The Vietnam War was one such war, and there were others, in different guises, in several parts of Africa, in Central America, in Malaysia, the Philippines, and Indonesia, and in the Middle East. In some cases the United States was ultimately successful in containing communist expansion through conflicts of this kind, in others not. But strategically in the Cold War the United States silently abandoned its traditional opposition to imperialism, frequently preferring to ally itself with anticommunists, such as the French empire and later a French-oriented elite in Indochina, and with anticommunist, as opposed to anticolonial, forces in Latin America and the Middle East, rather than with emerging nationalism.

By the late 1950s, however, the economic dominance of the United States was already being challenged by the emerging economies of Western Europe and the Far East. American military and foreign-aid expenditures contributed to the difficulty of sustaining the fixed value of the dollar in relationship to the price of gold as agreed at the Bretton Woods Conference of 1944, which put at risk its status as global reserve currency and the consequent benefits of that U.S. global influence. These international factors contributed to a general challenging within the United States of several of the underlying assumptions of the liberal consensus.

The belief that American capitalism was a revolutionary force capable of generating abundance for every stratum of society was a fundamental pillar of this operational creed. Its adherents assumed that the incremental resources generated by a rapidly and endlessly growing economy would alleviate and then abolish all domestic problems without necessity for hard choices. By the 1960s such conviction had been called into question. If one of the premises of the consensus had been that American capitalism would continue to produce surpluses enough to pay for both invincible military strength and ever-increasing domestic prosperity for all, the experience of the 1970s and subsequent decades destroyed that premise. In the 1950s, economic growth was faster in some European countries, including France and Italy, than in the United States. Later, growth in Japan, South Korea, and ultimately China was even more dramatic, ridiculing the idea that the American way was the only path to expansion. Indeed, by the early 1970s the average incomes of American workers had all but ceased to rise. Economic growth continued, intermittently on a spectacular scale but more often at a level well below what was achieved during the long postwar boom. However, its product did not go to industrial workers or to the lower deciles of the economic ladder: it went overwhelmingly to a small category of owners, especially inheritors, of assets, and to a tiny percentage of very wealthy individuals, such as actors, sports stars, and a highly visible but numerically modest group of innovators and speculators.[24]

It had also been assumed, in the heyday of the consensus, that social problems in America were residual and could be "cured" by the action of government and nongovernmental organizations, informed by the new and essentially American social science. The founding fathers of social science like Karl Marx, Auguste Comte, Sigmund Freud, Max Weber, and Émile Durkheim were European. Their latter-day American counterparts, more reportorial and policy-oriented in outlook, as the Chicago school exemplified, were confident that the secrets of social transformation were in their grasp. In the 1960s, however, it began to appear that the problems of American society, notably the greatest and most intractable one, that of racial justice, might be immune to medication with expenditure.

It was not just that economic growth did not generate the money that would be needed to carry out fundamental social change. Except for the briefest of periods, government was not able to levy taxes on the scale that would be necessary. Political leaders soon gave up even trying to raise money on the requisite scale, because there was no adequate popular or democratic support for any such policies. On the contrary, from the beginning of the 1970s on, and culminating in the tax rebellion of Proposition 13 in California in 1978, there was a growing reluctance to pay taxes. We shall pay any price, John Kennedy had proclaimed, to assure the survival of freedom. He did not say "we shall pay any taxes."

Worse: the problems of racial justice, and other projects for equality between whites and blacks, men and women, simply did not seem to respond to the familiar methodology of identifying a problem and bombarding it with financial and human resources. So far from being easily curable in this way, the prosperous foundation donors and trustees, and the lawyers and academics of the eastern and western megapolises found that the profound underlying inequalities and injustices in American society could not be alleviated in the way they had confidently imagined. Instead their solution was dependent on America itself undergoing fundamental change.

A case in point, one of many, was the New York teachers' strike of 1968.[25] It resulted from the sacking of a Jewish teacher, Fred Nauman, by the local school board in Ocean Hill–Brownsville, a Brooklyn neighborhood once overwhelmingly Jewish but now half African American. To the citizens of that neighborhood, it appeared that Jewish teachers were being fired by black politicians. In 1963 Daniel Patrick Moynihan and Nathan Glazer had described New York as divided into five ethno-cultural tribes: Irish, Italians, Puerto Ricans, Jews, and African Americans. After the teachers' strike they admitted that "race had trumped religion" and that the only meaningful division was now between whites and blacks. But there was another dimension to the conflict. The devolution of power over schools to local school boards, intended to empower African Americans, did not come out of the black communities themselves. It was proposed by the Ford Foundation, led by one archetypal patrician, McGeorge Bundy, and adopted by the city under the leadership of another, Mayor John Lindsay.[26] The episode is only one of the best known of many that demonstrate how the WASP foundation elite misunderstood the realities of American society and how stubbornly it would resist liberal meliorism.

Worst of all, as I pointed out in my original 1976 book, they were discovering the social equivalent of Werner Heisenberg's uncertainty principle. "They had assumed," I wrote, "that they could study the world with objectivity. They had also assumed that they could change it by exerting money, or force, or both, with surgical dispassion, without themselves being changed. They found that can't be done"—from the Mississippi Delta to the Mekong Delta.[27] I might have added: the South Bronx, Detroit, and South Central Los Angeles.

As for the imminent disappearance of social class in American society, the proposition would be laughable were it not still so proudly avowed in some quarters. Inequality, so far from vanishing, is generally agreed to be more acute in the early twenty-first century than at any other time since the 1920s. The whole political system is now almost as structured in terms of class as in European countries. Before the mid-1960s it could be said that the two great political parties were not divided by ideology or class.[28] In those days I myself, if asked by a non-American what the basis of the parties' difference was, used to say that it was about things that had happened in the 1860s. Now it can be said that it is about things that happened in the 1960s.

Many historical developments and discoveries contributed to this change. The most important, perhaps, was the civil rights movement, and in particular the Voting Rights Act of 1965. After that, southern conservatives disappeared from the Democratic Party, which they had once ruled, while liberal Republicans disappeared from the Republican Party, in which they were once intellectually influential. As conservatives came to dominate the Republican Party, and African Americans overwhelmingly and women and Hispanics in substantial majorities voted for Democrats, who were relatively liberal, America now had a European-style ideological party system. Now haves confronted have-nots, led by a minority of haves. Consensus, liberal or otherwise, was now nowhere to be seen, and least of all on Capitol Hill.

More generally, in the mid-1970s the political weather changed all over the Western world. This shift, from the "thirty glorious years" of the social-democratic age to a more or less moderate conservative ascendancy, reflected many currents of thought and feeling. Everywhere the business class, for a start, having chafed impatiently at government interference and high taxation for decades, felt strong enough to reassert its interests, partly because with rising incomes it had been able to recruit enough allies from groups who no longer felt the need for government protection. Once economic growth no longer offered the luxury of avoiding the agonies of choice, government became less trusted and less respected, and more and more politicians were willing to entrust more decisions to the power of that equivocal savior, the market. There was disillusion with the failure of social-democratic institutions and policies to meet expectations. The liberal consensus died, as institutions often do, at the hands of a coalition between old enemies and the newly disillusioned.

Does It Matter That the Liberal Consensus Is No More?

My personal attitude to the liberal consensus was always divided. On the one hand, in the 1950s it appeared enviable that the American political world agreed about so many fundamental assumptions and goals, and was therefore not so blocked as British and European politics by ideological schism. On the other hand, even in the 1950s it was obvious that the consensus ignored many of the realities of American society. In the 1960s, under the hammer blows of racial upheaval and war in Vietnam, it was clear that many of its fundamental premises must be abandoned. Moreover, it became plain that the liberal consensus was essentially the credo of an elite. Political events on the left and right, from the rebellions by African Americans and feminists to the populist insurrections of George Wallace and the new conservatives, refuted comfortable assumptions of the liberal elite. It had been tempting to believe that inequality and injustice could be easily expunged by expertise and expenditure. But if, as it now appeared, the American people as a whole were not sure they wanted to commit themselves to that enterprise, consensus was problematic.

To the extent that the liberal consensus was the unrealistic ideology of an elite who had not taken much trouble to find support for their dreaming, we need not mourn its passing.

Yet something, surely, has been lost.

The liberal consensus, for one thing, was consciously a protection against extremism of left and right. It was insurgencies on the left that first rejected its centrist compromises. The reaction from the right was even stronger than the "alternative" vision of the 1960s and made possible the new conservatism, however. The decline of the liberal consensus also reflected a wider arousal of the "unyoung, the unpoor and the unblack," as Richard Scammon and Ben Wattenberg famously called the new majority.[29] As John Updike put it, for white American males in general, and for many women and non-whites as well, "the Vietnam era was no sunny picnic."[30] For them, Ronald Reagan's salute to "morning in America," the past dressed up as the future, was seductive.

It is not, I think, only the timid, the reactionary or the passionless who regret the ending of the "middle way." For along with its compromises, complacency, and smugness, there went a sense of the possible and an admirable ambition to do good. Along with the consensus, there disappeared that sense of a common project: that a democratic society could use the power of government to correct its own failings and to make life better.

To be sure, when it came to make life better for the inhabitants of other nations, who had not been consulted about their wishes, the foreign policy of the consensus, generous in its intentions, carried the seeds of its own dissolution. One reads with a stab of incredulity that John Kennedy said, in his great American University speech in the summer of 1963, that "the United States, as the world knows, will never start a war." Leaving aside the casuistry of pretext, the world now knows that the United States is all too likely to start a war every few years.

It is the domestic wing of the consensus that is most keenly missed. Since its passing there has been a sense of stasis. For many years now, American politics have been jammed. It is not just that even the most plainly necessary reforms require Herculean efforts with no certainty of success. The health system is a striking example. It costs twice as much as health care does anywhere else, yet delivers a miserable performance, simply because universal access is not guaranteed. But health care is not the only instance. In Congress, and for that matter in state legislatures too, extreme partisanship makes the most modest progress painfully hard. The very idea of an administration achieving the massive reforms the Johnson administration accomplished in 1964–66, in civil rights, health care, education, and immigration reform, has been unimaginable for decades. To be sure, the Johnson legislative triumphs were short-lived: today even a fraction of them would be inconceivable. They were victims of those same great forces—the disaster of the Vietnam War and the reaction to the racial revolution—that ended the liberal consensus itself.

In the age of the conservative ascendancy, it is not as if a new consensus has arrived. The country is bitterly divided, hardly between conservatism and liberalism—fewer than one in five now choose to call themselves liberals—but between Red and Blue. An irresolute moderation resists an ever more intransigent conservatism. The *res publica*, the public thing, drifts, like a Mississippi barge whose skipper is drunk at the wheel, toward the mud, its passengers cheerily confident that shale gas or something else will come to their rescue. At such a time, the liberal consensus, with all its failings and limitations, inspires a certain nostalgia.

Notes

1. For example, John Higham, who attacked the concept from the left. John Higham, "Beyond Consensus: The Historian as Moral Critic," *American Historical Review* 67 (1962): 609–26.

2. The use of the word "liberal" to denote a political party, *los liberales*, originated in Spain in 1812, though many of their ideas were drawn from the French Revolution and from the English Whig tradition.

3. Doug Rossinow, in his helpful *Visions of Progress: The Left-Liberal Tradition in America* (Philadelphia: University of Pennsylvania Press, 2009), distinguishes between left-radicals and liberal progressives.

4. Arthur M. Schlesinger Jr., *The Vital Center: The Politics of Freedom* (Boston: Houghton Mifflin, 1949).

5. Daniel Bell, *The End of Ideology: On the Exhaustion of Political Ideas in the Fifties*, rev. ed. (New York: Collier, 1961).

6. Frank S. Meyer, "What's Next for Conservatism?" *National Review*, December 1, 1964, 1057. For further discussion, see Geoffrey M. Kabaservice, *Rule and Ruin: The Downfall of Moderation and the Destruction of the Republican Party, from Eisenhower to the Tea Party* (New York: Oxford University Press), 135.

7. Godfrey Hodgson, *America in Our Time* (New York: Doubleday, 1976), 72.

8. Ibid., 75.

9. Ibid., 464–65.

10. Ibid., 120, but see also Godfrey Hodgson, "The Establishment," *Foreign Policy* 10 (Spring 1973): 3–40, an earlier and fuller treatment of the same ideas. I was encouraged to write the article by Richard Holbrooke, recently retired from the U.S. Foreign Service, and later to play an important part in American diplomacy during the Carter, Clinton, and Obama administrations until his sudden death in 2010.

11. See Edward H. Berman, *The Ideology of Philanthropy: The Influence of the Rockefeller, Ford and Carnegie Foundations on American Foreign Policy* (Albany: State University of New York Press, 1984). Other interesting treatments of the same subject are to be found in Joel L. Fleishman, *The Foundation: A Great American Secret—How Private Wealth Is Changing the World* (New York: PublicAffairs, 2007), which is largely uncritical; Inderjeet Parmar, *Foundations of the American Century: The Ford, Carnegie, and Rockefeller Foundations in the Rise of American Power* (New York: Columbia University Press, 2012), a sophisticated account, focusing on the role of the foundations in relation to foreign policy; and Warren Weaver, *U.S. Philanthropic Foundations: Their History, Structure, Management, and Record* (New York: Harper & Row, 1967), which emphasizes the varied contributions of the three big foundations, such as funding psychiatry in American medicine, promoting the Green Revolution and the Grameen Bank, and encouraging noncommercial television in the United States.

12. Richard Norton Smith, *On His Own Terms: A Life of Nelson Rockefeller* (New York: Random House, 2014).

13. John Andrew III, "Cracks in the Consensus: The Rockefeller Brothers Fund Special Studies Project and Eisenhower's America," *Presidential Studies Quarterly* 28 (1998): 535–52.

14. Prosopography is the historical study of groups and their interconnections and, in intelligence, the enemy's order of battle.

15. Ben Whitaker, *The Foundations: An Anatomy of Philanthropic Societies*, rev. ed. (New York: Penguin, 1979).

16. Godfrey Hodgson, *Woodrow Wilson's Right Hand: The Life of Colonel Edward M.*

House (New Haven: Yale University Press, 2006); Lawrence E. Gelfand, *The Inquiry: American Preparations for Peace, 1917–1919* (New Haven: Yale University Press, 1963). The Inquiry was even more dominated by men from Harvard, Yale, and Princeton than the members of the Rockefeller committees.

17. A Yale graduate and heir to a family firm, Miller and his wife left more than $600 million when they died. They had brought many of the greatest figures of modern architecture and art to ornament their small hometown of Columbus, Indiana. Miller was active in founding the National Council of Churches, which eventually proved too liberal for many of its membership.

18. Berman, *Ideology of Philanthropy*, 1–2.

19. Ibid., 162, 176.

20. I was not employed by the *Washington Post*, but as the Washington correspondent of the *London Observer* I was allowed to have a desk in the *Post* newsroom.

21. Although newspaper exposés appeared earlier, the boom in "muckraking" by investigative journalists like Lincoln Steffens, Ida May Tarbell, and Ray Stannard Baker was associated with magazines, beginning with *McClure's* in 1903 and spreading to the *American Magazine* and many others. It petered out within a few years.

22. *Time*, though favoring Republicans, was stoutly "internationalist" in foreign questions. *Newsweek* (though owned by billionaires, first an Astor, then the Meyer clan) was perceived as mildly liberal. Only David Lawrence's *US News and World Report* was openly conservative, its struggling place in the market making it the exception that proved the rule.

23. The adventurous documentaries of Edward R. Murrow and others are the exception that proves the rule: they encountered fierce criticism and were feebly defended by management.

24. The point has been demonstrated over the years by the successive studies of the Institute for Economic Policy and was made widely known by the success of Thomas Piketty, *Capital in the Twenty-First Century*, trans. Arthur Goldhammer (Cambridge: Belknap Press of Harvard University Press, 2014).

25. An excellent account is Jerald Podair, *The Strike That Changed New York: Blacks, Whites, and the Ocean Hill–Brownsville Crisis* (New Haven: Yale University Press, 2002).

26. Bundy and Lindsay feature in a classic study of the WASP elite, Geoffrey M. Kabaservice, *The Guardians: Kingman Brewster, His Circle, and the Rise of the Liberal Establishment* (New York: Henry Holt, 2004).

27. Hodgson, *America in Our Time*, 465.

28. In 1963, Robert Kennedy insisted to me that the United States was so divided—ethnically, racially, and by geographical sections—that it could not afford to be divided horizontally by class as well. In fact, the process by which the two great political parties did indeed essentially represent haves and have-nots was already under way as he spoke.

29. Richard M. Scammon and Ben J. Wattenberg, *The Real Majority* (New York: Coward-McCann, 1970).

30. John Updike, *Self-Consciousness: Memoirs* (New York: Knopf, 1989).

2

Historians and the Postwar Liberal Consensus

MICHAEL HEALE

The concept of a postwar liberal consensus, most fully articulated by Godfrey Hodgson in 1976, has enjoyed remarkable buoyancy over the last several decades. It is one of those terms that scholars have befriended, frequently employing it either in support or criticism, and it has become thoroughly embedded in academic and pedagogical literature. The "liberal consensus"—or some close variant—has become a standard title for textbook chapters, course handouts, blog discussions, and not least for those model essays that helpful agencies write for students.[1] Few studies in American history that examine the years on either side of 1960 can safely sidestep consensus liberalism. The success of the term, of course, owes much to the clarity and persuasiveness with which Hodgson advanced his argument, as it also owes something to its pithy invocation of key features of the period.

Once it was detached from its original moorings, the concept of a liberal consensus drifted widely across the literature, a testimony to the potential of its insights. It was frequently employed to characterize the fifteen or twenty years after 1945, although Hodgson himself clearly located it in the briefer era 1955–63, after the U.S. economy had demonstrated its miraculous potential and McCarthyite repression had been disavowed.[2] Further, Hodgson had focused primarily on political economy, although some scholars applied his ideas more widely, such as to foreign policy, about which Hodgson had said little beyond the conditioning role of anticommunism and the influence of the "foreign-policy establishment," and to cultural and artistic history.[3]

The concept also risked getting entangled with other theses that made use of consensual ideas. A substantial scholarship developed on the "Cold War consensus" that arguably emerged in the United States as the relationship with the Soviet Union took on a truly alarming aspect.[4] Specialists in foreign affairs and international relations wrote extensively on the bipartisan accord that could be found in U.S. foreign policy, but as Andrew Preston explains in this volume, it is questionable whether much was really consensual on this front. In another kind of scholarship, as discussed later, such terms as the "postwar social contract" were applied to those modern societies, including the United States, that sought to resolve class conflict by institutionalizing industrial relations and establishing a welfare state. Yet, while there are common elements, these formulations are not identical with the almost utopian vision that mesmerized the people Hodgson discusses, a vision that has exerted a distinctive influence of its own in historical literature.

The idea of a liberal consensus was the more readily accepted because it was congruent with other understandings of American history and society at the time. Among its intellectual roots was consensus history, the view that the American past is best thought of in terms of a pervasive "liberal" tradition and a common adherence to fundamental principles, a view that minimized domestic divisions. By the time Hodgson published his book, consensus history was in bruised retreat, but there was a case that the celebrated "end of ideology" was at least a postwar phenomenon. By the Eisenhower era the political convulsions of the New Deal years were safely in the past and the Cold War was encouraging Americans to close ranks against a foreign enemy. The very writing of consensus history was arguably evidence of some kind of intellectual or sociopolitical consensus in early Cold War America.

At about the same time, another group of scholars eager to learn from the behavioral sciences was advancing forms of American history that focused on organizations and systems. A so-called organizational synthesis examined large-scale bureaucratic transformations that caught up those within them, whether in politics, business, the military, or elsewhere. These studies often addressed a multitude of competing forces, but the very objective of a "search for order" was to replace a perceived disorder, to provide a turbulent society with stabilizing institutions. Consensus history might not be explicitly endorsed in this scholarship, but in projecting an urban-industrial society increasingly dominated by large bureaucracies characterized by impersonal rules and mechanisms for resolving conflict, the organizational synthesis offered an explanation for the allegedly conformist society of postwar America. These large bureaucratic organizations may sometimes be in conflict, accepted one scholar, "but they nevertheless shared certain modes of orientation, certain values, and certain institutionally defined roles."[5] In short, sociological studies seemed to provide some kind of evidential basis for the notion of a postwar social consensus.[6]

Accommodation was also a theme of broader studies of advanced industrial societies that identified an informal "social contract" in the postwar era. Modern governments, it was held, ensured the peace of their societies by promoting cooperation between capital and labor and by promising full employment, decent wages, and a reasonable welfare state.[7] In the United States this scholarship overlapped with that of labor historians discussing a new "civilized relationship" or "labor-capital accord" between management and unions.[8] The regulated bargaining system that had evolved since the New Deal, in this view, meant that in exchange for higher wages and fringe benefits employers could expect stability on the shop floor; labor arguably substituted consumerism and home ownership for the class struggle that had long been a central feature of American industrial relations. This served to explain the apparent absence of serious class conflict in the years around 1960, conveniently typifying the "liberal consensus."

The notion of a liberal consensus also chimed with contemporary literature about the American character. Americans were regularly told that theirs was an affluent society bereft of ideology and personified by "the organization man," a conformist society in which suburbs were increasingly spreading their bland homogeneity. The liberal consensus as formulated by Hodgson did not depend on popular sociology of this kind, but it seemed to offer some corroboration. So too did demographic studies, particularly those focused on the family. The 1950s arguably saw the heyday of the American family; by mid-decade more Americans were marrying than ever before and at younger ages, and these young people were having more children than their parents' generation. Endorsing and promoting this embrace of family life was a popular culture celebrating domesticity and a traditional family structure, reinforcing the notion of the home as a refuge from Cold War anxieties.[9] A stable family life seemed congruent with images of a placid society, one in which consensual values might take root. Treatments of American religious life also stressed elements of commonality. Will Herberg wrote of the shared values of the country's three major religions, and Robert N. Bellah identified a "well-institutionalized civil religion" reflected in "the common beliefs of ordinary Americans."[10]

Although a host of thoughtful historical, sociological, intellectual, and other studies functioned as buttresses of the idea of a liberal consensus, what immensely added to the appeal of Hodgson's thesis was its alignment with New Left history. By the mid-1970s, New Left historians were busily dismantling consensus history, even though some of its architects were hardly more admiring of the American past than the New Left revisionists. In a sense, Hodgson's version of the liberal consensus represented a merger of consensus with New Left history. Hodgson was clear that he was talking about ideology, not social reality, a fact that was not always grasped by his critics. He was as incisive as any New Left scholar in detailing the deep class and racial fissures disfiguring Cold War America.

Hodgson acknowledged that the ideology of the liberal consensus was "the creation of an elite," a "liberal elite" that controlled "enough of the expanding, powerful institutions of society to be without effective check or balance," and whose precepts were "more or less widely accepted by ordinary people."[11] He reasserts this position strongly in his essay in this volume, specifically arguing that the ideology was "formulated and fostered by the new, or newly ambitious, foundations," Rockefeller, Ford, and Carnegie, which is to say that it was "the working ideology of enlightened American capitalism." It was a liberal conservatism stretching from the anticommunist liberals of Americans for Democratic Action to the corporate liberals of Wall Street. Leading intellectuals explicated the reports of the major foundations. Authoritatively projected by sympathetic national newspapers and television networks, the acceptance of this ideology by the public apparently rested largely on the elite's prestige and powers of persuasion. This formulation of an ideological hegemony was almost Gramscian, as it was also strongly evocative of the New Left's Marxist guru, C. Wright Mills, and his analysis of a "Power Elite," with its interlocking relationships among the personnel atop of the major institutions of American society. Hodgson was not exactly invoking *la trahison des clercs*, but he noted how by the 1950s the great universities had been drawn into the ambience of the state, with its need for Cold War research in the social and natural sciences. The New Left scholars of the 1970s would have little trouble with this formulation, and there has been an extensive literature on the degree to which modern intellectuals, with their dependence on universities and foundation grants, have become more the agents than the critics of the power structure.[12]

The liberal consensus, then, was an illusion, a kind of false consciousness, a contrived consensus, wittingly or perhaps especially unwittingly manufactured by the elites.[13] Hodgson's stress on its faulty assumptions did nothing to dissuade other authors from appropriating the concept. The very cogency of Hodgson's argument, combined with the pedagogical appeal of its headline phrase and flanked by a mass of scholarship in related fields that served as corroboration, ensured its resilience.

In some respects further scholarship sustained some of Hodgson's themes, such as in explicating the conservative nature of postwar liberalism. A cluster of studies appeared over the next generation examining the trajectory of American liberalism from the New Deal through the 1960s and beyond, which argued that a crucial change of direction occurred as a result of wartime and early postwar experiences, when the radical aspirations that could be found in New Deal thought finally disappeared. Liberals ceased to contest capitalist structures and settled for Keynesian-style management and growth. Radical social-democratic options were closed off in favor of "growth liberalism."[14] The thrust of this scholarship abetted the tendency to date the liberal consensus from about 1945.

A growing literature in the 1970s showed how McCarthyite pressures also pushed leftists and liberals rightward.[15] More recently, Landon Storrs has documented the way in which right-wing interests used the loyalty programs to oblige those influential New Dealers surviving in the government bureaucracy to retreat from their former social-democratic stances and move to the cautious liberalism of the "vital center."[16] The moderate center also won recruits from the right as an increasing number of Republicans from the mid-1950s distanced themselves from a discredited McCarthyism and aligned with "Modern Republicanism," the term preferred by President Dwight Eisenhower, whose influential role in persuading at least some of his colleagues of the virtues of the "middle way" is explored by Robert Mason in this volume. For a time it seemed to be moderate or liberal Republicans like New York governor Nelson Rockefeller, characterized by Hodgson in his new essay as "almost an embodiment of the liberal consensus," who were assuming leadership positions in their party.[17] Whether these movements by both liberals and conservatives toward the center ground created a "consensus" may be debated (its problematic nature is pointed up in Mason's essay), but a conservative liberalism for a long moment occupied the mainstream.

Ideology functions in a number of ways, sometimes to summon true believers to a cause, but one objective of consensus liberalism was to influence public policy, particularly in the economic and social spheres. In this respect, some modern scholarship has endorsed Hodgson's characterizations. The natural and social scientists so often consulted by government in these years were themselves often deeply imbued with values of consensus liberalism, as Andrew Jewett has explained.[18] When politicians formulate practical policies, they are often obliged to adapt to political and legal realities. During the Kennedy era, as Gareth Davies has shown, pragmatic welfare reformers sought to frame legislation within an individualist ethos that could appeal to both liberals and conservatives, such as in the Public Welfare Amendments of 1962.[19] In this volume, Iwan Morgan demonstrates how Keynesianism, so central to consensus liberalism, was applied in both liberal and conservative ways by postwar administrations. The Employment Act of 1946 reflected a limited Keynesian consensus, though the high point of the ideology came in the Kennedy policies of the early 1960s. Morgan's chapter crisply delineates the relatively short life of the Keynesian ascendancy, closely corresponding to the years identified as the era of the liberal consensus.[20] David Stebenne's nuanced chapter broadly suggests that through the mid-twentieth century, differences between the parties over the welfare state were not that marked and were usually contained, thus offering some qualified support for the idea of a liberal consensus. Although one possible implication is that the exigencies of practical politics may have hidden deeper ideological divisions, interestingly Stebenne tacks in another direction, suggesting that differences may actually be exaggerated because of the need for liberals and conservatives each to appeal to their supporters on their respective wings. In the late twentieth century this did become a more visible feature of American politics, as increasingly the critical role of primary elections in particular encouraged the major parties to pitch to their more zealous partisans.

Some corroboration of Hodgson's argument also came from other studies. Interestingly counterpointing *America in Our Time* was Liz Cohen's *A Consumers' Republic*.[21] While Cohen's focus is very different from Hodgson's, with much less attention to what was happening in Washington, the broad outlines are not dissimilar. Her concern again was with American political economy between the 1940s and the 1970s, in the revolutionary potential of which Hodgson's liberals had such faith. She shifts the key from production to consumption, but otherwise her description of the prevailing ideology of postwar America is much the same. In her "consumers' republic," according to the governing classes, consumer purchasing power drove economic growth, which in turn promised to lift the bulk of Americans to a mass middle class, thus creating a republic of roughly equal citizens. Unhappily, as in Hodgson's America, the processes unleashed eventually created something like the opposite of the ideal. This too was partly the consequence of faulty assumptions, particularly that the working class was disappearing. For Hodgson, liberal overconfidence led to failure in Southeast Asia and in the ghettos, resulting in the splintering of the consensus into fragments. For Cohen, a strategy designed to promote an egalitarian affluence produced a suburbia and a culture segmented by class, race, and ethnicity, as well as a highly divided polity. The mechanisms promoting fragmentation were different, but in both studies consensual and egalitarian ideals eventually crumble before the reality of an increasingly splintered political society.

Other scholarship, advancing on different fronts, has been less supportive of the "liberal consensus" conceptualization of postwar America. In the last three decades of the twentieth century, the ever-widening chasm between rich and poor Americans and the increasing political polarization rendered suspect any notions of an authentic consensual past. A recent essay wearingly remarks that "historians have spent the past several decades dismantling the myth of the liberal consensus."[22] Foreign-policy scholars have even raised doubts about the broader concept of a "Cold War consensus," as Andrew Preston pointedly explains in this volume. On his analysis, there was a degree of accord on foreign policy for only a few years in the late 1940s, itself an "aberration," and not during the heyday of the liberal consensus as defined by Hodgson. Dismantling the notion of a Cold War consensus does little to further Hodgson's thesis, though it may be arguable that a liberal consensus came to characterize domestic but not foreign policy.

Nonetheless, the avalanche of studies called forth by the need to explain the (for many) unexpected triumph of Reaganite Republicanism in particular has threatened to bury the concept of a liberal consensus. Many mid-twentieth-century conservatives no longer seem very liberal or very consensual. Other studies, too, whether of evangelical religion, suburban expansion, big-city pathology, or civil rights, feminist, or other activism, have found either deep ideological divisions in the 1950s or a society of such heterogeneity that the notion of a liberal consensus seems hardly applicable.

The explosion of scholarship on modern conservatism, locating its roots firmly in mainstream America rather than on the fringes, questions the assumption that the postwar right could be dismissed as a "handful of dissidents" sulking outside Hodgson's "Big Tent" of consensus liberals.[23] Much of it has focused on local communities—variously dubbed "grassroots," "crabgrass roots," or even "grasstops"—allowing a whole range of activists to come into view, including suburban housewives, evangelical churchmen, local boosters, transplanted northern professionals, tradition-minded Catholics, southern migrants, disaffected urban workers, and others. With some exceptions, these grassroots figures were not the unreconstructed survivors of an earlier age but men and women engaged in the modern economy and civic affairs. Sometimes they were located in relatively affluent communities enjoying the benefits of Cold War defense contracts. They represented not so much a backlash against 1960s liberalism and disorder as a social and political movement that had long been developing networks and organizations. But it is in the nature of grassroots not always to be very visible.

A key role was played by businessmen, and labor historians were among the first to question conventional interpretations. In the 1980s, Howell Harris and Nelson Lichtenstein pointed to the success of corporate leaders at the end of World War II in delimiting union power and restoring their own "right to manage," that is, in maintaining their control over the workplace. Most industrialists, Lichtenstein pointed out, were not corporate liberals but conservatives determined to throw off governmental and union interference.[24] Subsequent scholars uncovered a remarkable range of programmatic ventures before the 1960s by determined businesspersons to nudge the American polity to the right. The idea of an authentic "labor-capital accord" in the postwar years became increasingly untenable.[25] In the 1990s and 2000s, Elizabeth Fones-Wolf and Kim Phillips-Fein affirmed the essentially anti-union thrust of significant business groups, with their promotion of free-market economics and lower taxes, bequeathing conservative agencies and a confident discourse to their heirs in the age of Reagan.[26] Elizabeth Tandy Shermer found that in Phoenix, Arizona, opportunistic businessmen even employed the state to limit the electorate and weaken unions as they fashioned an expansive commercial climate.[27] Jennifer Klein too demonstrated how far major corporations were prepared to go in offering welfare packages in order to deter government from expanding the welfare state.[28] The private sector was paramount. Some corporate leaders may have accepted the premises of the liberal consensus, but quite a few others were busily contesting them in the 1950s, including those associated with General Electric, fronted by the telegenic Ronald Reagan.[29]

From the mid-1990s, other scholars were discovering more varied roots for the New Right. Mary Brennan, Lisa McGirr, and Rick Perlstein uncovered legions of true believers who even before the Goldwater insurgency were working to place their supporters in Republican Party councils.[30] McGirr's canny middle-class conservatives were no backwoods provincials;

rather, attuned to the zeitgeist of an expanding, entrepreneurial, and patriotic Southern California, they assailed big-government liberalism in a contemporary vocabulary. Their values were hardly those of the liberal consensus. Subsequent scholars examined the political culture of American suburbs in the postwar years and found the basis for a conservatism that was inflected with racism but which also drew resilience from class and property issues related to housing, local taxation, schooling, and other matters of concern to a suburban community.

While the focus of this research tended to be the 1960s and beyond, it implicated the suburbanizing processes of the preceding years in fashioning a form of conservatism imbued with an "ethos of middle-class entitlement," and it enjoyed a broader appeal as it distanced itself from the crude racism of old.[31] Adjusting to a regional perspective, Sean Cunningham found somewhat similar processes in the rise of the right in the Sunbelt, where a "color-blind" conservatism eventually prevailed.[32] Demographic and religious trends also early served to pull an increasing number of Americans away from New Deal and consensus liberalism. Hodgson had excluded "southern diehards" and "rural reactionaries" from the liberal consensus, but huge numbers of southerners were leaving their section in the 1930s, 1940s, and 1950s, whites and blacks.[33] Some settled in the industrial cities of the North and border states and many on the West Coast. Poor whites, often reared in the fundamentalist culture of an unreconstructed South, could fall prey to the appeal of a populist right-wing conservatism.[34] Darren Dochuk published a highly suggestive study of southern migration to California, where the newcomers fashioned a cultural force at once evangelical and entrepreneurial. By the 1950s they were demanding "A New Age, Not a New Deal," and were soon promoting churches, schools, and organizations bent on defying the perceived secularism of the New Deal and fostering a crusading conservatism.[35]

An important group of local studies focused on constituencies that were once assumed to have been part of the New Deal coalition. Many working-class and middle-class whites in the cities in the 1940s and 1950s, it now appears, were not particularly comfortable with reform politics.[36] Thomas Sugrue, Arnold Hirsch, and John McGreevy drew attention to the near reactionary attitudes to be found among the white urban working classes, particularly when they acquired more black neighbors as competition for housing intensified and jobs became less secure.[37] Economic, ethnic, religious, and racial tensions eroded whatever attachment white workers may have had to the liberalism of Franklin Roosevelt and Adlai Stevenson.

Gary Gerstle underlined the racial element in this urban discontent in the "massive resistance" to integration in northern cities well before the civil rights movement crested in the 1960s.[38] In a review of the literature, Sugrue painted the 1950s as an age of insecurity rather than consensus, citing a plethora of studies documenting class, social, and particularly racial conflict.[39] While the focus of some of this writing was on behavior rather than political beliefs, the behavior in question betrayed a contemptuous rejection of the main principles of the liberal consensus.

Religious revivalism in the early Cold War years also chipped away at consensus liberalism. The growth of evangelical religion broadly served a conservative cause, although, as Uta Balbier shows in her chapter, the process was a complex one, since the success of Billy Graham's campaigns owed something to his capacity to tap into the optimistic and consensual values of the day. Nonetheless, his liberal ecumenicalism disturbed many fundamentalists, provoking a reaction that helps to explain the rise of the Religious Right. Recent scholars have examined other evangelical groups willing to promote unrestrained free enterprise and to take religion into politics, most notably Carl McIntire's fundamentalist American Council of Christian Churches. His organization expanded rapidly in the 1950s, when he not only helped to mentor several figures who were to emerge as prominent evangelists but also pioneered grassroots mass mobilization techniques and explored ways of cooperating with non-fundamentalist conservatives. McIntire has been credited with "paving the way to the renascence of conservative Christian political activism."[40]

Right-wing intellectuals, too, were not as rare as once assumed. Such figures as William F. Buckley and Ayn Rand, once seen as mavericks, have been recast in recent studies as core leaders.[41] One group whose influence has received increasing recognition was the Mont Pèlerin Society, incorporated in 1947 with some business funding. Intended by its intellectual sponsor, Friedrich Hayek, to promote an alternative to the Keynesian establishment through creating an elite network of classical liberals and libertarians, in the course of the 1950s it attracted high-profile figures in the United States and Western Europe. By the 1980s, it could be argued, Hayek's vision had been largely realized.[42]

Some of the contributors to this volume reinforce the view that a vibrant right-wing conservatism was well under way in Cold War America before the presidential candidacy of Barry Goldwater. Mason's chapter demonstrates that the deep-seated anti-labor animus within the Republican Party was a serious obstacle to Eisenhower's quest for Modern Republicanism.

Ironically, on this analysis, Eisenhower's consensual orientation provoked a conservative reaction within his party, ensuring that any liberal consensus would not long survive. This political reaction parallels the potent right-wing backlash to Billy Graham's expansive appeal that Balbier finds among religious fundamentalists. Focusing on the regional dimension, Shermer's chapter contends that there had never been a liberal-conservative accord in much of the South and the West. Sunbelt entrepreneurs, eager to build their businesses and attract outside investment, had no time for New Deal–type labor laws and were instrumental in the development of strong anti-liberal movements at state and local levels from the 1930s onward. Such business interests were happy to use government for their own ends, notably to develop regional infrastructure and sometimes to disfranchise potential Democratic voters. Conservative interests, perhaps mobilized by a chamber of commerce, often dominated local offices, and their credo of local control, well articulated before the civil rights movement gained momentum, would help make possible a cross-Sunbelt alliance. Shermer's perception that conservatives were eager to take over state governments is endorsed in Alex Goodall's examination of national-security debates around 1960, although he somewhat unconventionally focuses on Congress rather than the much-combed grassroots. On this issue at least, he demonstrates that shared hostility to an active Supreme Court allowed southern states' righters and northern businessmen to use anticommunism in a common cause, arguably anticipating Reaganite conservatism.

And there were dissenters on the liberal left too. There was more contention and variety in the 1950s than the image of a homogeneous society allows.[43] It has often been pointed out that even such figures as Richard Hofstadter and Louis Hartz, whatever they may have contributed to consensus theory, were far from uncritical admirers of the American past and were disenchanted with the present. They may have espied consensus, but they did not celebrate it. To Howard Brick their writing constituted "some kind of dissent" in a complacent conservative era, placing them somewhat closer to the radicals of the 1960s than the latter may have understood.[44]

More directly challenging the notion of the liberal consensus from the left have been those authors tracing a "long civil rights movement" back through the 1950s and before, courageously contesting the status quo.[45] This scholarship is not so much a criticism of Hodgson, who made clear the shortsightedness of his liberal opinion-makers on racial matters, as it is of looser applications of the concept and of notions that postwar America was a homogeneous society. George Lewis in this collection adds an interesting variant in arguing that the perception of the 1963 March on Washington as an exercise in consensus liberalism is a modern artifact, arising largely from the 1983 celebration of that event. In a way this is a tribute to the resilience of the concept, as it reshapes the past so as to elide the dread fears and the bloody struggles of civil rights activists. King, Lewis reminds us, was not the dominating figure in 1963 that some narratives assume, and a substantial part of the movement had little faith in liberalism (a skepticism significantly shared by King). Another recent study which jarringly demonstrates that the civil rights movement cannot be cast within the liberal consensus model is by Danielle McGuire, who has uncovered the extent to which it was a response by black women to the rapes and other sexual violence directed against them.[46] If the idea of the liberal consensus and the sanctification of King have been used to project a reassuringly rosy glow over the civil rights movement, did similar processes apply to other phenomena of the period?

There were certainly many forms of dissent that operated outside the parameters of cautious liberal centrism. The progressive stance of peace activists and feminist activists distinguished them from vital-center liberalism.[47] Instead of organized labor being complacent, as perceived by consensus orthodoxy, it was in the judgment of some scholars "remarkably combative" in the 1950s, as was manifest in the unusually high annual average of 352 major strikes over the course of the decade.[48] Indeed, there was a "flare-up of industrial conflict between 1958 and 1963," supposedly the peak period of the liberal consensus.[49] If labor leaders were sometimes seduced by the "corporate liberalism" of big business, below the surface tensions often simmered.[50] Other instances of 1950s and early 1960s diversity identified in recent scholarship embrace a lively gay network in Mississippi, organized lesbians in San Francisco, and fair-housing activists in such cities as Boston and Detroit.[51]

These left-leaning groups were operating in a changing environment. The chapter by Helen Laville in this volume, reinforced by that of Jonathan Bell, illustrates one of the most profound transformations in historical understanding of the last generation: the modern inescapability of gender. The liberal consensus, Laville demonstrates, was inherently gendered, the creation of white men (or as Bell bluntly puts it, "elite straight white men"). The postwar need for a strong economic revival meant that traditional gender roles were resuscitated, so that Rosie the Riveter and her companions were urged to leave the factory for the home and become model housewives, the key consumers in an economy of mass consumption, while their husbands manned the public world of work. Together these gendered roles drove the economy of abundance on which the liberal consensus rested. This analysis helps to explain rather than refute consensus liberalism. Laville goes further in highlighting the array of women's associations that provided a channel for civic activism beyond the home, albeit in a form that challenged gender roles more indirectly than frontally. Her chapter therefore endorses the notion of a postwar liberal consensus by adding a missing dimension, but its emphasis on women's civic and political activism implies that women's acquiescence in their lot would not be indefinite.

Recent studies of gender have also prompted some rethinking of the meaning of citizenship, and Bell's essay applies these new frameworks to California politics and locates supportive evidence in other parts of the country. Different political philosophies, Bell argues, projected different understandings of citizenship; there was the private citizenship of corporate culture, with its premise of an undifferentiated individualism, and the universalist citizenship of the liberal left, which wanted the state to underpin the security and well-being of all citizens, including a decent quality of life. A growing divergence between these two conceptions among California politicians in the 1950s, and evidence of similar features elsewhere, leads Bell to reject the thesis of a liberal consensus. He accepts that there was an ideology of this kind but argues that it did not arise from the kind of study and debate favored by Hodgson's intellectuals. Rather, its function was essentially disciplinary, designed to conceal deep-seated divisions and regulate dissent. By limiting economic, legal, and civil rights, "entire categories of people" could be excluded from effective citizenship. California's liberal Democrats determinedly contested this restrictive understanding, and by the end of the decade, in fighting for labor and civil rights, they were advancing a pluralist understanding of American society which recognized that each group—labor, children, the elderly, African Americans, and Latino Americans—had its own needs and that all had claims to the protective hand of government. This was a liberalism that had advanced beyond the limitations of the New Deal and was defiantly at odds with the ideology of corporate capitalism.

Liberalism, like conservatism, was naturally evolving as conditions changed.[52] If the New Right had its roots in the 1950s, the same likely applied to the new liberalism. Bell had previously elucidated the evolution of liberalism in postwar California, where a transformed Democratic Party ultimately succeeded in ending Republican dominance, employing grassroots organizing to fashion an extensive coalition embracing Latinos,

African Americans, gays, and progressive suburbanites. The liberalism of the New Deal was giving way to a new liberalism that anticipated the 1960s and later.[53] Jennifer Delton has recently argued that American liberals successfully adapted to the new postwar conditions, winning a wide acceptance for their view that "an activist state" could work within the framework of a market economy with an agenda embracing civil rights, social reform, and jobs creation. In her assessment, the Cold War ironically aided their cause by increasing the need to highlight the virtues of American civilization before the world.[54] Alan Petigny has intriguingly found an advancing permissiveness in 1950s America in the sense of a growing freedom from traditional constraints rather than wantonness. He distinguishes between "norms" or standards, which remained conservative in several spheres, and "values" and private behavior, which were "often concealed from public view."[55] Conformist norms in public discourse and permissive values in private were parting company with one another, only to close dramatically in the 1960s. Even under Truman and Eisenhower, on this evidence, the private views of Americans suggest that they were moving toward a more tolerant society, as they developed relatively relaxed notions of child rearing, more democratic marriages, and, for many, more liberal attitudes with respect to religion and sexual relations.

This image of early Cold War society sits awkwardly with those studies that focus on the rise of evangelical conservatism or unreconstructed businessmen, but it does accord with that recent scholarship which suggests that a vigorous liberalism survived through both the early and the later Cold War eras. While some scholars have liked to treat the late twentieth century as "the ascendancy of the right," others have preferred to stress fragmentation or polarization, depicting a society in which conservatives from Ronald Reagan to George W. Bush were challenged by resilient progressive impulses. The civil rights movement itself triggered a "rights revolution" as environmental, consumer, feminist, and other organizations gained momentum. Liberalism was changing rather than disappearing, reflecting less the labor constituencies of old and more the quality-of-life concerns of middle-class professionals and the rights of a range of ethnic, sexual, and identity groups.[56] Conservative businessmen and evangelicals were evidently very much on the rise in the 1950s, but the growing evidence of black, peace, feminist, fair-housing, labor, and gay activism, as well as such studies as those of Bell and Petigny, suggests that the cultural and political polarizations of the late twentieth century were already in the making.[57] As Hodgson himself pointed out, from about 1963 consensus liberalism was already being replaced by a "time of crisis" and then by a "time of polarization."[58]

Yet the flood of publications on the rise of the right and the conflict and diversity of the age of Eisenhower has not altogether written consensus liberalism out of the history books. There was much in the studies of postwar urban conflict, for example, with which Hodgson might have agreed. Hodgson himself emphasized the deep economic and racial fissures that those in authority had successfully concealed, including from themselves. In like vein, Sugrue contends that power rested with such entities as cultural elites, big business, and the media, who used it to silence dissent and maintain their dominance, sometimes by brutal means.[59] These elites do not seem so different from those identified by Hodgson, although they relied more on repression than persuasion and example, thereby creating a kind of conformity, a contrived consensus. Offering further support for this perspective, Alex Goodall's revisiting of consensus writing in this volume posits that consensus was really a "forced homogenization."

Other recent scholarship has pointed in the direction of a contrived consensus. Contentiousness was a principal feature of American religious life, according to Kevin Schultz, who has found that "anti-conformist and anti-consensus ideas circulated freely during the years following World War II." Catholic and Jewish groups determinedly challenged the curbs on their aspirations in the expanding universities and suburbs, demanding respect for the pluralist ideal. Nonetheless, if it was their contentiousness that persuaded the courts to clarify the principle of the separation of church and state, they could be said to be creating a broad public consensus around that principle.[60] Wendy Wall has shown how a consensus could be manufactured in an age of insecurity. "Why," she asked, "did a 'veneer of consensus' and civility reign?"[61] She strikingly dated the effort to create the ideology of the "American way" back to the late 1930s. In an age beset by anxieties triggered by depression at home and a menacing world abroad, and later by world war and cold war, government officials, businessmen, intellectuals, and religious leaders became involved in attempts to promote national cohesion. Whereas class conflict had appeared prominently in the discourse of the Progressive and New Deal eras, the pressures in a beleaguered United States were for Americans to pull together via an agenda emphasizing individual freedoms, rights, and social harmony. Motives were mixed—businessmen might link individual rights to free enterprise, but others saw an opportunity for promoting equality in the rhetoric of personal freedom. By the early 1950s these diverse groups had largely succeeded through their educational campaigns in fashioning "a fragile national consensus,"[62] one that seems rather similar to that which Hodgson encountered. It was a manufactured or contrived consensus, but perhaps it helps to explain how Hodgson's elites fell prey to their illusions.

Finally, the evidence that Hodgson, Jewett, and others gathered for the influence of an *ideology* of consensus liberalism cannot be lightly dismissed. Those tenets were being promoted by influential persons and agencies in the universities, government, and the media at a time when governments and experts generally commanded high public confidence.[63] As Daniel Rodgers has written, in these years "readings of the consensual strain in American society gained a traction never before equaled in the American past."[64] Iwan Morgan's chapter in this volume shows how a major component of the liberal consensus did shape public policy. It may be that the embrace of the liberal elite was not as far-reaching as once appeared, but its blindness is not difficult to understand. Much of the grassroots dissent around 1960 was still below the radar, for the most part unnoticed by the great and the good. The "labor-capital accord" did not fall into serious disrepute until the 1970s as it failed to deliver the promised security for working people. The process of postwar suburbanization may have been reshaping political culture, but the new studies for the most part say more about the decades after the mid-1960s than those before. Given the psychological theorizing popular in the years around 1960, liberals were no doubt too ready to dismiss dissidents as "extremists." Further, several studies of the emerging right concede that it was not yet fully formed. Lisa McGirr acknowledged that her Orange County movement was a "prototype," "the first functional form of a new kind of conservative milieu,"[65] and Darren Dochuk agreed that his conservative evangelicals had not secured dominance in California by the early 1960s. The doctrines of the liberal consensus were still holding sway, just, a reassuring myth, one clung to all the more firmly by society's elites. But the ideology was no more than a thin crust above the social and political turbulence below. As Hodgson has argued, it was shot through with faulty assumptions, and much of the recent work has not so much invalidated the concept as explained why it would be blasted apart so suddenly and with such vehemence.

Notes

1. Examples can be found by googling such terms as "ideology of the liberal consensus," "America's postwar consensus," and "the postwar consensus," which have received in aggregate over two million hits.

2. Godfrey Hodgson, *America in Our Time* (Garden City, NY: Doubleday, 1976), 136. While their definitions of the liberal consensus may vary, some scholars have dated the concept to earlier crises. Andrew Jewett, in a complex exercise in intellectual history, finds the origins of "consensus liberalism" in "the confluence of the struggle against totalitarianism with the domestic political battle of the late New Deal years." Jewett, *Science, Democracy, and the American University: From the Civil War to the Cold War* (New York: Cambridge University Press, 2012), 17; see esp. 232–34, 290–301, and 350–53 on the popularity of the concept among academics, especially social scientists. Similarly emphasizing the late 1930s and early 1940s in generating ideas of this kind is Wendy L. Wall, *Inventing the "American Way": The Politics of Consensus from the New Deal to the Civil Rights Movement* (New York: Oxford University Press, 2008), discussed later.

3. For the deployment of the liberal consensus concept in popular culture, see Peter Biskind, *Seeing Is Believing: How Hollywood Taught Us to Stop Worrying and Love the Fifties* (New York: Pantheon Books, 1983); and Charles Maland, "*Dr. Strangelove* (1964): Nightmare Comedy and the Ideology of Liberal Consensus," *American Quarterly* 31 (Winter 1979): 697–717.

4. See, e.g., Eugene R. Wittkopf and James M. McCormick, "The Cold War Consensus: Did It Exist?" *Polity* 22 (Summer 1990): 627–53. It is often argued that Cold War foreign and defense policies promoted a conservative consensus on the domestic front; e.g., Benjamin O. Fordham, *Building the Cold War Consensus: The Political Economy of U.S. National Security Policy, 1949–51* (Ann Arbor: University of Michigan Press, 1998), sees Cold War priorities crippling welfare reform and fostering campaigns against labor and other radicals.

5. Louis Galambos, "The Emerging Organizational Synthesis in Modern American History," *Business History Review* 44, no. 3 (Autumn 1970): 280. Galambos subsequently wrote that "the politics of institutional change involved above all the engineering of consensus and coalitions by organized interests which developed over the years elaborate networks to protect their interests." Galambos, "Technology, Political Economy, and the Professionalization: Central Themes of the Organizational Synthesis," *Business History Review* 57, no. 4 (Winter 1983): 471–93 (quotation on 492). See also Brian Balogh, "Reorganizing the Organizational Synthesis: Federal-Professional Relations in Modern America," *Studies in American Political Development* 5 (Spring 1991): 119–72.

6. This kind of history also resonated with the convergence theory that emerged in the 1960s, which held that advanced industrial and technological societies, notably including the United States and the Soviet Union, were increasingly becoming more alike, at least in forms of industrial organization, social stratification and bureaucratic structure: Clark Kerr et al., *Industrialism and Industrial Man: The Problem of Labor and Management in Economic Growth* (Cambridge: Harvard University Press, 1960); P. A. Sorokin, *The Basic Trends of Our Times* (New Haven: Yale University Press, 1964); and J. Kenneth Galbraith, *The New Industrial State* (Princeton: Princeton University Press, 1967).

7. Olivier Zunz, Leonard Schoppa, and Nobuhiro Hiwatari, eds., *Social Contracts under Stress: The Middle Classes of America, Europe, and Japan at the Turn of the Century* (New York: Russell Sage, 2002); "Scholarly Discussion: The Postwar Social Contract," *International Labor and Working-Class History* 50 (Fall 1996): 114–56; Thomas Kochan, "Wages and the Social Contract," *The American Prospect*, April 22, 2007.

8. Derek C. Bok and John T. Dunlop, *Labor and the American Community* (New York: Simon & Schuster, 1970).

9. Elaine Tyler May, *Homeward Bound: American Families in the Cold War Era* (New York: Basic Books, 1988).

10. Will Herberg, *Protestant-Catholic-Jew* (Garden City, NY: Doubleday, 1955); Robert N. Bellah, "Civil Religion in America," *Daedalus* 96 (Winter 1967): 1–21.

11. Hodgson, *America in Our Time*, 497.

12. See, e.g., Edward W. Said, *Representations of the Intellectual: The 1993 Reith Lectures* (New York: Pantheon Books, 1994); and Thomas Sowell, *Intellectuals and Society* (New York: Basic Books, 2009).

13. Cf. Jewett, *Science, Democracy, and the American University*: "Consensus liberalism solved all manner of problems for mid-twentieth-century human scientists by deeming them the authoritative spokesmen for American values" (234), and "In the 1940s and 1950s, those employing consensus liberalism similarly argued that the small minority of cultural leaders who sought to change the values of their fellow citizens were the true spokesmen for American values" (300).

14. Alan Brinkley, *The End of Reform: New Deal Liberalism in Recession and War* (New York: Knopf, 1995); Robert M. Collins, *More: The Politics of Economic Growth in Postwar America* (New York: Oxford University Press, 2000).

15. Mary S. McAuliffe, *Crisis on the Left: Cold War Politics and American Liberals, 1947–1954* (Amherst: University of Massachusetts Press, 1978).

16. Landon R. Y. Storrs, *The Second Red Scare and the Unmaking of the New Deal Left* (Princeton: Princeton University Press, 2013).

17. Geoffrey Kabaservice, *Rule and Ruin: The Downfall of Moderation and the Destruction of the Republican Party from Eisenhower to the Tea Party* (New York: Oxford University Press, 2012), chapter 1; Robert Mason, *The Republican Party and American Politics from Hoover to Reagan* (New York: Cambridge University Press, 2012), chapter 5.

18. Jewett, *Science, Democracy, and the American University.*

19. Gareth Davies, *From Opportunity to Entitlement: The Transformation and Decline of Great Society Liberalism* (Lawrence: University Press of Kansas, 1996), 29.

20. Very much the same years are characterized by Robert E. Lane as an "age of affluence" in which he identified the elements of a "politics of consensus." Lane, "The Politics of Consensus in an Age of Affluence," *American Political Science Review* 59 (December 1965): 874–95.

21. Liz Cohen, *A Consumers' Republic: The Politics of Mass Consumption in Postwar America* (New York: Knopf, 2003).

22. Matthew D. Lassiter, "Political History beyond the Red-Blue Divide," *Journal of American History* 98 (December 2011): 760. Lassiter was referring to postwar politics and also the broader New Deal order.

23. Hodgson, *America in Our Time*, 73.

24. Howell John Harris, *The Right to Manage: Industrial Relations Policies of American Business in the 1940s* (Madison: University of Wisconsin Press, 1982); Nelson Lichtenstein, "From Corporatism to Collective Bargaining: Organized Labor and the Eclipse of Social Democracy in the Postwar Era," in Steve Fraser and Gary Gerstle, eds., *The Rise and Fall of the New Deal Order, 1930–1980* (Princeton: Princeton University Press, 1989), 122–52.

25. Nelson Lichtenstein, *State of the Union: A Century of American Labor* (Princeton: Princeton University Press, 2002), sees the notion of an accord as a myth, at best an unstable truce.

26. Elizabeth Fones-Wolf, *Selling Free Enterprise: The Business Assault on Labor and Liberalism, 1945–1960* (Urbana: University of Illinois Press 1994); Kim Phillips-Fein, "'If Business and the Country Will Be Run Right': The Business Challenge to the Liberal Consensus, 1945–1964," *International Labor and Working-Class History* 72 (Fall 2007): 192–215; Kim Phillips-Fein, *Invisible Hands: The Making of the Conservative Movement from the New Deal to Reagan* (New York: Norton, 2009).

27. Elizabeth Tandy Shermer, *Sunbelt Capitalism: Phoenix and the Transformation of American Politics* (Philadelphia: University of Pennsylvania Press, 2013). Conservatives and businessmen, it has often been pointed out, were not averse to using the powers of the state when it suited their interests. The policies of the U.S. Department of Agriculture, Pete Daniel has shown, broadly served the interests of wealthy farmers at the expense of small black farmers, whose numbers plummeted. Daniel, *Dispossession: Discrimination against African American Farmers in the Age of Civil Rights* (Chapel Hill: University of North Carolina Press, 2013). See Kari Frederickson, *Cold War Dixie: Militarization and Modernization in the American South* (Athens: University of Georgia Press, 2013), for an account of how one poor, Democratic southern community became increasingly suburban, middle class, and Republican in the fifteen years after 1950, in no small part because of DuPont's corporate culture, heavy defense-industry expenditures, and settlement by professional northerners. In this perspective, the rise of southern Republicanism had less to do with race and more with a conservative commitment to national security.

28. Jennifer Klein, *For All These Rights: Business, Labor, and the Shaping of America's Public-Private Welfare State* (Princeton: Princeton University Press, 2003). See also Sanford M. Jacoby, *Modern Manors: Welfare Capitalism since the New Deal* (Princeton: Princeton University Press, 1998), on the survival and strength of corporate paternalism into the 1950s, esp. chapters 6 and 7.

29. The attempts by some businesses and corporations before the mid-1960s to relocate from the northern industrial belt to low-wage and non-union parts of the South, and even outside American borders, hardly suggested a commitment to liberal consensus values. See, e.g., Tami J. Friedman, "Exploiting the North-South Differential: Corporate Power, Southern Politics, and the Decline of Organized Labor after World War II," *Journal of American History* 95 (September 2008): 323–48; and Jefferson Cowie, *Capital Moves: RCA's 70-Year Quest for Cheap Labor* (Ithaca: Cornell University Press, 1999).

30. Mary C. Brennan, *Turning Right in the Sixties: The Conservative Capture of the GOP* (Chapel Hill: University of North Carolina Press, 1995); Lisa McGirr, *Suburban Warriors: The Origins of the New American Right* (Princeton: Princeton University Press, 2001); Rick Perlstein, *Barry Goldwater and the Unmaking of the American Consensus* (New York: Hill and Wang, 2001). Niels Bjerre-Poulsen, *Right Face: Organizing the American Conservative*

Movement, 1945–65 (Copenhagen: Museum Tusculanum Press, 2002), traces the political mobilization of right-wing activists to take back the Republican Party for conservatism in the two decades after World War II.

31. Matthew D. Lassiter, *The Silent Majority: Suburban Politics in the Sunbelt South* (Princeton: Princeton University Press, 2006), 3; Kevin M. Kruse, *White Flight: Atlanta and the Making of Modern Conservatism* (Princeton: Princeton University Press, 2005); Robert O. Self, *American Babylon: Race and the Struggle for Postwar Oakland* (Princeton: Princeton University Press, 2003). See also Donald T. Critchlow, *Phyllis Schlafly and Grassroots Conservatism: A Woman's Crusade* (Princeton: Princeton University Press, 2005).

32. Sean P. Cunningham, *American Politics in the Postwar Sunbelt: Conservative Growth in a Battleground Region* (New York: Cambridge University Press, 2014). Joseph E. Lowndes, *From the New Deal to the New Right: Race and the Southern Origins of Modern Conservatism* (New Haven: Yale University Press, 2008), traces the ultimate replacement of Democratic hegemony in the South with a Republican conservatism to configurations that were already emerging in the 1940s.

33. Hodgson, *America in Our Time*, 73.

34. James N. Gregory, *The Southern Diaspora: How the Great Migrations of Black and White Southerners Transformed America* (Chapel Hill: University of North Carolina Press, 2005); Kenneth D. Durr, *Behind the Backlash: White Working-Class Politics in Baltimore, 1940–1980* (Chapel Hill: University of North Carolina Press, 2003).

35. Darren Dochuk, *From Bible Belt to Sunbelt: Plain-Folk Religion, Grassroots Politics, and the Rise of Evangelical Conservatism* (New York: Norton, 2011), xviii. See also Michelle M. Nickerson, *Mothers of Conservatism: Women and the Postwar Right* (Princeton: Princeton University Press, 2012), on the role of Southern California housewives in 1950s right-wing activism, and Critchlow, *Phyllis Schlafly*.

36. See, e.g., contributions by Arnold R. Hirsch, Thomas J. Sugrue, and Gary Gerstle to the "Round Table" in *Journal of American History* 82 (September 1995): 522–86.

37. Thomas J. Sugrue, "Crabgrass-Roots Politics: Race, Rights, and the Reaction against Liberalism in the Urban North, 1940–1964," *Journal of American History* 82 (September 1995): 551–78; Thomas J. Sugrue, *The Origins of the Urban Crisis: Race and Inequality in Postwar Detroit* (Princeton: Princeton University Press, 1996); Arnold Hirsch, *Making the Second Ghetto: Race and Housing in Chicago, 1940–1960* (Cambridge: Cambridge University Press, 1983); Arnold Hirsch, "Massive Resistance in the Urban North: Trumbull Park, Chicago, 1953–1966," *Journal of American History* 82 (September 1995): 522–50; John T. McGreevy, *Parish Boundaries: The Catholic Encounter with Race in the Twentieth Century Urban North* (Chicago: University of Chicago Press, 1996), chapters 4 and 5. On Detroit see also Colleen Doody, *Detroit's Cold War: The Origins of Postwar Conservatism* (Urbana: University of Illinois Press, 2013).

38. Gary Gerstle, "Race and the Myth of the Liberal Consensus," *Journal of American History* 82 (September 1995): 579–86.

39. Thomas J. Sugrue, "Reassessing the History of Postwar America," *Prospects* 20 (October 1995): 493–509. See also Darren Dochuk, "Revival on the Right: Making Sense of the Conservative Moment in Post–World War II American History," *History Compass* 4/5 (2006): 975–99.

40. Markku Ruotsila, "Carl McIntire and the Fundamentalist Origins of the Christian

Right," *Church History* 81 (June 2012): 378–407 (quotation on 406), and *Fighting Fundamentalist: Carl McIntyre and the Politicization of American Fundamentalism* (New York: Oxford University Press, 2016). See Joel A. Carpenter, *Revive Us Again: The Reawakening of American Fundamentalism* (New York: Oxford University Press, 1997), on the remarkable and widespread revival of fundamentalism between the mid-1930s and the early 1950s, which created receptive conditions for Billy Graham. See also William Martin, *With God on Our Side: The Rise of the Religious Right in America* (New York: Broadway Books, 1997); Martin Durham, *The Christian Right, the Far Right and the Boundaries of American Conservatism* (Manchester: Manchester University Press, 2000); Daniel K. Williams, *God's Own Party: The Making of the Christian Right* (New York: Oxford University Press, 2010); and Kevin M. Kruse, *One Nation under God: How Corporate America Invented Christian America* (New York: Basic Books, 2015).

41. Jonathan M. Schoenwald, *A Time for Choosing: The Rise of Modern American Conservatism* (New York Oxford University Press, 2001); Patrick Allitt, *The Conservatives: Ideas and Personalities throughout American History* (New Haven: Yale University Press, 2010). Right-wing talk radio was also flourishing before the 1960s. See Heather Hendershot, *What's Fair on the Air? Cold War Right-Wing Broadcasting and the Public Interest* (Chicago: University of Chicago Press, 2011).

42. Niels Bjerre-Poulsen, "The Mont Pèlerin Society and the Rise of the Postwar Classical Liberal Counter-Establishment," in Luc van Dongen, Stéphanie Roulin, and Giles Scott-Smith, eds., *Transnational Anti-Communism and the Cold War: Agents, Activities, and the Networks* (Basingstoke: Palgrave Macmillan, 2014), 201–17. See also Philip Mirowski and Dieter Plehwe, eds., *The Road from Mont Pèlerin: The Making of the Neoliberal Thought Collective* (Cambridge: Harvard University Press, 2009).

43. One study to question images of conformity in 1950s culture is Peter J. Kuznick and James Gilbert, eds., *Rethinking Cold War Culture* (Washington, DC: Smithsonian Institution Press, 2001).

44. Howard Brick, "The Disenchantment of America: Radical Echoes in 1950s Political Criticism," in Kathleen G. Donohue, ed., *Liberty and Justice for All? Rethinking Politics in Cold War America* (Amherst: University of Massachusetts Press, 2012), 157–84 (quotation on 178).

45. Jacquelyn Dowd Hall, "The Long Civil Rights Movement and the Political Uses of the Past," *Journal of American History* 91 (March 2005): 1233–63.

46. Danielle L. McGuire, *At the Dark End of the Street: Black Women, Rape and Resistance—A New History of the Civil Rights Movement from Rosa Parks to the Rise of Black Power* (New York: Knopf, 2010).

47. Susan Lynn, *Progressive Women in Conservative Times: Racial Justice, Peace, and Feminism, 1945 to the 1960s* (New Brunswick, NJ: Rutgers University Press, 1992); Eugenia Kaledin, *American Women in the 1950s: Mothers and More* (Boston: Twayne, 1984); Joanne Meyerowitz, ed., *Not June Cleaver: Women and Gender in Postwar America, 1945–1960* (Philadelphia: Temple University Press, 1994); Jacqueline Casteldine, *Cold War Progressives: Women's Interracial Organizing for Peace and Freedom* (Urbana: University of Illinois Press, 2012).

48. Lichtenstein, *State of the Union*, 136. See Stanley Aronowitz, "The Unsilent Fifties," in *False Promises: The Shaping of American Working-Class Consciousness* (Durham,

NC: Duke University Press, 1992), 323–94, on the epidemic of wildcat strikes in the auto industry.

49. Mike Davis, *Prisoners of the American Dream* (London: Verso, 1986), 125.

50. George Lipsitz, *Rainbow at Midnight: Labor and Culture in the 1940s* (Urbana: University of Illinois Press, 1994).

51. John Howard, *Men Like That: A Southern Queer History* (Chicago: Chicago University Press, 1999); Marcia M. Gallo, *Different Daughters: A History of the Daughters of Bilitis and the Rise of the Lesbian Rights Movement* (New York: Carroll & Graf, 2006); Lily Geismer, "Good Neighbors for Fair Housing: Suburban Liberalism and Racial Inequality in Metropolitan Boston," *Journal of Urban History* 39 (May 2013): 354–77; Sugrue, "Crabgrass-Roots Politics," 572–77.

52. As remarked on in Lassiter, "Political History beyond the Red-Blue Divide," 760–64, the evolution of postwar liberalism has drawn little attention compared with that of conservatism.

53. Jonathan Bell, *California Crucible: The Forging of Modern American Liberalism* (Philadelphia: University of Pennsylvania Press, 2012).

54. Jennifer A. Delton, *Rethinking the 1950s: How Anticommunism and the Cold War Made America Liberal* (New York: Cambridge University Press, 2013). Delton insists that there was a "liberal consensus" (she dates it to the late 1940s) and that it embraced moderate Republicans and enlightened CEOs, though she presents it in much more positive terms than Hodgson. See also Andrea Friedman, *Citizenship in Cold War America: The National Security State and the Possibilities of Dissent* (Amherst: University of Massachusetts Press, 2014), on the way in which the contradictions of the national-security state in the 1950s provoked an extensive dissent that helped make possible the causes of the 1960s.

55. Alan Petigny, *The Permissive Society: America, 1941–1965* (New York: Cambridge University Press, 2009), 249.

56. See, e.g., Jeffrey M. Berry, *The New Liberalism: The Rising Power of Citizen Groups* (Washington, DC: Brookings Institution Press, 1999); and John B. Judis and Ruy Teixeira, *The Emerging Democratic Majority* (New York: Scribner, 2002). On the persistence of activist leftist movements in the 1970s and beyond, see Dan Berger, *The Hidden 1970s: Histories of Radicalism* (New Brunswick, NJ: Rutgers University Press, 2010): Michael Stewart Foley, *Front Porch Politics: The Forgotten Heyday of American Activism in the 1970s and 1980s* (New York: Hill & Wang, 2013); Bradford D. Martin, *The Other Eighties: A Secret History of America in the Age of Reagan* (New York: Hill & Wang, 2011); and the essays on "Rethinking the 1970s" in the *Journal of Contemporary History* 43 (October 2008): 617–700.

57. Cunningham similarly emphasizes the "resilient" nature of the liberal consensus in the two decades after 1945, even as it was challenged by growing numbers of conservatives in the South and elsewhere. Cunningham, *American Politics*, 89–91. For a discussion of cultural divisions in the early postwar era and the suggestion that it was only subsequently that conservative films less critical of American society gained prominence, see John Bodnar, "*Saving Private Ryan* and Postwar Memory in America," *American Historical Review* 106 (June 2001): 805–17.

58. Hodgson, *America in Our Time*, 136.

59. Sugrue, "Reassessing the History of Postwar America."

60. Kevin M. Schultz, *Tri-Faith America: How Catholics and Jews Held Postwar America*

to Its Protestant Promise (New York: Oxford University Press, 2011), 8; and Kevin M. Schultz, "The Irony of the Postwar Religious Revival: Catholics, Jews, and the Creation of the Naked Public Square," in Donohue, *Liberty and Justice for All?* 213–42.

61. Wall, *Inventing the "American Way,"* 5.

62. Ibid., 12. Movements to establish a middle ground were not confined to the United States in this period. In the United Kingdom in 1938, Harold Macmillan, then a Conservative backbencher and later prime minister, published *The Middle Way* (London: Macmillan, 1938), arguing for a centrist approach to political economy. The term had already been made popular by experiments in Sweden, Marquis Childs having published the bestseller *Sweden: The Middle Way* (New Haven: Yale University Press, 1936), a book in which Franklin Roosevelt showed considerable interest. It is suggestive that what in Europe went under the rather pragmatic term "middle way" in the United States became the patriotic "American way," perhaps offering support for Richard Hofstadter's observation that "it had been our fate as a nation not to have ideologies but to be one." Hofstadter, *Anti-Intellectualism in American Life* (London: Jonathan Cape, 1964), 43.

63. Lane, "Politics of Consensus," 877–78, 893–95; Seymour Martin Lipset and William Schneider, *The Confidence Gap: Business, Labor, and Government in the Public Mind* (New York: Free Press, 1983), chapter 1 et seq.

64. Daniel T. Rodgers, *Age of Fracture* (Cambridge: Belknap Press of Harvard University Press, 2011), 226. Rodgers pointed particularly to the power of a cultural consensus, as illustrated by Robert Bellah's "civil religion."

65. Lisa McGirr, "A History of the Conservative Movement from the Bottom Up," *Journal of Policy History* 14 (July 2002): 331–39 (quotation on 333).

3

The Reach and Limits of the Liberal Consensus

GARY GERSTLE

Godfrey Hodgson's *America in Our Time* is one of the great works of American political and social history written in the past half century. Few books capture the boundless confidence of the United States in 1945, the fear that settled on this society during the Cold War, and the tumult of the 1960s as vividly as this book does. Most of the major players in American politics and culture between 1945 and 1973 appear in Hodgson's narrative, from Presidents Eisenhower, Kennedy, Johnson, and Nixon to the hippies of Haight-Ashbury; from reactionaries like George Wallace to radicals like the Black Panthers; from anticapitalist student protesters of the New Left to the advertising executives who figured out early on how to cash in on the cultural revolution. Not all of Hodgson's assessments and judgments have stood the test of time, but all are advanced clearly and forcefully, and deeply engage the reader. I still teach this book, thirty years after I began doing so.

Of the core arguments that give thematic coherence to the book, none was more important than that of the liberal consensus. The consensus had arisen in the 1950s, Hodgson wrote, as "a strange hybrid" of liberal and conservative principles that "blanketed the scene and muffled debate."[1] Discussion of something like the liberal consensus had been percolating since the 1950s in the minds of Richard Hofstadter, Louis Hartz, Daniel Boorstin, Daniel Bell, John Higham, and other historians and social scientists of the postwar era.[2] Some in this group, such as Boorstin, thought that the liberal consensus was a positive development, a sign that the United States had been blessed with an exceptional nature and thus given the wherewithal to escape the deep ideological conflicts that had devastated Europe over the previous forty years.[3] Most who wrote about it, however, lamented its rise, for it signaled to them the death of the left and the consequent impoverishment of American politics. Hodgson shared in this lamentation. For him the demise of the left meant the loss of "an organized political force holding as a principle the need for far-reaching social and institutional change and consistently upholding the interests of the disadvantaged against the most powerful groups in the society." "The liberals," Hodgson acidly observed in an aside, "were never such a force."[4] The eclipse of the left, in his reckoning, helped to explain the deep frustrations of the 1960s. Stripped of left voices, the country was unable to get to the root of its problems, which lay far more with class inequality than with racial inequality or the alienation of university students.

Hodgson's argument about the rise of a liberal consensus captured salient elements of the 1950s: the successful attack on the left during the McCarthy era; the decline of labor as a dynamic, transformative force in American life; and the blandness that had apparently settled over so much of American politics and culture. But the liberal consensus interpretation has also, for a variety of reasons, met with considerable skepticism. Some have argued that Hodgson made too little of American liberalism's insurgent spirit, ignoring the times—the 1910s and the 1930s, for example—when activists marching under its banner had in fact done a great deal to advance the interests of the disadvantaged.[5] Others have emphasized that Hodgson slighted the race issue. That Hodgson dates the beginning of the liberal consensus to the very year (1954) when the great civil rights revolt erupted reveals how little race mattered in his thinking about the 1950s.[6] Hodgson also slighted the South, which could never be made to fit comfortably within a liberal consensus paradigm. How could it fit when, by 1955, white supremacists in former Confederate states were greeting civil rights initiatives with "massive resistance"? Hodgson was not unaware of these conflicts, of course, but he did partake of a mid-twentieth-century liberal/radical conceit, namely, that the South was an atavism that would soon have its rough edges removed—and perhaps be dissolved altogether—by the powerful currents of liberal modernity.[7]

There are reasons aplenty, therefore, to think about discarding the concept of liberal consensus, but I would like to suggest a different strategy for going forward: identifying the areas in which a liberal consensus ruled and the areas where it had little or no jurisdiction. On questions of foreign policy and political economy, I will argue, a liberal consensus did take shape, but on questions of race, religion, and sexuality it did not. The consensus that emerged on foreign policy and political economy is evident in the broad, bipartisan support garnered by three core ideas: first, the need to contain communism at home and abroad; second, the belief that capitalism could be regulated in some larger public interest; and third, the conviction that the federal government could be called upon to solve a great variety of social problems. Hodgson was right to argue that political economic principles formed the liberal consensus's core, though I would insist that agreement on these principles be understood as a compromise between liberalism and conservatism, not as capitulation by the former to the latter.

The kind of agreement achieved on questions of political economy did not, however, extend to a bevy of other questions, especially those concerning race, religion, and sexuality and reproduction. The sharpness of racial anger and conflict in the 1950s reveals that there was no national consensus on whether African Americans should be equal to white Americans in all respects. White Protestants may have been more ready by the 1950s to accept white Catholics and Jews than blacks as full-fledged Americans, but pushing God out of the public schools for the sake of religious neutrality—as had begun to happen by the early 1960s—infuriated the many evangelicals in their ranks. Finally, there was no agreement about the rights of individuals to make their own decisions about whom they would marry, what reproductive protections they might use, or what kinds of sexual practices they would engage in.

I want to explore the question of consensus and its boundaries by reference to a major institution in the middle of it all—the American state. The federal government is at the heart of Hodgson's account of liberal consensus. The New Deal and World War II had significantly expanded the powers of national government. These powers may well have been rolled back after World War II had ended, following the patterns of reversal that had emerged both after the Civil War and World War I, but the hardening of the Cold War in 1949–50 scuttled plans for reversal. Instead, the realization that the United States would remain at war indefinitely impelled Republicans to assent to principles they never would have accepted in peacetime: a large standing military, a steeply progressive mass taxation system to support it, and a large and dynamic federal government.

But other governments in the United States also mattered, namely, those of the states, and Democrats and Republicans found no accord over the proper scope of the activity of these units. The Constitution had vested state governments with extraordinary power. The right to regulate race and private life in the public interest rested largely with the states. By the 1950s, substantial numbers of Americans wanted to use the newly expanded power of the central government to uphold civil rights and liberties and, in the process, free individuals from the control that state governments exercised over them in matters of race, religion, and sexuality. But there was no consensus on the drive to use federal power in this way. Millions of whites were not ready to lose their racial supremacy, millions of Protestants were not willing to be told that they could not pray in public schools, and millions were not prepared to accept the proposition that decisions about marriage, sexuality, and reproduction should be entirely personal and private, free of communal, and civic, approval. The states themselves were no more ready than the white South to be swept into the dustbin of history. Bringing the states back into a history from which they have been largely excluded reveals in new ways the domains where a liberal consensus did not rule.

Where Consensus Ruled: Political Economy and the Federal Government

The reach of the federal government expanded rapidly across the 1930s. New Dealers established a significant welfare state, largely built around the Social Security Act of 1935. Through the 1935 Wagner Act they constrained the power of capital and enhanced that of labor. They also inserted themselves in unprecedented ways into the regulation of capital markets via laws establishing the Securities and Exchange Commission and separating investment from commercial banking. They made a similar intervention into housing markets by extending mortgage insurance to home buyers and to commercial banks. Meanwhile, New Deal farm regulation stabilized agricultural markets as they never had been before. The strong performance of the American economy under this regulatory regime during World War II strengthened the case for making the New Deal state permanent.[8]

Nevertheless, the commitment to regulated markets and to the establishment of a large welfare state might have been reversed after World War II, much as earlier government edifices had been dismantled following the Civil War and World War I. This was the goal of large and influential groups of Republicans energized by their success in the midterm congressional elections of 1946. But the stunning international events of 1949 and 1950 put an end to this GOP dream. America's nuclear monopoly ended abruptly in 1949 when the Soviet Union exploded its first nuclear device. Then came the "loss of China" to Mao and the Communists, which many Americans interpreted as a sign that all of East Asia, including Japan, might fall into the Soviet Union's orbit. The swift advances of Communists across the Korean peninsula in 1950 confirmed these fears among Washington policymakers. The United States responded by declaring its commitment to fighting Communism everywhere and with all its resources. Most immediately, this commitment involved the United States in a long and grinding land war in Korea. More generally, it compelled American policymakers and legislators to acknowledge that the Cold War would not be quickly or easily won.[9] The United States therefore required a big military for the foreseeable future. That in turn meant a large federal government to sustain it and pay for it. When Dwight D. Eisenhower, in 1953, became the first Republican president to occupy the White House in twenty years, he made clear his intention to maintain a large military and a government apparatus to manage it. He soon declared as well that his administration would carry on with the other responsibilities that the federal government had undertaken in depression and world war: regulating capitalism in the public interest and sponsoring a robust social-welfare apparatus to help those unable to help themselves.[10]

In stressing how conservative liberalism had become by the 1950s, Hodgson underplays how far to the political center Eisenhower moved the GOP when he acquiesced to the New Deal political order that had taken shape in the 1930s and 1940s. Many conservatives were not happy about the GOP's acquiescence, but few were willing to risk taking down the federal government that liberals had built across the New Deal–World War II years. To do so was deemed too great a risk in the fight against Communism.

Eisenhower's decision to maintain the liberals' system of progressive and mass taxation illustrates this acquiescence well. In the 1940s the federal government had imposed on the nation's biggest income earners marginal taxation rates exceeding 90 percent. These rates remained in place across Eisenhower's two terms as president. So, too, did the federal government's insistence that it had a right to tax virtually all income earners. A tradition of taxing the income of the wealthy stretched back to World War I. The New Deal had intensified this tradition with the Wealth Tax Act of 1935, which levied a tax of 75 percent on those making more than five million dollars a year. But the New Deal did little to broaden the base of taxpayers. As late as 1938, only 4 to 8 percent of the working population—the upper crust—paid any income tax at all.[11]

This "class" taxation system turned into a "mass" taxation system in World War II when the federal government deemed the taxation of virtually all income earners imperative to financing the war. The number of wage earners subject to taxation nearly doubled from 1939 to 1940, and then almost quintupled across the next four years. By 1945 nearly two-thirds of

American wage earners were paying income tax, in contrast to the single-digit percentage paying taxes in the 1930s. Annual tax receipts, meanwhile, rose twentyfold between fiscal year 1940 and fiscal year 1945, from $892 million to $18.4 billion.[12]

That this system of mass taxation emerged during World War II is not surprising in light of the revenue demands of total war. More surprising is that the system stayed in place after the war ended. Republicans who took control of Congress in 1947 wanted to roll back wartime taxation, and in 1948 they engineered a significant tax cut that was envisioned as a first step toward disassembling the new mass taxation system. Indeed, the percentage of taxpayers in the working population declined from its World War II peak of 65 percent in 1945 to 57 percent in 1949.[13] But as the Cold War heated up in 1949–50 the GOP's anti-tax efforts were thwarted. The United States accelerated its nuclear research and weapons program and geared up for a major land war in Korea, putting an end to talk of cutting defense expenditures and taxes.

By the 1950s the Republicans were ready to join a bipartisan coalition committed to a global struggle against Communism. This coalition understood that success depended on a system of mass revenue extraction. Representative Wilbur Mills of Arkansas, the conservative southern Democrat who held the chairmanship of the House Ways and Means Committee, was hardly profligate, but he appreciated the existing system's necessity. "We live in a complex and dangerous time and there is no use pretending on some happy day very soon we can cut expenditures to the point where we will no longer need large tax revenues," he said in 1959.[14] Most members of Congress on both sides of the aisle shared this sentiment, and serious objections came only from the largely irrelevant fringes of the right.[15]

It would be difficult to overstate the significance of the decision to perpetuate this high-tax system. Never before had such a substantial, regular, and long-lasting stream of revenue come into the central state's coffers. Much of that revenue went to support defense expenditures, of course. But the landscape of defense was itself changing, involving the maintenance not just of a large military but also of a robust arms industry, cutting-edge research facilities, a first-class educational system for the masses (K–12 + universities), a modern and well-maintained transportation infrastructure, and generous levels of foreign aid to allies. The federal government spent lavishly on private industry, universities, and roads, all in the name of national defense. The scale and variety of expenditures changed the horizon of possibility for what the federal government could do. It was in this new climate of possibility that one of the key axioms of Hodgson's consensus took hold, namely, that the federal government had the resources to solve any problem. The national government had acquired extraordinary resources, which in turn bred confidence that it was now endowed with exceptional ability to manage the economy and society, and even to address issues related to national security only tangentially if at all.[16]

Eisenhower's thinking on the question of mass taxation and the uses to which these augmented government revenues could be put reveals how far this new mind-set penetrated Republican circles. The president made his thoughts public in 1954 as he was steering a complex overhaul of the federal tax code through Congress. The bill was intended to codify the many changes in the taxation system that had occurred since 1939 and address the problems that those changes had generated. Eisenhower was especially concerned about tax exemption, a feature of the bill that, in his mind, threatened a cherished principle: all working Americans should pay income tax.

Tax exemption (declaring certain streams of income as wholly or partially tax free) was not in itself a new principle, as universities and religious institutions had been able to exempt their income from taxation for decades. But the 1954 bill was designed to dramatically widen the scope of tax exemption by extending its benefits from institutions to individual taxpayers. Republicans in Congress wanted to confer most of the new exemptions on wealthy Americans as a way of moderating the progressivity of the tax code. Democrats responded with amendments designed to grant working-class Americans exemptions of equal significance. The Democrats' demand for equality of exemption alarmed Eisenhower, who believed it would, if encoded into law, fatally compromise the entire mass taxation system. Thus, he went on national television and radio on March 15, 1954, to defend the federal income tax.[17]

The system's rationale, the president told the American people, was simple but powerful: paying income taxes to the federal government had become part of Americans' civic duty. While conceding that paying taxes was a burden, Eisenhower asserted that it was, like military service, one that "every real American is proud to carry." He had seen too many "examples of American pride" and "unassuming but inspiring courage" to believe that "anyone privileged to live in this country wants someone else to pay his own fair and just share of the cost of government."[18]

That a Republican president would choose to defend taxation in such civic terms was itself noteworthy. Equally striking was Eisenhower's vision of the uses to which revenues could be devoted. Defense, of course, topped his list, consuming "70 cents out of each dollar spent by your government." But Eisenhower dreamed of using tax revenues to do more, to implement a "great program to build a stronger America for all our people." "We want to improve and expand our social security program," he told his national audience. "We want a broader and stronger system of unemployment insurance. We want more and better homes for our people. We want to do away with slums in our cities. We want to foster a much improved health program."[19] Broadened Social Security, better unemployment insurance, urban renewal, and national health care—here, in embryo, was the vision that would animate the Great Society, the ambitious legislative program pushed through Congress by President Lyndon Johnson in the 1960s to complete the welfare state that Roosevelt and the New Deal had launched in the 1930s. Already in the 1950s, this liberal vision was being articulated not just by Democrats but also by a moderate Republican.

Here we can see the coalescence of a liberal consensus, the core of which, as Hodgson had shown, was a belief in the capacity of the federal government to solve economic and social problems. The policy successes of the New Deal in the 1930s and the federal government's achievements in the following decade—winning World War II and resuscitating capitalism—brought many Republicans on board. If not for the Cold War, this consensus would likely have crumbled in the midst of the conservative resurgence that followed the Allied victories of 1945. Instead, Cold War developments, particularly in 1949 and 1950, reinvigorated it and widened assent to the proposition that a large central state, armed with a powerful military and an efficient mass taxation system, could be a core feature of American politics for the long term. The new fiscal flushness of the central state impelled many citizens and politicians, including those on the GOP side of the aisle, to contemplate how the federal government might enter more and more areas of social life and engineer solutions to the problems they found there.

Where Consensus Did Not Rule: The States and Their Police Power

Confidence in the power and reach of the federal government impelled many to begin addressing as well inequalities of race and religion in American society. A concern for civil rights and civil liberties had been gathering force since the late 1930s. Recommitting the nation to its egalitarian principles took on new urgency in a world broken apart by war, Hitler's destruction of European Jewry, and totalitarian efforts by Communist and fascist regimes to render individuals powerless in the face of overwhelming government power. The emergence of India and other Third World nations from Western imperial domination gave people of color everywhere hope that that they too could achieve equality and independence. A reckoning with these global developments energized those in the United States who wanted to promote equality for African Americans and to create a society in which Jews and Catholics would be on an equal footing with white Anglo-Saxon Protestants. Movements for sexual equality and reproductive freedom had not yet gained similar prominence. Yet, integral to civil rights campaigns was an insistence that every individual American be treated with dignity and respect. Some began to find in this insistence a belief that every individual ought to be in charge of the most intimate decisions shaping his or her personal life: whom one might marry, whether or not to use birth control, how to express one's sexuality.

In this context, more and more Americans began calling on the federal government to use its authority to enlarge every person's zone of civil rights and liberties. The U.S. Supreme Court's stunning 9–0 decision in *Brown v. Board of Education* (1954), which adjudged that maintaining segregated school systems had denied American blacks "the equal protections of the laws," seemed to indicate that the federal government was prepared to act in this way. Some read into the unanimity of the Court's decision the existence of a society-wide consensus on the importance of using the federal government's power for achieving social equality.

But there was no consensus here. Millions of whites were not ready to relinquish racial segregation, whether formal or informal, public or private, and its associated assumptions of their racial supremacy. Millions of Protestants, meanwhile, were not ready to be told that they could not pray in public schools. And millions were not ready to accept the proposition that decisions about sexuality and reproduction should be entirely personal and private decisions, free of communal or civil constraint or approval.[20]

Those harboring these conservative sentiments expressed them through an array of influential institutions: churches and affiliated religious organizations, fraternal organizations, country clubs, and residential associations that, despite the Supreme Court's 1948 ruling outlawing racial covenants, still asserted the right of neighbors to control the racial and religious composition of the areas in which they lived. They also made their voices heard in government. They had the support, for example, of long-serving Democratic senators and representatives from the one-party South who dominated key committees in Congress. They could also aspire to control individual state legislatures, which the Constitution had invested with broad power, known as the "police power," to look after the "good and welfare" of the people living within a state's borders. For more than 150 years, states had issued thick sets of regulations about how people ought to live—morally, racially, and sexually. Segregation, bans on marriage between whites and blacks, the outlawing of homosexual practices, and the prohibition of commerce on the Sabbath were all held to be legitimate exercises of individuals states' police power.[21]

The Supreme Court, full of liberal FDR appointees by the mid-1940s, began taking steps to constrain the states' police power and to bind state legislatures to the Bill of Rights. But this was a slow process: it was not easy to reverse the exemption of states from the Bill of Rights that had stood for more than a hundred years. Moreover, the strengthened federal government that had emerged from the New Deal depended for its success on a series of legislative compromises that had actually enhanced the powers of the states, at least in the short term. Looking more closely at these compromises will reveal additional reasons why the federal government faced a tough challenge in taking on the states.

During the Great Depression, states were willing to accept a greater level of federal assistance than they had previously tolerated. This change of heart reflected the magnitude of the economic crisis and the insufficiency of resources available to the states from within their own borders. But many states, and those in the South in particular, attached conditions to federal aid, namely, that it not be allowed to upend the racial and class hierarchies that defined their polities' economic and social life.

Roosevelt and his New Dealers had to respect the wishes of southern states for two reasons. First, these states constituted a formidable power bloc in the Senate and the House of Representatives, thanks to the benefits of the seniority system, which gave long-serving southern legislators disproportionate influence within the standing committees of both bodies. FDR faced the prospect of making no headway with his ambitious New Deal reforms without getting the southern senators and representatives to support them. Second, the capacity of the central state in most policy areas, if measured by the number of officials in place relative to the size of the territory and the number of Americans to be serviced, was not adequate to the tasks taken on during the 1930s. The New Deal had created numerous agencies to do its work, but these needed the far more robust sets of governing institutions already extant in the states actually to deliver on promised benefits and services. These federal agencies also needed the revenues of the states, which during the 1930s were far larger in aggregate than those available to the federal government itself.[22]

These circumstances of mutual need explain the grand compromise that structured much of the New Deal order. On the one hand, the states allowed the federal government to expand its reach into the lives of their citizens in unprecedented ways. On the other hand, the states were given substantial discretion to administer the new federal programs. Consider agricultural reform, Social Security, and veterans benefits. The Agricultural Adjustment Act of 1933 directed the U.S. Department of Agriculture to pay farmers to limit their production. The revenues came from the federal government, but administration of the program was largely in the hands of state- and county-level institutions orchestrated by the Agricultural Extension units of state universities.[23] The federal government administered part of the Social Security program—the old-age pension—but state welfare agencies administered the other part—assistance to the widowed and orphaned, the disabled, and children living in households without fathers. Both levels of government contributed funds to this second part of Social Security, with the federal government agreeing to pay a certain amount for each dollar a state appropriated for welfare assistance. But the states determined the levels of support given those in need. In that way, they were able to control the size and composition of the welfare rolls in their jurisdiction.[24]

Similarly, the states played an outsized role in administering veterans benefits once Congress approved the Servicemen's Readjustment Act of 1944, better known as the G.I. Bill. Through this decentralized model of administration, states exerted considerable control over how the federal monies would be distributed. In the South, for example, state administrators distributed as little as they could to black World War II veterans. And states, South and North, found ways to channel large amounts of federal dollars to questionable destinations such as "commercial colleges" and private training programs set up overnight to cash in on federal largesse.[25]

Over the long term, the grand New Deal compromise between the states and the federal government benefited the latter more. Time (and war) gave the federal government an opportunity to enlarge its capacity, putting it in a position to take over administrative tasks it had initially delegated to the states. Likewise, the postwar decision to make the wartime federal mass taxation permanent gave the federal government access to fiscal resources that quickly dwarfed those available to the states. The shift in the portion of government revenue being raised by the federal government as opposed to the individual states was swift and stunning. In 1938 the federal government raised 41 percent of total government revenues and the states 59 percent. By 1948 the federal government's share had risen to 70 percent, with the state's share declining to 30 percent. This ratio would remain fairly constant during the first two decades of the Cold War. The dramatic change in the distribution of resources changed the entire landscape of federal-state relations. The federal government was now in the driver's seat of social policy, with the states, for the first time, in the back seat, and compelled to go along for the ride.[26]

That states by the 1960s were being pressured to accede to federal government mandates should not be interpreted as evidence of a broad consensus on the question of making Washington, DC, the preferred locus of public power. Many states wanted to sustain the pattern of the 1930s and 1940s whereby the national government supplied domestic program funds while decision making regarding allocation remained in their hands. The states' reluctance to cede power induced the federal government, through the Supreme Court, to chip away at the constitutional basis of their authority. The attack on the states began in the area of racial policy, specifically, the Court's declaration that southern states would no longer be permitted to maintain Jim Crow school regimes. It continued with the Court's declaration in 1962 that states and municipalities could no longer require children in public schools to say a prayer. And it intensified when the Court ruled in 1965 that states that prevented women from getting access to birth control were violating rights granted women by the Constitution. This campaign to use federal power to diminish the states and to enhance the civil rights and civil liberties of American citizens drew support from a broad coalition of groups, ranging from Supreme Court justices to officials across a wide range of federal agencies to the millions of ordinary citizens agitating for racial and gender equality. But this broad coalition did not reflect a society-wide consensus on the virtue of enlarging the scope of personal freedom and constricting the regulatory powers of state governments. An emphasis on consensus only serves to obscure the fault lines that divided Americans from each other on these intertwined issues.[27]

Deep disagreement over the proper use of government continues to this day. It is a principal reason for the chasm that currently separates Democrats and Republicans, and it has long paralyzed government action at the federal level. Some of the anti-government animus of conservatives reflects post-1960s developments. The GOP today would not nominate for the presidency a moderate Republican like Dwight D. Eisenhower, committed to mass taxation and to the broad deployment of federal power.

This post-1960s change in the GOP signifies that the consensus on political economy that once held sway in the United States in the 1950s and 1960s no longer exists. But there had never been an equivalent consensus on the use of federal power to redress racial, religious, and sexual (and reproductive) grievances. Redress here required an attack on the powers of the states in the name of civil rights and liberties. It demanded that the federal courts bind the states to the federal Bill of Rights after a 150-year period in which they had been exempt; and it required judges to declare that rights that were implied but not named in the Constitution took precedence over the right of state legislatures to determine what was good for the people whom they had been elected to represent. This attack on the power of states did not stem from a consensual belief uniting liberals and conservatives. The question of whether or not to strip the states of their power to legislate morality and standards for a good life divided Americans in the two decades after 1945, the heyday of Hodgson's liberal consensus. It continued to do so in the first two decades of the twenty-first century.

Notes

1. Godfrey Hodgson, *America in Our Time* (Garden City, NY: Doubleday, 1976), 73.

2. Daniel J. Boorstin, *The Genius of American Politics* (Chicago: University of Chicago Press, 1953); Richard Hofstadter, *The American Political Tradition and the Men Who Made It* (New York: Vintage Books, 1948); Louis Hartz, *The Liberal Tradition in America: An Interpretation of American Political Thought since the Revolution* (New York: Harcourt, Brace, 1955); John Higham, "The Cult of the 'American Consensus': Homogenizing Our History," *Commentary* 27 (January 1959): 93–100; Daniel Bell, *The End of Ideology: On the Exhaustion of Political Ideas in the Fifties* (New York: Free Press, 1960).

3. For discussion, see Hans Kohn, *American Nationalism: An Interpretative Essay* (New York: Macmillan, 1957).

4. Hodgson, *America in Our Time*, 89.

5. See, e.g., Alan Brinkley, *The End of Reform: New Deal Liberalism in Recession and War* (New York: Knopf, 1995).

6. Hodgson, *America in Our Time*, 71.

7. Gary Gerstle, "Race and the Myth of the Liberal Consensus," *Journal of American History* 82 (September 1995): 579–86.

8. William E. Leuchtenberg, *Franklin D. Roosevelt and the New Deal, 1932–1940* (New York: Harper & Row, 1963); Steve Fraser and Gary Gerstle, eds., *The Rise and Fall of the New Deal Order, 1930–1980* (Princeton: Princeton University Press, 1989); David M. Kennedy, *Freedom from Fear: The American People in Depression and War, 1929–1945* (New York: Oxford University Press, 1999).

9. Melvyn P. Leffler, *A Preponderance of Power: National Security, the Truman Administration, and the Cold War* (Stanford: Stanford University Press, 1992); John Lewis Gaddis,

The United States and the Origins of the Cold War, 1941–1947 (New York: Columbia University Press, 1972); John Lewis Gaddis, *Strategies of Containment: A Critical Appraisal of Postwar American National Security Policy*, revised and expanded ed. (New York: Oxford University Press, 2005); John Lewis Gaddis, *George F. Kennan: An American Life* (New York: Penguin, 2011); John Lewis Gaddis, *We Now Know: Rethinking Cold War History* (New York: Oxford University Press, 1997); Gar Alperovitz, *Atomic Diplomacy: Hiroshima and Potsdam: The Use of the Atomic Bomb and the American Confrontation with Soviet Power* (New York: Penguin, 1985); Vladislav Zubok and Constantine Pleshekov, *Inside the Kremlin's Cold War: From Stalin to Khrushchev* (Cambridge: Harvard University Press, 1996); Michael, J. Hogan, *Cross of Iron: Harry S. Truman and the Origins of the National Security State, 1945–1954* (New York: Cambridge University Press, 1998); Bruce Cumings, *The Origins of the Korean War*, 2 vols. (Princeton: Princeton University Press, 1981–1990); William Stueck, *The Road to Confrontation: American Policy toward China and Korea, 1947–1950* (Chapel Hill: University of North Carolina Press, 1981); William Stueck, *The Korean War: An International History* (Princeton: Princeton University Press, 1995); National Security Council Paper, "NSC-68: United States Objectives and Programs for National Security," April 14, 1950, http://fas.org/irp/offdocs/nsc-hst/nsc-68.htm.

10. Gary Gerstle, *Liberty and Coercion: The Paradox of American Government from the Founding to the Present* (Princeton: Princeton University Press, 2015), chapter 8.

11. *Historical Statistics of the United States, Millennial Edition Online*, "Federal Income Tax Returns—Individual: 1940–1992" [Table Ea740–747]; "Federal Income Tax Returns—Individual: 1913–1943" [Table Ea748–757]; "Population: 1790–2000 [Annual Estimates]," [Table Aa6–8]; "Labor Force, Employment, and Unemployment: 1890–1990" [Table Ba470–477]; "Military Personnel on Active Duty, by Branch of Service and Sex: 1789–1995" [Table Ed26–47]. For the history of taxation in the United States, see Sheldon Pollack, *War, Revenue, and State Building: Financing the Development of the American State* (Ithaca: Cornell University Press, 2009); W. Elliott Brownlee, *Federal Taxation in America: A Short History*, 2nd ed. (Washington, DC: Woodrow Wilson Center Press, 2004); W. Elliott Brownlee, ed., *Funding the Modern American State, 1941–1995: The Rise and Fall of the Era of Easy Finance* (Washington, DC: Woodrow Wilson Center Press, 1996); Sidney Ratner, *American Taxation: Its History as a Social Force in Democracy* (New York: Norton: 1942); Sidney Ratner, *Taxation and Democracy in America* (New York: Wiley, 1967); Carolyn Jones, "Class Tax to Mass Tax: The Role of Propaganda in the Expansion of the Income Tax during World War II," *Buffalo Law Review* 37 (1988–1989): 685–738; Mark Leff, *The Limits of Symbolic Reform: The New Deal and Taxation, 1933–1939* (New York: Cambridge University Press, 1984); John Witte, *The Politics and Development of the Federal Income Tax* (Madison: University of Wisconsin Press, 1985); and Julian Zelizer, *Taxing America: Wilbur D. Mills, Congress, and the State, 1945–1975* (New York: Cambridge University Press, 1998).

12. These totals reflect revenues received exclusively from personal income tax paid. Corporate taxes brought in another $16 billion, up from $1.2 billion in fiscal year 1940. *Historical Statistics of the United States Millennial Edition Online*, "Federal Government Revenue, by Source: 1934–1999 [OMB]" [Table Ea683–697]; Pollack, *War, Revenue, and State Building*, 261–62.

13. *Historical Statistics of the United States Millennial Edition Online*, "Federal Income

Tax Returns—Individual: 1940–1992" [Table Ea 740–747]; "Federal Income Tax Returns—Individual: 1913–1943" [Table Ea 748–757]; "Population: 1790–2000 [Annual Estimates]" [Table Aa6–8]; "Labor Force, Employment, and Unemployment: 1890–1990" [Table Ba470–477]; "Military Personnel on Active Duty, by Branch of Service and Sex: 1789–1995" [Table Ed26–47.

14. Wilbur D. Mills, "Are You a Pet or a Patsy?" *Life*, November 23, 1959, 62.

15. Romain Huret, *American Tax Resisters* (Cambridge: Harvard University Press, 2014).

16. Gerstle, *Liberty and Coercion*, chapter 8.

17. Dwight D. Eisenhower, "Radio and Television Address to the American People on the Tax Program," March 15, 1954, *Public Papers of the Presidents*, in Gerhard Peters and John T. Woolley, *The American Presidency Project*, http://www.presidency.ucsb.edu/ws. See also Witte, *Politics and Development of the Federal Income Tax*, 146–50; Iwan W. Morgan, *Eisenhower versus "the Spenders": The Eisenhower Administration, the Democrats, and the Budget, 1953–60*, (New York: St. Martin's Press, 1990), 67–68.

18. Eisenhower, "Radio and Television Address."

19. Ibid.

20. Gerstle, *Liberty and Coercion*, chapter 9.

21. Thomas J. Sugrue, *The Origins of the Urban Crisis: Race and Inequality in Postwar Detroit* (Princeton: Princeton University Press, 1996); Thomas J. Sugrue, *Sweet Land of Liberty: The Forgotten Struggle for Civil Rights in the North* (New York: Random House, 2008); Arnold R. Hirsch, *Making the Second Ghetto: Race and Housing in Chicago, 1940–1960* (New York: Cambridge University Press, 1981); Ira Katznelson, *When Affirmative Action Was White: An Untold Story of Racial Inequality in Twentieth-Century America* (New York: Norton, 2005); Ira Katznelson, *Fear Itself: The New Deal and the Origins of Our Time* (New York: Liveright, 2013); Kevin Kruse, *Atlanta and the Making of Modern Conservatism* (Princeton: Princeton University Press, 2005); Matthew D. Lassiter, *The Silent Majority: Suburban Politics in the Sunbelt South* (Princeton: Princeton University Press, 2006); Joseph Crespino, *In Search of Another Country: Mississippi and the Conservative Counterrevolution* (Princeton: Princeton University Press, 2007). On the states and their police power, see Gerstle, *Liberty and Coercion*, chapters 2 and 9.

22. Katznelson, *Fear Itself*; James T. Patterson, *The New Deal and the States: Federalism in Transition* (Princeton: Princeton University Press, 1969).

23. Gerstle, *Liberty and Coercion*, chapter 6.

24. Alice Kessler Harris, *In Pursuit of Equity: Women, Men, and the Quest for Economic Citizenship in Twentieth-Century America* (New York: Oxford University Press, 2001); Suzanne Mettler, *Dividing Citizens: Gender and Federalism in New Deal Public Policy* (Ithaca: Cornell University Press, 1998); Edward D. Berkowitz, *Mr. Social Security: The Life of Wilbur J. Cohen* (Lawrence: University Press of Kansas, 1995).

25. Katznelson, *When Affirmative Action Was White*; Mettler, *Dividing Citizens*; Kathleen Frydl, *The GI Bill* (New York: Cambridge University Press, 2009).

26. *Historical Statistics of the United States, Millennial Edition Online* (2013), "Total Government Revenue and Expenditure, by Level: 1902–1995" [Table Ea10–23].

27. Gerstle, *Liberty and Coercion*, chapter 9.

4

The 1930s Roots of the Postwar "Consensus"

WENDY L. WALL

In the waning months of World War II, Rabbi Louis Finkelstein addressed a gathering of diverse academics, business and religious leaders, foundation officials, and other American elites who had assembled at Columbia University for a symposium on "Unity and Difference in American Life." A leader of Conservative Judaism, Finkelstein was president of the Jewish Theological Seminary and director of its relatively new Institute for Religious and Social Studies, which had sponsored the symposium. In his remarks, the rabbi set the tone for the gathering, suggesting that Americans needed to be encouraged to think about their common interests "as against their diverse interests." Finkelstein acknowledged that America's "moral influence" was "indispensable" in the postwar world and could only be exerted if the nation "set its own moral house in order." Most of his comments, however, focused on the need for what he called a "mental reorientation" on the part of his countrymen. "[A] trade union may regard its interests as opposed to those of the employer; the southern Negro has his quarrels with the southern white," the rabbi observed.

> But the more thoughtful in each group will realize that beyond these divisive interests, there are centripetal ones, shared by opposing groups. The prosperity of an industry often has more effect on the lives of the employees and employers than the results of their struggle against one another. The prosperity and well-being of the South as a whole is more significant in the life of both whites and Negroes than is their relative position in the struggle for power.

Americans ignored such common ground at their peril, Finkelstein argued, for recent events around the globe had shown the threat "to all groups and institutions of democratic lands from emphasis on that which divides us rather than on that which unites us."[1]

Finkelstein's remarks were echoed—in a slightly different key—by a man who became during the war one of the most visible spokesmen for American industry. Eric Johnston, a Spokane businessman, was elected president of the U.S. Chamber of Commerce in May 1942. A frequent speaker and prolific writer, he argued in numerous venues that "the factors of conflict" between labor and management—indeed, between most groups in American society—were "real enough" but were "always smaller in extent than the factors of mutual interest." "Social peace," he suggested, depended on bringing contending parties together in conversation and encouraging them to concentrate on areas of agreement. The alternative, he suggested, was the kind of "family quarrel" that Americans had engaged in during the Depression, a quarrel "which seemed again and again to be spiraling towards the depths of disaster."[2]

Louis Finkelstein and Eric Johnston were very different men. Finkelstein was a Talmudic scholar, a lifelong New Yorker, and the scion of a rabbinical family whose parents had immigrated to the United States from Lithuania in the late nineteenth century.[3] The *New York Times* described Johnston as an "ebullient extrovert," a former marine and self-made businessman from Washington State, who could trace some of his ancestors to the American Revolution.[4] Finkelstein was alarmed by the rise of anti-Semitism both in the United States and abroad during the late 1930s, and he devoted much of his subsequent career to promoting the notion that America's "democratic way" was rooted in values shared by Christians and Jews alike. Johnston, by contrast, emphasized that Americans were "capitalists all," a fact that they had briefly lost sight of during the economic catastrophe of the Depression decade. As head of the U.S. Chamber of Commerce and later the Motion Picture Association of America, Johnston promoted labor-management cooperation and a consensual politics of consumption and economic growth.

In several critical ways, however, these men were quite similar. Both the rabbi and the businessman repeatedly emphasized—in speeches, in their writings, and through various actions—the need for Americans to "reorient" themselves and to focus on finding common ground.[5] Both proselytized during the 1950s and 1960s on behalf of their own versions of an American "consensus." And both did this because they were alarmed by social and political developments in the United States and abroad during the 1930s, a period that Finkelstein called the twentieth century's "slough of despond."[6]

Finkelstein and Johnston were hardly alone. In fact, in their efforts to awaken their fellow citizens to what each declared was America's "common ground," they were emblematic of a broad swath of American elites. Thus their stories suggest the need to reframe our understanding of the postwar "liberal consensus." For decades, both scholarly and popular commentators depicted the postwar years—particularly the 1950s and early 1960s—as a time of unusually deep and well-grounded national unity, a time when postwar affluence and the Cold War combined to produce a remarkable level of agreement about the nation's core values.[7] In recent years, scholars have challenged this picture of ideological cohesion, pointing to evidence of dissent on both the left and the right.[8] The views and activities of Finkelstein, Johnston, and many of their compatriots, however, suggest a third possibility, namely, that "consensus" was, above all, a political project. By defining the values on which "all Americans" supposedly agreed—and by promoting those values using an array of cultural forums—diverse elites sought to shape the nation's political culture in ways that furthered their own political and social agendas. They sought to define the nation's "circle of we" in ways that excluded those with whom they ideologically disagreed.[9]

Moreover, the stories of Finkelstein and Johnston suggest that the roots of this "consensus culture" can be found, not in postwar prosperity or even the Cold War, but in the turbulent years that immediately preceded U.S. entry into World War II. In the 1930s and early 1940s, Americans across the political spectrum worried that "foreign ideologies"—fascism or communism, depending on one's political perspective—were not only challenging the United States abroad but making inroads domestically as well. Some also worried about the effects of internal disunity on democratic political culture: many liberals and European émigrés, for instance, believed that only internal strife could explain the stunning collapse of France in 1940. Spurred by such fears, journalists, historians, cultural critics, and others sought to define a consensus on American values, while businessmen, political leaders, interfaith activists, and ultimately civil rights activists sought to create one. Into at least the early 1960s, the shared language of consensus—often cast in terms of an "American way"—masked real disagreement about national values and policies.[10]

Although this chapter focuses on the United States, the argument made here may also be relevant to the postwar politics of other nations. Beginning in the late 1930s, politicians and others in European countries ranging from Britain to Norway and Sweden began employing terms like "the middle way" and "consensus" to suggest the need for policy alternatives that "would allow for a broad alignment of democrats of all political faiths in the interests of unity against both . . . internal and external evils."[11] By the early 1960s, such terms were in widespread use, and scholars were noting the "decreasing political conflict and increasing political consensus" in "many post–World War II western political systems."[12] Any "consensus," however, may have been more prescriptive or rhetorical than real. Examining the case of Britain, Richard Toye recently concluded that politicians and commentators from the early 1940s through at least the Thatcher era "invoked the concept of 'consensus politics' in a variety of ways in order to advance a diverse range of agendas."[13] Certainly that was the case in the United States, as the stories of Finkelstein, Johnston, and many of their contemporaries suggest.

* * *

Few individuals better exemplify one strain in the consensus politics of postwar America than Rabbi Louis Finkelstein. Born in 1895 in Cincinnati, Ohio, to Lithuanian immigrant parents, Finkelstein was the son of an Orthodox rabbi. When Finkelstein was about seven, his father accepted a call to a Brooklyn synagogue and the family moved to New York City. Finkelstein attended New York public schools while also receiving a religious education. He earned his bachelor's degree at City College in 1915 and his doctorate from Columbia three years later. In 1919 he was ordained as a rabbi at the Jewish Theological Seminary and accepted a post at a growing Bronx synagogue. Finkelstein also taught at the seminary, publishing scholarly works on Jewish self-government in the Middle Ages, and the sociology and faith of the Pharisees. In 1931 he was promoted to full professor, left his congregation, and began to move up in the seminary's administration. Finkelstein was named provost in 1937 and president in 1940, a position he held for more than thirty years.[14]

Finkelstein's role at the Jewish Theological Seminary connected him to a broad circle of prominent Jewish New Yorkers. He was a close friend of *New York Times* publisher Arthur Hays Sulzberger and broadcast pioneer David Sarnoff, and a frequent correspondent with individuals ranging from New York governor Herbert Lehman to investment banking heiress and philanthropist Frieda Schiff Warburg. Many of these people came from German Jewish families with deep roots in the United States, and they had long considered themselves safe from most forms of anti-Semitism. In the mid-1930s, however, they watched with alarm as fascist anti-Semites surged to power in Europe and the Depression triggered an eruption of indigenous bigotry. More than one hundred anti-Semitic organizations emerged in the United States between 1933 and 1941; by one estimate, this was twenty times the number formed in the country up to that point.[15] In the past, domestic anti-Semitism had primarily taken the form of social or economic discrimination, but many of the new organizations resorted to violence. Some benefited from foreign support, even as they wrapped themselves in the mantle of Americanism.

Nothing alarmed Finkelstein and his associates more than the rising popularity of the charismatic "radio priest," Father Charles Coughlin.[16] In the early 1930s, Coughlin attracted an audience of millions to his weekly radio show, in which he assailed communism, railed against the gold standard, and called for the nationalization of the U.S. banking system. Coughlin initially allied himself with President Franklin D. Roosevelt, but he soon founded his own political organization and launched a weekly newspaper; by 1934 he was receiving more mail than the president. Throughout the 1930s, Coughlin blamed the Depression on "money changers" and "international bankers," and in 1938 he turned openly and stridently anti-Semitic. He repeatedly assailed "communistic Jews" and in one editorial lifted wording directly from Hitler's chief propagandist, Joseph Goebbels. Although Coughlin lost followers towards the end of the decade, a Gallup poll conducted in early 1938 showed that 10 percent of all American families with radios still tuned him in regularly and that 83 percent of those who listened approved of his message. Meanwhile, the Christian Front, a movement of Coughlin supporters, drilled its members in military tactics and stockpiled weapons. In cities such as Boston and New York, roving gangs of Christian Fronters smashed the windows of Jewish-owned stores and "engaged in open, Nazi-like brawls with Jews."[17]

Finkelstein attributed both Hitler's successes abroad and the rise of virulent anti-Semitism at home to the same cause: a general weakening of religious faith that was undermining democratic values. Finkelstein distinguished between democracy as a "mode of government" and democracy as a "way of life." The former emerged "in opposition to monarchy and oligarchy," rested (at least in the United States) on the Constitution, and focused on the legal rights of citizens. The latter, by contrast, sprang from scripture and began with "the concept of man as made in God's Image, having an immortal soul, and therefore possessing infinite dignity on which no one dares infringe."[18] It was this democratic *culture*, Finkelstein believed, that had long protected Jews both in the United States and abroad. "The real difficulty we must face . . . is the . . . heathenization or paganization of such a large part of the population both Jewish and Christian," he wrote to one associate in July 1939. "From the long range point of view, I do not know of anything we can do more important than to make some contribution to the preservation of religion as a vital force in America."[19]

As this suggests, Finkelstein believed that the best way to combat domestic anti-Semitism was by convincing Americans that they shared values rooted in religious tradition and by defining that tradition in a way that included Jews. In short, he sought to promote the notion that Judaism, Catholicism. and Protestantism were "the religions of democracy," diverse representations of the spiritual ideals and moral values that all Americans shared. It was from the "Judeo-Christian" tradition, he suggested, that Americans derived their belief in "the Fatherhood of God and the Brotherhood of Man," and it was this common belief that formed the cornerstone of "true democracy."[20]

Finkelstein was hardly alone in promoting a national consensus based on Judeo-Christian values. Others in his circle pursued similar projects from the late 1930s on, working through organizations and enterprises like the 1939 New York World's Fair, the American Jewish Committee, the National Conference of Christians and Jews, the United Service Organizations, and the Advertising Council.[21] Finkelstein's contribution to this cultural project came primarily through his establishment of several influential forums designed to bring together "men who differed widely among themselves" to allow them to "learn from one another" and to explore their common ground.[22] In 1938 he founded within the Jewish Theological Seminary the Institute for Interdenominational Studies (IIS), which gathered theologians and clergymen of various faiths for lectures, classes, and symposia devoted to highlighting "the common elements in the Jewish and Christian tradition, with especial reference to its significance in the struggle for preservation of American democratic ideals." Finkelstein hoped the IIS would help to combat "the pagan pseudo-religions of Fascism and Communism" by making "the idea [of a Judeo-Christian tradition] an integral part of American religious thought." The institute, he suggested, "is at once a tribute to American democracy, and a bulwark for its preservation."[23]

In 1940, two years after establishing the IIS, Finkelstein launched an even more ambitious initiative to strengthen the nation's "moral and spiritual fiber."[24] The Conference on Science, Philosophy and Religion in Their Relation to the Democratic Way of Life (CSPR) was an annual seminar that brought together prominent theologians, scientists, and other scholars—men and women like John Courtney Murray, Jacques Maritain, Harlow

Shapley, Enrico Fermi, Van Wyck Brooks, Alain Locke, Talcott Parsons, and Margaret Mead. Drawing on a wide range of moral, philosophical, and religious traditions, they sought to use face-to-face dialogue to develop "a comprehensive moral framework that would support democratic values."[25] In the words of political scientist Harold Lasswell, the goal of the CSPR was to create "an organized conscience for American civilization."[26]

Both the IIS and the CSPR continued into the postwar period, reflecting the desire of Finkelstein and many of his compatriots to create a "'one-for-all, all-for one' pattern of thought and behavior."[27] The IIS eventually evolved into the Institute for Religious and Social Studies, which sponsored a variety of programs designed to reduce intergroup tensions and promote national unity, including the symposium described at the beginning of this chapter. The CSPR met regularly through 1968, attracting participants who represented "a particularly weighty section of the American intelligentsia."[28] It also spawned an offshoot—the Institute of Ethics—that pursued similar discussions even more intensively. As Finkelstein explained in a 1948 letter to his friend Arthur Sulzberger, both programs were needed to combat the tendency for American groups and institutions to stress their own needs over the common good. "Unless the various component institutions are trained by their leaders to think of the whole," he wrote, "each group becomes a pressure group, self-seeking and dividing the nation against itself."[29] This was a lesson Finkelstein had learned in the cauldron of the 1930s.

* * *

Eric Johnston came to the politics of consensus by a very different route, but he too was profoundly shaped by the social and political turmoil of the 1930s. Johnston was born in 1895, the same year as Finkelstein, in Washington, DC, but his family moved west instead of east—first to Montana, and then to Spokane, Washington. Johnston's father repeatedly failed in business as a pharmacist, and when Eric was fifteen his parents divorced. Johnston matriculated at the University of Washington, paying his way in part by working as a longshoreman on the Seattle docks. Although he had hoped to become a lawyer, World War I ended Johnston's formal education. He enlisted in the Marine Corps, became an officer, fought with the American Expeditionary Force in Siberia in 1919, and then served as an assistant naval attaché in Beijing. While in China, Johnston got into a confrontation with locals and suffered a skull fracture. This and related sinus problems soon led to his medical discharge from the marines.[30]

Returning to Spokane in 1922, Johnston found a job selling vacuum cleaners door-to-door for a small retailer of electric appliances. Using money he had made speculating in Chinese currency, he soon bought a share in the enterprise, renamed it the Brown-Johnston Company, and built it into one of the largest distributors of lamps and household appliances in the Pacific Northwest. In 1933 Johnston organized the Columbia Electrical and Manufacturing Company, which became a leading regional manufacturer of electrical appliances. The same year, he took over the bankrupt Washington Brick and Lime Company, eventually restoring it to profitability and repaying its creditors.[31]

A gifted orator and classic western booster, Johnston was increasingly tapped for leadership positions in local business groups. In 1929 he served as president of the Inland Empire Manufacturer's Association, and two years later he was elected president of the Spokane Chamber of Commerce. In the late 1930s Johnston chaired the Washington State Progress Commission, which used public and private funds to promote tourism, industry, and investment in the state.[32] Then, in early 1942, Johnston burst onto the national scene. He had served the U.S. Chamber of Commerce in various capacities since 1934. Just after the start of World War II a group of younger, mostly western, members of the national Chamber revolted against the organization's reactionary older guard and elected the forty-six-year-old Johnston president.[33]

Johnston's rise in the Spokane business community coincided with the onset of the Great Depression. A sharp downturn in crop prices after the end of World War I had already brought a decade of lean times to rural parts of the Pacific Northwest. The stock market crash and its aftermath only exacerbated the region's troubles. In 1931 and 1932 a slew of Spokane banks failed, including three on the same day. Some cash-poor lumber mills in the Inland Empire paid their crews in scrip. Although Spokane's unemployment rate rose to 25 percent in the bleak winter of 1932–33, hundreds of unemployed workers arrived daily by boxcar, drawn by rumors that jobs were available out west. "The ever-increasing army that throngs to the freights is one of the most pathetic aspects of the depression," wrote one local journalist in October 1932. "The other morning, when a through freight slowed down as it entered Parkwater, more than 300 men, women, and children dropped from the train."[34]

The economic crisis of the early 1930s ended the Republican Party's long hold on Washington State and revived the state's tradition of militant radicalism and labor activism. The lumber camps, mill towns, mines, and docks of the Pacific Northwest had once proved fertile ground for socialists, the Knights of Labor, and the Wobblies, but the Red Scare that followed World War I left radicalism moribund for a decade. In the early 1930s the tide turned once again. Former socialists in Seattle attracted thousands to their newly formed Unemployed Citizens League, while radicals with ties to Upton Sinclair's End Poverty in California (EPIC) initiative worked to elect state officials who would support cooperatively owned factories and farms. In 1935 these EPIC sympathizers formed the Washington Commonwealth Federation and began running left-wing candidates for office from within the Democratic Party. They also built public support for unions, social programs, and old-age pensions. Organized labor too rebounded beginning in 1933. In May 1934, longshoremen in Seattle, Tacoma, and Bellingham, Washington, joined others from the Canadian to the Mexican border in a strike that shut West Coast ports for eighty-three days. The massive waterfront strike inspired similar actions by teamsters, loggers, sawmill workers, Filipino cannery workers, and others.[35]

New Deal policies—first the National Industrial Recovery Act and later the National Labor Relations (aka Wagner) Act—paved the way for such labor militancy by affirming the right of workers to join unions. The federal government also intervened in other ways. In an attempt to boost farm incomes, it paid farmers to leave wheat fields fallow and to slaughter excess livestock. In March 1933, President Roosevelt launched the Civilian Conservation Corps, and by August some forty-five CCC camps employing ten thousand young men were operating within one hundred miles of Spokane.[36] The Works Progress Administration put thousands more to work in the region building roads, sewers, and water mains. Most dramatically, the Public Works Administration oversaw construction of the Grand Coulee Dam on the Columbia River, a project that remade the Inland Empire by providing cheap hydroelectric power and irrigation. Such policies reflected the belief of many liberals in the late 1930s that the American economy had reached a mature stage of development that lacked dynamic elements of growth and needed government management to ensure it could deliver adequate levels of prosperity and employment.

Johnston's political views were forever shaped by both the economic crisis and the resulting reactions of workers, radicals, the federal government, and his fellow businessmen. "The black depression of the 1930s and the spread of various ideologies of despair" challenged "my basic beliefs," he wrote in 1944, and "impelled me, as they did millions of others, to take apart and appraise matters that had until then been accepted uncritically."[37]

For starters, Johnston concluded that the survival of America's capitalist economy depended on its ability to provide jobs. "Our people will not again stand for mass unemployment," he declared shortly after assuming the presidency of the U.S. Chamber of Commerce. "If you solve that problem you solve the whole problem of retaining the free enterprise system in one fell swoop."[38] At the same time, Johnston argued that Americans could retain their "civilization of abundance" if they maintained their characteristic optimism—their belief in "total wealth as ever-expanding"—and if they remembered that workers, farmers, and management "must flourish together."[39]

Like most businessmen, Johnston decried many aspects of the New Deal: its attempts "to legislate by administrative decrees"; its emphasis "upon negative and defeatist ideas and procedures, such as 'made' work [and] plowing-under"; and its "tendency to excessive centralization," which, Johnston warned, could produce "totalitarian governmentalism." But Johnston did not let business entirely off the hook. He acknowledged workers' legitimate desire for jobs and decent wages and argued that "business cannot save itself from a species of persecution and ultimate obliteration unless it meets the forces of social change halfway." For Johnston that meant embracing collective bargaining, while convincing both workers and the public that "the common ground between labor and management is invariably larger and more solid than the margins of disagreement." He also conceded the need for social security, for temporary relief for "all Americans in distress," and for some public-works projects—preferably ones controlled by states and localities. "In the spirit of the Middle Way for America," he declared, "these and a good many other New Deal measures can be absorbed and brought into alignment with a freely functioning private-enterprise world."[40]

Johnston may have drawn his reference to the "Middle Way" from European thinkers and economists.[41] But he used the term to highlight what appalled him most about the Depression decade: what he saw as its tone of animosity and rancor. "The main evil of the New Deal period," he argued, "was its spirit of vendetta and class warfare—its refusal to explore and exploit areas of agreement." Johnston clearly placed the primary blame for this on New Dealers and radicals, but he conceded that it "takes at least two to make a quarrel. . . . The business-baiters and the Roosevelt-haters proved equally lusty fellows."[42]

Johnston was a master of the optics of consensus, and World War II gave him the perfect stage. One of his first acts after being elected president of the U.S. Chamber of Commerce was to call on President Roosevelt—something no Chamber leader had done since the organization bitterly denounced FDR in 1935. He then sought out the presidents of the American Federation of Labor and the Congress of Industrial Organizations, William Green and Philip Murray, respectively, arguing to both that business and labor had a common stake in boosting production and preserving capitalism more generally.[43] Finally, he led a delegation—consisting of himself, Green, Murray, and the head of the National Association of Manufacturers—to the White House where they pledged to work together to develop "maximum and uninterrupted production."[44] Perhaps because of this show of solidarity, Johnston was widely, if erroneously, credited—in press accounts at the time, in his *New York Times* obituary, and in Wikipedia today—with persuading labor to make a no-strike pledge during World War II.

Johnston was a business moderate, but his overall approach was to "talk about the things [on which business and labor] see eye to eye" and to "take up other things later."[45] Thus, he downplayed issues on which he disagreed with labor leaders—for instance, the Wagner Act, the need for strikes, or the need for wage freezes to combat inflation. Instead, Johnston stressed business and labor's common interest in creating jobs through stepped-up production, in "decent" wages as a means of boosting consumption, and in the need to rebuild countries after the war to create new markets for American goods. His arguments for consensus and national unity ignored the power imbalance that had long existed between management and workers, but to many Americans they had the ring of common sense. During the war, Johnston made these points in numerous widely publicized speeches and articles—including in one February 1943 piece in *Reader's Digest* (titled "Your Stake in Capitalism") that was reprinted as a full-page ad in scores of newspapers and employee publications throughout the country.[46] In his 1944 book *America Unlimited*, Johnston coined the phrase "people's capitalism" to describe a capitalism of high productivity and high consumption—an economy "of the people, by the people, for the people"—that would contrast sharply with both the "capitalism of private monopoly and special privilege" and with the "bureaucratic capitalism" of Moscow and Berlin. This "people's capitalism," he argued, "is the essence of what we have called earlier the Middle Way."[47]

Johnston left the U.S. Chamber of Commerce in 1945 to assume the presidency of the Motion Picture Producers and Distributors of America. His new perch in Hollywood, together with his membership on the Committee for Economic Development, put him in an even better position to popularize the ideology of production, consumption, and class consensus.

Johnston told screenwriters in 1946, "We'll have no more films that deal with the seamy side of American life. We'll have no more films that treat the banker as villain." He called on Hollywood to purge the industry of "American proponents" of "European ideologies," and presided over the institution of the Hollywood blacklist. As Lary May has argued, Johnston and his allies "used the anticommunist crusade to alter the structure of power and ideology permeating the film capital." Whereas Hollywood films of the 1930s criticized class inequality and offered sympathetic portraits of strikers and the poor, films of the 1950s portrayed "a new Americanism rooted in big business, class consensus and consumer democracy."[48] The fervency with which Johnston promoted this message until his death in 1963 reflected his experiences during the Depression decade.

* * *

A few months after World War II ended, Eric Johnston warned a group of entertainment executives about "the salesmen of dissension, the rabble-rousers and hatemongers" who were "seeking to exploit post-war dislocations and post-war nerves." The nation, Johnston suggested, needed both a "program of group relations" designed to rebuild national unity and "a more conscious appraisal and defense of American values."[49] Three years later, Louis Finkelstein and his colleagues at the Institute for Religious and Social Studies called for "a permanent seminar or conference of leaders of various organizations in America for the purpose of formulating the 'Goals for America.'" Such a conference they suggested, would help leaders overlook the "particular interests" of their organizations and arouse in them an "awareness of common [national] goals."[50]

Neither Johnston nor Finkelstein undertook such an initiative, but roughly a decade later several other organizations did. The late 1950s and early 1960s saw an outpouring of concern about the "national purpose." In February 1960, President Eisenhower created a President's Commission on National Goals and later that year *Life* and the *New York Times* jointly published a series of essays on the topic.[51] The Rockefeller Brothers Fund (RBF) acted even sooner, launching a policy planning project in 1956 to "clarify the national purposes and objectives." Nelson Rockefeller chaired the study, and he chose Henry Kissinger to direct the project. Kissinger recruited more than one hundred prominent Americans—industrialists, government officials, academics, labor leaders, editors, philanthropists, generals, and theologians—and organized them into working panels to discuss topics ranging from international objectives and military policy to economics and education. Some individual panel reports appeared between January 1958 and September 1960. In 1961, all were compiled and published under the title *Prospect for America.*[52]

For Godfrey Hodgson and many scholars since, the RBF reports provide dramatic evidence of the existence of a postwar "liberal consensus." As Hodgson wrote in 1976, *Prospect for America* formed "a handbook of the shared assumptions of the American governmental and business elite."[53] The final product would appear to support this assessment. Yet a close look at the behind-the-scenes discussions of two panels which organizers deemed particularly important—those formed to address "The Moral Framework of National Purpose" and "The Power of the Democratic Idea"—tell a different story.

From the beginning, both Rockefeller and Kissinger agreed that the most important part of the study would be an opening chapter on "The Moral Framework of National Purpose." This chapter, Kissinger argued, would keep the project from floundering "in a sea of expediency" by focusing the debate on "the most fundamental questions." To draft this introductory chapter—to define the nation's common moral framework—Kissinger tapped Rabbi Louis Finkelstein and eight other stalwarts of the Conference on Science, Philosophy and Religion. They, after all, had been wrestling with just this question for some fifteen years.[54]

In a series of meetings held throughout 1957, the nine members of the panel tried to articulate a national moral consensus. They considered topics ranging from the moral implications of abundance to the values that should be used to set spending priorities or to set limits on the use of nuclear weapons. Kissinger prodded the group, posing questions like "What are we willing to die for in terms of values?" At one point, a frustrated Rockefeller stepped in, offering his own summary of what he saw as core American beliefs; these included "one God Almighty (by whatever name)," human dignity, religious dignity, international interdependence, and a "sound expanding economic life."[55] After multiple meetings, however, the panelists were unable to come to any conclusions. A few even began to question the assumptions underlying the effort. Rev. F. Ernest Johnson, a consultant to the National Council of Churches of Christ and a professor emeritus at Columbia Teachers College, wrote to Kissinger in September as the standoff between civil rights activists and segregationists in Little Rock, Arkansas, gathered steam. "'Consensus' is a very appealing and effective word as used here, yet I have misgivings as to its import," Johnson wrote. "Our national life is conspicuously marked by *dissensus* even on the most vital issues.

Does not the current strife over the essential equality of persons, which we have regarded as the moral foundations of our institutions, do great violence to our 'consensus'?" Johnson also questioned whether any consensus on values could be considered distinctively *American*. "Almost everything said in this manuscript about the consensus is quite as applicable to several other nations," he wrote. "I keep wondering what a Canadian, an English, a West German, or a Scandinavian reader would say about this 'American consensus.'"[56]

Meanwhile, those assigned to discuss "The U.S. Democratic Process: Its Challenge and Opportunities" were having similar troubles. When members of the panel were asked in early 1957 to propose a focus for their discussions, individuals ranging from W. W. Rostow to drugstore magnate Justin Dart emphasized the need for leaders to build public consensus over policy.[57] Nearly three years later, however, consensus on the panel was clearly lacking. "I have never myself presided over any conglomeration of points of view that even rivaled the conglomeration handed to me," lamented Dartmouth College president and panel chair John Dickey in September 1959. The following month, after talking to panel members, Carnegie Corporation president John W. Gardner concurred. "Strong divergences of viewpoint within the group made it exceedingly difficult to arrive at a consensus on any fragment of the subject," he reported.[58]

Ultimately, project organizers decided to scrap both panel reports in favor of a combined chapter on "The Power of the Democratic Idea" authored largely by philosopher Charles Frankel. Those assigned to review Frankel's work, however, continued to debate both the existence and the breadth of any American agreement practically until the document went to press. While some argued that Americans indeed had a "practical working consensus," others questioned this view or debated whether it extended beyond economics to race. "If you asked me what it is all Americans agree to, I can't say," Frankel himself declared. "The only thing I do know . . . is that most of the time most of them, a sufficiently large proportion, agree to certain rules of the game."[59]

What is striking about the ongoing discussions of both panel members and those overseeing the *Prospect for America* project is less the degree of consensus they achieved than the degree to which many believed that harmony and widespread accord were essential to a healthy democracy. In September 1960, Gardner drafted an introduction to the entire volume that began with a two-page discussion of the "American consensus." "Beneath the partisan conflicts of the moment lies a measure of consensus" that gives "durability and cohesiveness to our free society," he wrote. "This consensus is the rock on which we build. Without it our society would die from within."[60] This was a view shared by many members of Gardner's generation, men and women who came of age during the 1930s and World War II. It was shared as well by individuals like Finkelstein and Johnston, who belonged to a slightly older cohort. What bound these Americans together—and what separates them from many of their compatriots today—was not only their experience of postwar prosperity and war, hot and cold, but the lessons they took from the Depression decade.

Scholars would do well to remember this history as they assess the continuing relevance of the "liberal consensus" framework for understanding postwar American political culture. For nearly four decades, scholars have debated whether widespread agreement existed or not—whether Hodgson's "liberal consensus" was, in fact, myth or reality. The answer to that question depends, of course, on where and how deeply one looks: whereas most Americans in the two decades after World War II opposed communism, embraced some form of capitalism, and—at least in theory—supported equality for all, issues like military spending, support for the United Nations, wage and price controls, and school integration continued to generate controversy. Perhaps it is time to rethink the question. Instead of asking how widespread or shallow political agreement actually was, historians and others should ask why so many American elites chose to emphasize political agreement and to what ends they deployed the rhetoric of consensus. The answers to both questions begin in the 1930s.

Notes

1. R. M. MacIver, ed., *Unity and Difference in American Life: A Series of Addresses and Discussions* (New York: Institute for Religious & Social Studies, 1947; distributed by Harper & Bros.), 5–7.

2. Eric Johnston, *America Unlimited* (Garden City, NY: Doubleday, Doran, 1944), 18, 20.

3. Michael B. Greenbaum, "The Finkelstein Era," in Jack Wertheimer, ed., *Tradition Renewed: A History of the Jewish Theological Seminary in America*, vol. 1 (New York: Jewish Theological Seminary of America, 1997), 163–64; Ari L. Goldman, "Louis Finkelstein, 96, Leader of Conservative Jews," *New York Times*, November 30, 1991, 9.

4. "Eric Johnston Dies; Aided 3 Presidents," *New York Times*, August 23, 1963, 1.

5. Finkelstein used the word *reorient* in the speech quoted in the opening of this essay. For Johnston's use of the same word, see "Calls Chamber Board: Head of U.S. Body Says Session Will Weigh 'Reorientation,'" *New York Times*, July 15, 1942, 17.

6. Finkelstein to Henry S. Hendricks, May 13, 1938, quoted in Michael B. Greenbaum,

Louis Finkelstein and the Conservative Movement: Conflict and Growth (Binghamton, NY: Global Publications, 2001), 48.

7. One of the first—and still the most influential—scholarly overviews of the postwar "liberal consensus" was offered by Godfrey Hodgson in *America in Our Time* (Garden City, NY: Doubleday, 1976), 67–98. Since then, scholars ranging from Geoffrey Perrett and William L. O'Neill to William H. Chafe and James T. Patterson have posited a postwar consensus. Ironically, these scholars have sometimes treated the immediate postwar decades in much the same way that John Higham complained scholars of the 1950s were treating the broad sweep of American history. "Current scholarship," Higham wrote in 1959, "is carrying out a massive grading operation to smooth over America's social convulsions." Higham, "The Cult of the 'American Consensus': Homogenizing Our History," *Commentary* 27 (January 1959): 93–100 (quotation on 95). Also available at https://www.commentarymagazine.com/articles/the-cult-of-the-american-consensushomogenizing-our-history.

8. For an early overview of the literature stressing grassroots resistance on the left, see Thomas Sugrue, "Reassessing the History of Postwar America," *Prospects* 20 (Fall 1995): 493–509. In recent years, many more scholars have stressed conservative resistance. Some examples include Gary Gerstle, "Race and the Myth of the Liberal Consensus," *Journal of American History* 82 (September 1995): 579–86; Thomas Sugrue, *The Origins of the Urban Crisis: Race and Inequality in Postwar Detroit* (Princeton: Princeton University Press, 1996); Lisa McGirr, *Suburban Warriors: The Origins of the New American Right* (Princeton: Princeton University Press, 2001); Kim Phillips-Fein, *Invisible Hands: The Businessmen's Crusade against the New Deal* (New York: Norton, 2010); and Kevin Kruse, *One Nation under God: How Corporate America Invented Christian America* (New York: Basic Books, 2015).

9. I have borrowed this phrase from David Hollinger, "How Wide the Circle of We? American Intellectuals and the Problem of Ethnos since World War II," *American Historical Review* 98 (April 1993): 317–37. Hollinger used the phrase to describe the shift from a universalist, "species-centered discourse" to a particularist, "ethnos-centered discourse," but I find it equally useful for discussing the ideological boundaries of a national community.

10. For a more extended exploration of these issues, see Wendy L. Wall, *Inventing the "American Way": The Politics of Consensus from the New Deal to the Civil Rights Movement* (New York: Oxford University Press, 2008).

11. Daniel Ritschel, *The Politics of Planning: The Debate on Economic Planning in Britain in the 1930s* (Oxford: Clarendon Press, 1997), 325. See also Arthur Marwick, "Middle Opinion in the Thirties: Planning, Progress and Political 'Agreement,'" *English Historical Review* 79 (April 1964): 285–98; and Carl Marklund, "The Social Laboratory, the Middle Way and the Swedish Model: Three Frames for the Image of Sweden," *Scandinavian Journal of History* 34 (September 2009): 264–85.

12. Ulf Torgersen, "The Trend towards Political Consensus: The Case of Norway," *Acta Sociologica* 6 (1962): 159. The classic account of the rise of a British consensus in the postwar era is Paul Addison's *The Road to 1945: British Politics and the Second World War* (London: Jonathan Cape, 1975), which traces consensus politics to the domestic planning of the wartime coalition government.

13. Toye argues that politicians and political commentators used "the trope of consensus" to suggest that their opponents "did *not* belong to a wide and established national community of common sense," while others portrayed consensus "as a means used by the political establishment to shut out alternative viewpoints." Richard Toye, "From 'Consensus' to 'Common Ground': The Rhetoric of the Postwar Settlement and its Collapse," *Journal of Contemporary History* 48 (January 2013): 4–5, 7.

14. Greenbaum, "The Finkelstein Era"; Goldman, "Louis Finkelstein."

15. Leonard Dinnerstein, *Antisemitism in America* (New York: Oxford University Press, 1994), 112; Philip Perlmutter puts the number at roughly 120 in *Divided We Fall: A History of Ethnic, Religious, and Racial Prejudice in America* (Ames: Iowa State University Press, 1994), 234.

16. James Gilbert, *Redeeming Culture: American Religion in an Age of Science* (Chicago: University of Chicago Press, 1997), 69.

17. Alan Brinkley, *Voices of Protest: Huey Long, Father Coughlin and the Great Depression* (New York: Knopf, 1982), particularly 266–67.

18. Although Finkelstein made versions of this argument in speeches, correspondence, and other writings throughout the late 1930s, the most complete articulation I have found comes in a paper he prepared in late 1956 and early 1957 for Henry Kissinger, who was then organizing the Rockefeller Brothers Fund's Special Studies Project. See Louis Finkelstein, "American Values and American Foreign Policy" (12/56–1/57), folder 539, box 48, RG 4 (Special Studies Project), series G, Rockefeller Brothers Fund Records [hereafter RBF Records], Rockefeller Archive Center [hereafter RAC], Tarrytown, New York. Finkelstein was hardly alone in attributing the crises of the 1930s to a crisis of faith. For more on how such views reverberated through intellectual circles in the United States, see Gilbert, *Redeeming Culture*, chapter 4.

19. Finkelstein to Cyrus Adler, July 26, 1939, quoted in Greenbaum, *Louis Finkelstein*, 49.

20. Louis Finkelstein, J. Elliot Ross, and William Adams Brown, *The Religions of Democracy: Judaism, Catholicism and Protestantism in Creed and Life* (New York: Devin-Adair, 1941).

21. For more on such efforts, see Wendy L. Wall, "Symbol of Unity, Symbol of Pluralism: The 'Interfaith Idea' in Wartime and Cold War America," in Bruce J. Schulman, ed., *Making the American Century: Essays on the Political Culture of Twentieth Century America* (New York: Oxford University Press, 2014), 171–87.

22. Finkelstein's June 6, 1941, report to the Jewish Theological Seminary Board of Directors, quoted in Greenbaum, *Louis Finkelstein*, 55.

23. "Report on Institute of Interdenominational Studies as of February 20, 1940," folder labeled "Report on Institute, Feb. 1940," box 1, RG 16 (Institute for Religious and Social Studies), Special Collections Reading Room, Jewish Theological Seminary (JTS), New York City.

24. Finkelstein's April 1941 report to the JTS Board is quoted in Greenbaum, *Louis Finkelstein*, 51.

25. Fred W. Beuttler, "Organizing an American Conscience: The Conference on Science, Philosophy and Religion" (Ph.D. diss., University of Chicago, 1995), xiv, 6.

26. "Notes on the Amherst Conference" folder labeled "Conference on Science, Religion and Philosophy—5th—Sept. 7–11, 1944," box 31, RG 1 (JTS General Files), Special Collections Reading Room, JTS.

27. Greenbaum, "The Finkelstein Era," 177.

28. Gilbert, *Redeeming Culture*, 91.

29. Finkelstein's March 19, 1948, letter to Sulzberger is quoted in ibid., 179.

30. John Chamberlain, "Eric Johnston," *Life,* June 19, 1944, 96; "Eric Johnston Dies," *New York Times*, August 23, 1963, 1; Ralph A. Edgerton, "Hometown Boy Makes Good: The Eric Johnston Story," *Pacific Northwesterner* 33 (October 1989): 55–64.

31. "Eric Johnston Dies"; John N. Ingham, *Biographical Dictionary of American Business Leaders*, vol. 2 (Westport, CT: Greenwood Press, 1983), 677–79.

32. Ingham, *Biographical Dictionary of American Business Leaders.*

33. Ibid.

34. Jim Kershner quotes the *Spokesman-Review*'s Margaret Bean in his article "Modern Spokane Forged in Struggle," *Spokesman-Review*, December 14, 2008.

35. See *The Great Depression in Washington State: Pacific Northwest Labor and Civil Rights Projects, University of Washington*, http://depts.washington.edu/depress/index.shtml.

36. Kershner, "Modern Spokane Forged in Struggle."

37. Johnston, *America Unlimited*, 3.

38. "U.S. Chamber Head for Pay Stability," *New York Times*, May 18, 1942, 31.

39. Johnston, *America Unlimited,* 11, 15, 40.

40. Ibid., 17, 21, 84–85, 132.

41. British Conservative MP Harold MacMillan advocated a broadly centrist political philosophy in *The Middle Way: A Study of the Problem of Economic and Social Progress in a Free and Democratic Society* (London: Macmillan, 1938). Macmillan went on to implement much of this philosophy while serving as prime minister from 1957 to 1963. It is unclear whether Johnston ever read Macmillan's 1938 book, but his capitalization of this phrase is significant. Johnston also refers to Sweden's success "in combining free enterprise with a large degree of cooperative enterprise in which the government has no part, as well as public ownership of certain utilities and services." Johnston, *America Unlimited*, 93.

42. Johnston, *America Unlimited*, 75.

43. Johnston argued that labor, like business, had a stake in capitalism and limited government, because "you cannot strike against a government" and "you cannot even truly bargain with a government." Ibid., 89–90.

44. Louis Stark, "Labor, Employers Meeting for Unity," *New York Times*, July 24, 1942, 7.

45. Johnston, *America Unlimited*, 25.

46. Eric Johnston, "Your Stake in Capitalism," *Reader's Digest,* February 1943, 1–5.

47. Johnston, *America Unlimited*, 93, 95–96, 98.

48. Lary May offers an insightful discussion of Johnston's role in promoting the postwar ideology of consensus in *The Big Tomorrow: Hollywood and the Politics of the American Way* (Chicago: University of Chicago Press, 2000), chapter 5.

49. "'Militant' Unity Asked to Fight Bias," *New York Times*, December 15, 1945, 22.

50. "Institute for Religious and Social Studies Memorandum, 12/48," in box 6, RG 16, Special Collections Reading Room, JTS.

51. John W. Jeffries, "The 'Quest for National Purpose' of 1960," *American Quarterly* 30 (Autumn 1978): 451–70.

52. *Prospect for America: The Rockefeller Panel Reports* (New York: Doubleday, 1961), xv. For more background on the project, see John Ensor Harr and Peter J. Johnson, *The Rockefeller Conscience: An American Family in Public and Private* (New York: Scribner, 1991), 202–3.

53. Hodgson, *America in Our Time*, 69. Jeffries too stresses the "consensus" he sees embodied in much of the "national purpose" literature of 1960—a consensus that primarily revolved around the nation's Cold War mission. He notes, however, that "the very desire for common purpose, the consensus sought beyond the consensus at hand, led to shunting aside hard, divisive questions and thus militated against penetrating analysis or major new departures" ("The 'Quest for National Purpose' of 1960," 462). John Andrew III offers a slightly different assessment in "Cracks in the Consensus: The Rockefeller Brothers Fund Special Studies Project and Eisenhower's America," *Presidential Studies Quarterly* 28 (Summer 1998): 535–52. He argues that the project was "designed to forge a strong consensus over the future direction of American policy," but one that challenged the policies of the Eisenhower administration. As such, he sees the project as "one of the first public efforts to advance a critique of America's postwar policies" (535, 536).

54. See contents of folder 864, box 105, Nelson A. Rockefeller Personal Papers, series A (Activities), RAC. This paragraph and the following also draw on Beuttler, "Organizing an American Conscience," chapter 9.

55. Beuttler, "Organizing an American Conscience," 516–18.

56. Johnson to Kissinger, September 20, 1957, folder 565, box 49, RG 4, series G, RBF Records, RAC.

57. W. W. Rostow, "Suggestions Concerning Scope and Coverage for Subpanel VI Discussions," January 7, 1957. See also the suggestions submitted by Justin Dart, Arthur Smithies, and James Albert Pike. Interestingly, Lucius Clay, a retired U.S. Army general and still a close associate of President Eisenhower, disagreed. "I would like to raise one (perhaps lone) voice against so-called bipartisanship in any field. . . . I am sure that even in the field of foreign policy, an active opposition is essential to developing the will of our people and indeed in finding the right answer." All of these memos and letters can be found in folder 461, box 41, RG 4, series F, RBF Records, RAC.

58. "Transcript, Overall Panel Meeting—Sept. 17, 1959" and John W. Gardner to Laurence S. Rockefeller (October 7, 1959), both in folder 463, box 41, RG 4, series F, RBF Records, RAC.

59. Transcription of the report writing committee meeting held on January 27, 1960, folder 576, box 51, RG 4, series H, RBF Records, RAC. See also Morris Hadley to James Perkins, March 28, 1960, folder 567, box 50, and transcript of the Overall Panel meeting on May 17, 1960, folder 590, box 53, ibid.

60. Gardner's September 22, 1960, draft of the introduction to the overall volume can be found be found in folder 917, box 110, Nelson A. Rockefeller Personal Papers, series A, RAC.

5

The Keynesian Consensus and Its Limits

IWAN MORGAN

Keynesianism was a bedrock element of the liberal consensus as envisaged by Godfrey Hodgson.[1] Conceived as a prescription for the depressed economy of the 1930s, this doctrine found only limited acceptance by the New Deal but had far greater influence during the long boom of the postwar era. Every administration from 1945 to 1968 accepted the fundamental Keynesian tenet that, in the words of Arthur Schlesinger Jr., "central economic management may be reconciled with the decentralization of decision and the technical advantages of a price system and a free market."[2] Postwar political economy operated on the assumption that private enterprise would generate material abundance and the state would ensure economic stability and sustained growth. Presidents from Harry S. Truman to Lyndon Johnson relied on expert advisers to aid them in the management of prosperity, a task regarded as second in significance only to that of ensuring the nation's security.

Owing to its Great Depression pedigree, Keynesianism's contribution to the postwar consensus is conventionally regarded as liberal in intent. In reality, its applications are better considered as complex, constrained, and—for much of the time—conservative. This was hardly surprising given its intellectual pedigree. Never a radical or even a democrat in the fullest sense, British economist John Maynard Keynes was a post-Victorian elitist engaged in a quest for increased rationality in economic policy. Insofar as Keynes had an ideology, one scholar perceptively described it as "a confidence born of the humane Locke-Hume-Mill tradition that intelligence in human affairs is both essential and possible."[3] In essence, Keynes idealized expert-informed government activism to tame the business cycle and preempt the misery of mass unemployment. Whatever their somewhat tenuous association with the New Deal in the 1930s, his ideas were no less capable of being applied by enlightened conservatives as by enlightened liberals in discharging government's management of the postwar economy.

This was manifest in two cases bounding the high period of "liberal consensus" that Hodgson conceived as spanning the mid-1950s to the mid-1960s. In 1953–54, Dwight D. Eisenhower, the first Republican president since Herbert Hoover, put a bipartisan seal of approval on deficit budgets as a device to counter recession. Praising the Eisenhower administration's willingness to move away from "the clichés of a balanced budget and the unspeakable evils of deficit financing," liberal economist John Kenneth Galbraith commented in congressional testimony that it had "shown a remarkable flexibility of mind in the speed with which it has moved away from these slogans."[4] A decade later, the Kennedy-Johnson tax cut of 1964 represented a more expansive vision of economic management in seeking to enlarge the economy's productive capacity through a strategy that liberal economist Walter Heller called "Keynes-*cum*-growth." In celebration of its success, *Time* magazine put a picture of the long-dead John Maynard Keynes on the cover of an issue featuring an article headed "We Are All Keynesians Now."[5]

Such effusiveness implicitly airbrushed out of history Eisenhower's earlier response to recession that could also be characterized as Keynesian in inspiration even if this pedigree was never formally acknowledged. Self-evidently, Keynesianism meant something different to the Democratic economic policymakers of 1964 and their Republican predecessors of 1954. For the Eisenhower administration it entailed a relatively passive strategy of reliance on automatic fiscal stabilizers and discretionary monetary actions for counter-cyclical ends. For the Kennedy-Johnson administrations, in contrast, it entailed discretionary fiscal and monetary activism in pursuit of economic expansion. This chapter assesses whether these variants of Keynesianism accorded with the liberal consensus idea or whether their differing level of statism fundamentally challenged it.

To put both variants in historical perspective, it is necessary to consider an earlier iteration of Keynesianism that had gained liberal support in World War II. What social scientists Margaret Weir and Theda Skocpol characterized as "social Keynesianism" grew out of Depression-era stagnationist theory.[6] Under the intellectual leadership of Harvard's Alvin Hansen, the foremost American promoter of Keynesian ideas, its adherents regarded the 1937–38 recession that interrupted recovery from the slump of 1930–33 as proof of private investment's incapacity to make good any withdrawal of fiscal and monetary stimuli. In their assessment, the economy was now in a mature stage of development lacking the dynamic elements that had powered industrial growth in the past, notably population growth, territorial expansion, and new investment opportunities in emergent industries. Accordingly, Hansen and his supporters wanted the state to curb endemic joblessness through protracted deficit spending and to effect more equitable distribution of wealth through regulation, taxation, and social-welfare provision.[7] Despite the revitalization of America's economy in World War II, stagnationists still insisted that government planning was essential to sustain full employment and ensure equitable distribution of the material abundance with the return of peace. Though the congressional coalition of conservative Democrats and Republicans had succeeded in abolishing the New Deal's National Resources Planning Board (NRPB) in 1943, Hansen looked forward to its peacetime replacement by an even stronger planning agency that would act as "an economic government composed of specialists."[8]

A reluctant Keynesian at best in the 1930s, Franklin D. Roosevelt seemingly moved closer to Hansen's left-wing version as peace drew near. His 1944 State of the Union address included an economic bill of rights outlining ambitious social-welfare, full-employment, housing, and aid-to-education commitments, something the NRPB had recommended in 1942. Later, in an election-eve speech, he envisaged a postwar economy that generated 60 million jobs (compared with 48 million in 1940, when unemployment ran at 14.5 percent of the labor force). Finally, his budget message of January 1945 included a Keynesian accounting device in the form of a national budget showing the contributions of business, consumers, and government to national economic output. In its concluding section, FDR recommended an expansionary economic policy that included "provision for extending social security, including medical care; for better education, public health, and nutrition; for the improvement of our homes, cities and farms; and for the development of transportation facilities and river valleys."[9]

Roosevelt's death left unanswered the question of how far he would have sustained a peacetime commitment to social Keynesianism. The strength of opposition to its expansive statism became evident in the legislative struggle over the Full Employment bill introduced by Senator James E. Murray (D-MT) in early 1945. In pristine form, this proclaimed the right of all Americans to regular employment; endowed government with ultimate responsibility to guarantee this; established the National Production and Employment Budget as a planning mechanism under presidential supervision to estimate the private and public output needed for full employment; required federal spending ultimately to make up any deficiency; and mandated national government to act against monopolistic business practices that could counteract the bill's fundamental purpose. Despite removal of some liberal provisions to secure its enactment, Senate approval of the measure signaled the high-water mark of social Keynesianism.

The House of Representatives took up an alternative bill that was largely the work of the U.S. Chamber of Commerce (USCC). In common with other business organizations, this group had reviled deficit spending as the greatest threat to economic recovery and free enterprise in the 1930s. Unsurprisingly, the Murray bill with its underlying stagnationist convictions was anathema to the USCC. In a jointly written book, two of its economic researchers denounced "the Keynes-Hansen school" for propagating an ideology "not greatly distant from neo-Marxian thinking."[10] Yet opposition to such advanced statism did not preclude recognition that government should have an enlarged role in the peacetime economy. Acknowledging this necessity, USCC president Eric Johnston, a progressive-minded businessman from Spokane, warned that the return of mass unemployment in peacetime was "the one thing which might doom capitalism and rivet a bureaucratic slave state on us forever."[11] It was his conviction that no single sector of the economy was capable of forestalling a slump. Accordingly, the issue for the USCC was not to deny government's responsibility for economic management but to define its appropriate extent.[12]

The conference committee charged with reconciling the House and Senate measures came down heavily in favor of the former. What became the Employment Act of 1946 differed in both title and substance from liberal aspirations. Within the limits of maintaining "free competitive enterprise," it mandated an imprecisely stated government obligation to "promote maximum employment, production, and purchasing power" rather than an unambiguous commitment to full employment; eschewed reference to the right of employment; lacked any planning mechanism akin to the national budget; and was silent on what policies should be pursued to achieve its objectives. Bowing to political realities, congressional liberals accepted that there was no hope of obtaining any stronger guarantee of jobs. The reconciled measure consequently won huge majorities in both chambers and received presidential signature on February 20, 1946.[13]

Shorn of its stagnationist features, the Employment Act's passage into law marked the emergence of a limited Keynesian consensus. Its fundamental insistence on the primacy of free enterprise effectively assigned the state a secondary, indirect, and ill-defined responsibility to maintain high levels of national output, demand, and employment through encouragement of private economic activity. According to one approving conservative analyst, "some domestication of Keynes—some adaptation to traditional values as well as greater recognition of the facts of the economic and political system—was necessary before Keynesianism could become national policy."[14] In a mirror image of this assessment, a disapproving liberal contended that the Employment Act had produced "a congeries of scattered and *ad hoc* short-range efforts" rather than planned economic policy, lacked any redistributive intent, did not provide for transfer of resources from the private to the public sector to achieve necessary national objectives, and facilitated "obsessionary [*sic*] preoccupation" with inflation rather than jobs.[15]

Nevertheless, the measure's broadly formulated commitment to maximum employment offered scope for more expansive interpretation than intended by its conservative creators. It had effectively anointed the president as chief manager of prosperity in requiring him to submit an annual *Economic Report* to Congress and establishing the Council of Economic Advisers (CEA) within the Executive Office of the President to assist in this task. Presidents now had a formal responsibility to ensure high levels of employment and could draw on the institutionalized advice of the CEA, the bailiwick of professional economists in every postwar administration, in pursuit of this end. In the hands of "a determined chief executive," economist Robert Lekachman remarked, these new arrangements "could be turned into powerful agents of public action."[16]

In the first decade and a half of its history, interpretation of the Employment Act broadly followed the stabilizing budget idea promulgated by the Committee for Economic Development (CED). This group filled the vacuum in progressive business leadership following the USCC's reversion to balanced-budget preferences under new leadership more attuned to rank-and-file conservatism. A research-based organization formed in 1942, the CED operated in the techno-corporatist tradition that traced its origins to the Progressive Era's National Civic Federation, found further expression in Herbert Hoover's concept of the associative state, and was briefly manifest in the support of business corporatists like Henry Harriman and Gerald Swope for early New Deal cartelization. It idealized objective expertise that addressed public policy from a technical rather than political perspective. It was "very important," CED chair Paul Hoffman informed trustees in 1947, that "we as a group think of ourselves not as 'right,' 'left,' 'conservative' or 'radical' but 'responsible.' What we are trying to do is get at the facts about the way this economy functions . . . and then go down the roads indicated."[17] This supposed empiricism meant searching for solutions that were inherently ideological in identifying the national interest with the well-being of American capitalism.

Economic stability was essential if American business were to bring to profitable fruition ambitious plans for postwar expansion. The CED looked to address this need through a "middle way" fiscal policy that eschewed annually balanced budgets regardless of economic conditions and anti-recession deficit spending that could fuel inflation because of its likely continuation during recovery. In its seminal fiscal policy statement of 1947, the group advocated a stabilizing strategy that operated primarily through the revenue side of the budget. This entailed a fixed-rule approach of setting tax rates to deliver surpluses for debt reduction at a high level of employment and national income. In recession, declining tax revenues in combination with rising outlays on unemployment insurance would automatically generate expansionary deficits; in recovery, the reverse would occur to produce surpluses that doused inflationary pressures. Somewhat arbitrarily, the CED set 4 percent joblessness as the high-employment level based on the belief that "most involuntary idleness is of the between-jobs variety." It was uninterested in pursuing full employment for fear that this would fuel inflation and justify a stronger federal presence in the economy.[18]

The guiding principle of stabilizing budget strategy was automaticity—namely, reliance on the automatic fiscal stabilizers to counteract cyclical fluctuations in economic performance. Only in the exceptional circumstances of a serious slump did the CED acknowledge need for discretionary fiscal activism. In stark contrast, the group railed against continuation of fixed-rule monetary policy established in wartime. The "peg" agreement of 1942 obliged the Federal Reserve to support Treasury securities at predetermined price levels. This arrangement restricted the central bank's ability to meet changing economic conditions. Calling for its termination, the CED insisted that flexibility was "essential to wise monetary action." A group that counted leading bankers among its members had utter confidence that Federal Reserve officials would respond swiftly and sagely to business-cycle movement. The Treasury-Fed Accord of 1951 eventually liberated monetary policy to play its part in stabilization strategy. Outgoing central bank chair Thomas McCabe, a founding trustee of the CED, acknowledged that the group's policy views had shaped his determined opposition to continuing the "peg."[19]

The stabilizing strategy conferred on the Employment Act an operational clarity lacking in its terms of enactment. In dispensing with contestable discretionary measures, fiscal automaticity consolidated the Keynesian consensus embodied in the 1946 legislation. It received the imprimatur of academic respectability when a group of economists issued the so-called Princeton Manifesto (they were attending a National Planning Association conference at the university) that endorsed the principle of automatic flexibility in fiscal response to changing economic conditions.[20] In essence, the CED had adapted the balanced-budget rule idealized by traditionalists to the inevitability of cyclical fluctuations that modern economics looked to tame. Through a combination of economic circumstance, political considerations, and—in the Eisenhower administration's case—personnel transfer, its formula for economic stability largely shaped presidential management of prosperity from the late 1940s to the early 1960s.

Impatient with theory, Harry S. Truman instinctively held pay-as-you-go preferences that were appropriate in the inflationary circumstances of the early postwar years. Stabilizing strategy therefore provided a practical rationale for his economic management. Facing an opposition-led Congress in 1947–48, he thrice vetoed a Republican bill that substantially reduced wartime taxes but was finally overridden after its sponsors removed inequities that offended Democratic legislators. Advancing a starve-the-beast justification for the measure, Senate Majority Leader Robert Taft (R-OH) declared, "The best reason to reduce taxes is to reduce our ideas of the number of dollars that government can properly spend in a year." In contrast, Truman employed stabilization rationale to oppose a tax cut that even when watered-down equaled the GDP size of its 1964 successor. "The time for tax reduction," he asserted, "will come when general inflationary pressures have ceased and the structure of prices is on a more stable basis than now prevails."[21] In recession-hit 1949, however, counter-cyclical imperatives induced presidential abandonment of plans to repeal the Republican tax cut with support from the new Democratic Congress. This inaction represented the most significant discretionary response to the downturn. Otherwise, automatically generated fiscal imbalances proved sufficient to facilitate economic recovery. Facing deficit-elimination demands from bipartisan conservatives and business groups like the U.S. Chamber of Commerce, Truman offered a compensatory defense right out of the CED playbook: "We cannot expect to achieve a budget surplus in a declining national economy."[22]

Dwight D. Eisenhower's adherence to stabilizing strategy was never really in doubt—not least because it was perfectly attuned to the "middle way" ideals inherent in his conception of what historian Robert Griffith dubbed the "corporate commonwealth."[23] Another depression, he told J. P. Morgan vice president and Council of Foreign Relations chair Russell Leffingwell, would be "a national tragedy." As a consequence there could be "no disagreement among responsible citizens about the proper role of the Federal Government as a preventive agent in times of economic stress." Recognizing that a trade-off was sometimes necessary between balanced budgets and economic stability, Eisenhower asserted, "If conditions require, we shall not hesitate to subordinate the first of these criteria to the second." The president similarly confided to his brother Milton, "Maintenance of prosperity is one field of governmental concern that interests me mightily. In these days I am sure that government has to be the principal coordinator and, in many cases, the actual operator for the many things that the approach of depression would demand."[24]

The recession of 1953–54 provided an early test of Eisenhower's resolve. With business fearful that the downturn could turn into a slump, his administration debated the need for fiscal activism but remained circumspect about whether conditions warranted this. A CEA contingency plan for a $6 billion program of anti-recession outlays never got beyond the blueprint stage. Fiscal activism was more evident on the revenue side of the budget, but only as the incidental consequence of previously scheduled reductions in personal taxes, the expiry of Korean War taxes, and a major revision of the tax code. Significantly, Eisenhower used every means at his disposal to defeat a congressional Democratic proposal to boost low-income consumption by raising the personal tax exemption from $600 to $800. If enacted, its removal of approximately one-third of taxpayers from the rolls would have resulted in long-term loss of revenue.[25]

The combination of automatic fiscal stabilizers and discretionary monetary relaxation ultimately proved sufficient to generate recovery after four quarters. Eisenhower had fulfilled his Employment Act responsibilities without incurring expensive new commitments in the name of fiscal activism. Thanks to post–Korean War defense retrenchment, the deficit actually contracted over the course of the downturn, from 1.7 percent GDP in fiscal year (FY) 1953 to 0.8 percent GDP in FY 1955. CEA member Neil Jacoby, a CED alumnus, later remarked that Keynesianism had played "a key role" in shaping the administration's response to recession, but this was only true in a passive sense.[26]

The recession of 1957–58, the sharpest downturn between the Great Depression and the oil-shock recession of 1974–75, proved a tougher challenge for Eisenhower's economic management. GDP declined by 4.3 percent in real terms over its duration (compared to 2.7 percent in 1953–54). Meanwhile, the unemployment rate grew from 4.3 percent to 7.4 percent as the jobless total surpassed 5 million for the first time since 1941. The recession was a symptom of the broader economic slack evident in the gap between actual and potential output once the early surge of postwar growth tapered off. From 1948 to 1955, unemployment averaged 4.3 percent and total employment grew yearly by 1.2 percent, compared with 5.6 percent and 0.6 percent, respectively, from 1956 to 1960.[27]

This record suggested that Eisenhower had not discharged his obligation to promote maximum employment. Instead the president focused on his corollary duty to safeguard maximum consumption. In his assessment, inflation represented the greatest threat both to America's economic well-being and its capacity to wage the Cold War. The 2.5 percent annual rise in consumer prices in the 1955–57 recovery cycle was a matter of considerable concern to him. In recent times, U.S. involvement in World War II and the Korean War had been the main source of inflationary pressure, but the nation was now at peace. Accordingly, Eisenhower and his advisers worried that the economy was in the grip of "creeping inflation" that would steadily erode the dollar's value. In their assessment, its continuation threatened to weaken purchasing power and breed inflationary psychology among consumers. Ongoing price instability could also undermine the dollar's status as global reserve currency under the terms of the Bretton Woods agreement of 1944, which had fixed the greenback's value in relation to gold ($35 an ounce) as a means of underwriting the liquidity of the postwar international monetary system. If foreign dollar-holders suspected that inflation might compel dollar devaluation, the consequent demand to transfer currency assets into gold threatened to exhaust U.S. reserves.[28]

From Eisenhower's perspective, the greatest source of inflation was government spending. "If the budget is too high," he remarked in 1957, "inflation occurs, which cuts down the value of the dollar, so that nothing is gained and the process is self-defeating."[29] Despite a Gallup poll in March 1958 showing unemployment as the major issue of public concern for the first time since 1940, the president eschewed fiscal activism to counter the recession lest this fuel inflation. On this occasion there was no contingency planning for counter-cyclical spending in case of need. In the face of intense political pressure to increase government outlays, the administration relied on automatic stabilizers and monetary relaxation to pull the economy out of its tailspin. Eisenhower told his first-term CEA chair, Arthur Burns of

Columbia University, "It is vital to have statesmen and economists in controlling positions. . . . I realize that to be conservative in this situation—and flatly to say so—can well get me tagged as an unsympathetic, reactionary fossil. But my honest conviction is that the greatest public service we can do for our country is to oppose wild-eyed schemes of every kind."[30]

Presidential animus focused on the anti-recession spending program that congressional Democrats had cobbled together to boost employment in sectors such as home construction, highway improvement, and public works. Eisenhower's determined opposition and occasional use of the veto ensured that no expenditure measure of note made it onto the statute books without significant modification to meet his insistence that discretionary initiatives should not lay the foundation for large fiscal imbalances.[31] Deficit concerns further governed his resistance to temporary tax reduction that the CED and other business groups supported as a fast-acting stimulant. Eisenhower suspected that Congress would amend any administration proposal for a time-limited tax cut into a permanent one, causing long-term loss of revenue. The fact that inflation remained at pre-recession levels during the downturn worried him more than any short-term rise in joblessness.[32] His chief cabinet ally, Treasury Secretary Robert Anderson, was of like mind. A journalist close to this onetime CED notable, Edwin Dale, reported his willingness "as the lesser of evils, to accept a condition of fairly serious unemployment all through 1958, as long as the jobless situation is showing some little improvement."[33]

The recovery that began in mid-1958 seemingly justified Eisenhower's adherence to stabilizing budget strategy, but seasonally adjusted industrial production was still below pre-recession levels at year's end. This was a critical factor in the GOP's heavy defeat in the midterm elections. In the new Congress, the swollen Democratic ranks looked to enact a raft of liberal expenditure measures deemed essential for national purposes and hitherto stymied by Eisenhower's second-term parsimony. In the words of Senate Majority Leader Lyndon Johnson, their concern was "to determine the full potential of our economy and how it can be realized for the benefit of our people."[34] This agenda encompassed increased funding for post-*Sputnik* defense expansion, school construction, health care, assistance to depressed areas, and infrastructure projects. Anticipating "the bloodiest battle we have ever had" to control spending, Eisenhower mounted a public campaign to depict what he called the "spender wing" of the Democratic Party—a distinction that enabled him to appeal for support from conservative southerners—as the agent of inflation. This was a strategy, one administration official observed, that cast Republicans as being "*for* an honest dollar rather than *against* public services."[35] Its success was soon evident in opinion polls attesting to popular concern about prices and the inflationary effects of deficits. Meanwhile, the Democrats found they had the votes to pass budget-expanding bills but not to override the presidential veto. As *New Republic* columnist Richard Strout lamented, Eisenhower had turned the tables on their liberal aspirations "with the bogey words 'inflation,' 'spenders,' and 'deficits.'"[36]

What impelled Eisenhower to stand his ground was his determination to balance the FY 1960 budget following the recession-affected FY 1959 deficit, which was the largest of the postwar era both in current-dollar ($12.8 billion) and GDP (2.5 percent) sizes. Anderson had carried back from an International Monetary Fund–World Bank meeting in New Delhi in late 1958 the warning that foreign anxiety about this bumper imbalance could generate a run on America's gold reserves. A strong assertion of stabilizing strategy appeared vital to reassure foreign dollar-holders of the administration's intent to curb inflation.[37] However, the unprecedented single-year movement from substantial deficit to small surplus denied the economy the fiscal adrenaline needed to sustain expansion. As a consequence the recovery cycle—the briefest of the postwar era hitherto—ended with the onset of what was effectively a double-dip recession in late 1960.[38]

The weak recovery on the heels of sharp recession changed the terms of debate over political economy. Eisenhower-era annual growth of 2.5 percent was far beneath the Truman-era rate of 4.5 percent. The slowdown prompted development of a liberal, dynamic, and expansion-oriented Keynesianism in opposition to Eisenhower's conservative, constrained, and inflation-focused version. Envisioning the U.S. economy's endless possibilities, the 1960 Democratic Party national platform avowed: "Economic growth is the means whereby we improve the American standard of living and produce added tax resources for national security and essential public services."[39] Synthesizing this imperative in his closing statement in the final televised presidential debate, John F. Kennedy declared it incumbent on the next president "to get this country moving again, to get our economy moving ahead, to set before the American people its goals, its unfinished business."[40] As historian Robert Collins observed, "The interpenetration of growth economics and liberal politics produced a defining feature of public life in the 1960s—the ascendancy of what might be labeled 'growth liberalism.'"[41]

What became the "new economics" of the Kennedy-Johnson era traced its lineage to Truman's second term. The 1950 *Economic Report of the President* proffered an optimistic vision of growth as the best route to full recovery from the recent recession. "Maximum production and maximum employment," it declared, "are not static goals; they mean more jobs and more business opportunities in each succeeding year. If we are to attain these objectives, we must make full use of all the resources of the American economy."[42] Amid the general intensification of the struggle with the Soviet Union, the Korean War provided the opportunity to test the possibilities of growth strategy in place of stabilization. CEA chair Leon Keyserling persuaded Truman that the war should be funded through expansion of national output rather than transfer of resources from civilian to military sectors. The experiment was short-lived because Chinese intervention presaged a longer conflict than originally anticipated. Accordingly, Truman felt obliged to institute a general price freeze, raise taxes, and stretch out defense procurement to control inflation for the duration.[43]

Thanks mainly to Keyserling's tireless advocacy, this was only a temporary setback for growth economics. After service in the Truman administration, he created a personal think tank, the Conference on Economic Progress, to promote his ideas. Under his influence as vice-chair, Americans for Democratic Action (ADA) became the first significant political group to espouse growth as its primary economic goal. Its 1956 platform proclaimed that excessive concern with stability had blinded both Republicans and Democrats to the limitless potential of the American economy to deliver ever-rising living standards.[44] Keyserling's influence reached its peak through membership of the Democratic Advisory Council (DAC), created by the Democratic National Committee in 1957 to develop agenda ideas for the 1960 election. Its statements throughout 1958 hammered home the message that "the basic domestic economic issue . . . [is] stagnation with inflation, against real growth without inflation." In December the group voiced commitment to a 5 percent annual growth rate, a target later endorsed by the 1960 Democratic platform.[45]

The 1960 campaign for the presidency signaled the emergence of a broad consensus on the economy's potential for substantial year-on-year growth to fulfill America's promise of abundance. Denying that the country could be "governed into perpetual prosperity," the GOP standard-bearer, Vice President Richard Nixon, warned that Democratic efforts to do so would result in inflationary deficits.[46] Nevertheless, a head of steam in support of growth had already built up in Republican ranks. Liberal grandee Governor Nelson Rockefeller of New York became strongly associated with the issue after a Rockefeller Brothers Fund report of March 1958 proclaimed 5 percent annual growth an achievable target.[47] Nixon himself made similar public declarations in advocating a supply-side strategy of tax reduction to incentivize investment as the means of recovery from recession. The need to placate Eisenhower pulled him back into the anti-inflationary bunker in 1959, but he broke out again in 1960 in negotiating the so-called Compact of Fifth Avenue on the terms of the Republican platform with Rockefeller just prior to the GOP national convention. Its key provision specified that "the rate of our economic growth must, as promptly as possible, be accelerated by policies and programs stimulating our free enterprise system—to allow us to meet the demands of nation defense and the growing social needs and a higher standard of living for our growing population."[48] Despite holding out against "government manipulated growth," Nixon campaigned against Kennedy as a pro-growth Republican. In October he expressed support for "a maximum growth rate" that could be 3 percent, 4 percent, or 5 percent in accordance with economic conditions and national need.[49]

Consensus over the goal of growth did not extend to the means of achieving it, even among Democrats. Keyserling insisted that a higher level of government expenditure would have the dual benefit of expanding the economy and funding domestic and defense programs that had atrophied under Eisenhower. In his assessment, the federal budget should be "a bold weapon of progress rather than a defeatist weapon of regression." To this end he advocated a National Prosperity Budget, an adaptation of the stagnationist model, to set national goals for employment, production, investment, and consumption in pursuit of growth.[50] Such thinking precipitated the eclipse of his influence within the DAC. Other economists in this body, notably John Kenneth Galbraith, charged that Keyserling's strategy was a recipe for inflation if pursued during prosperity. This was enough to scare off the political members of the group who were already worried by the success of Eisenhower's anti-spender campaign.[51]

In its December 1958 statement extolling a 5 percent annual growth, the DAC had followed Keyserling's line on spending. A year later, it issued a new statement hailing monetary relaxation as the engine of expansion while surplus budgets constrained inflation amid prosperity. The inspiration for this idea was the congressional Joint Economic Committee's recent report on alternative growth strategies based on exhaustive investigation under the direction of Otto Eckstein of Harvard University. In its assessment, easy money and cheap credit could generate a 4.5 percent annual expansion if fiscal policy operated on stabilizing budget principles to prevent cyclical excess.[52] Thanks to DAC promotion, these recommendations found their way into the Democratic platform of 1960—albeit with the growth target rounded up to a more marketable 5 percent. The trouble was that Federal Reserve chair William McChesney Martin was not party to this strategy. International concern that a Democratic president would limit central bank independence to fight inflation in the interests of growth led to a preelection gold drain. To stem this, Kennedy unequivocally vowed on election eve to preserve the dollar at current value if elected. As further reassurance, he committed to lowering only long-term interest rates to boost domestic investment and production rather than short-term rates carried by most foreign-held obligations.[53] These pledges soothed the money markets but closed off the easy-money route to growth.

Through a process of elimination, the only avenue of expansion still open was that of tax reduction. This was the preferred option of the Keynesian economists appointed to the Kennedy CEA under the chairmanship of Walter Heller of the University of Minnesota. Their "new economics" ideas found cogent expression in the council's 1962 report, which launched an assault on stabilizing strategy as a fiscal drag on growth because the automatic increase in tax revenues as the economy moved from recession to recovery impeded the growth of private income before the attainment of full employment. In the CEA's assessment, the consequent retardation of economic expansion was the main cause of the estimated $50 billion performance gap between potential and real GDP in 1960. A fiscal policy that aimed to balance the economy rather than balance the budget was the way to close this. The CEA advocated a "full-employment budget" based on the hypothetical level of receipts at the full-employment level of 4 percent. A "full-employment deficit" provided stimulus to boost economic output; a "full-employment surplus" would keep inflation around 2 percent when the economy was at maximum capacity.[54]

Heller and his colleagues recommended consumption-boosting personal tax reduction within the framework of the "full-employment budget" as the most efficient agency of economic growth. This challenge to orthodoxy did not find ready reception from the deficit-conscious president, Congress, and business. Heller's patient tuition persuaded Kennedy to endorse the "new economics" by mid-1962 amid signs that recovery from the final Eisenhower-era recession was stalling.[55] The president consequently embarked on a public campaign to promote broader support for tax reduction. This may not have generated a tide of congressional and popular enthusiasm for the measure, but it persuaded the corporate community that tax-induced deficits could generate inflation-free growth. "I gave them straight Keynes and Heller," Kennedy reported in delight to the CEA chair following his very successful appearance before the Economic Club of New York in December, "and they loved it." In response, Heller urged that the time was now right to send a tax bill to Capitol Hill. "Congress may be lukewarm," he remarked, "but powerful groups throughout the country are *ready for action.* When the Chicago Board of Commerce, the AFL-CIO, the CED, and the Chamber of Commerce are on the same side—when repeated editorials in *Business Week* are indistinguishable from those appearing in the *Washington Post*—the prospect for action cannot be wholly dim."[56]

With powerful conservative elements in both parties still dedicated to balanced-budget ideals, the tax cut became the subject of a protracted legislative battle. Kennedy did not live to see its final enactment in the early months of Lyndon Johnson's presidency. The ensuing mid-decade boom marked the high point of growth liberalism: in 1965 economic expansion exceeded 6 percent, unemployment fell to 4.1 percent, inflation held steady around 2 percent, and the deficit actually declined to a mere 0.2 percent GDP because the lower tax rates yielded higher revenues. Growth thereby became the word that meant all good things. As new economist and former CEA member James Tobin of Yale remarked, it had come to occupy "an exalted position in the hierarchy of goals of government policy." Heller expressed this view more emphatically: "Gone is the countercyclical syndrome of the 1950s. Policy now centers on gap closing and growth, on realizing and enlarging the economy's non-inflationary potential."[57]

The new economists' joy would soon turn to tears, of course, but this study is not concerned with the economic problems of the second half of the 1960s and beyond. Its purview is to consider whether the political debates and disputes over economic management in the period between the passage of the Employment Act of 1946 and the enactment of the 1964 tax cut uphold the liberal consensus paradigm. Review of the historical evidence points to a positive assessment, albeit with qualifications.

Whatever their differences, stabilization and growth strategies were hewn from the same oak of what Robert Lekachman dubbed "commercial Keynesianism."[58] In contrast to the stagnationist version of Keynesianism embodied in the Full Employment bill, both succeeding variants looked to achieve their ends through encouragement of business enterprise as the main source of prosperity. Neither sought to redistribute wealth, reallocate resources from the private economy to the public one, and pursue actual full employment. Both courted the support of business more than labor in the belief that corporate confidence was the critical element in the economy's well-being.

Each Keynesian variant was entwined with Cold War concerns: Eisenhower's battle against inflation reflected belief that it would eventually undermine America's capacity to meet the communist challenge; the late-1950s emergence of growthmanship reflected post-*Sputnik* anxiety about the Soviet Union's growing productive capacity; the sense that America's leadership of the Western Alliance required it to match the impressive growth rates of its European partners had a part in Kennedy's conversion to the new economics.[59]

Despite its greater ambition, the new economics had the same legislative root as stabilizing strategy. As the 1962 *Council of Economic Advisers* report acknowledged, "The mandate of the Employment Act renews itself perpetually as maximum levels of production, employment and purchasing power rise through time. The weapons of stabilizing policy—the budget, the tax system, control of the supply of money and credit—must be aimed anew, for their target is moving."[60]

The main difference between Eisenhower economics and the new economics was one of priorities. Both wanted growth and low inflation but placed different emphasis on their attainment. Eisenhower summed up his conviction in a 1959 press conference: "I believe that economic growth in the long run cannot be soundly brought about except with stability in your price structure."[61] For the new economists, expanding the productive capacity of the economy was the best safeguard against inflation ensuing from the rise of aggregate demand. As a corollary to this, they also disagreed about how much inflation was acceptable—Eisenhower's concern about creeping inflation put a premium on near-zero price instability; the new economists accepted 2 percent annual inflation as the trade-off for high employment.

However, the Keynesian consensus was not all-embracing, as there were outliers on the right of the political spectrum. Conservative Republicans and southern Democrats continued to regard balanced budgets as the fundamental safeguard against expansion of big government. Despite their belief that taxes were too high, this was why GOP legislators voted 126–48 against the Kennedy tax cut when it gained House approval in September 1963. With Johnson urging passage in memory of the dead president, a majority of Republicans backed it 21–10 in the Senate. One of the nays was Senator Barry Goldwater of Arizona, soon to become the GOP presidential candidate. It was his conviction that an orderly reduction of federal spending through domestic program transfer to the states was necessary to achieve tax reduction within the framework of a balanced budget. This would enable individuals to have maximum freedom to dispose of the fruits of their labor, the prerequisite for economic growth.[62]

The economic boom generated by the tax cut helped to put Johnson back into the White House. The lesson that some conservative Republicans drew from this was that it was not necessary to balance the budget before taxes were cut. Ronald Reagan would draw on this when promoting enactment of the Economic Recovery Tax Act in 1981. Despite deficits growing to unprecedented levels, Reagan ran for reelection on the growth benefits of this measure in the face of Democratic demands that he raise taxes to restore budgetary control. Throughout the 1984 campaign he posed as the true heir of John F. Kennedy's growth economics. As one analyst later noted, "In the past, as the party of responsible finance, Republicans would try to cut spending and deficits; generally they were successful at neither. Under Reagan they have abandoned tasks at which they failed in the past in favor of others that are easier to accomplish."[63]

By the 1980s, of course, the liberal consensus was long gone. The opportunities unlocked by growth economics had a considerable role in its downfall. As Heller remarked, growth was "both an end in itself and an instrumentality, both the pot of gold and the rainbow." The prosperity it generated put at presidential disposal as nothing else could "the resources to achieve great societies at home and grand designs abroad."[64] Johnson expressed the same optimism more directly, telling an aide in 1964, "Hell, we've barely begun to solve our problems. And we can do it all. We've got the wherewithal."[65] Such hubris underlay simultaneous overreach to fight communism in Southeast Asia and to build the most ambitious set of reform programs since the New Deal at home. The political fractures resulting from these enterprises did much to undermine the liberal consensus. Moreover, the expansion of public demand in a full-employment economy generated by the Vietnam War and the Great Society brought the inflationary genie out of its bottle. Failure to put it back in presaged the decline of Keynesianism's ascendancy over American political economy.

The consensus around a domesticated Keynesianism had endured for some twenty years after the passage of the Employment Act of 1946. It was sufficiently flexible to accommodate the competing objectives of stability and growth that vied for preeminence within its framework. Within the limitations of its ambitions, the Keynesian consensus was successful in balancing high employment, low inflation, and solid economic growth until the late 1950s. The chronic slack of the final Eisenhower years made it increasingly difficult to achieve a satisfactory trade-off between these ends. The emergence of growth liberalism was an attempt to resolve this dilemma. At first the new economics appeared to have solved the conundrum of inflation-free growth, but the consensus in its support rapidly unraveled when this proved not to be the case. As the 1960s drew to an end, one of its luminaries acknowledged that the "task of combining prosperity with price stability stands as the major unsolved problem of aggregative economic performance," but he predicted that a "satisfactory compromise" between these ends would be found in the next decade.[66] Keynesianism's failure to square this circle ensured that the postwar consensus about its utility was never reborn.

Notes

The author expresses gratitude to graduate student James Hillyer for perceptive comments on a draft of this chapter.

1. Godfrey Hodgson, *America in Our Time* (Garden City, NY: Doubleday, 1976).
2. Arthur M. Schlesinger Jr., *The Politics of Hope* (Boston: Houghton Mifflin, 1962), 91.
3. Robert Lekachman, *The Age of Keynes* (London: Allen Lane, 1967), 256. For a biography, see Robert Skidelsky, *John Maynard Keynes: 1883–1946: Economist, Philosopher, Statesman* (London: Penguin, 2013).
4. U.S. Congress, Joint Committee on the Economic Report, *January 1955 Economic Report of the President, Hearings*, 84th Cong., 1st sess., 1955, 326.
5. Walter Heller, *New Dimensions of Political Economy* (Cambridge: Harvard University Press, 1966), 70; *Time*, December 31, 1965, http://content.time.com.
6. Theda Skocpol and Margaret Weir, "State Structures and Social Keynesianism: Responses to the Great Depression in Sweden and the United States," *International Journal of Comparative Sociology* 24 (March 1983): 4–29.
7. Hansen's key writings on this score are *Full Recovery or Stagnation?* (New York: Norton, 1938); "Economic Progress and Declining Population Growth," *American Economic Review* 29 (March 1939): 1–15; and *Fiscal Policy and Business Cycles* (New York: Norton, 1941). For a stagnationist manifesto by his Harvard and Tufts disciples, see Richard Gilbert et al., *An Economic Program for American Democracy* (New York: Vanguard, 1938). Their misconceptions are analyzed in Alexander Field, *A Great Leap Forward: 1930s Depression and U.S. Economic Growth* (New Haven: Yale University Press, 2012).
8. Robert Collins, *The Business Response to Keynes, 1929–1964* (New York: Columbia University Press, 1981), 96 (quotation), 99–100.
9. "State of the Union Message to Congress," January 11, 1944; "Address at Soldiers'

Field, Chicago, Illinois," October 28, 1944; and "Annual Budget Message," January 3, 1945, all in *Public Papers of the Presidents* [hereafter *PPP*], in Gerhard Peters and John T. Woolley, *The American Presidency Project*, http://www.presidency.ucsb.edu/ws [hereafter *APP*].

10. Ernst Swanson and Emerson Schmidt, *Economic Stagnation and Progress: A Critique of Recent Doctrines on the Mature Economy, Savings and Deficit Spending* (New York: McGraw Hill, 1946), 186–87.

11. Eric Johnston, *America Unlimited* (Garden City, NY: Doubleday, 1944), 140.

12. See Collins, *Business Response to Keynes*, 102–3.

13. Stephen Bailey, *Congress Makes a Law* (New York: Vintage Books, 1950), 228–32.

14. Herbert Stein, *The Fiscal Revolution in America: Policy in Pursuit of Reality*, 2nd ed. (Washington, DC: AEI Press, 1996), 132–33.

15. Leon Keyserling, "The Keynesian Revolution and Its Pioneers: Discussion," *American Economic Review* 62 (May 1972): 136–37.

16. Lekachman, *The Age of Keynes*, 148.

17. W. Walter Williams, "A Program to Increase Understanding of the American Economy," *Michigan Business Review* 2 (July 1950): 22–27 (quotation on 24). Authored by a Seattle businessman who succeeded Hoffman as CED chair, this article also discusses the group's aims and achievements. For the CED's history see Collins, *Business Response to Keynes*, 81–87, 205–8.

18. CED, *Taxes and the Budget: A Program for Prosperity in the Free Economy* (New York: CED, 1947), quotation on 22.

19. CED, *Monetary and Fiscal Policy for Greater Economic Stability* (New York: CED, 1948), quotation on 45; Thomas McCabe, *The Role of CED Today* (New York: CED, 1951).

20. The signatories were an eclectic group that included liberals like John Kenneth Galbraith and Paul Samuelson and onetime New Deal critics like Sumner Slichter. See "Federal Expenditure and Revenue Policy for Economic Stability," *American Economic Review* 39 (December 1949): 1263–68.

21. "The Text of Senator Taft's Address at Republican Leaders' Dinner at Columbus," *New York Times*, August 1, 1947; "Veto of Bill to Reduce Income Taxes," June 16, 1947, *PPP, APP.*

22. "Special Message to the Congress: The President's Midyear Economic Report, 11 July, 1949," *PPP, APP*.

23. Robert Griffith, "Dwight D. Eisenhower and the Corporate Commonwealth," *American Historical Review* 87 (February 1982): 87–122.

24. Eisenhower to Leffingwell, February 16, 1954, and to Milton Eisenhower, January 6, 1954, Ann Whitman Files–Dwight D. Eisenhower Diary Series [hereafter AWF-DDEDS], box 5, Dwight D. Eisenhower Presidential Library [hereafter DDEPL], Abilene, Kansas.

25. Iwan Morgan, *Eisenhower versus "The Spenders": The Eisenhower Administration, the Democrats and the Budget, 1953–60* (New York: St. Martin's Press, 1990), 60–70.

26. Neil Jacoby, "A Memoire on Service as a Member of the Council of Economic Advisers," Neil Jacoby Papers, box 6, DDEPL.

27. Wilfred Lewis, *Federal Fiscal Policy in Postwar Recessions* (Washington, DC: Brookings Institution, 1962), 131–43, 193–94.

28. Arthur Burns, *Prosperity without Inflation* (New York: Fordham University Press,

1957); Robert Anderson, "The Balance of Payments Problem," *Foreign Affairs* 38 (April 1960): 419–32.

29. "Memorandum of a Conference with the President, October 30, 1957," AWF-DDEDS, box 27, DDEPL.

30. Eisenhower to Burns, March 12, 1958, AWF-DDEDS, box 31, DDEPL.

31. Helen Hill Miller, "Politics and Recession: The 1958 Handicap," *New Republic*, February 10, 1958, 12–14; Morgan, *Eisenhower versus "The Spenders,"* 106–18.

32. Eisenhower to Arthur Burns, March 10, 1958, AWF-Administration Series, box 9, DDEPL

33. "Treasury Is Firm in Its Opposition to a Tax Cut Now," *New York Times*, April 6, 1958. For a critical assessment, see Hans Landsberg, "We Cannot Afford This Recession," *The Reporter*, May 15, 1958, 10–14.

34. Johnson to Senator Paul Douglas, February 14, 1959, Paul Douglas Papers, box 266, Chicago Historical Society; Leon Keyserling, "Is Inflation the Problem?" *New Republic*, February 9, 1959, 18–22.

35. "Memorandum of a Meeting in the President's Office, November 3, 1958," AWF-DDEDS, box 37, DDEPL; Eisenhower to Ralph McGill, February 26, 1959, AWF–Name Series, box 23, DDEPL; Don Paarlberg, Memorandum for General Wilton B. Persons, January 24, 1959, Gerald Morgan Records, box 4, DDEPL.

36. T. R. B., "Washington Wire," *New Republic*, September 14, 1959, 2. Senator Barry Goldwater of Arizona, a critic of the president's earlier toleration of unbalanced budgets, now remarked that his "[conservative] firmness is rubbing off on the Republican Party." See Goldwater to Eisenhower, May 29, 1959, White House Central Files, Office Files, box 561, DDEPL.

37. Dwight D. Eisenhower, *The White House Years: Waging Peace* (London: Heinemann, 1966), 461–62; Anderson, "The Balance of Payments Problem," 429.

38. Stein, *Fiscal Revolution in America*, 366–69.

39. "Democratic Party Platform of 1960," July 11, 1960, *APP*.

40. "Presidential Debate in New York," October 21, 1960, *APP*.

41. Robert Collins, *More: The Politics of Economic Growth in Postwar America* (New York: Oxford University Press, 2000), 61.

42. *The Economic Report of the President 1950*, 2, *APP*. For contemporary discussion, see Leon Keyserling, "A Policy for Full Employment," *New Republic*, October 24, 1949, 13–15; and Richard Lester, "Truman Economics—1950 Model," *New Republic*, January 23, 1950, 11–13.

43. Keyserling's remarks are in Erwin Hargrove and Samuel Morley, eds., *The President and the Council of Economic Advisers: Interviews with CEA Chairmen* (Boulder: Westview, 1984), 77–82; and Alonzo Hamby, *Beyond the New Deal: Harry S. Truman and American Liberalism* (New York: Columbia University Press, 1973), 415–18, 447–48, 453–54.

44. Leon Keyserling, "'Liberal' Government Is Not Enough," *The Reporter*, May 31, 1956, 17–18; ADA Press Release, "Testimony of Leon H. Keyserling on Behalf of ADA before the Resolutions Committee, Democratic National Convention, August 8, 1956"; Steven Gillon, *Politics and Vision: The ADA and American Liberalism, 1947–1987* (New York: Oxford University Press, 1987), 112–14.

45. Democratic Advisory Council, "Three Great Deficits of the Eisenhower-Nixon Administration," October 5, 1958, and "The Democratic Task in the Next Two Years," December 7, 1958, Paul Butler Papers, box 29, University of Notre Dame, South Bend, Indiana.

46. "Address at New York University," October 20, 1960, U.S. Senate, Committee on Commerce, Subcommittee on Communications, *Senate Report 994: Part II: The Speeches of Vice President Richard M. Nixon, Presidential Campaign of 1960* (Washington, DC: Government Printing Office, 1961), 685–91.

47. See the later published version, Rockefeller Brothers Fund, *Prospect for America* (Garden City, NY: Doubleday, 1961), 325–30.

48. Theodore White, *The Making of the President 1960* (New York: Atheneum, 1961), 434–36.

49. "Statements of the Candidates on Growth," *New Republic*, October 10, 1960, 16.

50. Leon Keyserling, "A *New* Economics for America," *The Progressive*, November 1959, 13–16; Keyserling, DAC Discussion Paper, "Towards Economic Growth: Priorities and Justice—Policies for Balanced Progress without Inflation," Butler Papers, box 14.

51. Galbraith to Keyserling, April 22, 1958, and to Charles Tyroler, July 31, 1959, John Kenneth Galbraith Papers, box 22, John F. Kennedy Presidential Library, Boston.

52. DAC, "The Decision in 1960: The Need to Elect a Democratic President," December 6, 1959, Butler Papers, box 14; U.S. Congress, Joint Economic Committee, *Staff Report on Employment, Growth and Price Levels*, 86th Cong., 1st sess. (Washington, DC: Government Printing Office, 1959); Paul Douglas and Howard Shuman, "Growth without Inflation," *New Republic*, September 26, 1960, 16–22.

53. Peter Bernstein, "Golden Hemorrhage," *The Nation*, November 1960, 339–42; "Text of Kennedy Pledge to Defend Dollar," *New York Times*, October 31, 1960.

54. *Annual Report of the Council of Economic Advisers 1962*, *APP*, especially 44, 78–81. See too Heller, *New Dimensions of Political Economy*, 64–70; James Tobin and Robert Solow, introduction, in James Tobin and Murray Weidenbaum, eds., *Two Revolutions in Economic Policy: The First Economic Reports of Presidents Kennedy and Reagan* (Cambridge: MIT Press, 1988).

55. For insightful discussion, see James Hillyer, "'Getting the Country Moving Again': Walter Heller, American Liberalism, and the Kennedy-Johnson New Economics," (MA diss., University College London, 2014).

56. Heller, *New Dimensions of Political Economy*, 35; Heller to Kennedy, December 16, 1962, Walter Heller Papers, box 22, John F. Kennedy Presidential Library.

57. James Tobin, "Economic Growth as an Objective of Government Policy," *American Economic Review* 54 (May 1964): 1; Heller, *New Dimensions of Political Economy*, vii–viii.

58. Lekachman, *The Age of Keynes*, 287.

59. For this, see Heller to Kennedy, "Paris Report No 1: Why Europe Grows Faster Than the U.S.," May 5, 1961, and "Report on Rome Monetary Conference," May 20, 1962, http://www.jfklibrary.org/Asset-Viewer/Archives/JFKPOF-063-019.aspx.

60. *Annual Report of the Council of Economic Advisers 1962*, 42.

61. "The President's News Conference of January 21, 1959," *PPP*, *APP*.

62. Barry Goldwater, *The Conscience of a Conservative* (Lexington, KY: Victor Books, 1960), 60–69.

63. Iwan Morgan, *The Age of Deficits: Presidents and Unbalanced Budgets from Jimmy Carter to George W. Bush* (Lawrence: University Press of Kansas, 2009), 103–7; Aaron Wildavsky, "President Reagan as Political Strategist," *Society,* May/June 1987, 58. See too Robert Mason, "Kennedy and the Conservatives," in Andrew Hoberek, ed., *The Cambridge Companion to John F. Kennedy* (New York: Cambridge University Press, 2015), 231–33.

64. Heller speech, Madison, Wisconsin, November 13, 1961, Heller Papers, box 17; Heller, *New Dimensions of Political Economy*, 11.

65. Richard Goodwin, *Remembering America: A Voice from the Sixties* (Boston: Little, Brown, 1988), 270.

66. Arthur Okun, *The Political Economy of Prosperity* (New York: Norton, 1970), 130.

6

Social Welfare in the United States, 1945–1960

DAVID STEBENNE

One of the more idiosyncratic aspects of Godfrey Hodgson's classic work, *America in Our Time*, was how little attention it paid to the topic of social welfare in the United States in the fifteen years after World War II. The book did, to be sure, discuss the G.I. Bill and the Employment Act of 1946 in some detail, but only a few other parts of the American welfare state were mentioned, and then just briefly. There was no effort to look at the whole *range* of social-welfare policies pursued then, or how they were related. To the extent there was a thesis about American social-welfare policy at that time, Hodgson's view was that moderately conservative Republicans of the Eisenhower-era variety had essentially accepted moderately liberal thinking of the New Deal–era sort, in a nation without other strong, competing political parties. Thus, he concluded, this area of public policy fit his overall postwar consensus thesis.[1]

The reason for this odd social-welfare gap in *America in Our Time* may well have had to do with the author's Anglocentric perspective. When compared to the Beveridge Plan and the work of the postwar Labour government, the American welfare state of 1945–60 likely struck Hodgson as comparatively puny, especially when compared with the huge amounts of money the United States was spending then on armies and armaments. He hinted as much in a passage on that latter subject:

> Between 1945 and 1967, according to Senator Fulbright, the federal government spent $904 billion on "military power," as against $96 billion on . . ."social functions," such as education, health and welfare, that were often thought so remarkable that they justified calling the United States a "welfare state."[2]

What Hodgson appears to have missed was how different the American welfare state was, both in origins and in subsequent development, from the British model. Close attention to that topic will help clarify what Hodgson's Anglocentric perspective distorted and will offer an interesting insight into whether his overall consensus thesis accurately described social-welfare policy in the United States from 1945 to 1960.

The origins of social-welfare provision in the post–World War II United States are still being debated. Theda Skocpol argues that the pension scheme for Northern veterans of the Civil War marked the birth of social provision in the United States. Given how many men served in the Grand Army of the Republic, as it was called, how generous the pension benefits approved by Congress ultimately were, and how long aging veterans collected them, Skocpol argues that something of a forerunner to the Social Security system first came into being in the United States in the late nineteenth century. Even she concedes, though, that the system was not permanent. As the veterans and their spouses died off in large numbers around the turn of the century, so, too, did this first mass system of social welfare.[3]

Other scholars, such as Roy Lubove, David Moss, and John Witt, point to the creation of workers compensation programs in the first two decades of the twentieth century as the beginning of a *permanent* system of social provision. Workers compensation was intended to address the very serious problem of work-related injuries in the major industrial countries. Germany had pioneered in the workers compensation area in the mid-1880s, and the British government had followed that example in passing a landmark workers compensation statute in 1897. In those countries, the basic idea was for the government to require employers and employees to contribute to a fund that insured against work-related injuries. (Germany's long-standing guild system and Britain's labor unions were the mechanisms through which workers contributions would be collected.) The amounts paid by the insurance fund were not intended to protect those injured from all of the medical expenses and lost income caused by such industries. Instead, workers compensation funds paid only a lesser amount that enabled those injured (and the families they supported) to live decently. By requiring *workers* as well as employers to contribute, the moderately conservative framers of such legislation thought, a significant deterrent would be created to excessive or fraudulent claims, lest the required worker contributions go up.[4]

Influenced by those precedents, American state legislatures had begun experimenting with workers compensation laws in the first decade of the twentieth century. The courts had struck down early versions of that kind of law passed by the legislatures in Maryland, Montana, and New York then as an unconstitutional taking of property without due process of law, because of the measures' requirement of mandatory employer contributions to fund the system. (Those laws had not required worker contributions, because the United States had neither a guild system nor a big enough system of labor unions to make that approach workable.) By 1917, however, more limited versions of that same basic idea survived legal challenges. That year, the U.S. Supreme Court found three different approaches constitutional in a trilogy of cases that arguably mark the start of a permanent American welfare state. Historian David Kennedy has argued that it was no coincidence that those rulings came just as the United States entered World War I. He sees the emergence of the modern American state, including its welfare-state component, as having first taken place during that time. Only the pressure of a major wartime emergency, Kennedy contends, was sufficient to overcome business community resistance to a larger governmental role in the provision of social welfare.[5]

Still other scholars, most notably William Leuchtenburg, tend to see the passage of the Social Security Act of 1935 as having brought the modern welfare state into being in the United States. Historians of the New Deal and Social Security emphasize how far-reaching its provisions were when compared with the earlier workers compensation statutes. From that point of view, the great breakthrough in the creation of the American welfare state came almost twenty years later than the students of workers compensation tend to suggest.[6]

The focus of this chapter is on social-welfare policy in the United States from 1945 to 1960, but one should keep in mind that no matter what starting date one uses, the American welfare state had begun earlier. Postwar social welfare thus was informed by earlier precedents and built upon preexisting structures. That was, to be sure, also true in the United Kingdom, and in that way the American and British models were similar. How all of the parts fit together and what they added up to in the immediate postwar period are less well understood, even today, and it is in those areas that the divergence of the American and British models after 1945 becomes clear. One needs to keep in mind, too, that differences between liberals and conservatives over social-welfare policy in the postwar years had to do not just with specific parts of the system but also its overall philosophy and direction.

The first major part of the postwar approach to social welfare was passed by Congress in 1944 and signed into law by Franklin Roosevelt on June 2 of that year. This was the Serviceman's Readjustment Act of 1944, more commonly known as the G.I. Bill of Rights. It deserves to be designated as the first postwar addition to social welfare, because it did not go into effect in any significant way until after the Japanese government surrendered in August 1945. Among its most important provisions were federal mortgage assistance with buying homes and starting businesses; federal aid to finance education at all levels, from primary through professional school; health care for the disabled through an expanded system of veterans hospitals; monthly allowances (known colloquially as "the 52–20 club") to help support returning veterans as they looked for work; and priorities for many jobs. Extensive and expensive, the G.I. Bill of Rights reflected in miniature what advanced New Dealers wanted to accomplish in the realm of social welfare for all Americans. Almost 13 million Americans were directly eligible in the first year after the war ended. Many millions more benefited indirectly, because they belonged to families and/or households of which those 13 million veterans were a part. The system also satisfied many conservatives, the more moderate of them especially, because government benefits were based on a traditional conception of entitlement. Recipients "earned" the G.I. Bill's benefits for having served the country during wartime, often at great risk to life and limb. In that limited sense, the G. I. Bill legislation marked the emergence of a kind of postwar "consensus" on social-welfare policy. The most advanced New Dealers in Congress and the conservative Democrats and Republicans serving there still disagreed, to be sure, on *why* they supported the law, but support it they did.[7]

Next came the Employment Act of 1946, a federal statute that *required* the federal government to use the means at its disposal to promote a "high employment economy" consistent with stable prices. Moderately liberal Democrats of the New Deal–era variety liked the explicit federal government obligation to promote high levels of employment, though they grumbled about not having aimed even higher so as to promote *full* employment. Moderately conservative Republicans in Congress (and leading southern Democrats there) liked what they saw as the realism in the act's more limited objective. The Business Advisory Council to the U.S. Commerce Department had debated this issue earlier, when planning for postwar economic policy. So, too, had the Committee for Economic Development, which the Business Advisory Council created. Moderately conservative Republican business leaders such as Eastman Kodak's Marion Folsom and Lamson Machine's Ralph Flanders played leading roles in both groups, and they believed strongly that full employment in a country like the United States was not truly feasible, and certainly not without inflation that diminished the real incomes of the poorest. At the same time, however, the experiences of the Depression and the war had led such business leaders to favor an enlarged federal government role in promoting overall economic stability and prosperity. The limited nature of that role, which was confined to using the government's power to modify economic aggregates while not interfering with management prerogatives over hiring and investment, also appealed to moderately conservative Republicans. So, too, did the fairly small size of the government machinery created to carry out that work, which suggested that the federal role would be kept within proper boundaries. What the statute meant in practical terms was that the federal government now had an affirmative obligation to use its expanded powers to fight hard against economic downturns, and that a new but not very big entity, the Council of Economic Advisers, had been created expressly to help the federal government do so. Failures to act of the sort that had marred Herbert Hoover's presidency were no longer merely inhumane or unwise; they had actually become illegal. The result was that there were no long-term periods of high unemployment from 1945 to 1960. When recessions arose, as they did in 1949–50, 1954, and 1957–58, federal government intervention did much to end them.[8]

The next addition to the social-welfare system was the emergence of privatized benefits systems in the unionized sectors of the economy. That development stemmed from an inability to win from Congress a comprehensive public-health system like the one begun by the British government in the late 1940s or a more generous and comprehensive Social Security pension system, due to stiff resistance from the coalition of fiscally conservative southern Democrats and Republicans dominant in Congress since 1939. Forced to lower their sights, American trade unionists and their liberal allies instead focused their efforts then on winning health and pension benefits via collective bargaining, backstopped by litigation and a helping hand from the Truman administration. The big breakthrough came in 1949, when the influential Steelworkers Union won a pension plan from management through skillful lawyering, tough collective bargaining, and adroit federal government mediation. The United Mine Workers had earlier won such a plan, but not until the Steelworkers followed was it clear that such an approach would spread throughout the heavily unionized manufacturing, transportation, and construction sectors of the economy. Even many *non*-union employers felt compelled to follow that emerging pattern in order to compete successfully for the best workers.[9]

Like the G.I. Bill and the Employment Act, the emergence of what scholars now call the "privatized benefits system" was something of a compromise. New Deal liberals liked the greater degree of social provision for many members of the working and lower middle classes. Moderate conservatives of the Eisenhower-era variety liked the "earned entitlement" approach (benefits went to employees and their dependents), the way the private benefits system tended to keep the public welfare state smaller than it would otherwise likely be, and the tendency of the system to strengthen patriarchal family organization. The typical recipient of health and pension benefits, in a direct sense, was a male head of household. Women and children tended to benefit indirectly, through him, with far-reaching consequences. Thus, the privatized benefit system tended to work the same way the G.I. Bill of Rights did; both had conservative qualities as well as more obviously liberal ones.[10]

The next development took the form of a fundamental shift in the nature of the Social Security system. From its inception in July 1935 through January 1951, the system had functioned more as a welfare program for the aged poor than as a social-insurance program for retired contributors regardless of financial need. In February 1951, for the first time, total social-insurance payments to retired contributors exceeded welfare payments based upon financial need rather than contribution. That shift stemmed from the growing number of retirees who had contributed significant amounts to the pension system since it first began operating and thus were entitled to monthly pension checks. That pattern only grew more pronounced as the 1950s went along. By 1960, Social Security had clearly assumed its modern form: a system mostly of social insurance for contributors irrespective of need. This was the period when Social Security's reach was broadened via legislative amendment to cover ever more employment categories and when benefits paid became somewhat more generous. Those legislative amendments added 10.5 million people to the system, made its reach almost universal, and increased monthly pension benefits by 13 percent. Another, related change took the existing patchwork of federal social-welfare entities and combined them to create the new, cabinet-level Department of Health, Education and Welfare (HEW). That reorganization both elevated the visibility of social-welfare policy and made its overall formation much easier to undertake. All of these changes passed in the Republican-controlled

Eighty-Third Congress of 1953–54 with a strong push from the Eisenhower administration.[11]

Like the other aspects of social-welfare provision already mentioned, those changes constituted something of a compromise that appealed to liberals and conservatives in different ways. At the start of the legislative amendment process, New Deal liberals expressed concerns that expanding Social Security to more employment categories would tend to work against the goal of obtaining more generous benefits. Eisenhower-era Republicans, on the other hand, tended to think that New Deal liberals were overly cautious about expanding Social Security out of a desire to increase excessively the benefits of those already in the system. The 1954 amendments thus were a compromise in that they made the system almost universal *and* substantially improved benefit levels (though not as much as New Deal liberals would have wished). There was also a significant disagreement over basic purposes, with New Deal liberals emphasizing what Social Security experts called "adequacy" (guaranteeing a decent benefit to all participants regardless of their contributions) and the Eisenhower Republicans emphasizing "equity" (making sure that people who paid more into the system received more for their money). The overall result of the 1954 legislative amendment process pleased New Deal liberals, who liked expanding Social Security to more employment categories when coupled with more generous pension payments. Moderate liberals could see, too, both the symbolic and practical value of a cabinet-level social-welfare department. While the GOP's congressional right wing, whose most notable member then was Arizona senator Barry Goldwater, strongly opposed such changes, Eisenhower-era conservatives, the so-called Modern Republicans, liked the earned entitlement aspect, the way ever more universal and generous Social Security old-age pensions tended to strengthen patriarchal family arrangements, the continuation of a strong correlation between the amount contributors paid into the system and the size of the benefits to which they would be entitled, and the more coherent approach to social-welfare policy that HEW's creation had facilitated.[12]

Next came the creation of a federal disability insurance program in 1956, what Europeans called "sickness insurance." That addressed one of the biggest gaps in the American social-welfare system when compared with Northern and Western European ones. Most of them had adopted sickness insurance first. Even in the United States, sickness insurance had been the first kind of social insurance to be seriously urged and studied. The reason it emerged later had to do mostly with the peculiarities of American constitutional interpretation and the timing of the Great Depression. The emergence of sickness insurance faced insuperable judicial obstacles during the heyday of laissez-faire constitutionalism from 1897 to 1937. A series of U.S. Supreme Court rulings, of which *Lochner v. New York* (1905) was the most memorable, erected a legal barrier to its development. The Court viewed mandatory employee contributions to fund such a system as a violation of workers' "liberty of contract," in the employment setting. Most American social-insurance programs had instead emerged during the Depression, when lawmakers' attention was focused on the problem of unemployment caused by economic conditions, not ill health. Even the old-age pensions part of Social Security, which seemed to address a physical cause of unemployment, had more to do then with lawmakers' desire to move older workers out of paying jobs and thereby create more opportunities for younger unemployed people. Only later did the rationale for old-age pensions shift to promoting the physical comfort and well-being of the elderly.[13]

The heart of the federal disability act of 1956 provided insurance for the permanently disabled over the age of fifty. The social provision aspect pleased New Deal liberals, as did the fact that the new disability insurance program would be officially overseen by a federal government agency rather than by the state governments, as Eisenhower and his aides had wanted. They liked most the limits on coverage, which prevented the program's cost from ballooning out of control then, and the fact that most administration of this "federal" program would be carried out by state governmental agencies.[14]

The last major development in social welfare during the 1945–60 period emerged in the late 1950s, when proposals to create a health insurance program for the elderly gained traction. New Deal liberals envisioned Medicare, as it came to be known, as something to which all Social Security recipients sixty-five and older would be entitled. New Deal liberals wanted such a program to pay for the cost of hospitalization and for surgical and medical costs. Eisenhower Republicans had a more limited conception of those to whom Medicare ought to be available. In keeping with the moderately conservative idea that social-insurance programs ought to insure against only those contingencies that caused a substantial decrease in income, they insisted that only the aged and disabled who lost income as a result of their medical problems should receive Medicare payments, not all elderly Social Security recipients. Seemingly a difference over details, that division reflected a more profound conflict over basic social-welfare principles and ultimate purposes. The Medicare debate of the late 1950s showed better than anything else the limits of the postwar "consensus" in welfare-state policy. That very contentious debate also helps explain why Medicare did not emerge until the consensus era broke down in the mid-1960s. The nature of the split over Medicare also helps explain why it was the most hotly debated social-welfare issue in the late 1950s and featured so prominently in the 1960 presidential campaign. That the major-party candidate who publicly endorsed Medicare ultimately prevailed over an opponent who did not was no coincidence, and helped propel the idea forward to fruition five years later.[15]

As well as the specific new additions to social welfare in the United States made and proposed from 1945 to 1960, existing programs such as workers compensation and unemployment insurance were (with the federal government's encouragement) made more comprehensive and generous by many state governments in this era. Generally speaking, those improvements were most pronounced in the major industrial states of the Northeast, Midwest, and West Coast, where union power was greatest. Similarly, the minimum wage, first mandated by federal statute in 1938, was also raised significantly. New Deal liberals wanted to increase it in the mid-1950s from 75 cents per hour to $1.00, while the Eisenhower Republicans favored a smaller increase (to 90 cents) so as to avoid a self-defeating increase in overall price inflation. Both camps of moderates favored extending the minimum wage's coverage to include workers in such low-wage sectors as textiles, sawmills, and sugar refining, but strong opposition from the most conservative people in Congress from both major parties (the southern Democrats especially) blocked that reform. These changes in the prewar parts of social-welfare provision made the system more generous (if not always more extensive) and more expensive.[16]

To understand the American social-welfare system as a whole, one must also keep in mind how federal tax policy and more direct federal government subsidies contributed to it. The federal tax burden in the years between 1945 and 1960 was high and progressive by historical standards. By 1950, not just moderate liberals but also moderate conservatives had come to support such an arrangement strongly. The transformative events in persuading moderate conservatives to take such a view were the Chinese Revolution and the related outbreak of war in Korea. Cold War necessities thus created a centrist consensus on the broad outlines of federal tax policy by 1950, which also helped support the American welfare state through heavy subsidies for such things as child rearing and home buying.

For example, perhaps the most accurate way of understanding the postwar emergence of mass suburbia was as one part of overall social-welfare provision. This was because virtually every facet of its development, from houses to roads to schools, was so heavily subsidized by federal, state, and local government, via the tax code (through the generous deduction for home mortgage interest) and through direct federal and federal-state subsidies in such forms as the G.I. Bill and the Federal Aid Highway Act of 1956. Although somewhat different from the Western European approaches of direct subsidies to families having children (so-called family allowances) and the construction of huge, inexpensive apartment buildings in major metropolitan areas, the overall purposes served were much the same. Here is where Hodgson's Anglocentric perspective appears to have thrown him off the most, because the partly public, partly private nature of the American system of social welfare in the postwar period differed significantly from the British one. His tendency to think that direct federal government spending on public welfare-state programs was a sufficient indicator of the overall size and scope of the American welfare state was more than a little misleading.[17]

What, then, does this history of social-welfare provision in the postwar United States tell us about the notion of a consensus there? Overall, it clearly indicates that differences between New Deal liberals and moderate conservatives over social welfare narrowed in important ways but still remained meaningful. Both sides agreed that a complete system of social insurance had become a necessity in the modern, wage-based economy. Both saw it as even more essential given the need to restabilize American society after the worst economic catastrophe ever during the 1930s and the most destructive war in human history that followed it. Both sides wanted to get away from means-tested programs, which were demeaning to those who benefited from them and less publicly supported than universalist ones based upon recipient contributions. Both believed that the state would have to expand in order to make such programs possible. And both believed that Social Security, the most important such program, had to be organized and run at the federal level, given the enormous sums of money required to fund it. Both sides agreed, too, that requiring recipients to contribute helped restrain pressures for excessive benefits, because greater benefits would likely mean higher Social Security taxes.[18]

Despite those basic areas of agreement, there remained five significant differences between New Deal liberals and Eisenhower-era Republicans. The first of these related to welfare entitlement. The most ardent and cosmopolitan New Deal–era liberals, such as United Auto Workers head Walter Reuther, looked to British and Scandinavian models of social welfare for inspiration. Their ultimate goal was a more comprehensive, citizen-based, public model of social-welfare entitlement. In contrast, Eisenhower-era Republicans such as presidential speechwriter and welfare-state-law expert Arthur Larson thought more in terms of insuring only male "breadwinners" against major and prolonged losses of income. Related to that was a vision of American life in which that kind of household became the norm for the overwhelming majority. Sustaining such a view had been the experience during the years from 1945 to 1960, when households of that sort became ever more numerous and influential. [19]

Second, the two groups split over issues of federalism. New Deal liberals tended to favor the creation of federal welfare programs as the swiftest route to a comprehensive system. They also tended to favor federal government administration of all social-welfare programs. To leave social welfare to the state and local governments would only perpetuate regional inequalities in a country where those kinds of disparities were very great indeed. Eisenhower Republicans tended to favor accomplishing as much as possible (in terms of program creation and administration) through state and local governments, leaving the federal government with only a residual administrative role. As the most articulate spokesman for the latter view, Arthur Larson expressed that thought by saying "if a thing must be done by the government, it should be done at as local a level as possible, and only if it cannot be done by the state should it be done by the federal government."[20] The alternative was, in Eisenhower's words, "the growth of a swollen, bureaucratic monster government in Washington, in whose shadow our state and local governments will ultimately wither and die."[21] Here can be seen the much greater doubts among moderate conservatives that the national state would be able, in a country as big and regionally diverse as the United States, to administer effectively welfare-state programs entirely or mostly by itself.

Third, New Deal liberals tended to favor broader coverage and more generous compensation levels, and Eisenhower Republicans less so, out of a greater sense of the danger of inflating program costs and undermining effective program administration, and also out of a belief that ordinary citizens ought to save more to address ordinary health and welfare needs and rely more on extended family and private charity for help when savings alone were not enough. This would tend to put a brake on excessive, abusive, and overly burdensome use of social-welfare programs, which were mainly meant to insure against big health-care-related expenses, or so Modern Republicans believed. Arthur Larson made that clear in an essay from the early 1950s:

> We have become so insurance-minded in this country that we are in danger of forgetting what the real function of insurance is. It is, or should be, to provide a fund at a time of emergency to meet an expense or loss that the insured cannot possibly cope with by using his ordinary resources. The impulse to liberalize social insurance benefits has frequently taken the regrettable direction of covering smaller and smaller emergencies and expenses, thereby enormously increasing administrative cost and diverting funds that could much better go to deal with real catastrophes.[22]

Fourth, New Deal liberals and Eisenhower Republicans differed in their publicly stated rationales for the modern welfare state. Liberals defended it first and foremost for humanitarian reasons. Moderate conservatives tended to emphasize the need for such programs as a way of preventing more radically leftist alternatives and as a means to head off severe recessions by maintaining household purchasing power even during periods of economic decline. Such conservatives also tended to defend Social Security as promoting the old-fashioned virtue of thrift, albeit in a new way. They similarly tended to describe social-insurance programs as "income insurance" ones, thereby putting distance between them and the Socialist label, and to point out how these strengthened the "traditional" family. The crucial differences here were ones of tone and emphasis. New Deal liberals, sensitive to criticism from those farther to the left of the American welfare state's imperfections, tended to highlight how much it had done, despite its faults, to alleviate the plight of those who did not have very much. Eisenhower Republicans were more concerned with quieting objections from those farther to the right by emphasizing those aspects of the American welfare state that seemed most conservative. One consequence was to make New Deal liberals sound more leftist than they actually were in the postwar period, and to make Eisenhower Republicans sound more conservative than they were at that time. Here is a reminder that even during its heyday, the postwar "consensus" in welfare policy was contested by those farther to the left and right. Those less moderate critics could not do much to shape policy then, but pressure from them did affect the way in which welfare-state policies were publicly discussed.[23]

Fifth, the overall system of social welfare that emerged from 1945 to 1960 satisfied moderate liberals and moderate conservatives most, but they were not the only kinds of political actors then. Strongly left-wing Americans of the sort associated with Henry Wallace's ill-fated campaign for president in 1948 and the American Communist Party pointed to the gaps in the system, which operated more to the benefit of the upper working and lower middle classes, the middle three-fifths of the income distribution, than it did to the poorest Americans. For example, those with the lowest incomes tended to suffer the poorest health, something that led to their disproportionate exclusion from military service and the system of benefits stemming from it. Over a third of those who received draft notices during World War II were ultimately rejected as unfit for service, and the poorest Americans experienced that rejection most. The creation of the G.I. Bill thus widened the gap in social-welfare provision, leaving the poor with much less. So, too, did the ever more generous Social Security pension system, which required stable employment over time in covered sectors to build up a substantial old-age monthly benefit payment. The poor tended to work more casually and were disproportionately concentrated in agricultural and domestic jobs, which were not covered sectors during the first few decades of Social Security's existence. Furthermore, they were disproportionately concentrated in nonunion jobs, which largely excluded them from the reach of the private benefits system, although there were some indirect, spillover effects in terms of raising standards for compensation and benefits.[24]

There was also a regional aspect to this pattern. The nation's poorest regions—the South and the Mountain West—benefited less because their economies then were heavily based on agriculture. The major industrial states of the Northeast, Midwest, and West Coast, on the other hand, had much more diversified economies in which the bulk of the population was covered by welfare-state programs by the 1950s. Thus did their creation contribute to a widening of living standards in which the already more affluent parts of the country moved ahead faster than the poorest ones.[25]

Other parts of the nation's postwar social-welfare system produced similarly unsatisfactory results. The poor were excluded from mass suburbia precisely because they could not afford to buy a house. Marriage among the poor was typically much less stable, and so a social-welfare system that depended so heavily on stable marriages in order to benefit fully tended to work much less well for the poorest.[26]

That a disproportionate number of them were also not white only intensified strongly left-wing Americans' dissatisfaction with the postwar system of social welfare. That was especially true among black radicals such as the actor and activist Paul Robeson. From their perspective the steadily expanding postwar welfare system seemed to be just another example of the discriminatory treatment that limited the hopes of racial minorities for a better life.[27]

And then there were strongly left-wing straight women, as well as gays and lesbians, who chafed against a social-welfare system that tended to strengthen patriarchal arrangements. In the repressive atmosphere of the 1950s, that perspective tended not to be voiced publicly, but it nonetheless existed under the surface. By far the most numerous members of this group were straight women of a radically leftist orientation, who resented the American social-welfare system's tendency to deepen dependency on men, be they fathers, brothers, or husbands.[28]

Some of the same complaints could also be heard from strongly *conservative* people in the decade and a half after World War II. Republican senators Robert Taft of Ohio and Barry Goldwater of Arizona articulated those views on behalf of their impassioned supporters. They grumbled most, however, about the overall cost of the system, the heavy taxes needed to support it, the ever greater intrusiveness of the national state, the consequent decline in entrepreneurial initiative, and the adverse implications for international competitiveness of such a highly compensated labor force, in basic manufacturing especially. To those complaints was added a new, more potent one beginning in the later 1950s: the advent of persistent price inflation, in good economic times and in bad, which tended to increase conservative opposition to expanding social-welfare programs further. Strongly conservative people, such as Goldwater and *National Review* editor William F. Buckley Jr. argued forcefully toward the end of the 1950s for shrinking the size of welfare-state programs and for promoting private savings and charity instead. Goldwater's most famous statement of his views, his 1960 manifesto titled *The Conscience of a Conservative*, made that plain in his characteristically blunt way:

> Let welfare be a private concern. Let it be promoted by individuals and families, by churches, private hospitals, religious service organizations, community charities and other institutions that have been established for this purpose. If objection is raised that private institutions lack sufficient funds, let us remember that every penny the federal government does *not* appropriate for welfare is potentially available for private use—and without the overhead charge for processing the money through the federal bureaucracy. Indeed, high taxes, for

> which government Welfarism is so largely responsible, is the biggest obstacle to fund raising by private charities.[29]

And to the extent that some governmental role was needed in the area of social welfare, Goldwater and his supporters opposed playing it at the federal level. In his words, "If we deem public intervention necessary, let the job be done by local and state authorities that are incapable of accumulating the vast political power that is so inimical to our liberties."[30]

Although those kinds of pressures from the strongly left and right were contained from 1945 to 1960, the existence of a dissenting third of the overall population, as measured by polls, complicates the notion of a postwar consensus in the social-welfare realm, and more generally. That there was much greater agreement over social welfare in the mid-1950s than there had been ten or twenty years earlier was undeniable. And yet, even in the heyday of the postwar "consensus," the dissenters were there, more numerous than visible or influential to be sure, but still part of the political and social landscape. Accordingly, the fragility of the postwar "consensus" in welfare-state policy also helps explain why it declined so much thereafter. It therefore makes sense to moderate Hodgson's formulation somewhat. "The postwar moderate majority" is a more apt descriptor for the social-welfare domain than "the postwar liberal consensus," but the latter can still work as long as "liberal" is understood to mean "moderate" and as long as "consensus" is *not* understood to mean "universal," or nearly so.[31]

Notes

1. Godfrey Hodgson, *America in Our Time* (Garden City, NY: Doubleday, 1976), 53–54, 72, 75, 106–7, 130.

2. Ibid., 130. On the British Labour government's work in the social welfare policy area after World War II, see Arthur Marwick, *British Society since 1945* (Harmondsworth, Middlesex, UK: Penguin, 1982) 49–63.

3. Theda Skocpol, *Protecting Soldiers and Mothers: The Political Origins of Social Policy in the United States* (Cambridge: Harvard University Press, 1992).

4. Roy Lubove, *The Struggle for Social Security, 1900–1935*, 2nd ed. (Pittsburgh: University of Pittsburgh Press, 1986), 45–65; David A. Moss, *Socializing Security: Progressive-Era Economists and the Origins of American Social Policy* (Cambridge: Harvard University Press, 1996), 33, 68–71; John Fabian Witt, *The Accidental Republic: Crippled Workmen, Destitute Widows, and the Remaking of American Law* (Cambridge: Harvard University Press, 2006). For an early statement of this perspective by a law professor who became undersecretary of labor in the Eisenhower administration, see Arthur Larson, "The Nature and Origins of Workmen's Compensation," *Cornell Law Quarterly* 37 (Winter 1952): 206–34.

5. Lubove, *The Struggle for Social Security*, 45–65; Moss, *Socializing Security*, 33, 68–71; Witt, *The Accidental Republic*; Larson, "Nature and Origins of Workmen's Compensation"; and David M. Kennedy, *Over Here: The First World War and American Society* (New York: Oxford University Press, 1980), 93–143.

6. See William E. Leuchtenburg, *Franklin D. Roosevelt and the New Deal, 1932–1940* (New York: Harper & Row, 1963), 131–33.

7. See John Morton Blum, *V Was for Victory: Politics and American Culture during World War II* (New York: Harcourt, Brace, 1976), 247–50; and on the G.I. Bill and its consequences generally, see Suzanne Mettler, *Soldiers to Citizens: The G.I. Bill and the Making of the Greatest Generation* (New York: Oxford University Press, 2007); Kathleen J. Frydl, *The GI Bill* (New York: Cambridge University Press, 2009); and Edward Humes, *Over Here: How the G.I. Bill Transformed the American Dream* (Orlando: Harcourt, 2006). On the important role played by conservative southern Democrats in shaping the bill, see, too, Ira Katznelson, *Fear Itself: The New Deal and the Origins of Our Time* (New York: Liveright, 2013), 205, 368.

8. On the Employment Act of 1946 and its consequences, see Stephen Bailey, *Congress Makes a Law: The Story behind the Employment Act of 1946* (New York: Columbia University Press, 1950); Ruth Ellen Wasem, *Tackling Unemployment: The Legislative Dynamics of the Employment Act of 1946* (Kalamazoo, MI: W. E. Upjohn Institute, 2013); David Stebenne, "Thomas J. Watson and the Business–Government Relationship, 1933–1956," *Enterprise and Society* 6 (March 2005): 45–75, esp. 39; Robert Collins, *The Business Response to Keynes, 1929–1964* (New York: Columbia University Press, 1981), 13, 88, 99–101, 104–9, 154, 198–99; and Katznelson, *Fear Itself*, 380–82. For a perspective that the measure had only limited significance, see Alan Brinkley, *The End of Reform: New Deal Liberalism in Recession and War* (New York: Knopf, 1995), 259–64.

9. On the emergence of the privatized benefits system, see Nelson Lichtenstein, "From Corporatism to Collective Bargaining: Organized Labor and the Eclipse of Social Democracy in the Postwar Era," in Steve Fraser and Gary Gerstle, eds., *The Rise and Fall of the New Deal Order, 1930–1980* (Princeton: Princeton University Press, 1989), 142–44; and David Stebenne, *Arthur J. Goldberg: New Deal Liberal* (New York: Oxford University Press, 1996), 66–67, 74–75, 142–43. On the federal government's response to the first three postwar recessions, see A. E. Holmans, "The Eisenhower Administration and the Recession, 1953–5," *Oxford Economic Papers* 10 (1958): 34–54; and Iwan W. Morgan, *Eisenhower versus "The Spenders": The Eisenhower Administration, the Democrats and the Budget, 1953–60* (New York: St. Martin's Press, 1990), 9–13, 93–126.

10. For the New Deal liberal perspective, see Stebenne, *Arthur J. Goldberg*, 142–43. For the Eisenhower Republican one, see David L. Stebenne, *Modern Republican: Arthur Larson and the Eisenhower Years* (Bloomington: Indiana University Press, 1986), 90–91, 111–13, 139. For the way American welfare-state measures tended to encourage a patriarchal social system, see Barbara A. Nelson, "The Origins of the Two-Channel Welfare State: Workmen's Compensation and Mother's Aid," in Linda Gordon, ed., *Women, the State and Welfare* (Madison: University of Wisconsin Press, 1990), 123–51; Linda Gordon, *Pitied but Not Entitled: Single Mothers and the History of Welfare* (New York: Free Press, 1994); Michael Willrich, "Home Slackers: Men, the State and Welfare in Modern America," *Journal of American History* 87 (September 2000): 460–89; Alice Kessler-Harris, *In Pursuit*

of Equity: Women, Men, and the Quest for Economic Citizenship in 20th-Century America (New York: Oxford University Press, 2001); and Margot Canaday, *The Straight State: Sexuality and Citizenship in Twentieth-Century America* (Princeton: Princeton University Press, 2009), 91–173.

11. On the shift during the 1950s in Social Security's basic nature, see Edward D. Berkowitz, "The Historical Development of Social Security in the United States," in Eric R. Kingson and James H. Schulz, eds., *Social Security in the 21st Century* (New York: Oxford University Press, 1997), 28; and Brian Gratton, "The New Welfare State: Social Security and Retirement in 1950," *Social Science History* 12 (Summer 1988): 172–74. On the New Deal liberal and Modern Republican perspectives and the 1954 expansion of Social Security and creation of HEW, see Stebenne, *Arthur J. Goldberg*, 75–77; Stebenne, *Modern Republican*, 108–9, 114, 123–26, 128, 135–36, 141, 144, 165; Edward D. Berkowitz, *Robert Ball and the Politics of Social Security* (Madison: University of Wisconsin Press, 2003), 86–95; and Richard Norton Smith, *On His Own Terms: A Life of Nelson Rockefeller* (New York: Random House, 2014), 218–25, 229–34.

12. Stebenne, *Arthur J. Goldberg*, 75–77; Stebenne, *Modern Republican*, 108–9, 114, 123–26, 128, 135–36, 141, 144, 165; Berkowitz, *Robert Ball*, 86–95; and Smith, *On His Own Terms*, 218–25, 229–34.

13. For the early creation of sickness-insurance systems in other major industrial countries, see Deltev Zollner, "Germany," 24–27; Yves Saint-Jours, "France," 111; A. I. Ogus, "Great Britain," 182–87; and Herbert Hofmeister, "Austria," 285–87, 302–6, all in Peter A. Kohler and Hans F. Zacher with Martin Partington, eds., *The Evolution of Social Insurance, 1881–1981: Studies of Germany, France, Great Britain, Austria and Switzerland* (London: Frances Pinter, 1982); and International Labour Office, *An Introduction to Social Security* (Geneva: Kundig, 1970), 10–12. On the lateness of sickness insurance to arrive in the United States, see Stebenne, *Modern Republican*, 101–2, and the sources cited therein.

14. For the creation of the disability insurance program, see Edward Berkowitz and Daniel M. Fox, "The Politics of Social Security Expansion: Social Security Disability Insurance, 1935–1986," *Journal of Policy History* 1 (July 1989): 236–37, 247–49; Edward Berkowitz and Kim McQuaid, *Creating the Welfare State: The Political Economy of Twentieth-Century Reform* (New York: Praeger, 1980), 153–55; Sanford M. Jacoby, "Employers and the Welfare State: The Role of Marion B. Folsom," *Journal of American History* 80 (September 1993): 525–56; and Stebenne, *Modern Republican*, 102–3, 11–12, 136. A good short explanation of the law's major provisions is in "A Chronology of Significant Events in Social Security, 1935–1985," in Gerald Nash, Noel H. Pugach, and Richard F. Tomasson, eds., *Social Security: The First Half Century* (Albuquerque: University of New Mexico Press, 1988), 317.

15. On the origins of the Medicare debate and the program's eventual creation, see James Patterson, *Grand Expectations: The United States, 1945–1974* (New York: Oxford University Press, 1996), 572–74; Berkowitz, "The Historical Development of Social Security," 32–35; J. Douglas Brown, *An American Philosophy of Social Security: Evolution and Issues* (Princeton: Princeton University Press, 1972), 197–98; and W. Andrew Achenbaum, *Social Security: Visions and Revisions* (New York: Cambridge University Press, 1986), 52. For the Eisenhower Republican perspective and the importance of the Medicare issue in the 1960 election, see Stebenne, *Modern Republican*, 103, 230–32, 243, 256–57.

16. Stebenne, *Modern Republican*, 105–6, 131–33, 136–37.

17. See the passage quoted earlier from Hodgson, *American in Our Time;* Stebenne, "Thomas J. Watson," 64–65; John Patrick Diggins, *The Proud Decades: America in War and Peace, 1941–1960* (New York: Norton, 1988), 177–88; and Marty Jezer, *The Dark Ages: Life in the United States, 1945–1960* (Boston: South End Press, 1982), 117–46, 176–99. For a perceptive study of mass suburbia as it was in the 1950s, see Herbert J. Gans, *The Levittowners: Ways of Life and Community in a New Suburban Community* (New York: Columbia University Press, 1967). For the contemporaneous approach to social welfare in Western Europe, see Marwick, *British Society since 1945*, 49–63; Robert O. Paxton, *Europe in the Twentieth Century*, 2nd ed. (New York: Harcourt, Brace Jovanovich, 1985), 521–42, 599–603; and Olivier Zunz, ed., *Social Contracts under Stress: The Middle Classes of America, Europe and Japan at the Turn of the Century* (New York: Russell Sage Foundation, 2004).

18. For the New Deal liberal perspective on the welfare state, see Marquis Childs, *Sweden: The Middle Way*, 2nd ed. (New York: Penguin, 1948); Leuchtenburg, *Franklin D. Roosevelt and the New Deal*, 345; Nelson Lichtenstein, *The Most Dangerous Man in Detroit: Walter Reuther and the Fate of American Labor* (New York: Basic Books, 1995), 281–82, 337–38; and Stebenne, *Arthur J. Goldberg*, 43, 74–76, 152. For the Eisenhower Republican perspective, see Stebenne, *Modern Republican*, 108–14, 123–26, 141–42, 165–68. On the need to restabilize American society and similar ones in the wake of the Depression and World War II, see, generally, Charles S. Maier, *In Search of Stability: Explorations in Historical Political Economy* (New York: Cambridge University Press, 1988), 121–84.

19. Childs, *Sweden*; Leuchtenburg, *Franklin D. Roosevelt and the New Deal*, 345; Stebenne, *Arthur J. Goldberg*, 43, 74–76, 152; and Stebenne, *Modern Republican*, 108–14, 123–26, 141–42, 145–48, 165–68.

20. Stebenne, *Modern Republican*, 110 (quotation) and 111; and Stebenne, *Arthur J. Goldberg*, 43, 74–76.

21. "Address at the Cow Palace on Accepting the Nomination of the Republican National Convention," August 23, 1956, *Public Papers of the Presidents*, in Gerhard Peters and John T. Woolley, *The American Presidency Project*, http://www.presidency.ucsb.edu/ws.

22. Arthur Larson, "The American System: Structure, Coverage, and Current Issues," in the file on Larson at the Archives Services Center, University of Pittsburgh, Pittsburgh, Pennsylvania, 88. See, too, Stebenne, *Modern Republican*, 113, 136–37, and the sources cited therein.

23. On this difference in publicly stated rationales for the welfare state, see Stebenne, *Modern Republican*, 124–26, 142.

24. For the long-standing CPUSA view of the American welfare state as essentially fraudulent, see Earl Browder, *Democracy or Fascism* (New York: Workers Library Publishers, 1936), 17–18. For the 1948 Wallace campaign and its followers' perspective, see Thomas W. Devine, *Henry Wallace's 1948 Presidential Campaign and the Future of Postwar Liberalism* (Chapel Hill: University of North Carolina Press, 2013). On the unequal way in which the draft and the G.I. Bill operated, see David M. Kennedy, *Freedom from Fear: The American People in Depression and War, 1929–1945* (New York: Oxford University Press, 1999), 631–37, 709–13, 764, 771–74. On the tendency of the Social Security system's initial design to increase the distance between the middle three-fifths and the bottom fifth, see ibid., 257–73.

25. On the tendency of the postwar welfare state to replicate and even intensify such

regional disparities, see Lichtenstein, "From Corporatism to Collective Bargaining," 134–45.

26. On the inegalitarian consequences of mass suburbia as it emerged after World War II, see Kenneth T. Jackson, *Crabgrass Frontier: The Suburbanization of the United States* (New York: Oxford University Press, 1987), 231–45. On the instability of marriage among the poor and the welfare state's insensitivity to that problem, see Nelson, "The Origins of the Two-Channel Welfare State"; Gordon, *Pitied but Not Entitled*; Willrich, "Home Slackers"; and Kessler-Harris, *In Pursuit of Equity*.

27. On the plight of racial minorities in postwar America, see Patterson, *Grand Expectations*, 375–406. For Robeson's experience with race prejudice and radically left-wing perspective, see Martin Duberman, *Paul Robeson* (New York: Knopf, 1989).

28. On the unhappiness among women who resisted patriarchal arrangements in the postwar period, see Joanne Meyerowitz, *Not June Cleaver: Women and Gender in Postwar America, 1945–1960* (Philadelphia: Temple University Press, 1994). With respect to the gay and lesbian perspective, see Canaday, *The Straight State*, 137–73.

29. Barry M. Goldwater, *The Conscience of a Conservative* (1960; Princeton: Princeton University Press, 2007), 69. On the growing discontent among strongly conservative people with the postwar welfare state, see Rick Perlstein, *Before the Storm: Barry Goldwater and the Unmaking of the American Consensus* (New York: Hill and Wang, 2001), 4–95; and Stebenne, *Modern Republican*, 187–88, 216–18, 226–28. For Robert Taft's views, see James T. Patterson, *Mr. Republican: A Biography of Robert Taft* (Boston: Houghton, Mifflin, 1972).

30. Goldwater, *The Conscience of a Conservative*, 69.

31. On the fragility of the "consensus" generally by the late 1950s, see Patterson, *Grand Expectations*, 407–41.

7

Red-Hunting and Internal Security

Conflict in the Age of Consensus

ALEX GOODALL

> [The Red Scare] has charged the atmosphere of the national life with a fear that has become familiar. We cannot interpret it in terms of a single politician, whether he be McCarthy or someone who might succeed him. The hope has always been raised that by discrediting the personal villain in the redscare drama the drama itself would end. This is as delusive as the belief on the international plane that "we are the most revolutionary nation on earth." For it is of the very essence of our unusual response to Communism, whatever its immediate sources may be in national groups or political alignments, that it reflects an absolute "Americanism" as old as the country itself.
>
> Louis Hartz, *The Liberal Tradition in America: An Interpretation of American Political Thought since the Revolution* (1955)

The witness who had been testifying before the Senate Judiciary Committee's Subcommittee on Constitutional Rights for the past several hours was the compelling, loquacious Harry P. Cain, former Republican senator from Washington. Between his election to the Senate in 1946 and his defeat in 1952, Cain had been not so much a textbook McCarthyite as a caricature of one, sitting somewhere to the right of Senator Robert A. Taft of Ohio in the Republican Party's conservative wing on nearly all issues of note. Elected after running one of the first red-baiting smear campaigns of the postwar era, Cain distinguished himself as a vocal opponent of the New Deal and Fair Deal, federal infrastructure spending, Social Security, and the minimum wage. He supported the Taft-Hartley Act and boasted of his leading role as the voice of the landlord in the fight against rent control, which he compared to involuntary servitude.[1] He opposed efforts to eliminate discrimination against Catholics and Jews in the 1948 Displaced Persons bill, and voted against efforts to revise the rules on Senate cloture to weaken the southern filibuster. On foreign affairs he had been an outspoken critic of the Truman administration: standing out as one of only two senators to oppose an increase in the size of the air force from fifty-five to seventy groups; to resist providing aid to nationalist China, Greece, Turkey, Korea, the Philippines, and any of the NATO signatory countries; and opposing Point Four aid to developing nations. After the Korean War broke out, he repeatedly decried the administration's perceived efforts to tie the hands of General Douglas MacArthur, and introduced a quixotic resolution in early 1951 that demanded Congress either issue an open declaration of war against China or call for the complete withdrawal of troops from the Korean Peninsula. "Harry P. Cain," concluded columnists Joseph and Stewart Alsop, "is endowed with matchless ignorance on foreign affairs."[2] In a survey conducted by the *New Republic* in March 1952, where political scientists had been asked to rate the performance of sitting senators, Cain had been ranked ninety-first of ninety-five—just ahead of Joseph McCarthy of Wisconsin and William E. Jenner of Indiana, who ranked bottom and second-from-bottom, respectively, but below the equally aggressive McCarthyite Democrat, Pat McCarran of Nevada.[3]

After Cain's defeat in 1952 by Henry M. "Scoop" Jackson, his close friendship with and support for McCarthy saw him move to a position on the Subversive Activities Control Board (SACB), which had been established under the 1950 McCarran Internal Security Act to lead the hunt against Communists supposedly hiding in government. Here he served for three years. However, as the tide began to turn against McCarthy in 1954, Cain underwent a rapid and dramatic conversion. He began complaining that the loyalty-security apparatus that had swelled under Truman and Eisenhower was not only a source of injustice but potentially even a threat to the Constitution. In the aftermath of the Senate's censure of McCarthy in December, Cain began appearing in the most unlikely locations, speaking to meetings of the American Civil Liberties Union, giving speeches reprinted in the *New Republic* that spoke of the "shortsightedness, ruthlessness, smugness and brutality" of the loyalty-security review process at its worst, and appearing on *Face the Nation* to explain his remarkable change of heart.[4] In the final stages of what quickly became known as the "Cain Mutiny," in the spring of 1955, the former senator told the press that Attorney General Herbert Brownell had been misleading the president about the effectiveness of the loyalty apparatus. He was rebuked by presidential assistant Sherman Adams and dropped from the SACB soon after.[5] "The gyrations of Harry 'Pinwheel' Cain have become somewhat dizzying," the *National Review* observed, with something less than sympathy.[6]

The testimony Cain was giving to the Subcommittee on Constitutional Rights in June 1956 was therefore quite unlike what one might have expected from a longtime McCarthyite fellow traveler. The committee, chaired by Senator Thomas Hennings of Missouri—a Democrat who had been fighting McCarthy since his own election to Congress in 1950 and had, in his biographer's words, "contributed as much as any single public figure to McCarthy's decline in power"—was conducting a systematic examination of McCarthy-era violations of the First and Fifth Amendments, and Cain was participating as a friendly witness during its second set of hearings.[7] As well as warning in general terms that the path of unchecked executive supremacy led to fascism, Cain presented a series of specific examples of how the loyalty-security process had led to the unjust treatment of citizens, both in and out of government. These included one individual who, after working for the federal government for a quarter century, had been declared a loyalty risk based on the sole testimony of an anonymous informant who turned out to be a rival from a different department. After more than two years of legal challenges and private investigations, the accused had eventually been able to uncover details of the charges leveled against him, which had previously been classified, and hunted down witnesses who conclusively disproved them. The victim was then briefly reinstated before retiring on a full pension. Shortly afterward, he was the recipient of a form letter of thanks, sent to him for his long service by the same deputy undersecretary of state who had approved his dismissal, and which read: "I shall never forget the loyal and effective assistance which you rendered me during periods which at times were rather difficult."[8] Hearing this, the gathered reporters, senators, and committee staff members began to laugh, presumably in disbelief at the tendency of bureaucracy to veer toward the absurd, even in its most repressive moments. In one sense, laughter was an unremarkable response. But the ripple of amusement that passed through the audience testified powerfully to the fact that the pervasive climate of fear which had characterized Washington for much of the previous decade had begun to dissipate.

* * *

Godfrey Hodgson argued that the age of consensus began sometime around 1954 or 1955, in the "pudding time when moderation came back into fashion after the acerbities of the Korean War and the McCarthy era"—when politicians and public servants could laugh again while discussing the politics of internal security, after a half-decade of intense seriousness.[9] Certainly, Cain's decision to abandon his erstwhile ally reflected the wider isolation McCarthy had fallen into by mid-decade. Following the erosion of support for him during the televised Army-McCarthy hearings in the summer of 1954 and a growing chorus of public figures speaking out against "political hysteria," the congenitally cautious Senate finally acted to discipline its most troublesome member. Harvey Matusow, who, incidentally, had been sent by McCarthy to campaign for Cain in his failed reelection bid, revealed to the Senate Internal Security Subcommittee (SISS) in February 1955 that he had been encouraged by McCarthy and Roy Cohn to perjure himself in testimony given against alleged Communist Party agents, and later in the year published his memoir, *False Witness*, giving further details of his murky life as a FBI-sponsored anticommunist witness. Shortly afterward, Attorney General Brownell announced that the bureau would no longer retain paid witnesses on regular salaries as "consultants." That spring a "McCarthy Day" celebration in Boscobel, Wisconsin, an event of the sort that once fetched crowds in the tens of thousands, only attracted fifteen thousand attendees—many of whom, it was noted, "were members of high school bands."[10] Even before McCarthy's decline into alcoholism, his spell was broken, and many politicians and citizens alike breathed a collective sigh of relief. "The Washington summer is as hot as ever," wrote DC reporter John B. Oakes in August, "but in one way this Washington summer differs sharply from several that have preceded it. The difference is not in the temperature but in the atmosphere. There is a relaxation of tension, particularly over the great issue of individual liberty vs. national security that has characterized so much of Washington life, conversation and politics for so long."[11]

The dominant strain of politics in Hodgson's age of consensus seemed to be anticommunist, but also anti-McCarthy, then.[12] But although many agreed that there was a change in the political climate, they disagreed as to both its causes and significance. For some, the new tone came from politicians' gradual discovery that McCarthy did not have the terrifying power attributed to him during the 1950 elections. For others, the victory of the Republicans in 1952 had simply eliminated the political utility of red-baiting. Others, contradictorily, emphasized the shift in 1955 to a Democratic Congress, with its attendant effect of removing Republicans from the chairs of the major committees. Centrists credited Eisenhower's temperate strategy for McCarthy's defeat: by rising above the cheap theatrics of the senator from Wisconsin, it was said, the president helped to build a new spirit of decorum. The left, by contrast, criticized him for not moving fast enough, for depending too heavily on conservatives in his party, and for expanding the loyalty-security apparatus in order to defend his own security credentials and outflank the senator.[13] Moderate conservatives, meanwhile, claimed that the fear of communism was in decline for a wholly different reason: because the problem had largely been solved. The spirit of vigilance that produced the attorney general's list of subversive organizations and the passage of more than five million federal employees through the loyalty-security apparatus, a half-decade of congressional hearings, and efforts by official and private organizations across the country to exclude radicals from American life had, according to this view, succeeded. "The program has accomplished its purpose of restoring respectability to Federal employment as well as protecting the national security," one senior administration official argued. Voices further to the right agreed that the politics of security was on the back foot but mourned McCarthy's defeat, blaming it on a conspiracy of powerful elites and liberal journalists who had invented a demon of "McCarthyism" in order to reinvigorate Rooseveltian radicalism. "Some of them are almost indecently eager to assure the fellow-travelers that Ogre Joe is dead and that it's all right to come out now," complained *Human Events*.[14]

Indeed, almost as if to prove that McCarthy's censure should offer no simple lessons on anticommunism and civil liberties, the Senate passed a resolution soon afterward, in early 1955, reaffirming their right in principle to investigate subversive activities.[15] The post-McCarthy armistice may have exposed a temporary exhaustion of ammunition among the warring parties, then, but in the words of a contemporary commentator, it did not suggest that "deep-seated conflicts over this question have been resolved. They have not."[16]

Political scientist Thomas S. Langston has argued that, "As an ideology that failed, 'McCarthyism' helped to establish the boundaries of the postwar consensus. Anticommunism abroad would be the focus of major American politicians for the remainder of the Cold War; anticommunism at home would hereafter be left at the margins."[17] But the truth is that there was little consensus to be found on domestic security even after the defeat of McCarthy; nor did it become a marginal issue for groups on the right that continued to use fear of American communism as an issue on which to find out whose side individuals were on. It may have been that, absent the simplifying figure around which most news coverage oriented, the mainstream press turned its attention elsewhere. It was certainly true that the defeat of McCarthy was both a product of and a stimulant to a broader backlash from civil liberties activists who had for several years been silenced. Outgunned by a nationalist enemy, liberals and leftists in the early 1950s had been capable only of guerrilla skirmishes, but by the middle of the decade these minor actions had, cumulatively, begun to undermine the more sweeping aspects of the security state. The U.S. Supreme Court duly began to impose new limits on executive and judicial power. However, as Louis Hartz had presciently noted, it was a mistake to presume that "by discrediting the personal villain in the redscare drama the drama itself would end."[18] Liberal advances were met by howls of anger from a right wing that continued to believe in the danger of communism at home as well as abroad, that was unaffected by McCarthy's slouch from the political stage, energized by new fears of social dislocation, and eager to respond to challenges from the left with innovations in political strategy and rhetoric of their own. The battle to defend the machinery of internal security in a time of retrenchment turned out to be a critical point of encounter between states' rights southern Democrats and pro-business Republicans, groups who had stymied Roosevelt's New Deal before World War II and would come to play a major role in the Republican revival of the 1970s and 1980s.[19] In this sense, conflicts over security politics in the "age of consensus" exposed similar political fault lines to those seen in the generations before and after, and were fought on similar terrain, as Americans continued their never-ending debate over the appropriate balance to be struck between individual liberty and national security.

* * *

Senator Hennings's Subcommittee on Constitutional Rights was one of three committees that Senate liberals used to shift public perceptions away from anticommunist orthodoxy in the aftermath of McCarthy's fall from grace.[20] Hubert Humphrey of Minnesota, who had been a joint sponsor in 1954 of the notorious Communist Control Act (a measure outlawing the Communist Party that was supported by Democrats almost exclusively for political reasons, and which had almost no effect), had sensed the changing political climate and launched investigations into anticommunist excess.[21] Meanwhile, South Carolina's Olin Johnston used his position on the Committee on the Post Office and Civil Service to conduct his own investigations into the loyalty apparatus, following dubious claims about its effectiveness circulated by Richard Nixon.

As McCarthy had shown more effectively than anyone, the congressional investigation had become a powerful tool for political advocacy, mainlining talking points into the veins of the national press corps. Even the most cogent unfriendly witnesses struggled to challenge a narrative constructed by committee researchers, investigators, and counsel, not least because congressional hearings had few of the structural safeguards built into the judicial process. As a result, the anti-McCarthy committees were able to draw attention to the failings of the security system that had been constructed in such haste in the early Cold War years. For instance, the chief administrator of the Bureau of Security and Constitutional Affairs, Scott McLeod, who appeared (alongside an army of advisers and lawyers) before both Hennings and Johnston to defend the loyalty system, was forced to reveal that it was customary for the U.S. Passport Office, which had denied travel rights to hundreds of American citizens after World War II, to take anonymous denunciations into consideration when deciding whether or not to initiate a security investigation of an individual who applied for a passport. The FBI would then be asked to indicate whether it had any information on file that might have a bearing on the individual's security status. The bureau rarely revealed its sources, so allegations would often reach the passport administrators without meaningful contextualization against which to weigh their merits. But since the FBI also denied that it was drawing any conclusion as to the security status of the individual from the information it passed on—its "raw files" were intended to gather information, not assess its quality—it was the Passport Office that was technically supposed to adjudicate. This meant than an individual could be denied a passport on the basis of information that was hidden not only from the accused but also in part from the administrator charged with reaching the verdict:

> Senator HENNINGS. How could you evaluate, Mr. McLeod—I do not believe I quite understand—maybe we are not using the word with the same meaning—how can you evaluate information from sources of which you know nothing—how do you go about evaluating such information?
>
> Mr. McLEOD. The process of evaluating the information is most difficult, as I am sure you will understand.[22]

Such hearings tended to focus on minor individuals in government who had been subjected to damaging smear attacks. As Landon Storrs has recently shown, many senior figures with socialist or social-democratic histories had also been harassed, but often they chose not to take a public stand, hoping to remain in, or return to, political life.[23] The most-well-known individuals who testified were therefore not government employees, but private figures more willing to risk antagonizing the Eisenhower administration. One of the more famous was the biochemist Linus Pauling, whose passport had been issued and revoked repeatedly because of his association with the nuclear peace movement. Testifying before Hennings, Pauling listed dozens of awards, honorary doctorates, and degrees given to him over the years, alongside the honors he received for his work on explosives and jet propulsion during the war, culminating in the Medal of Merit. He disclaimed all interest in or support for communism. He explained that, at the time his passport was being denied on grounds of being a secret member of the party, he was also being attacked in the Soviet press as an agent of capitalism. Pauling was reissued a permanent passport only in 1954, when the administrators noticed that the latest request had been sent in so that he could go to Stockholm to pick up the Nobel Prize for Chemistry.

Coming in quick succession, and with abundant, carefully gathered evidence, the investigations helped to transform the public image of the loyalty-security apparatus from a shield of the republic to an arbitrary and incompetent bureaucratic mess: Washington as reimagined by Kafka. However, as Richard Fried has observed, the testimony "fell short of the 'Hiss-case-in-reverse' that journalist Joseph Alsop predicted the security program would eventually produce," not least because most congressional liberals sought to present themselves as cautious reformers of a malfunctioning loyalty-security program rather than sweeping critics of the basic principle of domestic counter-subversion.[24] Conservatives quickly realized that they could appropriate these same efficiency arguments for their own purposes, endorsing the principle of reform but in practice seeking to entrench, rather than roll back, the powers of the state to police its citizens' politics. Indeed, the Commission on Government Security created in response to Humphrey's hearings, whose membership included HUAC chairman Francis Walter of Pennsylvania, asserted that the threat from domestic communist conspiracy remained "real and formidable," recommended a broadening of the security program, and defended the anonymity of intelligence sources, even as it claimed to be eliminating the potential for future miscarriages of justice.[25]

In the judiciary, the post-McCarthy era also witnessed movement away from the more extreme policies of previous years, but along a similarly erratic course, subject to multiple reverses and intense opposition on the right. The Vinson court had supported the anticommunist legislation of the Roosevelt and Truman years, and Earl Warren was slower to take a stand for civil liberties than against segregation upon his accession to the chief justice's position in 1953. Even after he joined William A. Douglas and Hugo Black as a regular member of the Court's liberal wing, the majority—a combine of conservatives and Cold War liberals—sought to avoid controversial security decisions, preferring to delay or issue negative rulings on procedural grounds rather than confront the legislature directly. By the middle of the decade, taking a stand for the Bill of Rights had begun to look less risky. In the term beginning in the fall of 1955, the justices began to defend individual rights more assiduously: *Cole v. Young* overturned Eisenhower's expansion of the loyalty-security apparatus from nine sensitive departments to all federal agencies, and *Pennsylvania v. Nelson* asserted that federal counter-subversive laws had "preempted" state sedition laws and thereby invalidated dozens of regional statutes that had been used to prosecute radicals across the country. Further rulings followed in the 1956 term, culminating with the four decisions of "Red Monday," June 17, 1957. Most significant among these, *Yates v. United States* freed over a dozen low-level Communist Party members who had been convicted under the Smith Act, on grounds that made it virtually impossible to continue to use the law to prosecute individuals for simply belonging to a revolutionary organization. Effectively eliminating the principle of guilt by association that had crept into security law over the previous generation, the *Yates* decision was, in Michael Belknap's words, "a devastating blow to the Justice Department's war on the Communist Party."[26]

Hugo Black, the most courageous member of the Supreme Court in the McCarthy era, had famously written in his *Dennis* dissent of 1951 that he hoped "in calmer times, when present pressures, passions and fears subside, this or some later Court will restore the First Amendment liberties to the high preferred place where they belong in a free society." Many liberals concluded that such times had now come, and were quick to celebrate. The editors of the *New York Times* called Red Monday "A Day for Freedom."[27]

Even as these rulings reined in the executive, however, they generated an outpouring of anger that, when combined with the continuing fury over the *Brown* decision, stimulated the greatest wave of hostility to the Supreme Court since the anti–New Deal decisions of Roosevelt's first term. A particular point of contention was the doctrine of preemption, applied in the *Nelson* decision and elsewhere, which held that state laws were rendered invalid when a federal law was passed dealing with the same subject. Preemption was being used by the Supreme Court across a wide range of policy areas in the 1950s to strike down conservative state-level laws in favor of (typically more liberal) federal jurisprudence. But it was the application of the doctrine to the Smith Act of 1940, which had established a peacetime sedition law for the first time, that produced some of the most furious responses, not least because the man who gave his name to the act, Representative Howard W. Smith of Virginia, was still in Congress and insisted that he and the other drafters had absolutely no intention to replace state-level counter-subversive measures with their own act, only augment them. As the *National Review* complained, "the Court has implicitly claimed the power not merely to 'find' in congressional legislation an intent to supersede state laws even when Congress has neither expressed nor implied one, but also to find such an intent when Congress has explicitly disclaimed one."[28] J. Edgar Hoover said that the Court's use of what he called a "technical rather than logical interpretation of the law" was tantamount to "commit[ting] national suicide."[29] "The boys in the Kremlin may wonder why they need a fifth column in the United States so long as the Supreme Court is determined to be helpful," the *Chicago Tribune* concluded.[30]

In hearings before SISS in the summer of 1956, chaired by the segregationist James Eastland of Mississippi, anticommunists denounced the Supreme Court as inspired by radical, even communist, tendencies. Joseph McCarthy was asked to give the opening testimony. The *Nelson* decision, he averred, was "the most flagrant instance of judicial legislation that has ever come to my attention." When Eastland asked McCarthy whether there was "any more certain road to the destruction of the American system of government than an irresponsible Supreme Court usurping the powers of the Congress?" he replied that the mistake had been in confirming "as Chief Justice of the Supreme Court a man who had no judicial experience, who had practically no legal experience except as a district attorney for a short period of time, and whose entire experience was as a politician."[31]

Anger with the Warren Court over internal security built consistently over the next two years. Far from confined to the radical fringes, opposition to judicial activism could be found at the American Bar Association, at state and national chambers of commerce, and at the annual conventions of state governors and state chief justices.[32] In the wake of the successful *Sputnik* launch and the highly publicized failure in December 1957 of the United States' Vanguard missile, an event some put down to sabotage, calls began to be heard for tightened military security and a renewed spirit of vigilance of a sort rarely voiced since the end of the Korean War.

Seeking to capitalize on this anger, congressional conservatives introduced a raft of bills, more than seventy in the 84th Congress alone, to rebuild the domestic security state.[33] Most sought to recreate aspects of internal security laws that had been undermined by the Court, but two went further. Howard Smith had unsuccessfully proposed a States' Rights bill (H.R. 3) in January 1955 to outlaw federal preemption altogether. Resurrected by anti-Court forces in the wake of *Nelson* and *Yates*, this retroactive measure not only would have revived state sedition laws like the one in Pennsylvania struck down in *Nelson*, but also would have destroyed dozens of other postwar rulings that used the preemption doctrine to override conservative state laws. Even more explosively, Senator William Jenner of Indiana offered a bill that would have removed the Supreme Court's jurisdiction on matters of internal security entirely. If passed, this would have represented the single most substantial limitation to the principle of judicial oversight in the history of the United States—and in its most sensitive area. Warren Murphy described it as "the most fundamental challenge to judicial power in twenty years."[34]

After some delay due to political maneuvering, the major Court-curbing bills passed comfortably through the House in 1958.[35] Liberals were able to respond more effectively in the Senate. In committee, both the Jenner bill (now "Jenner-Butler") and H.R. 3 were forced to roll back their most sweeping elements to focus on challenging the Supreme Court on internal security alone. Despite this, even in modified form, the passage of either measure would have been deeply damaging to both the Court and the Eisenhower administration, as well as profoundly altering historians' subsequent perceptions of conservatism's relative political weakness in the late 1950s. Senate Majority Leader Lyndon Johnson of Texas—seeking to appear a moderate as part of his not-so-hidden agenda to win the presidency in 1960—was able to secure a majority to table the Jenner-Butler bill when it came to the floor, but his mythic reputation for vote-counting nearly came undone when a similar effort to end debate on H.R. 3 was defeated by seven votes. In the aftermath of the defeat, the chamber fell into "pandemonium."[36] Johnson was forced to stand at his desk on the Senate floor, demonstratively marking down on a list the way senators voted in order to intimidate his peers into an overnight adjournment, then had to stretch his political ingenuity to the utmost to defeat the bill the next day.[37] Not until five o'clock in the evening had he managed to bully sufficient numbers into changing their votes, and even then he and his aide Bobby Baker were forced to drag Oklahoma senator Robert Kerr bodily from the floor of the Senate to stop him from supporting the rebellion. A hard-won tie was eventually broken by the retreat of a strongly anti-Court figure, Utah's Wallace Bennett, who acquiesced only to avoid forcing the vice president and Senate chair, Richard Nixon, into an embarrassing vote of his own to defend the administration.[38]

Determined to see McCarthyism as an aberration whose time had passed, many liberals wrote off these events as simply a "steam letting operation."[39] Similarly, historians have tended to stress the consistent failure of Court-curbing bills to pass and the gradual shift away from domestic security law as a hot-button issue in the early 1960s.[40] Not only were anti-Court proposals stymied by Johnson's control of the Senate and the possibility of a liberal filibuster, but Eisenhower would almost certainly have vetoed all but the most minor of measures had they made it to his desk. As a consequence, the preemption doctrine survived, but the battle over H.R. 3 remains a moment of high legislative drama no less worthy of historical attention than the Supreme Court crisis of 1937—an event whose legislative tally was also zero. Indeed, as legal scholar Arthur J. Sabin notes, at certain points more senators supported anti-Court legislation in 1958 than had voted against FDR's "Court-packing" plan.[41] Although support for Court-curbing was weakened after the 1958 midterms produced a Democratic landslide, several bills were reintroduced in 1959, and the most committed conservatives continued to make their case into the 1960s. More importantly, even without legislative validation, the conservative backlash produced a retreat by the Court on civil liberties in the late 1950s, as attorney Robert M. Lichtman has convincingly shown.[42] Justice Felix Frankfurter led the forced march back from the Supreme Court's assertive position on Red Monday, and the majority repeatedly reaffirmed the basic thrust of the McCarthy-era decisions on internal security throughout these years. Only with the sudden retirement of Frankfurter following a stroke in 1961, and his replacement by the consistently liberal Arthur J. Goldberg, did the Court finally present a consistent line against the populist impulses of the legislature: not at the beginning of the era but at the time that the age of consensus was, according to Hodgson, supposedly coming to an end.[43]

The political significance of the conservative backlash against the Court was greater still, and persisted long after the judicial and legislative elements had been effectively settled. The Court-curbing fight was a formative moment in the early history of the modern conservative movement as the missing link between the McCarthy era and the emerging New Right. Until Barry Goldwater's run for the presidency in 1964, no single campaign was able to mobilize conservatives across the country as effectively, not least since Court-curbing offered the first sustained opportunity for cross-sectional collaboration on an issue that, superficially at least, did not seem to be about race. In January 1961, for instance, the radical right-wing John Birch Society launched a national campaign to impeach Chief Justice Warren, and advertisements calling for his removal appeared across the country. Although the head of the John Birch Society, Robert Welch, denounced the *Brown* decision as "the most brazen and flagrant usurpation of power that has been seen in three hundred years," he also pointed to *Nelson* and other civil liberties decisions to make the case against the chief justice.[44]

Of course, as the "Red Monday" moniker (echoing the "Black Monday" of the *Brown* decision) and the routine use of states' rights language revealed, the Court-curbing bills were clearly intended in part to hit back at Warren for striking down *Plessy v. Ferguson*. Anticommunist attacks on reformers had long been used by southern segregationists to defend the existing racial order, and it became central to their case after World War II, when more explicit forms of white supremacy had fallen out of favor. It was, however, by no means an unproblematic rhetorical tool. As George Lewis notes, the militant anticommunism of the streets that had been promoted by the Massive Resistance movement had damaged the segregationist cause among northern audiences, putting southerners on the wrong side of the law-and-order debate, and by the later 1950s it had largely run out of steam. While many in the South had admired McCarthy's patriotism, some still felt ambivalent about the federal power that was being amassed in the name of national security in the early Cold War years.[45] Moreover, whatever else he was, Senator McCarthy was an unabashed partisan. Even ideologically supportive southern Democrats had therefore been forced to come to terms with a campaign intended to win Congress and the White House back for the GOP. By contrast, the Court-curbing effort of the post-McCarthy era brought states' rights constitutionalism, law and order, and anticommunism back into alignment, and without the presence of a figure as polarizing as McCarthy. For this reason, as counterintuitive as it sounds, southern elites found it easier to fight the Supreme Court for restraining the executive branch on internal security than to support the executive's acquisition of those selfsame powers just a few years earlier.

As a recent generation of scholars have stressed, southern politics can only fully be understood by integrating it into a larger national narrative.[46] George Wallace's campaigns for the presidential nomination and the presidency in 1964 and 1968, respectively, would show most clearly that white southerners seeking to reinvigorate their arguments at the national level had to tone down their racism and play up their anticommunism. But the enemies of the Court had been engaged in these efforts long before Wallace set his cap for the White House.[47] Eastland, among the most determined of the southern anticommunists, had red-baited supporters of the civil rights movement during World War II, in conflicts over the poll tax and the Fair Employment Practices Commission (FEPC), and had been complaining about "communistic" Supreme Court decisions since *Smith v. Allwright* abolished all-white Democratic primaries in 1944. LBJ had once said of his Senate colleague that he could be "standing right in the middle of the worst Mississippi flood ever known and he'd say the niggers caused it, helped out by some communists." Nevertheless, Eastland generally took care to situate his anticommunism within a national and legislative, rather than local and militant, framework, working closely with the FBI and SISS to promote his views as part of a shared struggle for national security that just so happened to benefit southern segregationists.[48] Apparently unaware of the arrival of an age of consensus, in the wake of McCarthy's censure the Mississippi senator launched a blistering attack on the national media for supposed liberal bias and opened SISS hearings into communist influences at the *New York Times*.[49] By the time of the *Nelson* decision, he had assumed the chair of the Judiciary Committee, which he used to investigate, and assail, the new spirit of judicial activism.[50]

Another southern "nationalizer," Senator Strom Thurmond of South Carolina, was also a forceful presence in the Court-curbing fight. "If the Supreme Court can assume power without rebuff," this Democrat warned some years before crossing the floor to join the GOP, "the complete tyranny of the judiciary is close at hand. Then the Federal Government will cease to be Federal and become national in stature, imposing its will upon the states and local governments of this great country."[51] Thurmond biographer Joseph Crespino notes the importance of the anti-Court campaign to the senator's political evolution, describing it as "the starting point for his anti-Communist crusade that would mature several years later."[52] It was Thurmond's threat to introduce H.R. 3 as an amendment to every bill before the Senate that forced Johnson into agreeing to a floor debate, and Thurmond was instrumental in building the backroom coalition that would deliver the vote against tabling the bill that so unsettled the political equilibrium.[53]

In seeking to appeal to northern voters through anticommunist discourse, southern rhetoricians stressed affinities between the Jim Crow system and modern capitalism that would have been anathema to their antebellum forefathers. This effort can be traced back to Congressman Martin Dies's investigations of the CIO and southern unionization in the late 1930s, and became increasingly common in the 1940s. In 1944, for instance, Senator Walter F. George of Georgia had complained that the FEPC would "strip owners of private rights in private property" and "convert the present economic system into a communistic or national socialistic system."[54] However, this connection took on a new intensity in the 1950s, as business groups began to fear that the preemption doctrine might be used to revoke state-level right-to-work laws that conservative activists were using to undermine the Wagner Act and other pro-union legislation.[55]

As the conservative movement reconstructed itself from the grassroots, business groups had come to see that they could control state legislatures more easily than the national Congress, and that by extension they had almost as much to gain from states' rights as southern segregationists. The nexus of common interest found expression in Goldwater's defense of states' rights and his resulting popularity in the Old South in 1964.[56] In *The Conscience of a Conservative* (1960), the Arizona senator complained that it had become a matter of routine for "the federal government to threaten to move in unless state governments take action that Washington deems appropriate."[57] The Southern Manifesto's resurrection of interposition thus meshed with the hostility of northern business interests to preemption, and organizations such as the U.S. Chamber of Commerce and the National Association of Manufacturers, through congressional allies such as Francis Walter, Noah Mason, Styles Bridges, John Marshall Butler, Karl Mundt, John Bricker, and William Jenner, moved in to support the campaign against the Court. The amendment of H.R. 3 to focus solely on internal security would ostensibly have posed no problem for its supporters had they been motivated by domestic security alone. It was therefore revealing that Howard Smith refused to accept the compromised version, which would have sustained the principle of preemption in labor relations, insisting that, if necessary, he would reintroduce the original, more sweeping version by amendment: this attitude won him no friends among the congressional leadership, and ultimately contributed to the bill's demise, but it sent a clear signal to business conservatives that the measure was designed to support their interests as well as the South's.[58] Indeed, given this context, even the failed bill might have achieved its larger objective:

Supreme Court preemption would likely have gone much further had the two-year backlash to *Nelson* not been so intense.

Court-curbing allowed conservatives on both sides of the Mason-Dixon to play the victim, a role in which many had traditionally felt comfortable but which by no means implied that they had given up the fight. McCarthyism had been traumatic in the conservative North as well as the South, and for similar reasons. Indeed, the divisions on the right caused by McCarthy's excesses prefigured the dilemmas conservatives would face later in the century, in government, as they struggled to fuse small-government idealism with a desire to use elected office to promote social and political conformity.[59] Eminent conservatives such as Whittaker Chambers and Russell Kirk had disassociated themselves from McCarthyite histrionics in much the same way that southern senators had steered clear of more militant forms of southern anticommunism under Massive Resistance. Nevertheless, as George Nash notes, the debate over McCarthy had been "intense and virtually impossible to avoid."[60] As well as bringing North and South together, the post-McCarthy return to the defensive therefore also helped to clarify the conservative struggle for its participants, reenergizing the movement and allowing the right to reclaim their credentials as defenders of reason, balance, and the constitutional order after several years of successful liberal efforts to show they were undermining it.

* * *

On matters of internal security, then, there was no consensus in the age of consensus. The pendulum had moved toward liberalism, but the right remained actively concerned with domestic security, and campaigns against supposed liberal apathy provided important early opportunities for conservatives of different stripes to build new collaborative relationships. Whether one sees these campaigns as the last gasp of the old McCarthyism or as the birth pangs of the New Right, it was clear that conservatives were far from quiescent in the late 1950s and early 1960s.

Like the laughter provoked by Harry Cain's testimony to Senator Hennings, in the end, the language of consensus owes more to the relief of commentators and historians that McCarthy's brief moment in the sun had come to an end than to any agreement that had been reached on the balance between individual rights and national security. "Consensus" was a term that had been evoked in early Cold War texts such as Daniel J. Boorstin's *The Genius of American Politics*, and was returned to by implication in Richard Hofstadter's later essay, "The Paranoid Style in American Politics"—theses that differed substantially but shared a tendency to characterize radical dissent as abnormal. At one level, both of these works implied that all but the most marginal or disturbed American citizens endorsed a set of core, liberal norms. And yet even a cursory exploration would show that each was scarred by the antipathies, anxieties, and divisions of postwar security politics. Boorstin's evocations of a natural unity in American life were part of an effort to explain away his youthful flirtation with communism, which had been investigated by Congress and threatened to destroy his career. Hofstadter, meanwhile, attacked the politics of countersubversion to which Boorstin was acquiescing, a politics that had shaken his presumptions of academic security.[61] In both cases, forced homogenization somehow emerged as "consensus." In later years the term would be read and invoked as representative of the era while the mechanics of its gestation were forgotten.

Nor *could* such a permanent balance between individual rights and collective responsibilities be struck, for there is ultimately no timeless solution to the question of security. Reading the reports of James Reston or Walter Lippmann, one might believe that, through painful struggle, the United States had acquired a singular voice on such matters—one that was anticommunist but also opposed to McCarthy and his methods. However, this was to ignore or dismiss those who disagreed with the liberal majority, often vehemently, on the right as well as the left. Ultimately, the idea of consensus, a vision of political continuity emerging from agreement and consent rather than competition and force, is the stuff of ideology, not history. It is a mythic evocation that drifts above the nation without regard to evidence on the ground, floating alongside its equally hazy sibling in foreign affairs, exceptionalism. In fact, in matters of domestic security, as in many others, the Age of Consensus was infused at every level with conflict.

Notes

1. Richard L. Neuberger, "Washington's 'Dry Run' Primary," *The Nation*, April 8, 1950; "Explanation of Senate Voting Chart," *New Republic*, October 9, 1950.

2. Joseph and Stewart Alsop, "The Evolution of Foreign Policy," *Washington Post*, June 15, 1947. For other disparaging press commentary on Cain, see "Winning without a Third World War," *New Republic*, October 9, 1950; Robert C. Albright, "Resolutions for War or Withdrawal Are Offered by Cain in Debate," *Washington Post*, April 18, 1951; "The Choice in Korea," *New Republic*, April 30, 1951; "The GOP Choice," *New Republic*, July 7, 1952; "Knights and Knaves in Eisenhower's Great Crusade," *New Republic*, July 28, 1952.

3. Byron L. Johnson and W. E. Butt, "Rating the Senators," *New Republic*, March 3, 1952.

The other two senators below Cain were Republican George W. Malone of Nevada and Democrat Kenneth McKellar of Tennessee.

4. Harry P. Cain, "Security of the Republic," *New Republic*, January 31, 1955; Harry P. Cain, "Faith in Persons and Authority," *New Republic*, March 28, 1955; "Cain Urges Respect for Freedoms," *Washington Post*, June 6, 1955.

5. "Cain Sees Ouster from U.S. Board," *New York Times*, May 18, 1956; "Cain Is Leaving Security Board," *New York Times*, July 26, 1956. On Cain's impact, see Robert Justin Goldstein, *American Blacklist: The Attorney General's List of Subversive Organizations* (Lawrence: University Press of Kansas, 2008), 205–6.

6. "On the Left," *National Review*, January 4, 1956. By mid-1956 he was advising Richard Nixon to stop using the fear of Communists in government as a campaign issue. "Nixon Advised by Cain Not to Use Reds Issue," *Washington Post*, June 18, 1956.

7. Donald J. Kemper, *Decade of Fear: Senator Hennings and Civil Liberties* (Columbia: University of Missouri Press, 1965), 23.

8. "Security and Constitutional Rights," *Hearings before the Subcommittee on Constitutional Rights of the Committee on the Judiciary*, U.S. Senate, 84th Cong., 2nd sess., June 12–13, 1956, 890.

9. Godfrey Hodgson, *America in Our Time* (Garden City, NY: Doubleday, 1976), 71.

10. Thomas C. Reeves, *The Life and Times of Joe McCarthy: A Biography* (New York: Stein and Day, 1982), 668; David M. Oshinsky, *A Conspiracy So Immense: The World of Joe McCarthy* (New York: Oxford University Press, 2005), 502.

11. John B. Oakes, "The Security Issue: A Changing Atmosphere," *New York Times*, August 14, 1955.

12. In a more reductive sense, "consensus" could simply be used to describe the fact that nearly all Americans were, at some basic level, anticommunist; it is used this way in William Bragg Ewald's *McCarthyism and Consensus?* (Lanham, MD: University Press of America, 1986). On these narrow grounds it seems hard to deny a degree of unity in the 1950s, or at any time—although even here, the question of the process through which unanimity was arrived at suggests that "consensus" might not be the most appropriate word.

13. On Eisenhower and McCarthy, see Richard M. Fried, *Nightmare in Red: The McCarthy Era in Perspective* (Oxford: Oxford University Press, 1990), 133–35; Jeff Broadwater, *Eisenhower and the Anti-Communist Crusade* (Chapel Hill: University of North Carolina Press, 1992); Oshinsky, *A Conspiracy So Immense*, chapter 16.

14. Oakes, "The Security Issue"; Handicapper, "Those 'Liberal' Journalists," *Human Events*, December 22, 1954.

15. Fried, *Nightmare in Red*, 172.

16. Oakes, "The Security Issue."

17. Thomas S. Langston, "Ideology and Ideologues in the Modern Presidency," *Presidential Studies Quarterly* 42 (December 2012): 742.

18. Louis Hartz, *The Liberal Tradition in America: An Interpretation of Political Thought Since the Revolution* (1955; New York: Harcourt, Brace, 1991), 306–7.

19. Indeed, in one case, Howard W. Smith of Virginia, the same individual was involved in the conservative coalition of the 1930s and the anti-liberal backlash of the 1950s. James T. Patterson, "A Conservative Coalition Forms in Congress, 1933–1939," *Journal of American History* 52 (March 1966): 757.

20. Lawrence Speiser suggests, persuasively, that the Hennings committee was modeled on the 1930s La Follette Committee, which was intended to bring about a similar effect in publicizing abuses of authority, albeit in the private sector. Speiser, "The Constitutional Rights Subcommittee: The Lengthened Shadow of One Man," *Missouri Law Review* 26 (November 1961): 449–69.

21. Mary S. McAuliffe, "Liberals and the Communist Control Act of 1954," *Journal of American History* 63 (September 1976): 351–67.

22. *Hearings before the Subcommittee on Constitutional Rights of the Committee on the Judiciary*, U.S. Senate, 84th Cong., 1st sess., November 16, 1955, 195–96.

23. Landon R. Y. Storrs, *The Second Red Scare and the Unmaking of the New Deal Left* (Princeton: Princeton University Press, 2013), 179. For a tentative estimate of the impact of the elimination of the socialist left from government, see discussion in chapter 7 of the same book.

24. Fried, *Nightmare in Red*, 183.

25. "Study Proves Red Threat Both 'Real, Formidable,'" *Chicago Daily Tribune*, June 23, 1957; "Summary of Recommendations on Federal Security," *New York Times*, June 23, 1957.

26. Michal R. Belknap, *The Supreme Court under Earl Warren, 1953–1969* (Columbia: University of South Carolina Press, 2004), 248.

27. "A Day for Freedom," *New York Times*, June 18, 1957.

28. "Intent of Congress," *National Review*, August 1, 1959.

29. J. Edgar Hoover, "Two Enemies within Our Gates: The Twin Threats of Communism and Crime," *Human Events*, October 12, 1957.

30. "The Supreme Court Jumps the Track," *Chicago Daily Tribune*, June 19, 1957.

31. "Jurisdiction in Sedition Cases," *Hearings before the Subcommittee to Investigate the Administration of the Internal Security Act and Other Internal Security Laws of the Committee on the Judiciary*, U.S. Senate, 84th Cong., 2nd sess., May 11, 1956, 2, 8.

32. "State Justices Rebuke High Court: Historic Document Analyzes Court's Leftward Trend," *Human Events*, September 1, 1958; Arthur Sabin, *In Calmer Times: The Supreme Court and Red Monday* (Philadelphia: University of Pennsylvania Press, 1999), 97.

33. Warren F. Murphy, *Congress and the Court* (Chicago: University of Chicago Press, 1962), 97.

34. Ibid., 156.

35. Sabin, *In Calmer Times*, 196.

36. Murphy, *Congress and the Court*, 211.

37. Robert A. Caro, *The Years of Lyndon Johnson*, vol. 3, *Master of the Senate* (London: Jonathan Cape, 2002), 1031–33.

38. Murphy, *Congress and the Court*, 211–17.

39. "Letting Off Steam," *Washington Post*, July 19, 1958.

40. See, e.g., Michael Belknap, *Cold War Political Justice: The Smith Act, The Communist Party, and American Civil Liberties* (Westport, CT: Greenwood, 1977).

41. Sabin, *In Calmer Times*, 196.

42. Robert M. Lichtman, *The Supreme Court and McCarthy-Era Repression: One Hundred Decisions* (Urbana: University of Illinois Press, 2012), chapters 9–10.

43. Frankfurter got little credit from conservatives for his switch in time. Speculating eagerly about his retirement, *Human Events* proposed he be replaced by none other than

Irving Kaufman, the judge who had presided over the trial of the Rosenbergs and ordered their executions. It was concluded that he would "doubtless improve the present Court, with its continuing spate of 'Red Monday' decisions." *Human Events*, December 29, 1958.

44. Quoted in D. J. Mulloy, *The World of the John Birch Society: Conspiracy, Conservatism, and the Cold War* (Nashville: Vanderbilt University Press, 2014), 111. For more on state-level and grassroots anticommunism in the post-McCarthy era, and the role of the John Birch Society, see Michael J. Heale's two studies, *American Anticommunism: Combating the Enemy Within, 1830–1970* (Baltimore: Johns Hopkins University Press, 1990) and *McCarthy's Americans: Red Scare Politics in State and Nation, 1935–1965* (Athens: University of Georgia Press, 1998); Richard Gid Powers, *Not without Honor: The History of American Anticommunism* (New York: Free Press, 1995); and Lisa McGirr, *Suburban Warriors: The Origins of the New American Right* (Princeton: Princeton University Press, 2001).

45. George Lewis, *The White South and the Red Menace: Segregationists, Anticommunism, and Massive Resistance, 1945–1965* (Gainesville: University Press of Florida, 2004), 171–72; Broadwater, *Eisenhower and the Anti-Communist Crusade,* 170.

46. For a summary of this historiographical trend, see Matthew D. Lassiter and Joseph Crespino, eds., *The Myth of Southern Exceptionalism* (New York: Oxford University Press, 2009).

47. Dan T. Carter, *The Politics of Rage: George Wallace, the Origins of the New Conservatism, and the Transformation of American Politics* (New York: Simon and Schuster, 1995).

48. LBJ quoted in Keith M. Finlay, *Delaying the Dream: Southern Senators and the Fight against Civil Rights, 1938–1965* (Baton Rouge: Louisiana State University Press, 2008), 76.

49. Chris Myers Asch, *The Senator and the Sharecropper: The Freedom Struggles of James O. Eastland and Fannie Lou Hamer* (Chapel Hill: University of North Carolina Press, 2008), 155.

50. Ibid., 137.

51. *Human Events*, March 17, 1958.

52. Joseph Crespino, *Strom Thurmond's America* (New York: Hill and Wang, 2012), 103.

53. Murphy, *Congress and the Court,* 207.

54. George quoted in Finlay, *Delaying the Dream,* 80.

55. See, e.g., Elizabeth Tandy Shermer, *Sunbelt Capitalism: Phoenix and the Transformation of American Politics* (Philadelphia: University of Pennsylvania Press, 2013), 93–105.

56. Murphy, *Congress and the Court,* 92.

57. Barry Goldwater, *The Conscience of a Conservative* (1960; Princeton: Princeton University Press, 2007), 19.

58. Murphy, *Congress and the Court,* 95.

59. Julian E. Zelizer, "Reflections: Rethinking the History of American Conservatism," *Reviews in American History* 38 (June 2010): 367–92.

60. George H. Nash, *The Conservative Intellectual Movement in America* (New York: Basic Books, 1976), 117–18.

61. To understand how anticommunist investigations had pushed Boorstin into reductive assertions of national consensus in order to explain away his Communist Party membership when a Harvard undergraduate in 1938–39 , see his testimony in "Communist Methods of Infiltration (Education)," *Hearings before the Committee on Un-American Activities, House of Representatives*, 83rd Cong., 1st sess., February 25–27, 1953. See too

Michael Robbins, "The Cosmic Significance of Trivia," *Washington Post*, August 12, 1973; Robert E. Treuhaft, "A Reunion to Remember," *The Nation*, July 7–14, 1984; Jon Weiner, "A Life in History: The Odyssey of Daniel Boorstin," *The Nation* , September 26, 1987; and, of course, Daniel J. Boorstin, *The Genius of American Politics* (Chicago: University of Chicago Press, 1953). Richard Hofstader originally published "The Paranoid Style in American Politics" in *Harper's Magazine*, November 1964, 77–86. A longer version appeared in his book *The Paranoid Style in American Politics and Other Essays* (New York: Knopf, 1965), 3–40.

8

Containment

A Consensual or Contested Foreign Policy?

ANDREW PRESTON

Probably nothing defines the postwar liberal consensus more than the Cold War. Indeed, one of the most common analogues to the phrase "liberal consensus" is "Cold War consensus." According to this interpretation, celebrated at the time and repeated ever since, the period between the mid-1940s and the mid-1960s—from the glorious end of World War II to the ignominious stalemate in Vietnam—saw Americans of virtually all political persuasions agree on the need to contain the spread of global communism. In an age of industrial warfare, mass ideologies, totalitarian dictators, and nuclear weapons, the requirements of national defense were too important to be the plaything of domestic politics. As Senator Arthur Vandenberg, a Michigan Republican who worked closely on national-security issues with the Democratic administration of President Harry Truman, declared at the dawn of the Cold War, "politics stops at the water's edge."[1]

Under the leadership of Truman and his secretary of state, Dean Acheson, a consensus, forged mostly by Democrats and moderate Republicans, cohered around three related, mutually reinforcing ideas: a liberal internationalist world order underwritten by American power; the containment of international communism; and, in a fast-moving age that required quick decisions, deference to the executive in the making and wielding of foreign policy. Alternatives to this overall vision came from figures such as Progressive Party presidential candidate Henry Wallace on the left (who rejected containment and advocated cooperation with the Soviets) and Senator Robert A. Taft of Ohio on the right (who favored neo-isolationist retrenchment into a "fortress America"), but these were exceptions to the general rule, and by 1950 liberal internationalism, containment, and presidential power had carried the day. Anticommunist extremists sometimes proposed a more vigorous response to the Soviet Union, known as "rollback," but they did little to alter the reigning paradigm. Only the disaster in Vietnam could weaken liberal internationalism, question containment, and challenge presidential authority.

Until recently, historians have reiterated and reinforced Vandenberg's pronouncement. "The President, like most Americans," observes James T. Patterson in a passage on Dwight D. Eisenhower and the 1950s, "reflected a consensus that the Soviets were unbending and that signs of softness in dealing with them were tantamount to 'appeasement.' Most liberals and conservatives agreed on these apparently unchanging facts of world order."[2] In a standard, widely used textbook on postwar American history, William H. Chafe argues that Americans found national agreement that capitalism and democracy were the ideal bases for a just and prosperous society, and that "anchoring the entire consensus was a bipartisan commitment to anti-communism and containment of the Soviet menace."[3] Moreover, in the historiography on postwar American society, the Cold War's impact in creating a broadly conformist, paternalist, consumerist, religious, and capitalist culture has been equally pronounced.[4]

On closer inspection, however, containment does not appear to be as consensual as is often assumed. Instead, as historians have recently observed, U.S. foreign policy during the Cold War was the source of tremendous debate and partisan division, with the exception of the years between 1946 and 1950.[5] Wallace and Taft, after all, were not exactly peripheral figures in American politics; they may have represented minority positions, but they were popular figures and taken seriously by millions of Americans. But even within the very heart of Arthur Schlesinger's "vital center" of liberal anticommunism, containment provoked opposition or, even when the parties agreed on the need to resist communism, led to bitterly partisan political warfare.[6] Mythologizing the first two decades of the Cold War as a time of consensus, when dissent was supposedly confined to the radical fringes of public life, distorts the diplomatic history of the Cold War, and the history of postwar American society more broadly. This is especially true of the moment when the Cold War consensus supposedly broke down after President Lyndon Johnson took America to war in Vietnam.

* * *

To be sure, there's a very good reason why the idea of a Cold War consensus is so powerful and easy to accept at face value. For two decades after the end of World War II, Americans did indeed fear and loathe communism, both as an ideology and as a security threat, and the vast majority of Americans thought its spread should indeed be contained.

This was nothing new, however—Americans had never liked the Soviet Union. Communism had attracted condemnation in the nineteenth century and into the twentieth, even from organized labor and other left-liberal groups.[7] Americans were aghast at the Bolshevik Revolution in Russia in 1917, and President Woodrow Wilson sent U.S. troops to help suppress it in the civil war that followed the revolution, though to no avail.[8] At home the United States underwent a thoroughgoing moral panic over communism in 1919–20, and the federal government rounded up thousands of suspected communist agitators who were either imprisoned or deported, or both, among them the radical firebrand Emma Goldman.[9] Wilson's intervention was halfhearted, short-lived, and not even remotely successful, and with the Great War over it was uncertain whether communism represented a threat to American security. Evidently most Americans felt it did not, as nothing akin to the Cold War strategy of containment emerged in the interwar decades. Communism was definitely seen as an internal threat, but fears about it eased somewhat after the Red Scare hysteria of 1919. Yet despite nascent commercial exchanges in the 1920s, involving U.S. corporations such as the Ford Motor Company and the investment firm Brown Brothers Harriman, and the establishment of official diplomatic ties in 1933, a latent mistrust of both the Soviet Union and communist ideology lingered throughout the era.[10]

During the interwar period, especially the late 1930s, ferocious foreign-policy debates did not focus on communism. Instead, Americans vigorously argued whether they should intervene in the world crisis that was eroding international order in Europe and East Asia.[11] The intensity of these debates between interventionists (the forerunners to the architects of containment) and so-called isolationists echoed the partisan passion of earlier foreign-policy debates around imperialism in 1899–1900 and the League of Nations in 1919–20. Both of these earlier moments of rancor, when politics definitely did not stop at the water's edge, pitted Democrats against Republicans in fierce partisan combat. In the 1930s the great debates over intervention against Germany in Europe and Japan in Asia recalled these earlier moments of division, although interventionists and isolationists could be found in both parties. But in December 1941, the Japanese attack on Pearl Harbor settled the issue decisively in favor of the internationalist/

interventionist camp, and Americans of all political persuasions grasped the mantle of great-power leadership.

During World War II the Soviet Union had been a key ally of Britain and the United States in the Grand Alliance against Nazi Germany, but Franklin D. Roosevelt had to overcome a great deal of anticommunist suspicion to extend Lend-Lease to Moscow.[12] And despite its massive contributions to the Allied victory, the Soviet Union could never fully gain the trust of the U.S. government or the American people. For example, the British and Canadians were full partners in the Manhattan Project and were thus party to America's atomic secrets, but the Soviets were always kept in the dark (however, in a sign of mutual mistrust, Stalin knew full well of the secret through his espionage network, which was active in the United States). The *New York Times* was not a typical source of red-baiting, so its wariness of communism was telling. Cooperation between Washington and Moscow, argued the newspaper at the height of the war, would have to be the bedrock for a permanent postwar peace settlement, yet this did not mean that Americans had to embrace or even accept communism: "Nobody in his senses will court a conflict with Russia, but on the contrary will gladly welcome her into the family of nations," the *Times* editorialized in April 1943. But there was one condition: "as long as she confines her Bolshevist system to her own borders. But if Russia uses Communist Trojan horses either as agents of world revolution or as shock troops of a Bolshevist imperialism, neither peace nor the Four Freedoms will remain secure anywhere."[13] In a subsequent editorial the *Times* identified one potential Trojan horse: the small, powerless Communist Party of the United States under the leadership of Earl Browder. "The 'American' Communist party," the newspaper's editors warned, "is not a political party operating within the American political party system. It is an organization inspired by an alien ideology and having as its goal the conquest of America through internal revolution for the purpose of establishing a 'dictatorship of the proletariat' in a 'Soviet America.'"[14]

The end of the war brought with it new uncertainties about the Soviet Union. With the New Deal over and wartime nationalism in full flow, ideological hostility toward communism already began to harden in 1945–46. After nearly two years of fitful relations with Moscow, which lurched from confrontation to cooperation, the Truman administration essentially declared the start of the Cold War against the Soviet Union with several initiatives from March to July of 1947: in sequence, the Truman Doctrine, the

Marshall Plan, George Kennan's "X" article in the journal *Foreign Affairs*, and the National Security Act.[15] At a time when domestic politics was becoming increasingly fraught with partisan bitterness and ideological strife, this was the period in which Truman and the Republican-dominated 80th Congress actually cooperated on foreign policy and put in place the foundational architecture that would last throughout the entire Cold War. Such bipartisan cooperation on implementing containment in Europe continued into 1949 with the passage of the North Atlantic Treaty, which created the first permanent military alliance in American history. With the memory of partisan divisions and failed foreign policies from the late 1930s still fresh, Republicans and Democrats sought a united front in the interests of national security. The cost to Truman's progressive domestic agenda was high—anticommunism helped kill his Fair Deal initiatives[16]—but it enabled the smooth implementation of containment. It was at this moment, during the frenetic crisis years between 1947 and 1949, that Vandenberg alleged that politics stopped at the water's edge and the idea of the Cold War consensus was born.

* * *

At a fundamental level, the consensus was genuine: Americans more or less agreed that international communism was a menace. But such an observation is banal to the point of vapidity; it explains hardly anything at all, and certainly nothing causal. Americans had never liked communism, but by waging a global struggle against it, from 1947 onward, they embarked upon something new in their national history. The notion of a Cold War consensus also elides the diversity of opinion on foreign policy and bleaches out all the color from what was in fact an era of intense politicking and posturing over foreign policy. Beyond the very general notion that America should contain communist expansion, there was often intense disagreement—ideologically, strategically, and politically—on exactly what containment entailed or required. Thus it would be misleading to conclude that an anticommunist consensus shaped a general consensus on foreign policy. It would be akin to a historian, three or four decades from now, concluding that the early twenty-first century, a time when bitter partisanship and political gamesmanship were possibly at their most intense, was an era of consensus simply because Americans thought global Islamist terrorism was a menace.

The bipartisanship epitomized by the cooperative relations between Truman and Vandenberg existed, and it was powerful; but it was an aberration, not the norm.[17] It lasted for only two or three years, reached broad agreement on what to do about Soviet power in Europe but not the spread of communism in the rest of the world, and disappeared in the heated domestic debates that escalated in 1949 over Soviet atomic weapons, the "fall" of China to communism, and domestic subversion and espionage. This brief moment of bipartisanship rested upon an unusual degree of congressional deference to executive authority, which began to ebb in 1949–50.[18]

Beyond generalities about the evils of communism, Americans living in the early Cold War were deeply divided on how to deal with it, particularly in East Asia. When China "fell" to Mao Zedong and the Chinese Communist Party (CCP) in October 1949, the Truman administration discovered just how intense the politics of national security could be. Until then, supporters of Chiang Kai-shek and the Nationalists believed that the CCP was being kept at bay and prevented from seizing power. The Chinese Civil War had been brewing off-and-on since the late 1920s, but the Japanese invasion of China in 1937 brought a temporary truce. In 1945, with the Japanese defeated, the Communists and Nationalists resumed their struggle for the control of China. Although it was clear to experts in the State Department that Chiang was corrupt and that the Nationalists were inferior fighters, the CCP's victory in 1949 came as a total shock to most Americans. There quickly emerged the theory, nurtured and promoted by conservative Republicans, that Mao could only have triumphed with the help of communist sympathizers in high places in the United States—especially the State Department.

Thus began a sustained attack on "China hands," experts such as John Paton Davies and John Stewart Service. In the years leading up to 1949, Davies and Service formed nuanced, balanced assessments of the situation in China and recommended a non-interventionist policy for the United States. In the fearful climate of the early Cold War—the Soviets had only just successfully tested an atomic device six weeks before, thus breaking the American nuclear-weapons monopoly—the China hands were accused of betraying their country by siding with the communist enemy.[19] Republicans in Congress, led by Senator Joseph McCarthy of Wisconsin, excoriated Foreign Service officers, particularly experts on East Asia, and forced a purge of the diplomatic corps. Under such pressure, Washington refused to recognize the CCP government, and the United States and the People's Republic of China (PRC) did not establish official diplomatic relations until 1979.

Given that the State Department had been in Democratic hands since

FDR came to power in 1933, and that the China hands were liberals suspected of harboring socialist leanings, the Democratic Party also became a target for criticism. Under the leading question of "Who lost China?" conservative Republicans saw the ascent of Mao and the CCP as a golden opportunity to score political points against the liberal Democrats who had dominated federal politics for nearly two decades. This was not simply a case of political opportunism; Republican accusations that the Democrats were "soft on communism" were undoubtedly sincere, such was the intensity of communist-hating among conservatives and so entrenched was their view that the New Deal was tantamount to socialism. But such scorched-earth politics were just as undoubtedly partisan as ideological, motivated by a desire not simply to stop the spread of communism to East Asia but also to stop the rule of Democrats in Washington. Thanks to the Red Scare at home, American politicking not only went beyond the water's edge; it stretched all the way to Beijing, Nanjing, and Taipei.[20]

The CCP's victory in October 1949 also triggered a series of events in Northeast Asia that resulted in the outbreak of the Korean War in June 1950 and led to the next major round of partisan political warfare in the United States. After indicating that the Korean Peninsula lay beyond America's core national-security interests, the Truman administration reacted to the communist offensive by instantly committing the United States to the defense of South Korea. Encouraged by the Soviet Union and eventually backed by Chinese troops, a communist army from North Korea crossed an internationally recognized frontier to invade and subjugate non-communist South Korea. The fact that Stalin and Mao sharply disagreed over Korea was unknown to Americans at the time (Stalin encouraged the invasion, while Mao thought it was a risky, unnecessary distraction).[21] Rather than a divided communist world and a war that resulted from Stalin's outmaneuvering of Mao, it instead appeared to Americans that communism was on the march and that containment was under threat. So apparent was communist aggression that the United Nations agreed to commit troops to defend South Korea. Here was about as clear a war of containment as there could possibly be.

And yet the Korean War was never a popular war, certainly not in the United States. Weary after enduring the greatest crisis in the history of capitalism and waging a global war on two transoceanic fronts, Americans followed Truman into Korea unenthusiastically. If the need to do so seemed apparent in the summer of 1950, when communist aggression was clear and incontrovertible, intervention was still a reluctant crusade. When U.S.

forces and their allies suffered losses, as in the summer of 1950 or after Chinese troops intervened in October 1950, public support for the war, or at least Truman's handling of it, wobbled. Even more damaging to American morale was the brutal, bloody stalemate that settled over the conflict in the summer of 1951 and lasted for the next two years. If there really was a Cold War consensus, the Truman administration would have been able to take public support for granted, especially in a time of war when the American people usually rallied around the flag and reflexively backed their commander-in-chief. But beyond a general distrust of communism, the Cold War consensus was fragile, and after July 1951 public opinion turned sharply against Truman and the war itself. Even the Supreme Court, normally deferential to presidential authority in a time of war, rebuked Truman in the 1952 "Steel Seizure Case."[22] To be sure, there was no antiwar movement to speak of, but neither was public opinion all that supportive of the president. As a result, the Truman administration conducted the entire war on the back of a desperate but increasingly effective public-relations offensive to shore up public support. Truman had to "sell" the war to Congress and the American people, and make a hard sell at that. If there was a consensus, it had been forcefully manufactured.[23]

The war in Korea came to an end in the summer of 1953, when new Republican president, Dwight D. Eisenhower, came to terms with the North Koreans and Communist Chinese. A career military man and (relatively) moderate Republican, Eisenhower adhered to a slightly more conservative version of the liberal internationalist norm established by Truman and his secretary of state, Dean Acheson. Eisenhower's more conservative approach could be seen in his own fiscal caution and unwillingness to request the ever-increasing amounts on defense spending Truman had authorized.[24] But it could also be heard in the administration's rhetoric, which occasionally indulged in the rollback fantasies of the Republican Party's right wing; Secretary of State John Foster Dulles, otherwise an archetypal founding member of the Cold War consensus, was especially prone to speculating about beating back communism rather than simply containing it.[25] Overall, though, Eisenhower's New Look differed little in basic outlook from his predecessor's strategy of containment—while the means were often different, the ends were largely the same—and the United States continued to maintain a broadly anticommunist foreign policy.[26]

Still, the Eisenhower presidency did not stimulate a return to bipartisanship or legislative deference to the executive. There were of course instances of cooperation across party and institutional lines, but they were not standard practice. In 1954, for example, the Eisenhower administration deliberated whether to intervene to rescue the beleaguered French garrison at Dien Bien Phu from the communist Viet Minh. Dulles was firmly in favor, as was Admiral Arthur Radford, chairman of the Joint Chiefs of Staff. But Eisenhower ran into unexpected resistance when he privately consulted members of Congress, and he eventually abandoned the idea even though it meant also abandoning the northern half of Vietnam to communism; it was the most serious blow to containment since the Chinese communists had come to power five years before, but public opinion remained silent.[27] Elsewhere, beyond the difficulties posed by the mountains and jungles of Indochina, the Cold War remained contested terrain when it came to partisan politics and public opinion. A broad spectrum of Americans, and not simply liberals, questioned the administration's continued isolation of the PRC: according to pollsters, approximately half the population wanted at least economic and informal diplomatic relations with China, and during the 1958 military standoff in the offshore islands crisis 91 percent wanted the UN to mediate the dispute.[28]

On the other hand, the ideological fire had not completely gone out of America's Cold War. Containment was alive and well, despite its critics, and Americans did not expect their nation simply to give up resisting communist expansionism. When such moments arrived, popular anticommunism could be intense. However, they rarely led to bipartisan consensus. In fact, in the 1950s foreign policy provided a site of contest for Democrats and Republicans to continue their partisan battles by other means. Usually this meant that Democrats in Congress were given opportunities to attack the foreign policy of the incumbent Republicans in the executive branch. The launch of the Soviet satellite *Sputnik* in 1957 led to one of the biggest issues of the 1960 presidential campaign, the spurious "missile gap" controversy.[29] Similarly, the Cuban Revolution in 1959–60 offered Democrats a chance to avenge their suffering from the "Who lost China?" debate a decade before, an objective they pursued with relish.[30] Rather than creating common ground for bipartisan consensus, the Cold War provided the terrain for the most intense battles of partisan political warfare.

* * *

The most pernicious consequence of accepting the notion of a Cold War consensus at face value is that it leads to assumptions about causality—namely, that the pressure of the Cold War made U.S. military interventions inevitable. This is especially problematic when considering the origins of the Vietnam War. In hindsight, the war seems foreordained due to the overwhelming pressures of the Cold War consensus. As George C. Herring puts it in perhaps the most authoritative and influential survey of the war, "U.S. involvement in Vietnam was a logical, if not inevitable, outgrowth of a world view and a policy—the policy of containment—that Americans in and out of government accepted without serious question for more than two decades."[31] In thrall to the Cold War, policymakers were plagued by a lack of originality and an inability to question conventional wisdom, a problem Irving L. Janis memorably characterized as "groupthink."[32] Other scholars have pointed out that policymakers did not operate in a vacuum; nor were they unrepresentative of wider congressional and public opinion. According to James Patterson, when Johnson and his aides appeared tough in 1964–65 and unleashed the forces of escalation, "virtually all political leaders agreed with them. . . . Preventing the spread of Communism, after all, remained the guiding star of American policy." There were only a handful of doubters, Patterson contends, and they had no influence on policy, because they "competed against a Cold War consensus that continued to rule American society, politics, and culture."[33] If policymakers could not conceive of an alternative to the rigorous application of containment, how could they be faulted for their decisions that led to a disastrous war? Blame is difficult to assign if the policymakers themselves didn't know any better and if the rest of the country blindly expected them to quash communism wherever it threatened to spread.[34]

But what if thinking on the Cold War in general, and even on Vietnam in particular, was not so consensual? What if there was little agreement in the period before the Americanization of the war in 1965 on whether the United States should even defend South Vietnam? What if policymakers *did* know better? What if the public and Congress were *not* pressuring, or even expecting, them to go to war? What if withdrawal was an option that was seriously considered and thoroughly debated? As Fredrik Logevall has persuasively argued, historians have been too quick to accept the causes of the war as "overdetermined," that is, as resulting from the momentum of forces, predominantly shaped by the Cold War, that made escalation and intervention virtually inescapable.[35]

The Vietnam War was not the inevitable product of Cold War groupthink. Instead, the misapplication of containment to Indochina was the result of contestation, not consensus. While popular protests against the war did not emerge until the teach-ins of the spring of 1965, and while a mass antiwar movement did not emerge until the following year, elite dissent within the Kennedy and Johnson administrations reached a peak *before* Americanization in July 1965. Once Johnson committed U.S. forces to take over the burden of fighting from the South Vietnamese, policy-making elites halted their internal debate and concentrated on making the policy work. Before then, however, opposition to U.S. intervention forced Kennedy and Johnson to manufacture a consensus, because there was no broad agreement over whether the Cold War should be waged in Southeast Asia.

Internal opposition was found predominantly within the State Department. Leading the way were two undersecretaries of state, Chester Bowles (who served for less than a year, from January to November 1961) and George Ball (December 1961 to September 1966), whose position made them the deputy to the secretary and thus the second-ranking officer in the U.S. Foreign Service. Their views had different sources and rationales, but both men were adamantly opposed to intervening in Vietnam long before the war became an American one. Bowles, who had been a Democratic congressman from Connecticut before joining Kennedy's State Department, encouraged U.S. involvement in developing and decolonizing areas of the world, but he believed the United States should be fostering economic and political development and engaging with nationalist movements even if it risked bringing left-wing regimes to power.[36] Bowles's self-righteous moralizing irritated Kennedy, as well as Secretary of State Dean Rusk, and he was replaced as undersecretary with Ball in late 1961. On the Cold War, Ball held rather more conventional views: he did not give much priority to the Third World, and instead focused on maintaining the health of the transatlantic alliance with Western Europe. In other words, Ball was an arch–Cold Warrior, shaped very much in an Achesonian mold. Yet it was precisely this prioritization of Europe that led Ball to oppose intervention in Vietnam, which he saw as a distraction from more strategically important regions of the world. Ball vehemently opposed sending U.S. troops to Indochina as early as the autumn of 1961, but he stepped up his antiwar stance in 1964 when Lyndon Johnson seemed to be edging closer to full-scale intervention. By 1965, when the Johnson administration divided sharply over Vietnam, Ball was in the vanguard of antiwar dissent.[37]

Antiwar sentiment was found throughout the ranks of the State Department, from the upper echelons of ambassadorial appointees down to the regional desk officers. None were radicals or pacifists, and many had participated in the devising of containment. Ambassador to the United Nations

Adlai Stevenson, who had cabinet-level seniority and had twice run as the Democratic candidate for president, warned Johnson against escalation in Vietnam and cooperated with UN Secretary-General U Thant on an ill-fated peace proposal.[38] John Kenneth Galbraith, the Harvard economist whom Kennedy appointed as U.S. ambassador to India, visited Saigon and sent a stream of cables to Washington on the folly of applying containment to Vietnam; after returning from India, Galbraith kept sending antiwar missives to Johnson.[39] Assistant Secretary of State for the Far East W. Averell Harriman, who had served as ambassador to Moscow during World War II and oversaw the implementation of the Marshall Plan, initially wanted to make U.S. policy in Vietnam work, but after the overthrow of Ngo Dinh Diem in November 1963 he quietly advised Johnson to find a way out.[40] Thomas L. Hughes, the director of Intelligence and Research, the State Department's own in-house unit for intelligence assessment and analysis, was deeply pessimistic about America's ability to fend off the Vietcong; his role was not to offer policy recommendations, but his reports made it clear that military intervention was unlikely to work and was thus a mistake.[41]

Pessimism about the efficacy of American intervention could be found elsewhere in the Kennedy and Johnson administrations. In the Central Intelligence Agency, for example, high-level analysts such as Harold P. Ford echoed Hughes's warnings and suggested that withdrawal was the best option.[42] Chester L. Cooper and James C. Thomson Jr. of the National Security Council staff pushed for an exit from the Vietnam crisis, even if it meant South Vietnam falling to communism.[43] In the Defense Department, McNamara's top civilian advisers, such as John T. McNaughton, Alain Einthoven, and Adam Yarmolinsky, were skeptical that direct U.S. military involvement would turn the tide against the Vietnamese communists.[44] Even the military brass feared the effects of escalation and worried that another ineffectual, stalemated land war in Asia, such as the unloved Korean War, would do irreparable harm to the armed forces. Army Chief of Staff General Harold K. Johnson and Marine Corps Commandant General David M. Shoup were especially pointed in their criticism of Vietnam policy.[45]

Even stronger dissent could be found in the halls of Congress, particularly among the Senate leadership. In December 1962, Majority Leader Mike Mansfield, a Democrat from Montana and previously a firm proponent of defending South Vietnam from communism, began sending Kennedy strongly worded advice to reconsider the American commitment; he increased his dissent in 1963 and continued it into 1964 and 1965.[46] He even invoked the example of Korea—its strategic difficulties and uncertainties and its unpopularity at home—as a reason not to go to war in Vietnam.[47] And Mansfield was by no means alone. Famed for his openly antiwar Senate hearings in 1966, which supposedly marked a break with the Johnson administration, J. William Fulbright from Arkansas, chair of the Foreign Relations Committee, was already opposed to intervention in 1964–65 and advised Johnson to seek a way out of Vietnam.[48] In late May of 1964, Richard B. Russell of Georgia, chair of the Senate Armed Services Committee and Johnson's onetime mentor, flatly told the president that Vietnam was "the damn worst mess I ever saw." America's position was "deteriorating. . . . It's a hell of a situation. It's a mess. And it's going to get worse." Unlike Bowles, Ball, Stevenson, Mansfield, and many of the other Vietnam skeptics, Russell was hardly a liberal: as a conservative southern Democrat, he advocated high levels of defense spending, opposed civil rights and even more basic moves toward desegregation, and championed America's anticommunist crusade in the world. On Vietnam, however, he failed to see the need for perseverance. "I don't think that the American people are quite ready to send our troops in there to do the fighting," he confessed to Johnson. "If it got down to . . . just pulling out, I'd get out." When LBJ asked Russell how "important" South Vietnam was to U.S. national security, he replied: "It isn't important a damn bit."[49]

Vice President Hubert Humphrey shared these concerns. Until he became Johnson's running mate in 1964, Humphrey, a Minnesota Democrat, was a longtime, powerful voice for liberalism in the Senate. In early 1965, then, he had two perspectives on government policy, from the legislature and the executive. In February of that year, as the Johnson administration was beginning to contemplate a massive bombing campaign against North Vietnam and even the deployment of ground troops to South Vietnam, Humphrey sequestered himself for several days with the State Department's Thomas Hughes and drafted what is possibly the most prescient warning on Vietnam by an administration insider. What is most revealing about Humphrey's memo is that its principal concerns were not strategic, but domestic. He predicted that a war in Vietnam "would not make sense to the majority of the American people," thus doing incalculable damage to the Democratic Party and its progressive policies. Like Mansfield, he raised the specter of Korea: "From a political viewpoint, the American people find it hard to understand why we risk World War III by enlarging a war under terms we found unacceptable 12 years ago in Korea, particularly since the chances of success are slimmer." If there was a national consensus on the Cold War, Humphrey seemed to be saying, it was wary of pursuing containment to its logical conclusion.[50]

With the exceptions of major papers like the *Chicago Tribune* and the *Los Angeles Times*, the press was similarly wary of the United States becoming bogged down in another Asian land war. In the summer of 1963, the editorial pages of the *New York Times* began their long critique of U.S. military policy in Southeast Asia by endorsing French president Charles de Gaulle's call for a diplomatic settlement and the neutralization of Indochina. But unease with a possible war in Vietnam was prevalent throughout the print media, including in regional newspapers such as the *Des Moines Register*, the *Hartford Courant*, the *Indianapolis Times*, the *Miami Herald*, the *Milwaukee Journal*, the *St. Louis Post-Dispatch*, and the *Salt Lake City Tribune*. Even newspapers that could normally be counted on for their reflexive support of containment, such as the *Washington Post* and the *Wall Street Journal*, had mixed feelings about Vietnam and speculated about the soaring costs, political and economic, of military escalation.[51]

The presidents themselves were ambivalent about South Vietnam, reluctant to bear the burden of protecting it from communist subversion but also unwilling to pay the price of simply walking away from a longstanding commitment. Both Kennedy and Johnson leaned toward lending U.S. support to South Vietnam, even at the risk of war, but both were hesitant and privately questioned the need for the United States to be in Indochina; both could probably have been swayed either way. By 1963–64, then, the forces of a Cold War consensus were hardly pushing the Kennedy and Johnson administrations into a war for Indochina. Though certainly difficult, withdrawal was still a feasible option.[52]

In the face of this widespread unease and outright dissent among elites and ambivalence among the presidents, interventionist officials in the Kennedy and Johnson administrations mounted a strong counteroffensive. Much was at stake. With considerable support from McNamara and Rusk, National Security Adviser McGeorge Bundy led the charge to uphold the commitment to South Vietnam. Bowles was swiftly marginalized, but Ball, Mansfield, and others proved more difficult. Each time they advised Kennedy or Johnson to withdraw, Bundy, often joined by McNamara and/or Rusk, provided a firm rebuttal. Because unease with the war was constant, and constantly increasing, Bundy's interventionist counteroffensive remained in high gear from November 1961, when Kennedy first mooted the idea of deploying regular U.S. ground troops, to July 1965, when Johnson finally decided to Americanize the conflict.

The Kennedy and Johnson administrations did not blindly stumble into the jungles of Vietnam without knowing any better. It was not only "in retrospect" that officials saw the war as a mistake.[53] Well before there was an antiwar movement, Vietnam was the subject of intense deliberation and outright dissent among the policymaking elite. A narrow band of officials at the very highest levels escalated in the teeth of this dissent in full knowledge of the risks and full awareness of the alternatives. The Vietnam War, then, was not the inevitable product of a Cold War consensus, largely because there was not much of a consensus to begin with.

Thus the flip side of this shibboleth, that Vietnam smashed the Cold War consensus, also requires clarification. Certainly the war called into question some of the fundamental assumptions about American virtue and strength that suffused popular and political culture in the twenty years following World War II.[54] Vietnam also undoubtedly led to a surge of congressional involvement in foreign affairs.[55] And the famous "Vietnam syndrome," which made presidents wary of becoming embroiled in foreign conflicts, persisted well into the 1980s and gave rise to strategic doctrines that aimed to constrain presidential war powers and limit the instances in which U.S. troops were deployed overseas. But the Vietnam War didn't smash the Cold War consensus, because there wasn't much of a consensus to smash. By the time Johnson Americanized the war, the Cold War consensus was long since dead. Vietnam did not unravel a foreign-policy consensus; if any war had that effect, it was Korea. Indeed, it is remarkable how similar U.S. foreign policy was both before and after Vietnam: the United States continued to be active abroad, and foreign policy continued to be the subject of intense partisan maneuvering and bickering. The politics of national security have been constant. The exceptional historical moment was instead the short-lived Cold War consensus of 1946–49, which achieved its purpose in Europe and then died on the shores of the Asian mainland. May it rest in peace.

Notes

1. Quoted in Julian E. Zelizer, *Arsenal of Democracy: The Politics of National Security—From World War II to the War on Terrorism* (New York: Basic Books, 2010), 5.

2. James T. Patterson, *Grand Expectations: The United States, 1945–1974* (New York: Oxford University Press, 1996), 280–81.

3. William H. Chafe, *The Unfinished Journey: America since World War II*, 7th ed. (New York: Oxford University Press, 2011), 99.

4. For examples, see Elaine Tyler May, *Homeward Bound: American Families in the Cold War Era* (New York: Basic Books, 1988); Stephen J. Whitfield, *The Culture of the Cold War*, 2nd ed. (Baltimore: Johns Hopkins University Press, 1996); Lizabeth Cohen, *A Consumers' Republic: The Politics of Mass Consumption in Postwar America* (New York: Knopf, 2003); Wendy L. Wall, *Inventing the "American Way": The Politics of Consensus from the New Deal to the Civil Rights Movement* (New York: Oxford University Press, 2008); Kevin M. Schultz, *Tri-Faith America: How Catholics and Jews Held Postwar America to Its Protestant Promise* (New York: Oxford University Press, 2011); and Kevin M. Kruse, *One Nation under God: How Corporate America Invented Christian America* (New York: Basic Books, 2015).

5. See, e.g., Melvin Small, *Democracy and Diplomacy: The Impact of Domestic Politics on U.S. Foreign Policy, 1789–1994* (Baltimore: Johns Hopkins University Press, 1996); Campbell Craig and Fredrik Logevall, *America's Cold War: The Politics of Insecurity* (Cambridge, MA: Belknap, 2009); Zelizer, *Arsenal of Democracy*; and Andrew Preston, "Beyond the Water's Edge: Foreign Policy and Electoral Politics," in Gareth Davies and Julian E. Zelizer, eds., *America at the Ballot Box: Elections and Political History* (Philadelphia: University of Pennsylvania Press, 2015), 219–37.

6. Arthur M. Schlesinger Jr., *The Vital Center: The Politics of Freedom* (Boston: Houghton Mifflin, 1949).

7. M. J. Heale, *American Anti-Communism: Combating the Enemy Within, 1830–1970* (Baltimore: Johns Hopkins University Press, 1990), 5–41.

8. Lloyd C. Gardner, *Safe for Democracy: The Anglo-American Response to Revolution, 1913–1923* (New York: Oxford University Press, 1984).

9. Heale, *American Anti-Communism*, 60–78; Alex Goodall, *Loyalty and Liberty: American Countersubversion from World War I to the McCarthy Era* (Urbana: University of Illinois Press, 2013), chapters 2–3.

10. Goodall, *Loyalty and Liberty*, chapters 4–6.

11. The literature is enormous, but for an excellent introduction to the key debates immediately before American entry into World War II, see Justus D. Doenecke, *Storm on the Horizon: The Challenge to American Intervention, 1939–1941* (Lanham, MD: Rowman & Littlefield, 2000).

12. George C. Herring, *Aid to Russia, 1941–46: Strategy, Diplomacy, the Origins of the Cold War* (New York: Columbia University Press, 1973); Steven Merritt Miner, *Stalin's Holy War: Religion, Nationalism, and Alliance Politics, 1941–1945* (Chapel Hill: University of North Carolina Press, 2003); Andrew Preston, *Sword of the Spirit, Shield of Faith: Religion in American War and Diplomacy* (New York: Knopf, 2012), 353–61. Roosevelt's political difficulties between 1941 and 1945 are often forgotten amid nostalgia for "the good war," a time when Americans seemed united against the evil of Nazism. For a useful corrective

that illustrates how controversial even the war could be after Pearl Harbor, see Steven Casey, *Cautious Crusade: Franklin D. Roosevelt, American Public Opinion, and the War against Nazi Germany* (New York: Oxford University Press, 2001).

13. "Peace and Communism," *New York Times*, April 26, 1943, 18.

14. "The 'American' Communists," *New York Times*, May 29, 1943, 12.

15. The literature on the origins of the Cold War is vast and contentious, but for an excellent treatment see Melvyn P. Leffler, *A Preponderance of Power: National Security, the Truman Administration, and the Cold War* (Stanford: Stanford University Press, 1993).

16. See Jonathan Bell, *The Liberal State on Trial: The Cold War and American Politics in the Truman Years* (New York: Columbia University Press, 2004).

17. This point is made by Zelizer in *Arsenal of Democracy*, 5.

18. See, e.g., the shift from bipartisanship in 1946–49 to partisan strife from 1950 onward in Robert David Johnson, *Congress and the Cold War* (New York: Cambridge University Press, 2006), 1–68.

19. Hannah Gurman, *The Dissent Papers: The Voices of Diplomats in the Cold War and Beyond* (New York: Columbia University Press, 2012), 71–110.

20. James Peck, *Washington's China: The National Security World, the Cold War, and the Origins of Globalism* (Amherst: University of Massachusetts Press, 2006), 48–139.

21. On Sino-Soviet divisions over Korea, see Sergei Goncharov, John Lewis, and Litai Xue, *Uncertain Partners: Stalin, Mao, and the Korean War* (Stanford: Stanford University Press, 1993); Chen Jian, *China's Road to the Korean War* (New York: Columbia University Press, 1995); and Richard C. Thornton, *Odd Man Out: Truman, Stalin, Mao, and the Origins of the Korean War* (Washington, DC: Brassey's, 2000).

22. Maeva Marcus, *Truman and the Steel Seizure Case: The Limits of Presidential Power* (New York: Columbia University Press, 1977).

23. Steven Casey, *Selling the Korean War: Propaganda, Politics, and Public Opinion in the United States, 1950–1953* (New York: Oxford University Press, 2008).

24. Aaron L. Friedberg, *In the Shadow of the Garrison State: America's Anti-Statism and Its Cold War Grand Strategy* (Princeton: Princeton University Press, 2000).

25. For a thoughtful assessment, see Richard H. Immerman, *John Foster Dulles: Piety, Pragmatism, and Power in U.S. Foreign Policy* (Wilmington, DE: Scholarly Resources, 1999).

26. John Lewis Gaddis, *Strategies of Containment: A Critical Appraisal of American National Security Policy during the Cold War*, rev. ed. (New York: Oxford University Press, 2005), 125–96.

27. Fredrik Logevall, *Embers of War: The Fall of an Empire and the Making of America's Vietnam* (New York: Random House, 2012), 454–80.

28. Michael H. Hunt and Steven I. Levine, *Arc of Empire: America's Wars in Asia from the Philippines to Vietnam* (Chapel Hill: University of North Carolina Press, 2012), 180.

29. Christopher A. Preble, *John F. Kennedy and the Missile Gap* (DeKalb: Northern Illinois University Press, 2004).

30. Aleksandr Fursenko and Timothy Naftali, *One Hell of a Gamble: Khrushchev, Castro, and Kennedy, 1958–1964* (New York: Norton, 1997), 65–80.

31. George C. Herring, *America's Longest War: The United States and Vietnam, 1950–1975*, 4th ed. (Boston: McGraw-Hill, 2002), xiii.

32. Irving L. Janis, *Victims of Groupthink: A Psychological Study of Foreign-Policy Decisions and Fiascoes* (Boston: Houghton Mifflin, 1972).

33. Patterson, *Grand Expectations*, 604, 610.

34. Confronted with their disastrous errors on Vietnam, policymakers have explained themselves by invoking their ignorance about Vietnam, which in turn stemmed from reflexive, unthinking assumptions about the Cold War. See, e.g., Robert S. McNamara with Brian VanDeMark, *In Retrospect: The Tragedy and Lessons of Vietnam* (New York: Times Books, 1995).

35. Fredrik Logevall, *Choosing War: The Lost Chance for Peace and the Escalation of War in Vietnam* (Berkeley: University of California Press, 1999), xvi–xix.

36. Howard B. Schaffer, *Chester Bowles: New Dealer in the Cold War* (Cambridge: Harvard University Press, 1993), 234–35, 302–15.

37. Ball's internal dissent on Vietnam is covered in virtually every history of American escalation and intervention. But for good overviews of Ball, his worldview, and how it related to Southeast Asia and affected his policy recommendations on Indochina, see David L. DiLeo, *George Ball, Vietnam, and the Rethinking of Containment* (Chapel Hill: University of North Carolina Press, 1991); and James A. Bill, *George Ball: Behind the Scenes in U.S. Foreign Policy* (New Haven: Yale University Press, 1997).

38. Walter Johnson, "The U Thant–Stevenson Peace Initiatives in Vietnam, 1964–1965," *Diplomatic History* 1 (July 1977): 285–95; Logevall, *Choosing War*, 185–87, 295–96, 342–43, 354, 489n42.

39. John Kenneth Galbraith, *Ambassador's Journal: A Personal Account of the Kennedy Years* (Boston: Houghton Mifflin, 1969), 254–69; John Kenneth Galbraith, *A Life in Our Times: Memoirs* (Boston: Houghton Mifflin, 1981), 461–79.

40. Rudy Abramson, *Spanning the Century: The Life of W. Averell Harriman, 1891–1986* (New York: Morrow, 1992), 637–39.

41. Logevall, *Choosing War*, 266, 330, 346.

42. Harold P. Ford, *CIA and the Vietnam Policymakers: Three Episodes, 1962–1968* (Langley, VA: History Staff, Center for the Study of Intelligence, Central Intelligence Agency, 1998).

43. Andrew Preston, *The War Council: McGeorge Bundy, the NSC, and Vietnam* (Cambridge: Harvard University Press, 2006), 184–88, 191–207.

44. Aurelie Basha i Novosejt, "Robert S. McNamara's Withdrawal Plans from Vietnam: A Bureaucratic History" (PhD diss., London School of Economics, 2014).

45. Robert Buzzanco, *Masters of War: Military Dissent and Politics in the Vietnam Era* (New York: Cambridge University Press, 1996), 81–186.

46. Report by Mike Mansfield, December 18, 1962, *Foreign Relations of the United States, 1961–1963*, vol. 2, *Vietnam, 1962* (Washington, DC: U.S. Department of State, 1990), document 330; Logevall, *Choosing War*, 26–27, 82–85, 90–93, 326–31, 380–81.

47. Mansfield to John F. Kennedy, August 19, 1963, *Foreign Relations of the United States, 1961–1963*, vol. 3, *Vietnam, January–August 1963* (Washington, DC: U.S. Department of State, 1991), document 258; Mansfield to Lyndon B. Johnson, December 7, 1963, *Foreign Relations of the United States, 1961–1963*, vol. 4, *Vietnam, August–December 1963* (Washington, DC: U.S. Department of State, 1991), document 355; Mansfield to Johnson, January

6, 1964, *Foreign Relations of the United States, 1964–1968*, vol. 1, *Vietnam, 1964* (Washington, DC: U.S. Department of State, 1991), document 2.

48. Randall B. Woods, *J. William Fulbright, Vietnam, and the Search for a Cold War Foreign Policy* (New York: Cambridge University Press, 1998), 81–105.

49. Telephone transcript, Lyndon Johnson and Richard Russell, May 27, 1964, in Michael R. Beschloss, ed., *Taking Charge: The Johnson White House Tapes, 1963–1964* (New York: Simon & Schuster, 1997), 363–64.

50. Humphrey to Johnson, February 17, 1965, *Foreign Relations of the United States, 1964–1968*, vol. 2, *Vietnam, January–June 1965* (Washington, DC: U.S. Department of State, 1992), document 134.

51. Logevall, *Choosing War*, xviii, 282–84, 377.

52. This is the central argument in Logevall, *Choosing War*. See also Preston, *War Council.*

53. McNamara, *In Retrospect*. See also Bundy's reflections in Gordon M. Goldstein, *Lessons in Disaster: McGeorge Bundy and the Path to War in Vietnam* (New York: Times Books, 2008).

54. See Tom Engelhardt, *The End of Victory Culture: Cold War America and the Disillusioning of a Generation*, rev. ed. (Amherst: University of Massachusetts Press, 2007); Natasha Zaretsky, *No Direction Home: The American Family and the Fear of National Decline, 1968–1980* (Chapel Hill: University of North Carolina Press, 2007); Michael J. Allen, *Until the Last Man Comes Home: POWs, MIAs, and the Unending Vietnam War* (Chapel Hill: University of North Carolina Press, 2009); and Patrick Hagopian, *The Vietnam War in American Memory: Veterans, Memorials, and the Politics of Healing* (Amherst: University of Massachusetts Press, 2009).

55. Randall B. Woods, ed., *Vietnam and the American Political Tradition: The Politics of Dissent* (New York: Cambridge University Press, 2003); R. D. Johnson, *Congress and the Cold War*, 105–241.

9

Sunbelt Patriarchs

Lyndon B. Johnson, Barry Goldwater, and the New Deal Dissensus

ELIZABETH TANDY SHERMER

Historical interpretations of the 1964 presidential election conventionally present it as signaling either the climax or demise of consensus liberalism in postwar American politics. Viewed from the perspective of the Sunbelt, however, another explanation of its significance is possible.[1] For this emergent region, the contest marked the end of a protracted political struggle waged over the New Deal since the 1930s. It was a conflict fought at local, state, and federal levels over industrial development, union empowerment, progressive taxation, business regulation, and racial equality. As this chapter will demonstrate, this larger struggle was reflected in the personal histories of the 1964 presidential contenders, Democrat Lyndon B. Johnson and Republican Barry Goldwater. The politics of the Texas-born president and the Arizona senator had been forged in local, regional, and national fights over underdevelopment. Their careers attested to a fundamental conflict running through the New Deal, World War II, and postwar eras over how to achieve the economic reconstruction of the South and West.

Liberal Democrats and conservative Republicans hailing from this regional battleground found agreement on some issues pertaining to its development. They defended capitalism, considered corporate investment critical to regional uplift, and collaborated to direct federal dollars to their states and localities. On the other hand, liberals like Johnson embraced federal programs that empowered and uplifted the New Deal's various low-income and working-class constituencies. In contrast, conservatives like Goldwater, initially found in the ranks of local boosters, looked to disempower and disenfranchise these same electoral groups in order that business elites could harness state and local governments to circumvent, frustrate, and even dismantle the New Deal.

These small-town entrepreneurs turned to northeastern and midwestern manufacturers to aid their efforts. Through investment in the emergent Sunbelt, these Steelbelt executives collaborated with boosters to build antiliberal oases from the New Deal in the South and West. To attract new enterprise to their cities and region, local businessmen increasingly looked to hold elective office in order to overturn liberal tax, labor, and regulation policies, often doing so with the benefit of outside corporate donations. Once ensconced in city halls, state legislatures, and ultimately both chambers of the U.S. Congress, boosters like Goldwater became powerful agents of Sunbelt conservatism in national politics. Indeed, regional rivals—not only liberal Democrats like Johnson but also moderate Republicans—increasingly had to compromise on their progressive principles to remain in office.[2]

Such white flags very much shaped the outcome of the 1964 presidential election. Johnson had to surrender two critical liberal beachheads at the federal level: redistributive taxes and labor rights. This executive acquiescence did not represent the end of a liberal consensus. Presidential maneuvering instead dramatized the conflict present at all levels of American politics over the previous thirty years. Moreover, the campaign decisions of LBJ and Goldwater very much shaped the ways in which liberals and conservatives would fight over the nation's political, economic, and social agenda for the subsequent thirty years.

Pre-Sunbelt Poverty Politics

Neither Johnson nor Goldwater hailed from areas of peak strength for mid-twentieth-century liberalism. The industrialized Northeast, Midwest, and Pacific Coast were home to those later identified as the liberal establishment, whose power over both parties increasingly rankled both conservatives and radicals in the postwar period.[3] Yet the national influence of this elite was far from total, since it did not extend to the South or interior West, during either the New Deal or postwar eras. This reality sharply limited the capacity of liberal Democrats and their Republican counterparts to uplift impoverished southerners and westerners.

The politics of the South and West's extractive, commodity-based economy very much shaped the early lives, social stations, and worldviews of Johnson and Goldwater. LBJ came from the central Texas Hill Country, where his forebears had settled in the nineteenth century in the belief that it was situated within the fertile cotton belt but beyond the sphere of big planters and merchants, who were pushing many independent farmers into sharecropping, the regional form of serfdom, throughout much of the South. However, the area was not the yeomanry haven early settlers had anticipated, because water was scarce and the soil was poor. Save for the brief World War I cotton boom, Johnson grew up in a family that constantly struggled to make ends meet.[4] His efforts to escape destitution honed the political skills and liberal values that shaped his political career. Empathy for those trapped in poverty, such as the Mexican American children he taught at segregated Welhausen School in Cotulla in 1928–29, stayed with him in his rise to the presidency. "I remember even yet the pain of realizing and knowing then that college was closed to practically every one of those children because they were too poor," Johnson remarked before signing the 1965 Higher Education Act. "I made up my mind that this nation could never rest while the door to knowledge remained closed to any American."[5]

Born on January 2, 1909, just four months after Johnson, Barry Goldwater also grew up surrounded by poverty yet was no pauper, which helps explain his conservatism, but his family was more comfortable than wealthy. Goldwater's father had turned his department store, Goldwater's, into Phoenix's largest emporium and launched a successful Arizona chain. Goldwater's profits rose and fell with the price of cotton, much like the Johnsons' more meager fortunes. Unlike central Texas, Arizona had this crop in abundance, as well as copper and cattle. Nonetheless, the vagaries of supplying eastern and Pacific Coast manufacturers ensured that Phoenix experienced very hard times during the Depression.[6] Taking over the family business on his father's death in 1930, Goldwater left its running to store managers while he pursued his personal interests. The firm was renowned for its positive employee relations, medical benefits, and pension plans, perks intended to quell unionization. It also hired minority employees, but not for positions where they came into contact with the Anglo clientele. Goldwater manifested open distaste for Jim Crow, but in contrast to Johnson he "didn't pay attention" (the later words of a Phoenix civil rights lawyer) to the negligible differences between de jure and de facto segregation.[7]

The Phoenix Chamber of Commerce, the forum for the city's entrepreneurial class of professionals, retailers, bankers, lawyers, and newsmen, considered industrialization critical to ending regional subservience to cotton, copper, and cattle. As one of its luminaries, Goldwater welcomed early New Deal initiatives to improve infrastructure, shore up banks, and water arid land as vital to prepare the West for manufacturing investments. The influential presence of so many northeastern, midwestern, and Pacific Coast executives in new federal agencies offered reassurance that the Roosevelt administration was pro-business. Initially, therefore, local boosters found common cause with corporate progressives against the unreconstructed group of northeastern tycoons that founded the Liberty League to contest federal intervention as anathema to free enterprise.[8]

Business opposition to the New Deal became more widespread at national and local levels as concern grew that its emergency measures and social-welfare provisions were becoming permanently embedded in the fabric of American government. Even some of the high-level supporters of early stabilization measures came to question the direction of the reforms from 1935 onward. For Goldwater, the red light flashed with the Wagner Act's institutionalization of rights for organized labor, which he reviled as an effort to reconstruct capitalism. As guest editorialist for the *Phoenix Gazette*, he damned Roosevelt for "turn[ing] over to the racketeering practices of ill-organized unions the future of the working man." Another diatribe took aim at American businessmen who condemned the New Deal in private but were too fearful of doing so "in the open where [their] thoughts and arguments would do some good."[9]

The channels connecting central Arizona's merchants and professionals with outside conservative executives would help forge an alliance to contest liberalism. A goodly number of Phoenix Chamber of Commerce members had received undergraduate, law, and business degrees from top universities in the East, Midwest, and Pacific West. Their membership in extensive alumni networks complemented their affiliation with professional organizations and leading financial houses. Retailers like Goldwater often negotiated directly with leading manufacturers or bankers who sold products or made loans throughout the South and Southwest. These connections firmly linked this elite desert coterie to high-ranking executives who may have initially divided over New Deal liberalism but later united to fund and direct the postwar conservative movement from above.[10]

To participate in an anti-liberal alliance that would facilitate the kind of regional development it favored, the Phoenix Chamber of Commerce had to create a power base for business ascendancy in local and state politics. The odds on successfully challenging the Democratic establishment that dominated Arizona seemed bleak. Two legendary Senate liberals were Arizona's foremost representatives in national politics: Carl Hayden, architect of the federal Central Arizona Project irrigation system, and Ernest

McFarland, the principal force behind the G.I. Bill of Rights of 1944. Nevertheless, the pair were not emblematic of a Rooseveltian consensus on national government activism within a state party deeply divided between New Dealers, so-called Jeffersonian Democrats (who disliked federal intervention), and the commodity interests (who opposed the kind of industrial investment that could raise living and workplace standards, require new taxes, and undermine their control of company towns).[11] Getting control of Phoenix as the first step to state ascendancy initially looked beyond chamber of commerce capabilities, too. A commission system of municipal government that facilitated a spoils system of contract awards cried out for reform, but the forces of change were divided. The business elite wanted to modernize Phoenix without democratizing it, but liberal elements wanted to build a local version of the New Deal featuring improved public services, fair-employment guarantees, and housing projects.[12]

Periphery Politics in Washington

To promote the New Deal vision of southern and western development, FDR's federal appointees wanted to empower the grassroots rather than work through conservative elites. Tennessee Valley Authority director David Lilienthal, for example, considered federal spending as the agency of relief, recovery, and reconstruction, all of which necessitated popular oversight of government initiatives. Empowering the laity would in his view put "democracy on the march" against the outside investors, agricultural interests, and large mining outfits blocking the industrialization, unionism, and civic participation that liberals championed.[13]

Lyndon Johnson struck many New Dealers as ideally suited to the task of redeeming the South from the bottom up. Since first coming to Washington as aide to Congressman Richard Kleberg of Texas, he excelled at contacting key legislators able to help his boss direct federal dollars to projects back home. This political acumen was rewarded by appointment to head the National Youth Administration in Texas in 1935. Experience in this post convinced Johnson that young Americans needed opportunity, stability, and security just as much as the nation's middle-aged and elderly. Fifteen thousand Texan youngsters would benefit from the agency's support during his two years in charge. These included a significantly higher proportion of minorities than in most other states, a record he did not boast about in a racially conservative state.[14]

In general, Johnson kept his liberalism under wraps in order to maximize his political prospects. This enabled him to gain the support of influential politicians and businessmen who disdained New Deal reformism while also impressing top administration officials, not least FDR himself. The president monitored LBJ's successful 1937 campaign to fill a vacant congressional seat as an off-year test of his own popularity. After a meeting with the young victor during a visit to Texas, he commented to aides that "in the next generation the balance of power would shift south and west, and this boy could well be the first Southern president."[15] The newly elected congressman continued his political balancing act in boldly reaching out to prominent liberals, top journalists, and influential congressmen while endearing himself to the kinds of businessmen whose proclivities better matched Goldwater's. Johnson's most important business backers were lawyer Alvin Wirtz and Herman and George Brown, heads of a construction firm that eventually became a Halliburton subsidiary.[16]

This alliance was hardly unique. For the most part, the large administrative bureaucracies created by the New Deal did not blithely select contractors, initiate projects, or distribute monies. Communities had to apply for relief and infrastructure. In turn, their congressional representatives had to lobby for their constituents in sprawling, overlapping agencies. Boosters like Wirtz, Brown, and Goldwater may have detested New Dealers, but they still needed Johnson, Hayden, and McFarland to open Washington doors. Their personal wealth and civic standing made them important in turn to liberal legislators, who may have wanted to help the grassroots but nonetheless relied on local elites to request funding that was supposed to engender industry, uplift, and social democracy. This partnership hardly signified a broad consensus on redeeming Texas or Arizona, of course. Whatever their agreement on the need for infrastructure and industry to boost the West and South, liberals and conservative boosters disputed whether reconstruction should be undertaken in the name of social welfare or free enterprise and what kind of policy apparatus should support such an overhaul.[17]

Johnson was an eager collaborator with his Austin promoters within this dichotomous framework. Tutored by Alvin Wirtz in how to survive Texas and Washington politics, the new congressman secured important infrastructure projects that strengthened his home-district base. These pork-barrel benefits also pleased his business backers, who may have hated the New Deal's social-democratic ethos but were eager to procure the contracts that could build their wealth, further their political power, and better enable them to contest the New Deal both from below and within the administration. Johnson also made sure rank-and-file voters understood the value of the policies created to empower, enrich, and enfranchise them. For example, he promoted formation of Rural Electrification Administration cooperatives to maximize local control over cheap electricity. "Electric power," he reasoned, "doesn't have to run through the cash register of a New York power and light company before it gets to our lamps." Johnson also had a quick retort for any Texans questioning such infrastructure spending: "It's not coming out of your pocket. Any money that's spent here on New Deal projects, the East is paying for. We don't pay any taxes in Texas." That rejoinder foreshadowed the ways in which liberals like Johnson would have to sell their progressive programs in the more conservative, business-focused language of tax cuts, individual benefits, and local controls to a citizenry whom politicians implicitly recognized as skeptical of (if not hostile to) reform.[18]

Johnson's New Deal experiences prepared him for the political battles at home during World War II. New Dealers had not fared well in the recession-affected 1938 midterm elections. Republican gains enhanced the already budding conservative congressional coalition that stymied New Deal legislation from 1939 onward. The Roosevelt administration continued economic experimentation under the guise of victory abroad after the United States entered the global conflict. FDR issued decrees requiring construction of military installations and war-production factories in the interior and observance of fair-employment hiring practice. Administration appointees overseeing the business of war, particularly the executive dollar-a-year men supposedly on loan from the corporations receiving sizable military contracts, showed no interest in forcing their full-time brethren to hire minorities and only acquiesced to shifting production outside the Steelbelt when existing plants could not meet demand. In lobbying contractors, military officials, and dollar-a-year men for defense installations, western and southern boosters promised monetary support for industrial development, quiescent labor, and supportive state and local governments. Accordingly, Steelbelt CEOs became aware of the economic and political possibilities of the soon-to-emerge Sunbelt.[19]

Johnson's political ascent amid these developments illustrated the strength of anti–New Deal sentiment at local, state, and federal levels in the 1940s. Early success in bringing vote-winning defense dollars to Texas persuaded him to enter the 1941 Senate special election, which highlighted the deep divisions among state Democrats over the New Deal. Fraudulent ballots sent popular Governor Pappy O'Daniel, an FDR critic, to Washington.

Johnson remained in the House until some electoral deceit on his own part won him a seat in the upper chamber in 1948. Meanwhile, the Texan made himself wealthy through dealings that violated 1930s reform ideals. Stories circulated about kickbacks from military contractors and how his connections with the Federal Communications Commission and CBS transformed a small Austin radio station, bought in his wife's name in 1943, into a major financial asset, a pattern of shady dealing replicated in the acquisition of lucrative television stations in the 1950s. As a freshman senator, he seemingly epitomized the kind of southern Democrat who belied theories of a postwar consensus through his support for the conservative coalition. His spectacular first-term rise to become Senate Democratic leader owed everything to his acceptability to southern members of that body, but it would grow increasingly difficult for him to walk a middle way between conservatives and liberals in the late 1950s.[20]

While LBJ navigated the choppy waters of Democratic politics, Goldwater was emerging as a powerful critic of liberalism. During World War II, the Phoenix Chamber of Commerce doggedly competed with other southern and western promoters for defense investment. Training camps, airfields, and factories revived the once depressed city, but the return of peace threatened economic ruin. Interior bases and defense plants were quickly closed, not reconverted. Washington infighting all but guaranteed that liberals would be unable to prepare communities for demobilization. Thousands of wartime migrants were out of work, and defense boomtowns like Phoenix lacked the resources to meet their needs. Nevertheless, reconversion was as much a political opportunity for conservative elites as it was an economic disaster for working- and middle-class southerners and westerners. In Phoenix's case, liberals, veterans, small-business owners, and the unemployed all wanted Steelbelt investment in central Arizona's shuttered factories. Boosters persuasively argued that revitalization hinged on creating a haven from the New Deal that offered low taxes, anti-union laws, and utility deals. Chamber men, Goldwater foremost among them, used this anti-liberal investment platform to campaign their way into the city council, the state legislature, and the statehouse.[21]

This success hinged on both antidemocratic social engineering and old-fashioned party-building. Boosters across the nascent Sunbelt, not just in Phoenix, were behind a wave of municipal reform movements that placed urban economic elites in control of their towns. Goldwater was among the business founders of Phoenix's supposedly nonpartisan Charter Government Committee (CGC), which in 1948 promoted enactment of a new city charter instituting at-large election rules as a means of effectively eliminating working-class and minority voices on the council. The following year, Goldwater had a prominent place on the first CGC slate, which would dominate local politics long after larger ambitions removed him from city governance. The organization enjoyed victories in every council race for twenty-five years and remained a political force until Phoenix voters approved a district system in 1982.[22]

Although Phoenix boosters contested local elections on a nonpartisan basis, state and national contests required declaration of their party preference. Accordingly, Goldwater and his allies resurrected the Arizona GOP as a staunchly anti-liberal party that openly pledged to rewrite tax codes and legislative statutes in order to attract investment. They were remarkably successful in creating what would later be called a business climate, promoting tax breaks for aeronautic, electronics, and computer manufacturers and allowing business to subtract the amount of taxes paid to Washington when figuring what they owed Arizona. By 1957, Arizona firms paid just 32.7 percent of the state tax burden, a rate on a par with the low-tax South's overall average, lower than in high-growth California, and significantly lower than northeastern and Great Lakes states. Such investment environments hinged on voter support for business-first policies that not only attracted a remarkable flow of inward manufacturing investment but also served as a model for other southern and western boosters eager to industrialize and contest New Deal liberalism.[23] This strategy, furthermore, enabled Goldwater to dethrone the seemingly well-entrenched Ernest McFarland in his 1952 Senate campaign directed more against FDR's New Deal and Truman's Fair Deal than his actual opponent. Assailing the "Powercrats" of big government, the Republican challenger pledged to resist "waste and wild experiments, and giveaways of inflationary deficit spending that meant the consumer ultimately bore the cost for such reckless largesse."[24]

Once in Washington, Goldwater found himself angrier with moderate Republicans like Dwight Eisenhower than with Democrats like Johnson. "The Administration has succumbed to the principle that we owe some sort of living, including all types of care to the citizens of this country," he confided to friends. "I am beginning to wonder if we haven't gone a lot farther than many of us think on this road we happily call socialism." Republicans who supported the censure of Senator Joseph McCarthy of Wisconsin in late 1954 were a particular target for loathing as participants in "the merciless fight to destroy a United States Senator and the fight against communism."[25]

In contrast, Goldwater made common cause with conservative southern Democrats in defense of local control and free enterprise that served as the basis for a nascent cross-Sunbelt alliance. This was manifest in his accord with Senator Strom Thurmond of South Carolina when both served on the Labor and Public Welfare Committee in the late 1950s. Though best known as the presidential candidate of the States' Rights Party in 1948, Thurmond was an early promoter of the Sunbelt South as a governor with a strong record of industrial recruitment to his state. The Arizonan and the South Carolinian were in philosophical agreement in their anti-union, anticommunist, and antifederal ideals but were only partly in unison on matters of race. Infamously filibustered by Thurmond, the Civil Rights bill of 1957 gained Goldwater's approval as a justifiable effort to provide African Americans with legal protection against voting-right abuses. He also endorsed the kind of moderate challenge to segregation that many boosters already promoted at local level across the South and West. The Arizona senator had joined the NAACP when it successfully contested the racial separation of Phoenix public schools in 1953. On the other hand, he opposed the landmark *Brown* decision in the following year and the Civil Rights Act of 1964 as federal violations of state-local rights.[26]

Goldwater built his national reputation on stridently anti-liberal politics geared toward industrial development, not individual opportunity. He spent his first term helping Phoenix boosters promote the Valley of the Sun to military suppliers, aiding potential investors with government contracts, and traveling the country to deliver avowedly conservative speeches for the Republican Senate Campaign Committee. Service on the Senate's Select Committee on Improper Activities in the Labor or Management Field (better known as the McClellan Labor Rackets Committee) thrust him into the national spotlight. Though critical of infamously corrupt Teamster leader Jimmy Hoffa, Goldwater targeted Walter Reuther, who embodied his profound fear of increased trade union power both on the shop floor and in politics. During committee hearings in March 1958, he grilled the United Automobile Workers president about his union's financial contributions to Democrats, the aggressive nature of its organizing efforts, and his own pronouncements on domestic and foreign policy issues with little bearing to the interests of union members. During their exchanges, the Arizonan remarked that he would "rather have Hoffa stealing my money than Reuther stealing my freedom." Media coverage of the hearings, notably a piece in the *Saturday Evening Post*, profiled him as modern conservative with support among like-minded younger voters, the lower-middle classes, small-business owners, a smattering of corporate executives, and a gaggle of unionists.[27]

A strong home-state base enabled Goldwater to withstand the Democratic national landslide and a concerted AFL-CIO attempt to unseat him in the 1958 midterms. By now it was evident that a profound shift had occurred in Arizona's political character. The GOP's anti-liberal party-building had delivered victories in state and congressional races and resisted labor efforts to rescind the right-to-work law enacted initially in 1946. Some Jeffersonian Democrats had switched party affiliation, while many others had split their tickets. Liberals were also having second thoughts about launching direct attacks on the conservative economic principles most evidently associated with Goldwater. Carl Hayden, in particular, ducked a fight with the Steelbelt executives who had invested in Phoenix and now spent their money campaigning for local allies in business's larger war against the New Deal tradition.[28]

Executive Warfare

Goldwater showed no inclination toward moderation as his national profile grew. Reelected chairman of the Republican Senate Campaign Committee in 1959, he proclaimed himself "proud of being a conservative" and urged President Eisenhower to "quit copying the New Deal."[29] Conservatives in search of a presidential nominee to challenge establishment Republicans in the race for the 1960 presidential nomination turned to him. Powerful midwestern radio broadcaster Clarence Manion, who represented the rising significance of Roman Catholics in the conservative movement, engineered efforts to get the Arizonan to run.[30] This right-winger subsequently arranged for Goldwater to put his name to a manifesto for the coalescing conservative movement that was drafted on his behalf by William Buckley's brother-in-law, Brent Bozell. Brought out in 1960 by Manion's newly formed nonprofit publishing company, *Conscience of a Conservative* was a forthright statement of anticommunist, anti-statist, and anti-liberal opinion that became a runaway bestseller.[31] By 1964 it had racked up sales of 3.5 million, helped by right-wing organizations purchasing the volume in bulk and distributing it at a loss. To coincide with its publication, Goldwater was invited to South Carolina's Republican state convention. In a calculated appeal to Sunbelt solidarity, the Arizonan declared that the GOP was "the only place a conservative can go" while putting a bipartisan spin on his words by remarking, "I just wish to God we could find some more Strom Thurmonds in this country."[32]

Although Goldwater discouraged conservative efforts to promote him as a serious candidate in 1960, he drew the most heartfelt demonstration at the Republican national convention in Chicago. Following Richard Nixon's narrow electoral defeat, the GOP right regarded the Arizonan as the man to lead the party into battle against John F. Kennedy four years hence. Prominent businessmen began organizing a pro-Goldwater coalition as early as the summer of 1961. CEOs, including du Pont and Eli Lilly family members, Walt Disney, Walter Knott, and Charles Edison, donated generously to this project. Leading conservative economists, such as Milton Friedman, gave prestigious endorsement to his views.[33]

This was the base for Goldwater's successful campaign for the GOP nomination in 1964. As well as attracting support from business elites wanting to keep the Sunbelt safe for capitalism, however, the Arizonan was the beneficiary of a populist surge of conservatism against big government, high taxes, and racial liberalism in the region's rapidly growing and almost exclusively white suburbs.[34] In 1964, suburban wives went door-to-door to arouse the faithful, husbands handed out pro-Goldwater literature, and daughters dressed as cowgirls for the Arizonan's campaign. It was small wonder that the GOP's 1964 convention at San Francisco became such a boisterously enthusiastic affair that historian Robert Goldberg characterized it as "Woodstock for Conservatives." This erupted into prolonged applause when Goldwater declared in his acceptance speech the words that embodied outright rejection of anything akin to a liberal consensus: "Extremism in the defense of liberty is no vice! Moderation in the pursuit of justice is no virtue!"[35]

Kennedy's assassination meant that Goldwater would contest the presidency against fellow Sunbelter Lyndon Johnson. The Texan's inept and somewhat halfhearted campaign for the 1960 nomination had exposed his limited support in the party beyond Washington, DC. To liberal dismay, JFK had offered him the vice-presidential slot, most likely in the hope of benefiting from his erstwhile rival's support in the South. Such was Johnson's concern that Kennedy was too liberal for the country that he engineered a change in Texas law to allow him to also run for reelection to the Senate while on the national ticket. Kennedy's narrow victory by just 0.2 percent of the popular vote and consequently short coattails seemingly justified LBJ's concerns. In a footnote to the national election, Johnson easily won reelection to the Senate by 17 percent over GOP challenger John Tower, but this was a puny margin compared to his 85 to 15 percent triumph in 1954. Confirming the growing appeal of Sunbelt Republicanism in the Lone Star State, Tower went on to become the first Republican it had sent to the Senate since 1870 in winning the special election to fill LBJ's vacant seat in 1961, albeit by a mere 1 percent margin.[36]

This outcome indicated that Dixie Republicans had begun their advance with the sort of political strategizing and messaging that had tipped the balance in one-party western states like Arizona. Tower's victory owed much to good GOP organization, stay-at-home Democratic voters, and even liberal defections in protest at establishment control of the majority party. Nevertheless, it was possible to see some sign of a regional realignment in the making. Democratic senator Robert Kerr of Oklahoma remarked of Tower, "He's sort of a new economy model compact that runs on regular Goldwater." Reporters found that thousands of Texas Democrats had changed their registration out of enthusiasm for a Goldwater presidential run four years hence. As if to affirm his pedigree on arrival in Washington, Tower issued a personal manifesto that chimed very much with *Conscience of a Conservative*.[37] Despite Johnson's later prediction that his signature on the 1964 Civil Rights Act would deliver the South to the GOP, it was evident that conservative Republicanism had started to make inroads into this Democratic domain some years earlier.

Ideologies, policies, and constituencies pitted Goldwater and Johnson against each other before JFK's assassination. Johnson had found himself largely shut out of the White House inner circle, but he could still deploy the power of his office to send NASA's new space center to Houston, in the process giving longtime backer George Brown a powerful advisory role in the agency. Phoenix boosters found themselves with a costly failed bid. Johnson also may have used his seat atop the President's Committee on Equal Employment Opportunities to pressure the administration to go further and faster than it had been willing to go on civil rights. Johnson certainly pushed against the limits of mainstream politics once in the Oval Office. Presidential persuasion, bargaining, and cajolery helped to enact the far-reaching 1964 Civil Rights Act, which Goldwater staunchly opposed as an unwarrantable intrusion on the private sector. "I am unalterably opposed to discrimination or segregation on the basis of race, color, or creed," the Arizonan avowed, but "two portions of this bill . . . [,] which are of such overriding significance that they are determinative of my vote on the entire measure, are those which would embark the Federal Government on a regulatory course of action with regard to private enterprise in the area of so-called public accommodations and in the area of employment."[38]

Against a background of ghetto disturbances and white backlash in the summer of 1964, Goldwater requested a White House meeting with LBJ to discuss the election. Held on July 24, this produced agreement that the candidates would not inflame racial tensions in the campaign, an accord publicized in a subsequent press release. In both his memoirs, Goldwater claimed the pair had also confidentially taken Vietnam off the table as an election issue. Neither part of the deal was honored. The Republican candidate lambasted presidential toleration of communist advances in Southeast Asia. Going after the votes of the white South also impelled him to use coded messages on states' rights, crime, and law and order that had evident racial undertones, a tactic that would become a familiar part of future GOP electoral strategy. Strom Thurmond's dramatic change of party affiliation before Election Day also reinforced Republican identification with the white South. LBJ, meanwhile, had no compunctions about portraying Goldwater as divisive, extreme, and trigger-happy.[39]

If Johnson could not find consensus with Goldwater on race and Vietnam, he had reached agreement with corporate America on issues that had divided reformers and CEOs for three decades. The 1964 contest underscored how much liberals like Johnson were beholden to conservative businessmen. They had once been uncomfortable allies in promoting a national New Deal and reconstructing the South and West through warfare. Now the growing conservative movement within the GOP increasingly forced liberals to reject key components of the New Deal tradition. Although the president publicly campaigned to build a Great Society and to wage a federal War on Poverty, he also solicited corporate support with promises of federal budget cuts and continuance of Kennedy's 1962 business tax cuts. This was the kind of agenda that boosters had long promoted at local and state level to make the South and West into havens from Steelbelt labor-liberalism. LBJ's campaign promise to rescind some of the most draconian parts of Taft-Hartley may have signified his need for labor votes, but reluctance to follow this up once reelected indicated that the balance of interest group power had swung toward business. CEOs, for their part, took temporary refuge within Johnson's big-tent coalition because they were averse to wasting their funding resources on the obvious loser and sacrificing their influence over the executive branch.[40]

Liberal Retreat

Despite a landslide presidential victory with coattails that produced huge Democratic majorities in the House and Senate, Johnson recognized that his options to promote liberalism were far from limitless. In his assessment, there was a narrow, two-year window to build where possible on the New Deal. The president invested his political capital in promoting a dramatic expansion of federally guaranteed opportunity and empowerment in 1965–66. Thereafter, the growing costs of America's war in Vietnam would limit the possibilities of expanding what had become known as the Great Society. By then, however, it was evident that this reform program had no place for the kind of tax increases, business regulations, and trade-union protections so objectionable to Goldwater during the Roosevelt years. Their absence could be traced back to the New Deal's unwitting empowerment of corporate leaders to shape recovery initiatives in the 1930s and to oversee victory at home during World War II. This laid the foundations for the anti-liberal alliance of CEOs and boosters that would upend local politics in the South and West. The consequent emergence of the postwar Sunbelt proved fertile ground for a conservative strand of Republicanism that exerted potent influence on national politics from the 1960s onward.

It was a considerable irony that the 1964 Civil Rights Act, arguably the greatest liberal achievement of the Johnson presidency, unintentionally eroded private-sector unionism, an influential ally of liberalism. Among its provisions, this measure prohibited employment discrimination on grounds of race and gender. Although many CEOs shared Goldwater's concern that this would establish federal authority over hiring and firing, businesses soon discovered it was far cheaper to settle a lawsuit against a single case of discrimination than to raise wages (even by a dollar). That cost calculation hardly mattered in the Sunbelt, where boosters like Goldwater had already used the Taft-Hartley Act's right-to-work allowance to frustrate union organizing and collective bargaining. That calculus had real consequences in the emergent Rustbelt, the successor to the Steelbelt, where unionists increasingly made wage concessions to stop capital from fleeing.[41]

In another symbolic irony, LBJ's political career came to an unexpected end with his decision not to seek another presidential term in 1968, the year that Goldwater resumed his as Arizona senator. Johnson was exhausted by party divisions over Vietnam, civil rights, and the War on Poverty. Goldwater, in contrast, won election to the seat vacated by ninety-one-year-old

Carl Hayden, the erstwhile champion of the New Deal who had reached accommodation with the booster-executive alliance of late. On his return to Washington, the onetime presidential contender held firm to the principles that shaped the business revolt against the New Deal. In the economically troubled 1970s, his brand of hyper-growth, anti-union, low-tax, deregulatory peripheral politics had become post-industrial economic orthodoxy not only in national politics but also in state-local efforts across the country to develop environments friendly to business. Paradoxically, Goldwater's second Senate career was more notable for his libertarian resistance to the efforts of moral conservatives to criminalize abortion rights and limit gay rights.[42]

In the first phase of his political career, which ranged from activism in the Phoenix Chamber of Commerce to being the GOP standard-bearer, Goldwater embodied the absence of a liberal consensus at any stage in the developing South and West. The relative strength of unionism and liberalism in the Northeast, Midwest, and Pacific West eventually induced Steelbelt industrialists to join with local boosters to build anti-liberal, free-enterprise oases from the New Deal in what became the Sunbelt. No less than Goldwater, LBJ was instrumental as a young politico, senior senator, and president in helping anti-liberal boosters and CEOs regroup during World War II and the Cold War. The 1964 presidential contest was the culmination of fights over New Deal economic policy that had begun in the 1930s. In regaining the White House, Johnson had to concede two pillars of federal economic reform (progressive taxation and union empowerment) to the businessmen at the helm of the conservative movement that had already frustrated these liberal policies at the state and local level.

Notes

1. Indispensable on the Sunbelt phenomenon is Sean Cunningham, *American Politics in the Postwar Sunbelt: Conservative Growth in a Battleground Region* (New York: Cambridge University Press, 2014). For a valuable review, see too the introduction to Michelle Dickerson and Darren Dochuk, eds., *Sunbelt Rising: The Politics of Space, Place, and Region* (Philadelphia: University of Pennsylvania Press, 2011), 1–18.

2. For more extensive discussion, on which much of this chapter is based, see my previous works: "Origins of the Conservative Ascendancy: Barry Goldwater's Early Senate Career and the De-legitimation of Organized Labour," *Journal of American History* 95 (December 2008): 678–709; "Sunbelt Boosterism: Industrial Recruitment, Economic Development, and Growth Politics in the Developing Sunbelt," in Dickerson and Dochuk, *Sunbelt Rising,* 31–57; *Sunbelt Capitalism: Phoenix and the Transformation of American*

Politics (Philadelphia: University of Pennsylvania Press, 2013); and "Drafting a Movement: Barry Goldwater and the Rebirth of the Arizona Republican Party," in Shermer, ed., *Barry Goldwater and the Remaking of the American Political Landscape* (Tucson: University of Arizona Press, 2013), 43–66.

3. Godfrey Hodgson, "The Foreign Policy Establishment," in Steve Fraser and Gary Gerstle, eds., *Ruling America: A History of Wealth and Power in America* (Cambridge: Harvard University Press, 2005), 215–49; Charles Postel, *The Populist Vision* (New York: Oxford University Press, 2007), 269–90.

4. Robert A. Caro, *The Years of Lyndon Johnson: The Path to Power* (New York: Knopf, 1982), 1–65. For a more sympathetic biography that stresses its subject's devotion to the social gospel as the inspiration for his liberalism, see Randall Woods, *LBJ: Architect of American Ambition* (Cambridge: Harvard University Press, 2006).

5. "Remarks at Southwest Texas State College upon Signing the Higher Education Act of 1965," November 8, 1965, *Public Papers of the Presidents*, in Gerhard Peters and John T. Woolley, *The American Presidency Project*, http://www.presidency.ucsb.edu/ws/?pid=27356 (accessed August 17, 2016).

6. Rick Perlstein, *Before the Storm: Barry Goldwater and the Unmaking of the American Consensus* (New York: Hill & Wang, 2001), 17–42; Robert Goldberg, *Barry Goldwater* (New Haven: Yale University Press, 1995), 3–42.

7. Shermer, *Sunbelt Capitalism*, 101–3

8. Kim Phillips-Fein, *Invisible Hands: The Businessmen's Crusade against the New Deal* (New York: Norton, 2010), 3–25.

9. "A Fireside Chat with Mr. Roosevelt," *Phoenix Gazette*, June 23, 1938; "Scaredee-Cat," *Phoenix Gazette*, June 23, 1939.

10. Shermer, *Sunbelt Capitalism*, 39–70.

11. Thomas Sheridan, *Arizona: A History*, rev. ed. (Tucson: University of Arizona Press, 2012), chapters 13 and 14. For a memoir by a onetime Democrat who became Goldwater's campaign manager in his 1952 Senate race, see Stephen Shadegg, *Arizona Politics: The Struggle to End One-Party Rule* (Tempe: Arizona State University Press, 1986).

12. Shermer, *Sunbelt Capitalism*, 116–46.

13. Jordan A. Schwarz, *The New Dealers: Power Politics in the Age of Roosevelt* (New York: Knopf, 1993), 195–248; David E. Lilienthal, *TVA: Democracy on the March* (New York: Harper, 1944).

14. Robert Dallek, *Lone Star Rising: Lyndon Johnson and His Times* (New York: Oxford University Press, 1991), 93–184.

15. Schwarz, *The New Dealers*, 270.

16. Dallek, *Lone Star Rising*, 225–67.

17. Shermer, *Sunbelt Capitalism*, 39–92.

18. Schwarz, *New Dealers*, 264–84 (quotation on 276).

19. For the regional benefits, see Gerald Nash, *The Federal Landscape: An Economic History of the West* (Tucson: University of Arizona Press, 1993), 3–55; Gavin Wright, *Old South, New South: Revolutions in the Southern Economy since the Civil War* (New York: Basic Books, 1986), 81–239. For a local case study, see Thomas Scott, "Winning World War II in an Atlanta Suburb: Local Boosters and the Recruitment of Bell Bomber," in Phillip

Scranton, ed., *The Second Wave: Southern Industrialization from the 1940s to the 1970s* (Athens: University of Georgia Press, 2001), 1–23.

20. Robert Caro, *Means of Ascent: The Years of Lyndon Johnson* (New York: Knopf, 1990), 80–118; Dallek, *Lone Star Rising*, parts 3 and 4.

21. Shermer, *Sunbelt Capitalism*, chapter 3.

22. David Berman, *Arizona Politics and Government: The Quest for Autonomy, Democracy and Development* (Lincoln: University of Nebraska Press, 1998), 181.

23. Shermer, "Sunbelt Boosterism," 49–51.

24. Shermer, *Sunbelt Capitalism*, 168.

25. Shermer, "Origins of the Conservative Ascendancy," 696; Jack Bell, *Mr. Conservative: Barry Goldwater* (Garden City, NY: Doubleday, 1962), 96–98; Godfrey Hodgson, *The World Turned Right Side Up: A History of the Conservative Ascendancy in America* (Boston: Houghton Mifflin, 1996), 96.

26. Joseph Crespino, *Strom Thurmond's America* (New York: Hill and Wang, 2012), 8; Donald Critchlow, *The Conservative Ascendancy: How the GOP Right Made Political History* (Cambridge: Harvard University Press, 2007), 50; Goldberg, *Barry Goldwater*, 89–91, 196–97.

27. Shermer, "Origins of the Conservative Ascendancy," 698–703 (quotation on 701–2); Paul Healy, "The Glittering Mr. Goldwater," *Saturday Evening Post*, June 7, 1958, 39.

28. Shermer, "Drafting a Movement," 60–63.

29. "Goldwater Urges President to 'Quit Copying New Deal,'" *Associated Press*, January 23, 1959.

30. On Manion, see Critchlow, *The Conservative Ascendancy*, 46–49.

31. Stephen Shadegg, *What Happened to Goldwater? The Inside Story of the 1964 Republican Campaign* (New York: Holt, Rinehart & Winston, 1965), 27; Barry Goldwater, *The Conscience of a Conservative* (Lexington: Victor Books, 1960).

32. Crespino, *Strom Thurmond's America*, 128–30.

33. Phillips-Fein, *Invisible Hands*, 115–49. See, too, Clifton White, *Suite 3505: The Story of the Draft Goldwater Movement* (New Rochelle, NY: Arlington House, 1967).

34. See, in particular, Lisa McGirr, *Suburban Warriors: Origins of the New Right* (Princeton: Princeton University Press, 2001), esp. 111–46.

35. Goldberg, *Barry Goldwater*, 181–209.

36. Sean Cunningham, "John Tower, Texas, and the Rise of the Republican South," in Robert Mason and Iwan Morgan, eds., *Seeking a New Majority: The Republican Party and American Politics, 1960–1980* (Nashville: Vanderbilt University Press, 2013), 110–12.

37. John Knaggs, *Two-Party Texas: The John Tower Era, 1961–1984* (Austin: Eakin Press, 1986), 16–17; Robert Mason, *The Republican Party and American Politics from Hoover to Reagan* (New York: Cambridge University Press, 2012), 190; John Tower, *A Program for Conservatives* (New York: Macfadden, 1962).

38. Dallek, *Flawed Giant: Lyndon Johnson and His Times* (New York: Oxford University Press, 1999), 3–121; Senator Barry Goldwater, "Civil Rights," *Congressional Record*, 88th Cong., 2nd sess., June 18, 1964, S14319.

39. Robert Johnson, *All the Way with LBJ: The 1964 Presidential Election* (New York: Cambridge University Press, 2009), 141–42; Andrew Johns, *Vietnam's Second Front:*

Domestic Politics, the Republican Party, and the War (Lexington: University Press of Kentucky, 2010), 71–73.

40. Shermer, *Sunbelt Capitalism*, 284–92.

41. Nelson Lichtenstein, *State of the Union: A Century of American Labor* (Princeton: Princeton University Press, 2002), 178–211.

42. Part 3 of Goldberg, *Barry Goldwater*, offers the best discussion of the second Senate career.

10

"Down the Middle of the Road"

Dwight D. Eisenhower, the Republican Party, and the Politics of Consensus and Conflict, 1949–1961

ROBERT MASON

On Labor Day 1949, speaking to the American Bar Association in St. Louis, Dwight Eisenhower diagnosed a problem of conflict in American society and then prescribed, as a solution, a quest for unity. Perceiving dissension—within this wider climate of conflict—to be strongest in the field of industrial relations, he called for "more economic understanding and working arrangements that will bind labor and management . . . into a far tighter voluntary cooperative unit than we now have." In his assessment, a tendency currently existed to view employers' interests and employees' interests as mutually exclusive. Eisenhower characterized such a perspective as "distorted doctrine [that] is false and foreign to the American scene where common ideals and purpose permit us a common approach toward the common good." In response to such challenges, and to calm the conflict they fomented, the direction for the United States to take, he said, was "down the middle of the road between the unfettered power of concentrated wealth on one flank, and the unbridled power of statism or partisan interests on the other." This was a vision that stressed the need for common purpose. But Eisenhower did not speak of consensus. Instead, he observed that "the center" was where "the contest is hottest, the progress sometimes discouragingly slow."[1]

As president between 1953 and 1961, Eisenhower would repeatedly look back to this American Bar Association address as a definitive statement of his political philosophy.[2] The pursuit of the "middle way" would inform his agenda as president, providing a key reason why, according to some contemporaries as well as some historians, this period was one of consensus in politics.[3] Because Eisenhower's interest in fashioning a consensus-oriented form of politics involved a quest—to shift the policy focus of the Republican Party and to amend the decision-making mechanisms of the post–New Deal federal government—the concept of consensus associated with the Eisenhower years involves a dynamic project emerging from a particular political vision, not a static descriptor of harmonious agreement in American society. Indeed, this quest for a middle way was far from consensual in design and in implementation; it was beset by controversy. Not only did Eisenhower ground his rationale for this middle way in the existence of political, social, and economic conflict, as he outlined in his St. Louis address. But also, rather as he predicted in his comments there, Eisenhower's middle-way politics met fierce opposition—most notably within the Republican Party, where it fostered a reassertion of anti-consensus conservatism.

The Labor Day speech was one of several interventions on questions of public controversy during 1949 by Eisenhower, newly able to do so after many years of military service. All indicated alarm about the long-term implications of New Deal liberalism, especially as Democrats under Harry Truman promoted a Fair Deal agenda of further programmatic innovation. The trajectory of big government was destructive of liberty, Eisenhower warned. He spoke of a "constant drift toward centralized bureaucratic government" that would lead to "a swarming of bureaucrats over the land" and to government ownership of property—"and finally you have to have a dictatorship as the only means of operating such a huge and great organization."[4] According to Eisenhower, "the fundamental struggle of our time" was "between those who would further apply to our daily lives the concept of individual freedom and equality; and those who would subordinate the individual to the dictates of the state."[5] It is certainly true that Eisenhower warned, as he did at his installation as president of Columbia University in 1949, of "[t]he power of concentrated finance," as well as the "the power of selfish pressure groups [and] the power of any class organized in opposition to the whole," as endangering liberty as much as "excessive power concentrated in the political head of the state." Yet his focus remained on "paternalistic government" and on the politics of interest-group pluralism as especially dangerous.[6]

In his Columbia University address, Eisenhower noted that "ready cooperation in the solution of human problems is the only sure way to avoid forced government intervention."[7] The following year, he outlined more comprehensively his prescription for America's challenges when he appeared at a forum on the role of government, the key question raised by the New Deal and then the Fair Deal—a question to which Republicans had struggled to find an electorally promising response. As president of Columbia, Eisenhower advocated "a convocation of leaders in every field with the faculties of some of our great universities" so that "the question would be rescued from the domain of prejudice, emotion, partisan politics and self-interest, and be subject to logical analysis and enlightened judgment," in order "to promote social and economic welfare without jeopardy to individual freedom." He assumed that such an ostensibly neutral, expertise-based approach would be against bigger government. "Their conclusions," he said, "would certainly emphasize the truth, 'More and more bureaus, more and more taxes, fewer and fewer producers; the final result is financial collapse and the end of freedom.'"[8] At the end of the 1940s, then, Eisenhower was articulating a need for the identification and pursuit of a common purpose, balanced between capital and labor, and emerging from harmonious exchange rather than political conflict—a vision of consensus. It was a vision that involved a political project to challenge the trajectory of New Deal liberalism, and the consensus idea was a goal and not a descriptor of contemporary politics and society. For historian Robert Griffith, Eisenhower's engagement with current problems, and with the larger challenges of modern society, involved a quest for "the corporate commonwealth." This was, Griffith writes, "an attempt to resolve what he saw as the contradictions of modern capitalism and to create a harmonious corporate society without class conflict, unbridled acquisitiveness, and contentious party politics."[9]

Eisenhower's prescription of a middle way, to harness common purpose among Americans, places him among the diverse people and groups identified by Wendy Wall as sharing the belief that it was necessary to promote proactively the "American way" during this period.[10] Although partisanship was among Eisenhower's targets, as he saw such debate as obstructing rather than assisting the pursuit of the nation's purpose, his analysis of the nation's challenges also had a partisan edge (even before Eisenhower publicly announced his Republican affiliation), rooted in the view that the GOP's long-term minority status had damaging implications for the two-party system as well as for public policy; anxiety about the party's future significantly shaped Republican thinking during this period, especially in the aftermath of Truman's surprise triumph over Thomas Dewey in 1948.[11] In responding to the Labor Day speech, Senator Arthur Vandenberg of

Michigan, one of the party's leading figures, signaled the potent interaction between Eisenhower's ideas and the Republican Party's mission both in electoral politics and in public policy. "The sane philosophy of the 'middle road' is indispensable to the preservation of our threatened American unity," Vandenberg told Eisenhower. "No one can lead this indispensable 'revival' quite so well as you."[12] In offering such praise, Vandenberg was just one among many Republicans who lobbied Eisenhower during this period, encouraging him to take forward such a cause within the party.[13]

The theme of unity in place of conflict was especially potent because many Republicans saw the Democratic Party's majority status as dependent on a form of interest-group pluralism that was hostile to good government.[14] During the 1930s, the paradigm of the "bought vote"—the view that the Democrats' electoral success was thanks to the support of the New Deal's direct financial beneficiaries—had influenced Republican understandings of the Roosevelt coalition.[15] When such programmatic spending declined in significance thanks to economic recovery, many nevertheless persisted in seeing "political patronage, political subsidies, political spoils," as a West Virginia Republican put it, as central to Democratic strength.[16] Representative Hugh Scott of Pennsylvania, chair of the Republican National Committee (RNC) in 1948 and 1949, maintained the paradigm of the bought vote within this amended landscape of government activism by writing of the Democrats' "vote buying through the pay-off of pressure groups."[17] Within this framework of interest-group pluralism, Republicans recognized, quite inescapably, that their party had acquired an external identity as the representative of socioeconomic privilege, but they often saw themselves instead, quite differently, as the defender of a larger national interest.[18]

Furthermore, Republicans at large shared the view outlined by Eisenhower that the liberal agenda friendly to interest groups was not only a destructive one but also foreign or alien to the United States—as non-American somehow.[19] "We are face to face with a situation," Scott warned fellow Republicans in August 1949, "in which our Party offers the only hope for the preservation of the American Republic and the economic system which has made that Republic the envy of the world."[20] This opposition to the politics of interest-group pluralism often targeted labor in particular, as an especially strong force within the Democratic Party, and as an especially significant challenge to business interests—but also, within the Republican conception of group politics, as corrosive to sound policymaking and as a key agent in fostering conflict inimical to the greater good.[21] Labor seemed powerful, but also vulnerable; opposition to organized labor had been a successful issue for Republicans on the way to capturing Congress in 1946, and the Taft-Hartley Act of 1947 was a key conservative achievement of the 80th Congress that followed.[22]

The international context of the Cold War, as well as the domestic framework of the Truman administration's Fair Deal agenda, fueled such perceptions; on the party's liberal side, Jacob Javits of New York, then in the House of Representatives (and later, from 1957 to 1981, a leading figure within the Senate's declining contingent of liberal Republicans), shared the perspective of more conservative Republicans in observing a choice "between a drift which could lead to a total state and the capability for the development of a uniquely American system to juxtapose to the life-and-death challenge of Communism."[23] For the midterm campaigns of 1950, Republicans embraced the theme of a fundamental contrast between their agenda and New Deal liberalism through the slogan of "liberty versus socialism." Altogether, the stakes seemed high in this period. "Our country is in the most critical period since the Civil War when we fought to make men free and to preserve the Union," wrote Iowa's Harrison E. Spangler, a former RNC chair, in early 1950; Spangler interpreted the Fair Deal as a similar threat to liberty.[24]

While Republicans embraced the need for national unity as an alternative to interest-group politics and as an imperative in face of the Soviet threat, their own party was characterized by factional disunity. As historian Michael Bowen demonstrates, in his study of the clashing visions for the party associated with Dewey on the one hand and Robert A. Taft on the other, strategic differences and personal rivalries were often more important than policy conflicts in fostering this disunity. To be sure, disagreements existed within the party on the policy response to New Deal liberalism—between Republicans who were more moderate and those who were more conservative—but the distance between these competing views was relatively small (on these domestic questions, though not on issues of foreign policy), certainly by contrast with the ideological spectrum covered by the big-tent Democratic coalition.[25] "The Democratic Party—that curious conglomeration of economic and social reactionaries . . . , of Communist fellow travelers, of corrupt city machines, of star-gazing amateur messiahs with a conviction that they must make over the world to their liking and profit—has only one cohesive element, namely, money from the federal treasury," wrote Herbert Brownell in 1945, then RNC chair and subsequently U.S. attorney general from 1953 to 1957.[26]

Factional conflict intensified in the aftermath of the Dewey defeat; Scott, a special target of Dewey's intraparty opponents because of his role as national chair during the campaign, complained about "the complete lack of any cooperative spirit on the part of some of these unconscionable bastards."[27] For many Republicans, the lessons of the 1948 disappointment were absolutely clear, that their party should underscore difference with the Democrats in order to achieve progress at the polls, a view that led to the embrace of the "liberty versus socialism" theme for the 1950 midterms.[28] Others disagreed, maintaining the posture that their opponents dismissively labeled "me-too," as intraparty conflict intensified. "Those who think they can get elected by saying they are going to repeal unemployment insurance, old age pensions or the Securities and Exchange Act, or by retreating into isolationism, are going to be in for a rude awakening and I am afraid may keep the Party out for another twenty years," Dewey told Alf Landon, the party's 1936 presidential candidate, at the end of 1949.[29] Dewey feared for the party's prospects if it "continues to sound as if it is going back to Ulysses S. Grant in a hurry."[30]

Dewey and his supporters would embrace Eisenhower as their candidate in opposition to Ohio's Robert A. Taft, the party's leader in the Senate and a front-running contender for the presidential nomination, and certainly Eisenhower's emphasis on harmony among different groups and on balance between different interests was much closer to the "me-too" strategy (stressing agreement with New Deal liberalism's goals) of moderate and liberal Republicans than the conservative alternative (stressing, more fundamentally, disagreement with its big-government methods). (In 1960, Richard Nixon would offer this characterization of such conservatism: "They are against any change whatsoever, including good change. Whenever we talk about good ends, they charge us with being 'me too.'")[31] Still, Eisenhower's middle-way response to New Deal liberalism offered something fresh.

Eisenhower's vision for a middle way shared much with Republican opposition to New Deal liberalism, then, while fashioning a new and promising focus for that critique. Yet it was the defense of bipartisanship in foreign policy that proved to be more influential in encouraging him to enter presidential politics. His challenge to Republicans skeptical of bipartisanship was also Eisenhower's most successful contribution to the construction of consensus. In his conceptualization of how "the ideology of the liberal consensus" developed, as outlined in chapter 1, Godfrey Hodgson stresses movement toward the center among Republicans on domestic policy, alongside a decline in dissent on bipartisanship in foreign policy among Democrats. To be sure, Henry Wallace's Progressives of 1948 were the most sharply critical of American foreign policy during the Cold War, but the Republican Party contained the more significant skeptics—the inheritors of its isolationist tradition, most powerfully exemplified by Taft. No longer isolationist, their outlook was nevertheless anti-internationalist in sounding concern about the postwar network of cooperative agreements that were at the heart of American foreign policy as the Cold War emerged. They believed, too, that bipartisanship sidelined Congress at the expense of an expanded, unresponsive executive branch, and they worried about the Cold War's expense. Eisenhower shared a concern that the Soviet threat would foster the development of a "garrison state" hostile to American values and damaging to economic vitality, but he also saw the critique of bipartisanship as dangerous to national security. In 1952, John Foster Dulles, soon to be Eisenhower's secretary of state, offered such a perspective when he spoke of the imperative for national unity in foreign policy within the international context of "deadly peril," both to instill confidence in allies and "to impress our enemies with the fact that our capacity for resolute action is not paralyzed by internal dissensions."[32] While Eisenhower's discussions of the middle way in 1949 demonstrated the significance of his engagement with domestic concerns, Taft's quest for the 1952 Republican nomination spurred his candidacy more directly because of differences on foreign policy.[33]

Eisenhower's defeat of Taft in securing the presidential nomination did not complete his challenge to those skeptical about bipartisanship, because this spirit remained strong among congressional Republicans at the start of his White House years. The clearest indicator of its vitality was the Bricker amendment, introduced as Senate Resolution 1 in 1953. Forty-three Senate Republicans joined their colleague John Bricker of Ohio, the party's 1944 vice-presidential nominee, alongside eighteen Democrats, as cosponsors of the proposed amendment, which harnessed concerns about the expansion of executive powers in foreign policy. While it was not straightforward for Eisenhower and his supporters to hold back the amendment, its defeat signaled the decline of anti-internationalist sentiment within the Republican Party, which had seemed significant during the Truman years. The vestiges of this sentiment remained visible in Republican responses to requests for foreign aid appropriations—congressional resistance to the administration's desired levels was persistent—but more broadly the party had coalesced around Cold War internationalism by the mid-1950s, the moment that Hodgson identifies as marking the arrival of the consensus ideology's heyday.[34] Eisenhower's leadership, together with party loyalty, had played an important role.

Even though disagreement with Republican anti-internationalists fueled his direct engagement with party politics, Eisenhower shared with them ideas about the Cold War that extended beyond the charge that Truman's leadership as president was deficient, not least with regard to the Korean War. His worries about the expense of the Cold War and about the threatened emergence of garrison-state priorities in spending led him to warn in 1953 that "by their military threat [the Soviet leaders] have hoped to force upon America and the free world an unbearable security burden leading to economic disaster," and that it was necessary to develop policy "in ways that do not undermine our freedom even as we strive to defend it." Challenging the NSC-68 assertion that 1954 represented "the year of maximum danger," he commented, "We live . . . not in an instant of danger but in an age of danger."[35] Within this context, he sought via the "New Look" to maintain the goals of containment in a more cost-effective way. When in the fall of 1957 New York Republican Frank Altschul protested to Eisenhower that security was more important than a balanced budget, the president underscored his view that the Cold War involved a lengthy project of defense for a "way of life" which, "over the long term, requires the observance of sound financial productivity so that the system may continue to work primarily under the impetus of private effort rather than by the fist of centralized government."[36]

Although Eisenhower's first engagement with domestic issues in 1949, before he became explicitly active in party politics, involved criticism of the status quo under the Democrats, his record in office was often interpreted as "me-too" politics in practice—as consensus-oriented. In the domestic arena, just as in the realm of foreign policy, his differences with the Democrats often seemed minor, crucially including the concerns of New Deal liberalism that had already defined American electoral politics for a generation. According to a *New York Times* journalist, writing in 1955, Eisenhower's "middle-of-the-road" agenda was one "in which there was nothing new but a diluted sort of New Dealism to which he was unwilling to put on too much pressure so as not to offend standpat members of his party in Congress and in his Cabinet."[37]

This perspective, however, understates the significance of Eisenhower's effort to challenge New Deal liberalism, taking forward the concerns he sounded in 1949; this effort emphasized both restraint on the federal government's expansion (including the federalism-grounded preference for state- or local-level initiatives in place of Washington initiatives where possible) and fiscal conservatism. Eisenhower himself, nevertheless, encountered difficulty in providing a definition of his agenda beyond the "middle way" label, variously defining himself and his supporters as "progressive moderates" and his agenda as involving "dynamic conservatism," before settling on "modern Republicanism" after his 1956 reelection victory, when he observed that the electorate had demonstrated support of such a philosophy but were unconvinced that the party at large had embraced it—comments that infuriated his intraparty opponents.[38] Two years later, again thinking about how to sell the party more effectively, this time in the aftermath of a midterm slump that sharply reduced Republican forces, Eisenhower pondered as a label "the 'Party of justice for all the people.'"[39] The concept, as Eisenhower saw it, explicitly tried to disconnect the party from its association with an elite, but it also reflected the enduring stress on national unity—the national interest, rather than special interests—as identifying the Republican agenda.

The party's platform of 1956 included a quotation from the president, another formulation that he often mentioned and that he linked with the Republican Party's Lincolnian inheritance: "In all those things which deal with people, be liberal, be human. In all those things which deal with people's money, or their economy, or their form of government, be conservative."[40] In seeking a balance between New Deal liberalism's goals and the defense of individualism, Eisenhower tended to place more emphasis on his challenge to, rather than acceptance of, activist government—despite the criticism he attracted as the exponent of "me-too" Republicanism. "What I mean by the 'Middle of the Road,'" he told an old army friend, "is that course that preserves the greatest possible initiative, freedom and independence of soul and body to the individual, but that does not hesitate to use government to use government to combat cataclysmic economic disasters which can, in some instances, be even more terrible than convulsions of nature."[41]

The record of the Eisenhower administration nevertheless reveals a straightforward acceptance of the key strands of New Deal liberalism: that the federal government should be proactively engaged with socioeconomic challenges and, as Iwan Morgan explores in chapter 5, that the federal government had a responsibility of economic management to promote prosperity. One element of this acceptance was the conviction, shared by moderate Republicans but often questioned by those on the Republican right, that it was a requirement of electoral politics. "Should any political party attempt to abolish Social Security, unemployment insurance, and eliminate labor laws and farm programs, you would not hear of that party again in our political history," Eisenhower wrote in 1954, in what would become a much-quoted observation. Those who advocated such a fundamental rollback of New Deal achievements were few and "stupid," he added.[42] Yet Eisenhower's middle-way agenda remained informed by the view that the expansion of the federal government's roles and responsibilities should be halted and that private and local remedies were preferable wherever possible. "The preceding Administration claimed a monopoly of the goals of a good society and their formula was always the same: a federal program financed by new federal taxes or new federal debt," Eisenhower told Oveta Culp Hobby in 1953. "Our task is to demonstrate that the goals our people want—in every field—can be achieved by other means than those that result in making Big Government bigger."[43]

Hobby was the first secretary of the Department of Health, Education, and Welfare, the creation of which, in 1953, numbered among the achievements of Eisenhower Republicanism. Among others, there were expansions of Social Security, including payment increases, the extension of coverage to previously uncovered groups, and the introduction of a new class of entitlement for disabled people. The Omnibus Housing Act of 1954 helped both the public and private sectors (though with a stronger market orientation) in promoting the building, purchase, and modernization of homes. A health reinsurance bill, however, did not achieve enactment, facing both liberal opposition (as inadequate) and conservative opposition (as expansive of federal government powers) in experiencing defeat. In tandem with these initiatives, the administration's fiscal conservatism remained strong, in promoting balanced budgets, restrained spending, and tax cuts where possible.[44] Although Eisenhower greeted his 1956 reelection victory as an endorsement of modern Republicanism, his second term would instead be defined by fiscal conservatism, notably with regard to the 1958 recession and its aftermath.[45]

The limitations of Eisenhower's middle way—its conservatism, rather than its liberalism—were evident, too, in its treatment of civil rights, issues that were achieving new significance during the 1950s. Although Eisenhower took steps against segregation where federal authority was clear, notably in the District of Columbia and within the armed forces, he saw no role for the White House as a "bully pulpit" from which to make pro-equality arguments and was reluctant to challenge state intransigence on civil rights. The restricted ambition and imagination of his political vision were clear in his response to the emergence of the modern civil rights movement; he employed his paradigm of the middle way in doing so, writing in February 1959 that he aimed to "inspire extremists on both sides to gravitate a bit more toward the center line, which is the only path along which progress in great human affairs can be achieved."[46] This was an understanding of extremism that equated civil rights activists with segregationists.

Eisenhower's consensus-oriented vision not only looked for a middle way on issues but also sought balanced representation of different interests in policymaking deliberations. "I will ask the advice and suggestions of all groups—public, management, and labor," he told the American Federation of Labor (AFL) annual convention in September 1952, adding that "labor will have an equal voice with all others."[47] In practice, however, "while labor and the laboring classes became partners in the corporate commonwealth," notes Robert Griffith, "they remained very junior members at best."[48] The opposition that Eisenhower signaled in his American Bar Association address to class politics and to interest-group pluralism suggested much common ground with the anti-labor sentiment that was strong in the Republican Party. Although the Taft-Hartley Act had significantly restricted union powers, many Republicans continued to see organized labor as a cornerstone of the Democratic Party's majority status—increasingly so, even, as a result of the 1955 merger between the AFL and the Congress of Industrial Organizations. They looked for ways to harness business energies in support of the party as a counterweight.[49] "Our party strength is poor," wrote a young AT&T executive in late 1960, active in local Republican politics, "because our good young people who are smart and ambitious gravitate naturally to business and not toward politics."[50]

Interested in tackling some aspects of Taft-Hartley considered unfairly anti-labor, Eisenhower nevertheless lacked adequate commitment to this project, a problem significantly reinforced by conservative opposition within the party.[51] Not only did the voice of business remain stronger than that of labor during the Eisenhower administration, but anti-labor sentiment among conservative Republicans continued to grow, further spurred by late-1950s controversies about union corruption, as Elizabeth Tandy Shermer explains in the previous chapter.[52]

While Eisenhower's corporate commonwealth was much more business- than labor-friendly, many in business viewed his project with skepticism. They saw the New Deal as having created an expanding state as well as excessive powers for labor (which, they believed, remained problematic despite Taft-Hartley), thus demanding much stauncher conservatism than modern Republicanism offered. In parallel to the somewhat contradictory strands of thinking within the party that identified association with business as damaging but that also hoped to mobilize business support more effectively, business leaders were stepping up extra-party efforts to promote such a brand of conservatism. These efforts included the resuscitation of the American Enterprise Association, a pioneering think tank against "the more or less steady trend toward a controlled economy," and they were especially visible at General Electric, where Lemuel Boulware, in charge of labor relations, led a diverse array of aggressive anti-union strategies. The 1958 midterms marked the maturation of this new business impetus for conservatism, through the promotion of "right-to-work" legislation that weakened labor—even if this quest, which took place across six states, achieved victory in only one, Kansas.[53]

The stridency of this business engagement in politics helps to expose the paradox underlying Eisenhower's quest for tranquility, in place of the storms of political conflict that had afflicted the United States during the Great Depression and then during the Fair Deal years. From the start, Eisenhower defined middle-way politics as controversy-beset. His politics of consensus certainly proved to be stormy, not tranquil, especially in his pursuit of "modern Republicanism." In 1956 he commented that "a turn to moderation and enduring principles can in itself be a revolution inciting the hatred and enmity of both extremes."[54] Yet, according to Eisenhower, "the extremes" had little support. "Most people," he told Nelson Rockefeller, the governor of New York and a presidential aspirant, in 1960, "believe that in general they belong to the 'middle-of-the-road' group."[55] In short, the middle way had popular support even if it struggled to mobilize elite support within his party, Eisenhower believed. As he put it in 1954, "If we could get every Republican committed as a Moderate Progressive, the Party would grow so rapidly that within a few years it would dominate American politics."[56] Providing substantiation to Eisenhower's suspicions, a contemporary study of political opinion among Republican politicians (sampled as convention delegates) and the party's supporters found that differences were significant—much more so than on the Democratic side. "Indeed, the conclusion is inescapable," its authors wrote, "that the views of the Republican rank and file are, on the whole, much closer to those of the Democratic leaders than to those of the Republican leaders."[57]

If Eisenhower did not employ the consensus concept directly, an aide who aimed to summarize Eisenhower Republicanism—and to underscore its connection with a majority among Americans—did. The president's success in meeting the concerns of "the American Consensus," which involved widespread agreement on the main issues, was a central theme of *A Republican Looks at His Party*, published in 1956 and written by Undersecretary of Labor Arthur Larson.[58] That success, Larson explained, was grounded in middle-way politics. The administration had "discovered and established the Authentic American Center in politics," Larson wrote, adding that "the man who holds the center holds a position of almost unbeatable strength," and echoing the charge that Republican ideas drew on American traditions but that the Democrats' New Deal liberalism was grounded in European ideologies.[59]

The view that a consensual approach to issues generated political controversy fostered in Eisenhower a certain suspicion of politics (especially party politics), and even an anti-democratic impulse.[60] More positively, it informed a project to achieve an organizational revitalization of the Republican Party, especially through Citizens for Eisenhower, the candidate-centered organization that first mobilized in support of his 1952 nomination campaign. Eisenhower hoped that the expansion of grassroots participation in the party, especially through the recruitment of the activists who had supported his candidacy, would have a moderating effect on the party at large. The project would fail, however.[61] Rather paradoxically—in view of Eisenhower's assumptions about the expansion of grassroots participation—the post-Eisenhower shift away from consensus-oriented politics in the Republican Party was closely associated with bottom-up mobilization, in support of Barry Goldwater.[62]

The "modern Republican" project, then, not only failed to establish the party as a force for middle-way politics but also helped to ignite conservatism's reassertion, kindled by sharp disappointment that the party's return to the White House for the first time since the Great Depression had failed to involve a more fundamental challenge to New Deal liberalism. Beyond the party, the challenge was liveliest within William F. Buckley's *National Review*, founded in 1955. "As a matter of fact," William Rusher, the magazine's longtime publisher, wrote Buckley in 1972, "modern American conservatism organized itself during, and in explicit opposition to, the Eisenhower Administration. Under your leadership."[63] Buckley's critique of Eisenhower was unsparingly wide-ranging. Eisenhower's foreign policy betrayed a deficient understanding of the communist threat, and his domestic policy made no effort to challenge New Deal liberalism, he charged. "The passion to federalize social and economic functions is as ardent today as it was in 1952, and beyond a few ritualistic rhetorical dampeners, Mr. Eisenhower has done nothing to check it," according to Buckley, writing in

1956. Furthermore, he added, "the forces of the Liberal left have gathered strength and determination from the victory, within the Republican party, of ideological toothlessness."[64]

While Buckley often took an anti-partisan view of politics (a view of parties as obstructing rather than facilitating his ideological odyssey), some conservative Republicans saw their president's agenda in a not dissimilar way, in perceiving consensus between New Deal liberalism and modern Republicanism. One activist captured the spirit of Buckley's critique yet more pithily and straightforwardly, stating that "there is no major difference between the Republican and Democratic parties as of 1959," and explaining that Eisenhower responded to a desire in 1952 for something new by offering nothing new. "It was a bitter disappointment," she wrote, "to see President Eisenhower travel down the same socialistic road that his predecessors have traveled so persistently."[65]

Senator Barry Goldwater of Arizona would emerge as the leader of this new conservatism. In April 1958 Goldwater responded to the administration budget by connecting Eisenhower with "the siren song of socialism" and "government by bribe"—deploying traditional Republican criticisms of New Deal liberals to attack the president.[66] Published in 1960 to buoy Goldwater's prospects for the Republican nomination, and ghostwritten by Buckley's brother-in-law L. Brent Bozell, *The Conscience of a Conservative* angrily denounced New Deal liberalism, but its anger toward Eisenhower Republicanism was barely more restrained. Goldwater criticized Arthur Larson's *A Republican Looks at His Party* as "an unqualified repudiation of the principle of limited government," no less than the ideas outlined by Dean Acheson, Truman's secretary of state, in a counterpart volume about the Democratic agenda.[67] Condemning excessively high levels of taxation and, yet more so, spending, Goldwater noted that "federal spending has greatly *increased* during the Republican years" (while acknowledging that the Democrats advocated more spending), so that "far from arresting federal spending and the trend toward Statism we Republicans have kept the trend moving forward."[68] He was no less critical of Eisenhower's record in foreign policy and of Cold War bipartisanship; containment's acceptance of global coexistence with the Soviet Union was dangerously defeatist, Goldwater argued.[69]

In making the case that the Republican Party should take a more conservative turn, Goldwater passionately deployed the paradigm that Eisenhower Republicanism offered little that was different from mainstream Democrats. He added the electoral claim that Republicans could expect defeat if following such a path, but that they could unlock new support by offering a conservative alternative to New Deal liberalism and Cold War internationalism. At the end of the Eisenhower years, Goldwater's stress was not so much on the expectation that the articulation of clearer-cut difference with Democrats would activate a currently latent vote for conservatism. Instead he emphasized that me-too Republican candidates, whose alternative to the Democratic agenda was insufficiently distinctive, failed to energize activists. Seeking to explain the history of Republican electoral failure in correspondence with Jacob Javits, he wrote, "the Republican workers would not buy their philosophy, and they didn't work and we did not win."[70] Goldwater, furthermore, responded to the 1960 elections by reigniting the claim that "pressure groups"—especially labor unions—were dominant in politics in a way that marginalized the needs of "the silent Americans, who . . . cannot find voice against the mammoth organizations which mercilessly pressure their own membership, the Congress, and society as a whole for objectives which these silent ones do not want." Within this framework, Goldwater detected opportunity for his party, thus adding, "The Republican party in this era in which so many pressure groups are seeking to dominate the total man is the vehicle and the voice for the dragooned and ignored individual, the forgotten American."[71]

Disappointment among Republicans in the Eisenhower agenda was not confined to the conservative wing. According to Emmet John Hughes, who had worked for Eisenhower as a speechwriter and who later acted as an adviser to Nelson Rockefeller, the president "set forth to remake the blurred image of the Republican party, but he merely ended by suffering himself to be remade in *its* image."[72] In 1960, challenging Nixon for the Republican nomination, Rockefeller not only spoke of a need to tackle society's problems and to promote economic dynamism more proactively, but also faulted the administration for investing inadequately in the nation's defenses, and for thus allowing the Soviet Union to develop an advantage in the Cold War. In this sense, viewing Eisenhower from the party's moderate wing, he shared something with Goldwater.[73] Many liberals, too, argued that under Eisenhower the United States was falling behind the Soviet Union, a theme that John F. Kennedy deployed on the campaign trail in 1960, especially in arguing that a "missile gap" existed.[74]

On the campaign trail against Kennedy in the fall of 1960, Nixon emphasized moderation in a way that fostered the perception that consensus, not conflict, characterized interparty competition at least at the national level.[75] (For columnist Joseph Alsop, Nixon's campaign was vague and even rather content-free: "a steady diet of pap and soothing syrup.")[76] Nixon's defeat then exacerbated factional tension. On the one side, William Rusher characterized his campaign as "stupid" for competing with Kennedy on programmatic activism, but also for inadequate toughness on the Soviet Union.[77] On the other, Senator Clifford Case of New Jersey read the results as supporting the argument that the party should take a moderate, centrist path. "I am sure you will not be surprised to hear me say," Case told the National Press Club at the end of 1960, "that we should not follow the advice of those who would have us turn our faces resolutely against what they term 'me-tooism,' raise the laissez-faire banner of Hayek and Von Mises and, eschewing our mistakes of the past, proclaim our allegiance to the Constitution according to its most literal exponents. To do this would make no sense in terms of the needs of America and the world. And it makes no sense politically."[78] Especially as the former argument gained strength within the party, it is little surprise that Eisenhower concluded that his project to connect the Republican Party with consensus-oriented politics had failed. In early 1964 he observed that the party "has been slow—and possibly too complacent—to recognize the value of and the need for adopting a doctrine of the center." He added that the failure to mobilize enough Republicans in support of his "middle way" vision was "[o]ne of the great disappointments of my eight years following 1953."[79]

While Eisenhower's leadership of the Republican Party helped to trigger an intraparty backlash that attacked consensus politics, and which would play an important role in the decline of the liberal consensus, other measures of his record suggest a more positive picture. Most historians have evaluated his administration's achievements more favorably than contemporaries did, in both domestic and foreign policy. Moreover, studies of public opinion toward the parties during this period suggested that the popular image of the Republican Party underwent a positive transition. No longer was the Republican Party seen as a threat to the achievements of the New Deal, a damaging association that had helped to explain the party's minority status. But the change in image was incomplete. Most Americans still saw Republicans as representing the party of socioeconomic privilege, whereas the Democrats were the party of the people.[80] Because the perception existed that the party catered "mostly for the rich and privileged and for big business," pollster Claude Robinson told the Republican National Committee in 1959, "The Republican Party . . . has the very important problem of getting rid of its class symbol and establishing its identity with the interests of a larger mass."[81] The persistence of this adverse association was a failure for Eisenhower's vision for a party that promoted the national interest by practicing a consensus-oriented politics, presented as a challenge to the Democrats' focus on special interests.

Despite its shortcomings in practice, under Eisenhower the Republican Party nevertheless pursued a consensus-minded outlook on politics, an outlook that critically shaped the emergence in the United States of what Godfrey Hodgson, writing in 1976, labeled "the ideology of the liberal consensus"—which was, indeed, not so liberal, but instead represented a "strange hybrid, liberal conservatism."[82] How Republicans responded to the period's key challenge—the outbreak of the Cold War—was a leading factor in this development, involving not only the specific goal of bipartisanship but also a larger concern that the United States should display unity behind national values at a time of superpower tension. So, too, were the dynamics of electoral politics. To suggest that a quest for consensus persuasively characterizes the Eisenhower agenda is not to argue that there was an absence of conflict about these goals. Indeed, Eisenhower's pursuit of a more tranquil politics inspired deep controversy, controversy that would lead the Republican Party to embrace an anti–liberal consensus vision during the 1960s.

Notes

1. "Text of General Eisenhower's Address before Bar Association," *New York Times*, September 6, 1949, 17.

2. See, e.g., Ann Whitman, diary entry, February 5, 1955, "ACW Diary February 1955 (5)," box 4, Ann Whitman Diary Series, Dwight D. Eisenhower Papers as President, Eisenhower Presidential Library, Abilene, Kansas; Dwight D. Eisenhower, diary entry, June 22, 1959, "[ACW] Diary June 1959 (1)," box 10, Ann Whitman Diary Series.

3. Robert Griffith, "Dwight D. Eisenhower and the Corporate Commonwealth," *American Historical Review* 87 (1982): 87–122.

4. "Eisenhower Sees Peril to Freedom," *New York Times*, February 13, 1949, 62.

5. "Gen. Eisenhower's Address at Columbia," *New York Times*, June 2, 1949, 24.

6. "Text of Eisenhower's Speech Pledging His Regime's Support to Keep Our Basic Freedom," *New York Times*, October 13, 1948, 21.

7. Ibid.

8. "Eisenhower Urges Parley on Welfare," *New York Times*, October 25, 1949, 1, 24 (quotation on 24).

9. Griffith, "Eisenhower and the Corporate Commonwealth," 88.

10. Wendy L. Wall, *Inventing the "American Way": The Politics of Consensus from the New Deal to the Civil Rights Movement* (New York: Oxford University Press, 2007).

11. Michael Bowen, *The Roots of Modern Conservatism: Dewey, Taft, and the Battle for*

the Soul of the Republican Party (Chapel Hill: University of North Carolina Press, 2011), 2, 75, 92.

12. Louis Galambos, ed., *The Papers of Dwight David Eisenhower*, vol. 10, *Columbia University* (Baltimore: Johns Hopkins University Press, 1984), 757.

13. Other examples around this time include Clare Boothe Luce and Thomas Dewey, leading toward the coalescing of an initially elite-driven movement to draft Eisenhower as a candidate for the Republican nomination. Robert H. Ferrell, ed., *The Eisenhower Diaries* (New York: Norton, 1981), 161–66.

14. The theme was at the heart of Dewey's campaign against Truman in 1948. Because of its failure, Dewey's focus on unity created a discouraging parallel; his Republican critics accused him of a content-free campaign that failed to mount an effective attack on Truman and liberalism. Confident of victory, Dewey did not want to alienate swing voters. Richard Norton Smith, *Thomas E. Dewey and His Times* (New York: Simon and Schuster, 1982), 516.

15. Robert Mason, *The Republican Party and American Politics from Hoover to Reagan* (New York: Cambridge University Press, 2012), 49–52. Historians have often overlooked the significance of the "bought vote" thesis among Republicans at a formative moment in the development of the Democrats' Roosevelt coalition, but the concept is much better remembered through the reported observation of Harry Hopkins, speaking in 1938, that the New Deal's success at the polls could be explained in these terms: "We shall tax and tax, spend and spend, and elect and elect." Jason Scott Smith, *Building New Deal Liberalism: The Political Economy of Public Works, 1933–1956* (New York: Cambridge University Press, 2005), 175.

16. Austin V. Wood, speech, August 14, 1948, folder 10, box 78, series 5, Thomas E. Dewey Papers, University of Rochester Library, Rochester, New York.

17. *The Chairman's Letter*, February 1949, "'The Chairman's Letter'—HS as Chairman of Repub. Natl. Comm.," box 6, Hugh Scott Papers, Albert and Shirley Small Special Collections Library, University of Virginia, Charlottesville.

18. Minutes, Meeting of Representatives of the Republican State Central Committees, March 13, 1949, "Minutes of Meeting of Representatives of Republican Central Committees: Chicago, Illinois," box 7, Scott Papers.

19. Robert A. Taft, speech, October 11, 1948, "Republican National Committee News," box 10, additional (10200-ab), Scott Papers.

20. Hugh Scott, report, August 4, 1949, "Printed Material re Republican National Committee," box 5, Scott Papers.

21. At the culmination of the 1946 midterm campaigns, Robert Taft noted, e.g., his emphasis "that the legislative program of the [Democratic] Party is dominated by the PAC with a program for complete regulation of the lives of all American citizens." Taft to J. D. Fisher, November 4, 1946, "Political—Republicans 1946," box 879, Robert A. Taft Papers, Manuscript Division, Library of Congress, Washington, DC.

22. The Psychological Corporation, "The Public's Attitudes toward Industrial and Political Issues in an Election Year," folder 5, box 39, series 2, Dewey Papers; Mason, *Republican Party*, 116.

23. Jacob K. Javits, "Modernizing the Republican Party," *New York Herald Tribune* reprint, June 28, 1951, "Newsclippings," box 7, Scott Papers.

24. Spangler to Robert A. Taft, January 10, 1950, "Republican Principles—1950," box 787, R. A. Taft Papers.

25. Bowen, *Roots of Modern Conservatism*; Barbara Sinclair, *Congressional Realignment, 1925–1978* (Austin: University of Texas Press, 1982), 37–72.

26. *The Chairman's Newsletter*, June 1, 1945, "Republican National Committee 1945–46," box 785, R. A. Taft Papers.

27. Scott to Earl Keisker, July 21, 1949, "Republican National Committee Correspondence," box 10, additional (10200-ab), Scott Papers.

28. See, e.g., transcript of Republican National Committee meeting, January 26, 1949, "Transcript of Luncheon Session of Republican National Committee, Omaha, Nebraska," box 6, Scott Papers; minutes, Republican Strategy Committee, December 13, 1949, in Paul L. Kesaris, ed., *Papers of the Republican Party*, part I: *Meetings of the Republican National Committee, 1911–1980* (Frederick, MD: University Publications of America, 1986), series A, reel 9; transcript, RNC Policy Committee, January 18, 1949, ibid.

29. Dewey to Landon, December 29, 1949, folder 3, box 24, series 10, Dewey Papers.

30. Dewey to E. G. Bennett, January 7, 1950, folder 3, box 4, series 10, Dewey Papers.

31. Nixon to Claude Robinson, April 9, 1960, "Robinson, Claude 1960 (3 of 3)," box 647, series 320, Richard Nixon Pre-Presidential Materials (Laguna Niguel), Richard Nixon Presidential Library, Yorba Linda, California.

32. John Foster Dulles, "National Unity in Foreign Policy," *Proceedings (American Bar Association, Section of International and Comparative Law)*, September 16–17, 1952, 24–28 (quotations on 24, 25).

33. William B. Pickett, *Eisenhower Decides to Run: Presidential Politics and Cold War Strategy* (Chicago: Dee, 2000), 51, 119, 210–11.

34. Mason, *Republican Party*, 151–52; Gary W. Reichard, *The Reaffirmation of Republicanism: Eisenhower and the Eighty-Third Congress* (Knoxville: University of Tennessee Press, 1975), 14–50, 69–96; Godfrey Hodgson, *America in Our Time: From World War II to Nixon—What Happened and Why* (Garden City, NY: Doubleday, 1976), 67, 71–72.

35. Dwight D. Eisenhower, "Radio Address to the American People on the National Security and Its Costs," May 19, 1953, *American Presidency Project*, http://www.presidency.ucsb.edu/ws/index.php?pid=9854 (accessed July 21, 2015); Robert R. Bowie and Richard H. Immerman, *Waging Peace: How Eisenhower Shaped an Enduring Cold War Strategy* (New York: Oxford University Press, 1998) 153.

36. Louis Galambos and Daun van Ee, eds., *The Papers of Dwight David Eisenhower*, vol. 18, *The Presidency: Keeping the Peace* (Baltimore: Johns Hopkins University Press, 2001), 514.

37. Thomas L. Stokes, "Democratic Tide—and Eisenhower Tide," *New York Times* magazine, May 15, 1955, 42.

38. "President Eisenhower's Administration Is Marked by a Middle-of-the-Road Policy," *New York Times*, August 23, 1956, 13; W. H. Lawrence, "President Calls Vote a Mandate for His Program," *New York Times*, November 15, 1956, 1, 26.

39. Eisenhower to Bob Woodruff, November 25, 1958, "DDE Dictation—Nov. 1958," box 37, DDE Diary Series, Dwight D. Eisenhower Papers as President [hereafter DDEDS], Eisenhower Presidential Library, Abilene, Kansas.

40. "Republican Party Platform of 1956," August 20, 1956, *American Presidency Project*, http://www.presidency.ucsb.edu/ws/?pid=25838 (accessed July 17, 2015).

41. Eisenhower to Bradford G. Chynoweth, July 20, 1954, "DDE Personal Diary Jan.–Nov. 1954," box 4, DDEDS.

42. Dwight D. Eisenhower to Edgar Eisenhower, November 8, 1954, "DDE Diary—November 1954 (2)," box 8, DDEDS.

43. Memo, Eisenhower to Hobby, July 30, 1953, "C. Preliminary Development," volume 41, series O, RG 4, Rockefeller Family Archives, Rockefeller Archive Center, Sleepy Hollow, New York.

44. Mason, *Republican Party*, 156–57; Roger Biles, *The Fate of Cities: Urban America and the Federal Government, 1945–2000* (Lawrence: University Press of Kansas, 2011), 47–81.

45. Iwan W. Morgan, *Eisenhower versus "the Spenders": The Eisenhower Administration, the Democrats, and the Budget, 1953–60* (London: Pinter, 1990).

46. Timothy N. Thurber, *Republicans and Race: The GOP's Frayed Relationship with African Americans, 1945–1974* (Lawrence: University Press of Kansas, 2013), 34–118 (quotation on 90).

47. Quoted in Steven Wagner, *Eisenhower Republicanism: Pursuing the Middle* Way (DeKalb: Northern Illinois University Press, 2006), 28.

48. Griffith, "Eisenhower and the Corporate Commonwealth," 109.

49. Mason, *Republican Party*, 164–165, 168–169.

50. Walter N. Thayer to Richard Nixon, December 27, 1960, enclosing letter to Thayer of December 19, "Nixon, Richard," box 7, Political Files, Walter N. Thayer, III Papers, Herbert Hoover Presidential Library, West Branch, Iowa.

51. Wagner, *Eisenhower Republicanism*, 27–42.

52. Elizabeth Tandy Shermer, "Origins of the Conservative Ascendancy: Barry Goldwater's Early Senate Career and the De-legitimization of Organized Labor," *Journal of American History* 95 (2008): 678–709.

53. Kim Phillips-Fein, "'If Business and the Country Will Be Run Right:' The Business Challenge to the Liberal Consensus, 1945–1964," *International Labor and Working-Class History* 72 (2007): 192–215 (quotation on 197).

54. Dwight D. Eisenhower to Milton S. Eisenhower, October 7, 1956, "Oct. '56 Miscellaneous (5)," box 18, DDEDS.

55. Eisenhower to Rockefeller, May 5, 1960, box 49, DDEDS.

56. Eisenhower to Clifford Roberts, December 7, 1954, box 27, Name Series, Dwight D. Eisenhower Papers as President, Eisenhower Presidential Library, Abilene, Kansas.

57. Herbert McClosky, Paul J. Hoffman, and Rosemary O'Hara, "Issue Conflict and Consensus among Party Leaders and Followers," *American Political Science Review* 54 (1960): 406–27 (quotation on 422).

58. Arthur Larson, *Eisenhower: The President Nobody Knew* (New York: Scribner, 1968), 45–46.

59. Quoted in David L. Stebenne, *Modern Republican: Arthur Larson and the Eisenhower Years* (Bloomington: Indiana University Press, 2006), 159, 161.

60. Griffith, "Eisenhower and the Corporate Commonwealth," 92–93, 110.

61. Robert Mason, "Citizens for Eisenhower and the Republican Party, 1951–1965," *Historical Journal* 56 (2013): 513–36.

62. Mary C. Brennan, *Turning Right in the Sixties: The Conservative Capture of the GOP* (Chapel Hill: University of North Carolina Press, 1995); Rick Perlstein, *Before the Storm: Barry Goldwater and the Unmaking of the American Consensus* (New York: Hill and Wang, 2001).

63. Rusher to Buckley, March 9, 1972, box 121, William A. Rusher Papers, Manuscript Division, Library of Congress, Washington, DC.

64. William F. Buckley Jr., "The Tranquil World of Dwight D. Eisenhower," *National Review*, January 18, 1956, 57–59 (quotations on 59).

65. Mrs. Joseph D. Kennedy to Charles P. Taft, July 23, 1959, "Case, Clifford," box 199, series I, Charles P. Taft Papers, Manuscript Division, Library of Congress, Washington, DC.

66. Quoted in Perlstein, *Before the Storm*, 33.

67. Dean Acheson, *A Democrat Looks at His Party* (New York: Harper, 1955); Barry M. Goldwater, *The Conscience of a Conservative* (1960; Princeton: Princeton University Press, 2007), 7.

68. Goldwater, *Conscience of a Conservative*, 58–59, 60.

69. Ibid., 81–120.

70. Goldwater to Javits, May 25, 1960, "Barry Goldwater 1960," box 9, subseries 2, series 5, Jacob K. Javits Collection, Special Collections, Stony Brook University Libraries, Stony Brook, New York.

71. Barry Goldwater, "The Forgotten American Part I," *Human Events*, January 27, 1961, sec. 2a, 57.

72. Emmet John Hughes, *The Ordeal of Power: A Political Memoir of the Eisenhower Years* (New York: Atheneum, 1963), 330.

73. Richard Norton Smith, *On His Own Terms: A Life of Nelson Rockefeller* (New York: Random House, 2014), 256–61.

74. James A. Nuechterlein, "Arthur M. Schlesinger, Jr., and the Discontents of Postwar American Liberalism," *Review of Politics* 39 (1977): 3–40, esp. 13.

75. Pollster Claude Robinson, who advised Nixon, was critical of the "middle way" concept, undertaking a pilot study to dissuade Nixon from emulating Eisenhower's rhetoric in this way: "Personally, I boggle at the phrase 'middle-of-the-road.' To many people it means 'fence straddling,' 'neither fish nor fowl,' 'no philosophy,' etc." Robinson to Nixon, May 3, 1960, "Robinson, Claude 1960 (3 of 3)," box 647, series 320, Nixon Pre-Presidential Materials.

76. Alsop to Paul Miller, October 6, 1960, "General Correspondence Joseph W. Alsop Sep–Oct 1960," box 16, series I, Joseph Alsop and Stewart Alsop Papers, Manuscript Division, Library of Congress, Washington, DC.

77. William A. Rusher to Christopher T. Bayley, November 21, 1960, folder 9, box 10, Rusher Papers.

78. Clifford P. Case, "The Future of the Republican Party," December 16, 1960, "Progressive Republicans 1960," box 36, subseries 2, series 5, Javits Collection.

79. Eisenhower to Walter N. Thayer, January 23, 1964, "Eisenhower, Dwight D. 1964," box 2, Political Files, Thayer Papers.

80. Angus Campbell, Philip E. Converse, Warren E. Miller, and Donald E. Stokes, *The American Voter* (New York: Wiley, 1960), 47.

81. Claude Robinson, "What Ails the GOP?" presented to Republican National Committee, January 22, 1959, "Robinson, Claude 1960 (1 of 3)," box 647, series 320, Nixon Pre-Presidential Materials.

82. Hodgson, *America in Our Time*, 73.

11

"We Have Run Out of Poor People"

The Democratic Party's Crisis of Identity in the 1950s

JONATHAN BELL

In September 1957, as former senator Bill Benton was considering a return to the Senate from his home state of Connecticut, he received some campaign advice from friend and former congresswoman Chase Going Woodhouse. "The Democrats need a new line," she wrote. "As somebody said we have run out of poor people. The Republicans have taken over our entire social security etc. program. . . . At three meetings I have tried out the idea of 'conformity,' of the need for angry young men such as were around Roosevelt, of individual freedom to speak and think etc and we reminded the audience that you were the only one with the courage to fight McCarthy at the height of his power. The response has been good. The changes in American life towards conformity and 'tranquillizers' . . . has troubled people."[1] The theme of how to adapt New Deal liberalism to the context of economic prosperity and the realities of the Cold War was also at the heart of Arthur Schlesinger Jr.'s 1956 article "The Future of Liberalism: The Challenge of Abundance," which set out his vision of how the heirs to FDR's legacy might recast their program for that year's presidential campaign. Schlesinger argued that what he termed "qualitative liberalism" concerning health, education, civil rights, and urban planning would replace the "quantitative liberalism" of the New Deal. "The issues of 1956 are no longer the issues of 1933," he wrote, "the issues that made the difference between starvation and survival." To Schlesinger, the burning question of the day was what he termed "the quality of civilization to which our nation aspires in an age of ever-increasing abundance and leisure."[2] Leaving aside the fact that these were in many respects rather crude interpretations of the

New Deal and its political legacy, it was clear to these liberal observers that Eisenhower's crushing victory in the election of 1952 and his adoption of what he called a "middle way" politics that accepted elements of New Deal statecraft while rejecting a planned economy had forced New Dealers to think afresh about what constituted the contours of the political spectrum.[3]

To Godfrey Hodgson, the author of the term that gave this volume its starting point, these examples of liberal soul-searching for a political purpose were symptomatic of a wider trend in American political life. The triumph of American capitalism after World War II and the political power of anticommunism in American life constrained the boundaries of political debate and limited the capacity of liberals in politics and the labor movement to expand the New Deal. Intellectual debate became obsessed by the possibility of nuclear annihilation and yet beguiled by what was termed in the Rockefeller study *Prospect for America* in the late 1950s "the inherent dynamism in our free enterprise economy." This study, heavily borrowed from by the Eisenhower administration in its official report on national goals in 1960, was the product of a bipartisan team of avid New Dealers like Chester Bowles and Adolfe Berle and pillars of the Republican establishment like Henry Luce and Henry Kissinger.[4] Few could be found who advocated economic policy experimentation practiced in the 1930s, and yet equally few in political life by the late 1950s denied the absolute importance of national defense and the Cold War as the dominant reality in shaping not just foreign policy but American governance in its totality. In replying to Woodhouse's stirring words of advice, which had concluded by warning against "too much emphasis on our responsibility in foreign affairs," Benton noted that "the launching of the Russian satellite certainly dramatizes mistakes the Republican administration have [*sic*] been making in cutting back on our defense budget."[5] In the context of an international arms race and a political culture in the United States unwilling to countenance the kind of state management of economic growth and public welfare practiced in other industrialized countries, Hodgson saw "an age of consensus. Whether you look at the writings of intellectuals or at the positions taken by practising politicians or at the data on public opinion, it is impossible not to be struck by the degree to which the majority of Americans in those years accepted the same system of assumptions."[6] Politicians with different political monikers or party labels represented different interests—labor or management, say—but did not differ markedly in their overall worldview, which placed the fundamental strength of American capitalism and its superiority over Soviet communism at its heart.[7]

Yet we know that more recent scholarship has altered our angle of vision when considering the political history of the postwar era. Looking back from a neoliberal triumph of the post-Reagan period characterized by the collapse of organized labor, the decimation of the New Deal regulatory and welfare systems, and grassroots Religious Right organizing, historians have increasingly seen the 1950s as bearing the roots of a "rightward bound" America that emphasized deep conflict over fundamental questions of political economy and social structure.[8] Histories of business politics have lent new credence to General Electric's public-relations guru Lemuel Boulware's frank comment to Raymond Moley in a letter of April 1960 that "the major labor problem of this country is not with the few bad union officials but with the many so-called 'good' ones."[9] To those entrepreneurs and economic boosters determined to extend corporate power and to attract inward investment to the growing Sunbelt region, there could be no accommodation with the kind of labor-management pact that had defined the New Deal order. The political tussles over supposed labor union racketeering and right-to-work laws in the 1950s represented more than just a sideshow that masked a deeper agreement over the legacy of 1930s labor laws. The decade saw the start of an all-out assault on the New Deal in which the very legitimacy of collective bargaining as a tool of economic management was at stake.

Historians working from a post–civil rights movement vantage point have also increasingly called into question the usefulness of "consensus" as a tool for understanding the postwar era, even from the perspective of elite politics. Informed by a scholarly awareness of the need to take apart and question the underlying assumptions of political debate, evaluating the language and rhetoric of political actors through a clearly defined analytical lens rather than presenting them on their own terms, a new scholarship has uncovered the ways in which consensus politics has been an ideological tool to hide or control deep-rooted gender, racial, and class divisions in American life. Margot Canaday has outlined the ways in which a "straight state" developed in the wake of the New Deal to regulate and control gender dissent. David Johnson highlighted this theme in his in-depth study of the federal government's crackdown on "sex perversion" in the early Cold War. Most recently, Marc Stein has uncovered the ways in which U.S. Supreme Court decisions since the early rights revolution have been constrained within specific notions of gender hierarchy.[10] To these historians, "consensus" is not arrived at by reasoned debate nor by political triumph of one party or group over another, but rather by a policy and legal agenda of coercion and regulation that defines who is included and who excluded from the confines of state patronage and acceptance. In this reading, the postwar period was one of a brutal crackdown on social difference in which every word of political debate of the kind documented by Hodgson hid entire categories of people who existed but who were not included in the benign embrace of a land of plenty but policed, surveilled, regulated, and sometimes imprisoned. Private capitalists and New Deal liberals alike had the regulatory power to offer or withhold patronage. It may have been true that the Eisenhower administration "accepted that the federal government must continue social security and other such New Deal programs" and "was ready to enforce due compliance with the law in civil rights, though reluctantly and with caution," but the very definitions of who lay within the confines of economic and civil rights citizenship were deeply contested, and any consensus on this point was achieved by airbrushing entire categories of people from the official record.[11] Reading American history—of any period—through an interpretive framework of consensus can only be achieved by an unabashed reproduction of the language of elite straight white men, who predominate in Hodgson's chapter on "the liberal consensus."

An investigation of electoral politics that bridges Democratic Party strategizing and grassroots activism reveals the ways in which liberal ideology and political strategy were evolving in this crucial decade of the 1950s. While I accept that consensus politics was a useful shorthand for the suppression of dissent, I also seek to understand how the language of liberal politics was making the transition from a New Deal politics of economic recovery and stability to a rights liberalism that came to serve as a vehicle for translating the civil rights movement into national policy. So my analysis of Democrats—by which I mean heirs to the New Deal in the North and West, using examples from my extensive research on California in these years—constructs a picture of liberal ideas at a crossroads between New Deal economic equality, which excluded and controlled, and civil rights equality, which was forced to question and reevaluate those notions of inclusion and exclusion.[12] The dilemmas of modern liberalism, responsive to sexual, racial, and social difference but also constrained by a limited political lexicon, can be traced back to this crucial period. Bitter electoral battles over the rights of labor and the role of a welfare state acted also as the beginnings of a link for liberals between economic rights and social equality. This link remained tentative and often coded in language that would resonate in a particular time and place, and we need to be careful not to extrapolate too much out of political rhetoric or electoral politics very much designed to win elections, not to act as a carefully scripted harbinger of future social change. But to take Democratic electoral politics of the 1950s seriously is to move beyond an impressionistic portrayal of 1950s politics as a preoccupation of elite actors conjoined in a consensual embrace over fundamental questions of the day in favor of a more complex story of how political ideas played out when paraded on a rapidly changing American electoral landscape.

Adlai Stevenson and the California Democratic Party

"I'm in mourning for the brains of the American people," wrote Los Angeles resident Eleanor St. Germain to Adlai Stevenson in the wake of his electoral defeat to Dwight Eisenhower in November 1952. "Because, if they're not dead, where are they?"[13] St. Germain was one of thousands of Californians who wrote to Stevenson during and after his campaign, excited at his candidacy and mobilized to support him. California's unique political context made the Golden State peculiarly receptive to his candidacy. There was no organized party structure, but rather a loose collection of political alliances based around individual officeholders and local leaders. "There is no cohesion within the [Democratic] party; there is, in fact, no party in the real sense," wrote one observer of the California political scene in 1950. "What the party consists of is a loose business alliance between various clots of opportunists who congeal about local 'strongmen.' . . . If there were a strong self-conscious liberalism here there would sooner or later grow up a liberal aggressive Democratic Party."[14] The California Republican Party dominated state politics, controlling almost all state offices in the early 1950s with the exception of attorney general. All but three newspapers supported the GOP. Organized labor often supported Republican candidates in order to gain patronage and favors in Sacramento.[15]

Without strong central direction, state politics provided a home for extremists on both sides of the political spectrum, and Democratic politics was a breeding ground for a popular front that survived the early Cold War and provided a sense of purpose for Californians actively engaged with issues of the day but frustrated by the inability of the state's political system to provide an outlet for a strong liberal program. Looking back on the 1950s, a decade that witnessed the growth of a vibrant Democratic organization in California out of the Stevenson campaign, Berkeley professor Paul Seabury reflected that continuous "defeat in state and local politics in the past made difficult the growth of responsible state-wide party organization; but it made it possible for the newly emergent Democratic organization in the state to be far more responsive to forces of 'modernity' within the party." He noted that "by and large it is something new in American politics, a broad movement of well-educated liberals whose political cohesiveness derives not from ethnic, or narrowly-based economic interest, but from a deep 'concern' with political issues transcending the 'self-interest' of the movement itself."[16] Many of those who came to form the backbone of a rejuvenated Democratic Party in California in the 1950s cut their teeth on the 1952 Stevenson campaign: Stevenson was to them in part a politician who had actively opposed McCarthyism (a sore point in a state that had seen bitter anticommunist campaigns, notably in the Senate race of 1950 between Richard Nixon and Helen Douglas) and in part a blank canvas onto which they could project their search for political meaning and belonging.

The Stevenson campaign in California sparked a network of "Stevenson for President" clubs independent of the official party organization; these would form the foundations of the new California Democratic Council in 1953. The growing movement for Stevenson during the early and mid-1950s was part of a rethinking of liberal politics for an age of prosperity. It also represented an attempt to import a New Deal electoral politics to a state that had voted for FDR but had never established his party as a dominant force. A summary of issues for the campaign by Los Angeles party operatives in October raised the question of Social Security as a New Deal triumph that could help bring Roosevelt's electoral magic to the West Coast of the 1950s. The report noted that Los Angeles County had more residents over the age of sixty-five than any other county in the country and that what was termed a "liberal view on old age and disability allotments [is] helpful for Southern California discussion." In Richmond, a naval city in the East Bay near San Francisco, the major issues were "reactivation of the shipyards, need for industrial water, Taft-Hartley, FEPC, Social Security, other progressive measures."[17] A significant addition to the roster of liberal concerns, one destined to reshape the American political world beyond recognition in future years, was the question of civil rights, a theme that came up repeatedly in dispatches to Stevenson party headquarters. Segregation in public housing in the Bay Area and Los Angeles and the lack of a state Fair Employment Practices law were underlined as key issues, ones Stevenson was encouraged to highlight in campaign visits.[18]

The stars began to align in California for Democrats in 1952 when organized labor in the state signaled its frustration with the GOP establishment and its growing willingness to risk the ire of Republican-controlled government by backing Democratic candidates. Smarting from a GOP gerrymander of the reapportionment of legislative seats in Sacramento that handed new districts to anti-labor right-wingers, William McSorley of the AFL's National Labor League for Political Education told delegates at the August 1952 Santa Barbara convention of the California branch that "this year of 1952 is indeed the most crucial year in the history of the American labor movement." He bitterly attacked the Republican-Dixiecrat coalition in Congress "that has served only one purpose: to delay, to disrupt and to destroy every single liberal, forward piece of legislation that has been brought up." He urged union members to "work politically to destroy reaction, to retire the peddlers of reaction from the halls of the United States Congress and the State Legislatures."[19] He was speaking to a receptive audience: member after member came to the floor of the pre-primary endorsement convention in San Francisco in April to express dissatisfaction with the California GOP and its links to labor, with one delegate lambasting what he called his union's prior "placation program. If we just don't kick you hard, will you please be kind to us next year?"[20] It would take until the divisive right-to-work campaign of 1958 in California for labor to align itself fully with a rejuvenated Democratic Party, but the process of realignment and the increasing schism between labor-liberalism and the right set the terms for a politics of economic citizenship that was anything but consensual.

The alliance between organized labor and the left-liberal activist cadre emerging in the newly formed California Democratic Council (CDC) in 1953 was in many ways wracked by suspicion and a product of happenstance as much as design. In 1957 George O'Brien of the AFL-CIO declared that "a state of war" existed between activist clubs and labor over the leadership and direction of the Democratic Party, and the coalition of interests that came together to take the governorship and defeat right-to-work in 1958 would prove difficult to maintain over the longer term.[21] But a 1955 analysis of California liberal politics underlined the importance of the political changes taking place: "What has happened is not a mere growth or development of the [Democratic] Party but its complete rebirth. Although the NEW Democratic Party is still young, it has all the potentialities necessary to make it an integrated, coordinated, disciplined and more efficient party than it has been in a generation." The new Democratic club structure established after the Stevenson campaign "made Democrats FEEL like Democrats, just as the addition of party labels made them VOTE like Democrats."[22] By November 1954 some 425 Democratic clubs had been set up across all but six of thirty congressional districts. "Only a forthright challenge of the Republican position all down the line will bring out the masses of voters who have 'had enough,'" wrote Dewey Anderson to CDC chair Alan Cranston in February 1954. The new organization had the task, he argued, of promoting "the welfare of the broadest possible body of our citizens."[23]

Emboldened by their organizational successes, California Democrats were no longer satisfied with the Adlai Stevenson of 1952; four years later they wanted to see in him the embodiment of truly liberal principles. Gerald O'Hara, active in San Francisco party circles, informed the Stevenson campaign headquarters in Chicago in April 1956 about what he was looking for in a Democratic standard-bearer. Stevenson, he wrote, may "in truth be the prophet of a new Democracy of 'moderation and conciliation' but if he is the voters don't understand it and won't buy it. If he is not the apostle of the Democracy that crusades for labor (by which I mean all work for wages), for the small farmer, for the old, the sick, and the jobless, for children, for Negroes, for peace, for the small businessman, for a better life for all Americans (especially the little fellow) without a ceiling . . . and a vigorous, unremitting fighter for the better life—then he is nothing as a Democratic candidate in 1956."[24] The response in San Francisco to a questionnaire sent out to local Democratic campaign outfits asking for the issues at stake to those working on the campaign trail was equally strident: "Governor Stevenson should tour our Howard Street flophouses and point up the human misery—still very real, if not as vivid as it has been. . . . He should visit our Hunter's Point 'temporary' housing where negroes live because they can't get good private housing at rates they can pay. He should dramatize his interest in these problems." In addition to highlighting poverty and the dangers of another economic downturn, especially in agriculture, the report urged the campaign to demonstrate how Stevenson could "consolidate and *advance* the Democratic gains in social and old age security, health preservation (district hospitals etc), health insurance (this need not touch the doctor-patient relationship but can cover all the costly incidentals of catastrophic illness such as hospital, laboratory, drugs, nurses, technical therapies), farm security, housing, SEC."[25] One Stevenson adviser called this emphasis on renewing and advancing the New Deal order "a start . . . toward developing a theme for the Age of Abundance. . . . I would cite health-education-welfare high on the list, with particular emphasis on the old folks."[26]

In California, at least, the notion that the Democrats had "run out of poor people" or that a politics of abundance was somehow incompatible with redistributive politics did not seem to resonate. On the contrary, a California public-relations company report for Stevenson painted a sort of Valley of the Dolls picture of psychiatrist couches, economic and consumer debt pressures, and the woes of working families: "One of the manifestations of the pressure on living standards here is a widespread pattern of two jobs per man in the hope of meeting mortgages and payments. A psychiatrist told us that his patients here show far more than the usual anxiety about earning enough to keep up in the rat race. . . . What this all adds up to is a kind of New Deal package. . . . The bread-and-butter package should appeal to the rapidly growing middle-class suburbs and might include such items and schools, water, taxes, and consumer debt."[27] The added issue in California by 1956 was activist passion over civil rights and desperate concern to get Stevenson energized on the issue. A bread-and-butter package of middle-class welfare and civil rights carried the seeds of a deeper debate yet to fully take flower of how to redefine the New Deal to take in the changing dynamics of social inclusion.

At the same time, anti-labor business interests in California were mounting their own challenge to those in the Republican Party committed to former governor Earl Warren and his allies' accommodation with labor and elements of the New Deal. A powerful group of conservative power brokers, including the Chandler family, owners of the *Los Angeles Times*, and Joe Knowland of the *Oakland Tribune*, forced Governor Goodwin Knight into swapping jobs for the 1958 campaign: Knight would run for William Knowland's Senate seat, and Knowland would run for the governorship. "California is becoming the most important state in the Union," one commentator noted, "and the conservative element is not willing to let it be a liberal state. They couldn't trust Knight to be conservative. Knight has been all things to all men." Another journalist emphasized the wider import of the switch: Knowland had built his case for taking over the governorship on his endorsement of a business-backed right-to-work referendum that would decimate labor's capacity to secure membership through a union shop. Knowland's "gamble on the right-to-work law paid off in consolidating the kingmaker group behind him."[28] One businessman commented that Knight's "complete leftist attitude in endorsing and supporting labor . . . has also severely damaged the Governor. The Governor's repeated statement that he would veto any 'Right-to-Work' legislation is another factor that has lost him Republican support throughout the state."[29] The Knowland challenge for the governorship represented the culmination of a process of business disenchantment with the enduring legacy of New Deal labor policy in California. The Taft-Hartley Act of 1947 had given states the right to repeal union shop provisions in favor of an open shop in which there was no obligation for employees to join a union at all. A decade later, however, only Indiana of the most industrialized states had passed an open-shop law. Many in California and elsewhere feared that open-shop states in the emerging Sunbelt region of the South and Southwest could lure business away.[30] By 1958, therefore, a major political schism was opening up between anti-labor conservatives and labor liberals in California and certain other industrialized states such as Ohio that would test the definitional limits of the word "consensus" in a major way. As labor leader Walter Reuther put it in July 1958, the American labor movement was trying "to bring about a basic realignment so that the two parties really stand for distinct points of view. And I think this is happening very rapidly. More and more the Democratic Party is coming to reflect the kind of programs and policies that the American labor movement can support, while the Republican Party more and more becomes the party of business."[31] Just as importantly, the manner in which the debate over labor was constructed and played out demonstrated ideological fissures in American politics that transcended the immediate questions being debated and set the terms of political divisions that would outlive any so-called Age of Consensus.

The 1958 Campaign and the Battle over Citizenship

It was clear nationally that the stuttering economy would make the 1958 midterms challenging for Eisenhower and the Republican Party. Despite the president's robust participation in the campaign, including in California, he could not prevent a landslide defeat for his party.[32] Yet the elections for governor and senator in the Golden State signaled a more profound political shift than just one of party control. Ideology assumed a far greater role in the dynamics of party politics there than ever before. In California the elections demonstrated unequivocally that the period between the passage of Taft-Hartley and the 1960s represented the inherent inability of business elites, labor, and Democratic liberals to agree on the internal dynamics of welfare capitalism. By the late 1950s this meant more than a disagreement about the scope of New Deal industrial pluralism that masked a wider general agreement about the robustness and promise of American capitalism. There was a genuine and substantive difference between labor-liberalism and right-to-work conservatism that was on one level a simple debate about "who runs America," the anti-labor slogan given rhetorical power by congressional investigations in the late 1950s into union corruption and links to organized crime, but on another level it was a more coded and contested debate over who came under the protective umbrella of state power, and why.

Fundamental to the battle over right-to-work in California was a contest over how citizenship should be defined and categorized. On one side, General Electric's public-relations manager, R. W. Jackson, appealed to a notion of "corporate citizenship" whereby leaders of industry, by virtue of their proven ability to manage the economy, had a duty to take a political stand on questions of economic power. "GE takes no sides in the campaigns of individuals for political office," Jackson declared, "but where vital public issues are involved, affecting the economic welfare of a community and its people, we believe it an essential part of good corporate citizenship to make whatever views we may have known."[33] GE was one of a formidable phalanx of corporate behemoths to come out strongly in favor of California's Proposition 18 to ban the union shop, portraying themselves not simply as guardians of good citizenship against the totalitarian impulses of "labor bosses" but even as embodiments of citizenship, a strategy that recalled the *Connecticut Life Insurance Co. v. Johnson* U.S. Supreme Court judgment of 1938. The case was notable for recently appointed Justice Hugo Black's dissent, in which he questioned the conflation of "person" and corporation in the majority's reading of the due process clause in the Fourteenth Amendment.[34]

In the Knowland gubernatorial campaign of 1958, a campaign totally dominated by the drive to pass the right-to-work referendum, citizenship was defined in universalist terms, eliding racial, class, or gendered distinctions in favor of a portrayal of a population united by a common understanding of freedom and anti-statism. Knowland decried his Democratic opponent's "special promises to special groups. By his promises to the racial minorities of this state he has set them apart as a special interest group seeking special legislation. Minorities should not be segregated but should have their rights protected as citizens of this great country."[35] Similarly, Knowland's anti–union shop stance was described as stemming from his revulsion at apparent union corruption and his desire to give "every worker in California freedom to decide for himself whether to join a union."[36] His opponent was "the captive candidate of the political labor bosses who have accumulated a one and a half million dollar slush fund from their members in an all-out attempt to seize power in California. . . . This is the road away from free enterprise and toward state labor socialist controls."[37] The Republican campaign aligned good citizenship with an undifferentiated individualism given structure by corporate leadership.

The Labor Committee against Prop 18, by contrast, deliberately targeted its media campaign at individual people, taking care to differentiate people's lives and make the argument against right-to-work personal to them. Labor radio spots were scripted to appeal to a variety of demographic groups, including housewives, merchants, workers, and businessmen. The campaign built gendered tropes of male workers and female household managers into a carefully crafted political portrait of a society bound together by higher living standards thanks to collective-bargaining rights. The campaign against right-to-work concerned a housewife's "family and home—her household budget and living standards. A NO vote will protect California's high wages and salaries—keep them going up, ahead of rising living costs."[38] A flyer put together by the San Francisco Local of the Waitresses Union contrasted working Americans in right-to-work states, who "work long hours, six days per week, and for practically no wages at all," with waitresses in California enjoying "the wage of $5.55 for just a three-hour lunch shift, plus meals, uniforms and all other fringe benefits."[39]

A Bay Area TV ad scheduled for Labor Day titled "Every Other House" sought in a similar way to personalize the collective-bargaining issue as a battle between ordinary wage earners and big capital. The ad consisted of "a series of reports and dramatic vignettes by residents (TV performers) of an imaginary block in a typical Bay Area community," and the narrator began his story with the assertion that "labor unions are people—people working together to accomplish desirable goals," before meeting these "residents" and creating a picture of individual union members as component parts of a wider community.[40] A precinct worker's handbook for anti–Prop 18 workers emphasized that "TALK is your most potent weapon in precinct work—plain talk, neighbor-to-neighbor talk. And it's used most effectively in personal visits to the voters at their homes."[41] This attempt to carry a personal appeal to voters was a deliberate attempt to counter the pro-right-to-work campaign's portrayal of unions as criminal outfits divorced from the concerns of working people. The tone and essential message of labor's campaign was specific to the context of the 1950s: labor had collective-bargaining rights, and their removal promised the collapse of the quality of life for which the Golden State had become known.

Though careful to avoid becoming too involved in the labor question, Democratic gubernatorial candidate Pat Brown widened the anti-right-to-work campaign's appeal to the needs and aspirations of individual citizens through the invocation of the protective powers of the state. In a speech titled "Government with a Heart" he argued that "public welfare involves the State's obligations to the aged—to needy children—to babies without homes—to the alcoholic—to wayward youth—to the mentally and physically ill—to crippled children and adults. . . . It is common sense to assist the needy of the state on two bases: Humanitarian considerations, and the ability of the State to pay the bills." In contrast to Brown's articulation of categories of citizens "who need our outstretched hand," and of a government "which respects the dignity of every last citizen in our State, including and down to the humblest and the poorest," the Knowland campaign portrayed "the average citizen as a faceless man" in a desperate attempt to deny the need for state regulation of economic relationships and social policy.[42] The political worldview portrayed here represented a deliberate strategy of associating redistributive liberalism with modernity: this was not now a Depression-era call for help to relieve general economic distress but rather a statement of society's moral obligation to ensure that a wealthy and prosperous nation provided for all its citizens. Like the anti-right-to-work campaign, Brown also spelled out how society was not simply an undifferentiated mass of individuals but a kaleidoscope of different social groups with differing social and economic needs.

The "Government with a Heart" speech—and the Democratic campaign more generally—was replete with cultural assumptions about poverty and exclusion that pathologized the so-called needy and used standard paternalist tropes. And in a sense the 1958 campaign represented the playing out of battles over how best to reconcile labor and management that had defined American domestic politics since the New Deal. Yet California had missed out on the political realignments of the 1930s, and the Democratic bid for power in the late 1950s was taking place at a time when social protections of the New Deal already existed, making the right's concerted effort to repeal them a much more deeply fought struggle than a "consensus" reading of the politics of the era allows, whatever terms of reference we use.

Following the Democratic Party's landslide election victory both in California and across the nation in 1958, including the defeat of ballot initiatives to roll back union rights in both California and Ohio, the *New Republic* provided its readership with a shopping list of legislative tasks for the now overwhelmingly Democratic Congress in Washington. The picture painted of the state of the nation at the end of the 1950s demonstrated clearly how liberals were having to redefine New Deal politics for an age of plenty while also continue to justify the existence of a social safety net. "The Democratic Party identifies itself as the party of the people," the article began. "It therefore behooves the Democratic majority to be *contemporary in its assumptions about who the people are.* Descriptions of the people which were accurate the last time the Democrats had a majority of present proportions are meaningless today, and the importance of working from modern descriptions cannot be overemphasized." This emphasis on modernity sprang from the argument that "lower or upper middle-class families are interested in facilities. Since many of them now have the staple consumer goods, they are more and more aware of the deficit in *community* goods—schools, roads, public services of all sorts."[43] As in the case of organized labor's reliance on general rising living standards as the justification for the union shop, 1950s liberals attempted to universalize the relationship between the individual and the state. No longer was the New Deal a response to the Depression or a safety net for the poor; it was a set of policies and goals to help all citizens navigate the economic travails of everyday life and get access to basic social commodities like education, public power and water, and transport infrastructure. The New Deal of the 1930s had itself possessed universalist policies, such as the Tennessee Valley Authority, but now the message of liberal intellectuals and politicians was that a common conception of economic citizenship backed by state authority was the central plank of their political project.

Two factors made this a deeply contested political worldview. The first, as we have seen, was that business conservatives and their allies were more concerned than ever to redefine citizenship as a private matter not subject to the guiding hand of the state, especially when it came to the economic relationship between labor and capital. The second was that in order to personalize their message about universal rights to access capital and services by means of the harnessing of governmental power, liberals increasingly had to define who needed the help of the state. In so doing, they had to assert that citizens, including those Brown defined as "wayward" and those the *New Republic* termed "contemporary," required access to publicly provided goods. In the words of one aide to Governor Brown in 1960, the administration should recognize "our rights as consumers to employ our government to arrange to scrutinize in our behalf products and services which the prudent consumer cannot feel confident of evaluating himself and to provide needed services that cannot be provided privately."[44] The provision of social services and of protective legislation such as a fair employment practices law gave government the opportunity to act as arbiter of social behavior, something that long predated the 1950s but was given new impetus in late-1950s California by the fact that the liberal victory was seen as new and requiring a fresh set of priorities.

Categories of the needy established earlier in the twentieth century, such as needy children and the elderly, acted in the early Brown administration as policy proving grounds for a political engagement with social diversity. The state's program for needy children, for example, was identified as a mechanism that, with amendment and improvement, could deal with "the entire scope of circumstances and events which subject children to conditions and situations which are inimical to their physical and moral welfare with particular attention being given to preventive activities and to the restoration and strengthening of family integrity and independence."[45] The key policy innovation to achieve this goal was the elimination in 1963 of the requirement that a parent be absent from the home for the child to qualify for benefits, a limited but genuine erosion of the New Deal link between traditional family structure (only widows and the abandoned needed government assistance) and social citizenship.[46]

Tellingly, a state government welfare adviser noted in 1960 that the California Department of Social Welfare had hitherto "been limited . . . by traditional notions concerning welfare which our more liberal legislature and Administration have discarded, thereby freeing the Department to plan in a positive way for the overall welfare of the needy and dependent." This new political climate allowed for a more universalist approach to the maintenance of social welfare of the citizenry. "Today there is a new climate at all levels—legislative, departmental, and executive. The time is opportune for a comprehensive statement embodying an inclusive program and philosophy." The report focused on the elderly, long an acknowledged category of the deserving, but argued that "old age is the great leveller," so an approach that privileged only the needy poor was no longer appropriate in a modern society that associated modernity with prosperity and health. "The health problem of the aged" was in part "an economic problem produced by a coincidence of declining earning power and growing need for increasingly costly drugs, hospitals and physicians," as well as a "medical problem of learning and employing rehabilitative techniques instead of treating the aged as though they were incurable invalids." The report argued that only a policy of state-provided health care for all elderly persons would allow older Americans the quality of life that all citizens deserved in the modern age.[47] Policy formation in the early Brown years acted as a laboratory for the reframing of social assumptions of citizenship well before the explosion of "rights talk" with the civil rights revolutions of the later 1960s.[48]

In this reading, welfare liberalism engaged increasingly with questions of social difference in California in the late 1950s, as politicians, policy advocates, and labor unions attempted to create a message of the state as benevolent overseer of economic justice in order to contest corporate control over economic citizenship. This process was inevitably patchy and full of contradictions. The growth of a complex social-welfare bureaucracy by the early 1960s placed social policy at the heart of the administration but encouraged the greater policing of the needy poor in ways that sat uncomfortably with the state government's stated acceptance of the reality of social diversity. The administration passed a civil rights bill to prohibit discrimination in the provision of goods and services in 1959, together with a Fair Employment Practices Act, but remained stubbornly unwilling to tackle the patent economic and racial injustice inherent in the bracero program of Latino migrant labor. But the 1950s witnessed a serious debate in California liberal discourse, electoral politics, and policy formation over the boundaries of economic and social citizenship that took place exactly at the moment that Republican politics was drifting rapidly rightward toward an association of good citizenship with free labor markets and corporate control over political debate. The explosion of civil rights and the launching of Johnson's Great Society in 1964 would place this political chasm front and center in national political debate and draw a line under Hodgson's era of consensus. But the roots of a bitter conflict between a "corporate citizenship" that effectively dismissed social difference as a factor in organizing or regulating society and a welfare liberalism that viewed the individual through the lens of state-supported rights are clearly located in the post-Taft-Hartley period.[49]

In the final analysis, any notion of consensus in politics can only be perceived from a particular and limited vantage point. It is true that the language of liberalism in most electoral contests or policy formulations of the 1950s was confined within capitalist and anticommunist boundaries that showed the bitter class conflicts of the 1930s to be a distant memory. Yet that decade witnessed in California the emergence of subaltern movements for legal and social rights unimaginable before World War II, including the nascent homophile movement and an increasingly confident array of civil rights movements.[50] Nor was the labor movement an impotent force buffeted by the uncontested march of corporate capitalism. The convoluted story of liberal Democratic politics in the Golden State of the 1950s is one of the elastic ideological possibilities of liberal politics, which set up the terms of the hotly contested battles over social inclusion and individual rights that took off in earnest in the wake of the 1960s.

Notes

1. Woodhouse to Benton, September 30, 1957, folder 5, box 282, William Benton Papers, Special Collections Research Center, University of Chicago Library.

2. Arthur Schlesinger Jr., "The Future of Liberalism: The Challenge of Abundance," *The Reporter*, May 3, 1956, in liberalism/conservatism file, box 7, Edmund G. Brown Papers, Bancroft Library, University of California, Berkeley.

3. The idea of a "middle way" is set out repeatedly in Eisenhower's own diaries. See Robert H. Ferrell, ed., *The Eisenhower Diaries* (New York: Norton, 1997).

4. See Godfrey Hodgson, *America in Our Time* (Garden City, NY: Doubleday, 1976), 69–70.

5. Benton to Woodhouse, October 8, 1957, folder 5, box 282, Benton Papers.

6. Hodgson, *America in Our Time*, 67.

7. Ibid., 72. The idea that the Cold War and an economics of abundance changed the fundamental character of American political discourse is common in historians' treatments of the early Cold War period in particular. See Alan Brinkley, *The End of Reform: New Deal Liberalism in Recession and War* (New York: Knopf, 1995); Jonathan Bell, *The Liberal State on Trial: The Cold War and American Politics in the Truman Years* (New York: Columbia University Press, 2004); Alonzo L. Hamby, *Liberalism and Its Challengers: FDR to Bush* (New York: Oxford University Press, 1992); and Robert Griffith, "Dwight D. Eisenhower and the Corporate Commonwealth," *American Historical Review* 87 (February 1982): 87–122.

8. The term "rightward bound" is the title of an edited collection on the 1970s, but a growing body of scholarship sees the mobilization of antistatist forces much earlier. See Bruce J. Schulman and Julian E. Zelizer, eds., *Rightward Bound: Making America Conservative in the 1970s* (Cambridge: Harvard University Press, 2008); Kimberly Phillips-Fein, *Invisible Hands: The Making of the Conservative Movement from the New Deal to Reagan* (New York: Norton, 2009); Elizabeth Tandy Shermer, "Counter-Organizing the Sunbelt: Right-to-Work Campaigns and Anti-union Conservatism, 1943–1958," *Pacific Historical Review* 78 (February 2009): 81–118; Elizabeth Tandy Shermer, *Sunbelt Capitalism: Phoenix and the Transformation of American Politics* (Philadelphia: University of Pennsylvania Press, 2013); and Kimberly Phillips-Fein and Julian Zelizer, eds., *What's Good for Business: Business and American Politics since World War Two* (Oxford: Oxford University Press, 2012).

9. Boulware to Moley, April 20, 1960, Boulware file, box 6, Raymond Moley Papers, Hoover Institution, Stanford University.

10. Margot Canaday, *The Straight State: Sexuality and Citizenship in Twentieth-Century America* (Princeton: Princeton University Press, 2009); David K. Johnson, *The Lavender Scare: The Cold War Persecution of Gays and Lesbians in the Federal Government* (Chicago:

University of Chicago Press, 2004); Marc Stein, *Sexual Injustice: Supreme Court Decisions from Griswold to Rose* (Chapel Hill: University of North Carolina Press, 2013).

11. Hodgson, *America in Our Time*, 72.

12. See Jonathan Bell, *California Crucible: The Forging of Modern American Liberalism* (Philadelphia: University of Pennsylvania Press, 2012).

13. Eleanor St. Germain to Stevenson, November 5, 1952, folder 5, box 115, Adlai E. Stevenson Papers, Mudd Manuscript Library, Princeton University.

14. Stanley Crook to James Loeb, director of Americans for Democratic Action [ADA], July 31, 1950, section 5, reel 57, ADA Papers, microfilm.

15. See Bell, *California Crucible*, chapter 1.

16. Paul Seabury to Samuel Beer of ADA, [ca. 1959], section 5, reel 57, ADA Papers.

17. Summary of major issues, Los Angeles and Richmond, October 10, 1952, file 5, box 230, Stevenson Papers.

18. Summary of major issues and background, San Francisco and Alameda Counties, September 3, 1952, ibid.

19. Address of William McSorley in Proceedings of the Pre–General Election Convention of the CLLPE, August 27, 1952, pp. 19ff., folder 7, box 7, California LLPE-COPE [CLLPE] Papers, Labor Archives and Research Center, San Francisco State University.

20. Jimmy Waugh speech to CLLPE pre-primary convention, April 7, 1952, p. 116, folder 6, box 7, CLLPE Papers.

21. Roger Kent to George O'Brien, July 30, 1957, Democratic Party Central Committee file, box 10, Alan Cranston Papers, Bancroft Library, University of California, Berkeley.

22. Miriam Deinard Coffey and Rudolph Pacht, "The New California Democratic Party: The Place of the California Democratic Council in the Democratic Party of California," CDC History material file, box 11, Cranston Papers. In 1952, party labels had been placed next to candidates' names on the ballot in California for the first time.

23. Anderson to Cranston, February 4, 1954, Dewey Anderson file, box 10, Cranston Papers.

24. O'Hara to Ken Hechler, April 26, 1956, folder 7, box 248, Stevenson Papers.

25. Reply to "Outline for local material" questionnaire, San Francisco, ibid.

26. Harry Ashmore to Stevenson, May 4, 1956, ibid.

27. Research report by Edward L. Greenfield and Co., "The Stevenson Campaign in California," folder 5, box 299, Stevenson Papers.

28. Memo, Will Davidson to Whitaker and Baxter PR company, November 20, 1957, re KQED program "Governor Knight—Did He Jump or Was He Pushed?" Operation switchover file, box 50, Whitaker & Baxter Campaigns, Inc. Records, California State Archives, Sacramento.

29. L. R. Hart of Sebastopol Fruit Growers Association to T. R. Dwyer, September 16, 1957, Political campaign, October 1957 file, William F. Knowland Papers, Bancroft Library, University of California, Berkeley.

30. Shermer, "Counter-Organizing the Sunbelt"; Melvin Dubofsky, *The State and Labor in Modern America* (Chapel Hill: University of North Carolina Press, 1994).

31. Henry Brandon, "A Conversation with Walter Reuther: How Do We Live with Bigness?" *New Republic*, July 21, 1958, 13–18.

32. The Democrats won a 64–34 margin in the Senate and a 282–154 margin in the

House. See Iwan Morgan, *Eisenhower versus "the Spenders": The Eisenhower Administration, the Democrats and the Budget, 1953–60* (London: Pinter, 1990), 123–26.

33. R. W. Jackson form letter, September 22, 1958, file 11, box 27, David F. Selvin Papers, Labor Archives and Research Center, San Francisco State University.

34. Connecticut General Life Insurance Co. v. Johnson, 303 US 77 (1938).

35. Knowland statement on civil rights, n.d., civil rights file, box 101, Knowland Papers.

36. Knowland speech at Kiwanis Club, September 2, 1958, Kiwanis Club speech file, box 102, Knowland Papers.

37. Knowland speech to Republican Assembly, Stockton, California, October 4, 1958, Stockton speech file, box 102, Knowland Papers.

38. Labor Committee against Prop 18 radio spot script, folder 10, box 27, Selvin Papers.

39. Waitresses Union Local 48 mailshot on right-to-work, Prop 18 file, box 115, Knowland Papers.

40. Dave Selvin memo to George Johnson re Labor Day TV ad, folder 11, box 27, Selvin Papers; script of TV ad, broadcast August 31 and September 1, 1958, KQED San Francisco, folder 10, box 27, Selvin Papers.

41. Precinct worker's handbook, folder 2, box 28, Selvin Papers.

42. Brown speech "Government with a Heart," Government with a Heart file, box 46, Brown Papers.

43. "Work Ahead for Congress," *New Republic*, November 17, 1958, 7ff.

44. Memo from Helen Nelson to Alexander Pope, Governor's Office, consumers file, box 73, Brown Papers.

45. J. M. Wedemeyer, Director of Department of Social Welfare, to Pat Brown, August 30, 1960, social welfare file, box 73, Brown Papers.

46. For an extended treatment of this theme see Jonathan Bell, "Social Democracy and the Rise of the Democratic Party in California, 1950–1964," *Historical Journal* 49 (June 2006): 497–524.

47. Memo from Harry Girvetz to Alexander Pope, Governor's Office, April 20, 1960, social welfare—general file, box 71, Brown Papers.

48. See Mary Ann Glendon, *Rights Talk: The Impoverishment of Political Discourse* (New York: Free Press, 1991).

49. Hodgson himself referred to the political upheavals sparked by the Vietnam War and civil rights movement as the "great schism" that marked the watershed terminating his era of consensus politics. Hodgson, *America in Our Time*, chapters 13 and 14. Yet it is difficult to view California politics of the 1950s, in particular the election of 1958, as a case of "the powerful emotions and interests that always work for conservative policies . . . opposed by a liberalism that was in effect hardly to be distinguished from a more sophisticated and less resolute conservatism" (ibid., 98).

50. See John D'Emilio, *Sexual Politics, Sexual Communities: The Making of a Homosexual Minority in the United States, 1940–1970* (Chicago: University of Chicago Press, 1998); Mark Brilliant, *The Color of America Has Changed: How Racial Diversity Shaped Civil Rights Reform in California, 1941–1978* (New York: Oxford University Press, 2010).

12

Billy Graham's Neo-evangelical Triumph and the Limits of the Liberal Consensus

UTA A. BALBIER

When Billy Graham preached on the steps of the Capitol in Washington, DC, on February 3, 1952, forty thousand people gathered in the drizzling rain to hear him. The center of U.S. political power stood behind Graham's pulpit, and American colors covered the rostrum. The audience included several senators and congressmen, displaying bipartisan support for Graham's cause, as well as military personnel. Curious non-Christian bystanders joined the crowd, as did conservative evangelicals, mainline Protestants, and a few Catholics and Jews. Graham preached two sermons during the one-hour revival meeting in which he called not only for personal conversion but also for an increase in military spending. He prayed for the capitalistic strength of the country and for lost souls. Moreover, in his sermon Graham asked for moral and spiritual regeneration to face the communist threat, which he saw as "a spiritual force [that] cannot be defeated on the field of battle alone."[1]

Graham's so-called crusades in the 1950s shaped and fostered a religiosity that represented the core features of the so-called liberal consensus: they celebrated confidence in the "perfectibility of American society" and simultaneously stirred anticommunist anxieties.[2] Never before had the close relationship between evangelicalism, patriotism, and civil religion been staged so persuasively. The Washington crusade not only highlighted the new political ambitions of neo-evangelicals who emerged as an important phenomenon in post-1945 U.S. Protestantism. The fact that Graham invited Catholics and Jews to attend the meetings also underlined the ecumenical shift that took place in the evangelical milieu and in the U.S. religious landscape more generally. Graham's crusades seemed to prove the core argument of Will Herberg's influential 1955 study *Protestant-Catholic-Jew* true: faith in the American way of life, marked by middle-class affluence and democracy, ruled out traditional religious divisions.[3]

The question of how far U.S. evangelicals embraced the Cold War liberal consensus, and how they participated in shaping it, has recently found interest among theologians, historians, and literary scholars. Jason Stevens shows persuasively how neo-evangelicalism underwent an important transformation during the early Cold War years and became a defining force in the way Americans made sense of the Cold War conflict.[4] This transformation, he argues, lays the foundation for the later rise of the Religious Right. Jonathan Herzog, in his inquiry into what he terms "the spiritual-industrial complex," argues for a close interplay between political and religious elites in fostering an ecumenical Cold War religious revival, in which a Christian consensus was created as a bulwark against the atheistic communist threat.[5] Yet, much more strongly than Stevens, he acknowledges the critics of this civic-engineered Cold War revival.[6] James Hudnut-Beumler, in his defining study of suburban religiosity in the 1950s, argues for a new emerging consensus in the religious landscape of the 1950s but also dedicates an important part of his analysis to these contemporary critics of consensual religiosity.[7]

Although academic works on Billy Graham address the criticism of his revival work, it plays only a minor role in a narrative of tremendous success.[8] The question remains whether Graham's revival meetings, which attracted millions of Americans over the years, were able to shape a unique religious consensus. Or did they, as Graham's critics claimed, reflect only a "myth of consensus" that excluded certain religious groups and even split the Protestant milieu?[9] This chapter argues that these critics' perspective must be considered to fully comprehend the nature of the consensus that emerged in the U.S. religious landscape of the 1950s and its limitations. Graham's critics allow us to see much more clearly the contours of this religious consensus, which developed between the liberal and the conservative, the traditional and the modern, the religious and the secular. It is this new consensus in the religious scene that, as Stevens has argued, created a foundation on which the Religious Right was later able to build.

This chapter uses Graham's religious triumph in the 1950s as a lens through which to explore the formation of this myth of a religious, liberal consensus and its limitations. Both aspects reflect the significant transformation that the U.S. religious landscape underwent in reaction to the perceived communist threat and the rise of consumerism in the early years of the Cold War. The first section shows how Graham incorporated significant aspects of liberal consensus ideology into his message to make it more inclusive and attractive. It investigates his firm stand on U.S. global power, military spending, and consumerism and his strong anticommunism. In this context, his commitment to ecumenicalism can easily be interpreted as Graham's very own liberal theological shift. The second section focuses on the contemporary controversies surrounding the Graham crusades to explore the limits of a consensual approach in the field of religion. In giving Protestant fundamentalists, mainline Protestants, Catholics, and Jews a voice, it explores the limitations of Graham's ecumenical offer and approaches the religious divisions that neither anticommunism nor the shared faith in the American dream could overcome. In many ways, these critics questioned not only the religious core of Graham's mission but also the cultural ramifications of the liberal consensus itself.

Consensual Evangelicalism

Americans attended the Billy Graham crusades in the 1950s in their thousands, a phenomenon that started with the young preacher's first revival meeting of national importance, which took place in Los Angeles in the fall of 1949.[10] From the start, Graham, a twenty-nine-year-old Southern Baptist preacher with a doctorate in anthropology from Wheaton College, began to present his new style of revival culture, which combined biblical quotations with current news headlines and salesman vernacular. Graham's new evangelicalism fused premillennial fears with political concerns reaching from anticommunism to military spending. Building on and departing from his fundamentalist predecessors of the 1910s and 1920s, Graham embraced American consumer culture, modern mass media, and national politics. Together with other influential neo-evangelical thinkers such as Carl F. H. Henry and Harold Ockenga, he discarded one important aspect of neo-evangelicalism's fundamentalist roots: his focus clearly shifted from the otherworldly to a distinct political and cultural involvement in public life. Protestant fundamentalists had always been politically and socially engaged, but never had they so fully and optimistically embraced U.S. secular culture and aimed to participate in political life.[11]

Graham's crusades fulfilled two goals. On the one hand, they shifted neo-evangelicalism into the heart and mainstream of U.S. society. On the other, they provided for a national spiritual renewal. At a time of shared anxiety caused by the experience of war and nuclear destruction as well as the beginning of the Cold War, Graham's revival meetings provided a forum for Americans to celebrate the Christian identity of their country. Dating back to his Los Angeles crusade, Graham established an inclusive rhetoric of national unity at his revival meetings that blurred the lines between anticommunism, civil religion, and evangelicalism. In Grant Wacker's words, Graham gave his audiences "tools to help them see themselves as good Christians, good Americans, and good citizens of the modern world all at the same time."[12]

In a radio interview Graham gave during his 1950 Portland crusade, he explained: "I believe at this very moment, there is a moving across the nation toward religion and back to the faith of our fathers. And I sincerely believe that the only hope of our present day is to reinject into American society the moral stamina which can be brought about by spiritual rearmament."[13] Graham argued that this spiritual rearmament was the only protection against the threat of communism, an ideology that he saw as "a religion that is inspired, directed, and motivated by the Devil himself who has declared war against Almighty God."[14] Against the godless religion of communism, Graham called Americans to return to their faith during his revival meetings, and he did not care what religious faith his followers found. He sent those who made a public commitment to Christ at his crusades back to the places of worship of their own choice, be these mainline Protestant, Catholic, or Jewish.

Graham's revival meetings, dressed in American colors and displaying American flags, were spaces of national unification supported by the U.S. government. President Dwight Eisenhower endorsed Graham's revival work through his well-publicized friendship with the young preacher, and high-ranking politicians attended his crusade meetings.[15] During the New York crusade in 1957, Vice President Richard Nixon joined Graham on the platform and bowed his head in a closing prayer together with the thousands in attendance.[16] In return, Graham symbolically endorsed government policies. He visited U.S. troops in Korea at Christmas 1952, a gesture he would repeat during the Vietnam War. During these visits and within his international evangelistic work in the 1950s, Graham carried the particular American gospel of freedom, military strength, and free-market capitalism to Europe, Asia, and Africa, where he not only preached in favor of moral rearmament but also defended military spending.[17] During the New York crusade of 1957, he published an article on Memorial Day in which he reminded his readers that through Jesus's death "our spiritual freedom was purchased at terrific cost by the most splendid youth that ever walked the shores of time."[18] The message rhetorically linked the Christian ideal of spiritual freedom with U.S. military conduct abroad, an important feature of Graham's preaching in the 1950s.

During his crusades, Graham persuasively linked the neo-evangelical movement's newfound political vigor and faith in the nation's Cold War mission. What other leading neo-evangelicals discussed in the circles of the newly formed National Association of Evangelicals (1942) or in recently founded evangelical institutions such as Fuller Theological Seminary (1947), Graham's revival meetings brought to the doorsteps of ordinary Americans. His revival meetings celebrated a nation "confident to the verge of complacency about the perfectibility of American society."[19] The particular way in which Graham addressed his audiences was illustrated during the sermon he preached at the end of his sixteen-week-long crusade in New York City:

> Let us tell the whole world tonight that we Americans believe in God. Let us tell the world tonight that our trust is not in our pile of atomic and hydrogen bombs but in Almighty God. . . . On this Labor Day weekend, here at the Crossroad of America, let us tell the world that we are united and ready to march under the banner of Almighty God, taking as our slogan that which is stamped on our coins: "in God we trust."[20]

Gone was the traditional fundamentalist rhetoric that reserved salvation to the chosen ones unwilling to share it with the entirety of a sinful nation. And gone was the traditional pessimistic look backwards. Graham's followers were ready to march forward into a bright American future.

The American community that Graham addressed was not an exclusively Protestant one. At a time when the terms "Christian," "Judeo-Christian," and "American" were nearly synonymous, Graham invited Catholics and Jews to attend his revival meetings and to join the crusade-planning committees. This indicated Graham's personal theological liberal turn. His ecumenical approach mirrored the consensus-oriented political culture. This also marked a clear break from the more exclusive traditional Protestant fundamentalist approach. A first attack on Graham by fundamentalist R. T. Ketcham, national representative of the General Association of Regular Baptist Churches, followed as early as October 1950. One year after Graham's national breakthrough in Los Angeles, Ketcham complained that Graham was unable to keep clear of Catholic and Jewish milieus. In reply, Jerry Beavan, Graham's public-relations manager, asked Ketcham to understand that "in this type of evangelistic work we refrain from attacking Catholics, Jews or any other group of race, color, or creed."[21] The new evangelicals aimed for a more consensual Christianity, a significant liberal shift from traditional Protestant fundamentalism.

Although Graham endorsed America's new global leadership role and its Cold War consensus, he upheld important conservative views that positioned him outside the liberal consensus. His message focused on personal salvation, not social change. This was particularly evident in the tumultuous years when the civil rights struggle reached its fever pitch. Whenever he was pressed on taking a stand to further the cause of racial or social justice, Graham beat around the bush.[22] Only through conversion of the individual could a socially just society be forged, he stated over and over again. Despite the fact that Graham's consensual rhetoric forbade him to speak openly against the welfare state, he did not endorse it, and his antistatism was an open secret.[23] His reasoning on racial justice evolved along the same lines. On the one hand, Graham refused to preach in front of segregated audiences, as he considered segregation an unjust system implemented by white supremacists. On the other hand, he refused to endorse human protest and action in order to change the system. In doing so, his position reflected the broader politics of the white evangelical milieu of the 1950s and 1960s, which, as Matthew Sutton observes, "indirectly (and sometimes directly) discouraged attempts to challenge the subordinate status of women and racial and ethnic minorities in American society."[24]

Instead, Graham endorsed the United States' cultural and social status quo through words, symbols, and practices. His inclusive message addressed in particular the rising white middle class, unburdened it from its social responsibilities, and endorsed its affluence.[25] Graham's gray flannel suits, which he wore onstage, became the symbol of his conformity with middle-class America of the 1950s. Graham acted onstage more like a slick salesman of religion than a traditional fire-and-brimstone preacher. He warned his followers of hell, damnation, and communism, but the revival meetings oozed with cultural optimism. Graham's lifestyle, which included air travel and playing golf, was widely publicized in crusade publications, thus endorsing the lifestyle of the entire Christian American middle class.[26]

Following his 1949 Los Angeles crusade, Graham accepted the financial support of groups such as the Christian Business Association in Los Angeles; leading businessmen such as Roger Hull, executive vice president of Mutual Life Insurance Company of New York, served on the organizing committees for his crusades. His crusades ran on budgets of up to $900,000, as in the case of the sixteen-week-long New York crusade. Graham's organization mirrored the new prosperity of the country, and the amount of every collection taken during the revival meetings reflected the new financial possibilities of the American middle class. The particular cultural milieu of his revival meetings explains their attractiveness to the rising suburban middle class. Despite Graham's insistence that he opened his meetings to African Americans, ethnic minorities, Catholics, and Jews, statistics indicate that the vast majority of his audiences had a white, Protestant background.[27]

In Graham's revival work, patriotism and consumerism, politics and business, and evangelicalism and lifestyle blended in a new consensual mix that proved particularly attractive to the white suburban middle class. Graham's own conservative offer became attractive through his ability to incorporate elements of the liberal Cold War consensus such as an outspoken anticommunism and the celebration of the American way of life in his revival work. But his audiences also displayed the limits of the liberal consensus: Graham might have reached out to African Americans and ethnic minorities, but they did not respond to his invitation in significant numbers. Some distanced themselves from Graham's Cold War religiosity by not attending his crusades, and others did so through outspoken criticism. Examining Graham's critics allows us to better assess how much he had shifted U.S. evangelicalism to the liberal mainstream, despite his persistent conservatism.

Faith beyond the Consensus

Graham's revival work evolved in the particular religious atmosphere of the post–World War II years when, as Will Herberg pointed out in 1955, religion seemed to hold the nation together. Church membership had reached an all-time high after the war. Polls revealed that nearly 95 percent of Americans believed in God and that 90 percent of the public still engaged in the private practice of prayer.[28] Religious publishing and church building flourished in the new economic climate, and religious nonfiction as well as Bible sales figures skyrocketed. The exploding economy and the baby boom led to church growth, and even mainline Protestant churches joined in the evangelistic fervor of the decade.[29] Secular newspapers fueled the revivalist atmosphere by running articles on the religious growth under headlines such as "High Tide of Faith" and "Religious Revival Runs at Flood Tide."[30] As William Martin writes of the spiritual atmosphere of the decade after the war, "for evangelists it was like being a stockbroker in a runaway bull market."[31]

But the consensual view of religion as a unifying force, as outlined by Herberg, must be careful not to brush over the factions that persisted in the U.S. religious landscape and those groups that resented and actively fought the emerging consensual faith Billy Graham represented during his revival meetings. During the Portland crusade in 1950, an interviewer questioned Graham's full support by local churches by asking: "I wonder if you are aware of the fact that . . . about 50 percent of the Christian people find themselves in vital areas of disagreement with you on a great many stands."[32] Carl McIntire, one of Graham's critics among fundamentalists, went even further seven years later when he stated that "Billy Graham is rapidly becoming the most controversial religious figure on the American scene."[33] Over the years, the question of whether to support or reject Graham's revival style increasingly split denominations. When Graham announced his San Francisco crusade to be held in 1958, the California fundamentalist leader G. Arch Weninger asked his Baptist followers not to cooperate with Graham's campaign team. One of his flock, however, assured *Christianity Today*, a pro-Graham periodical, that not all Baptists of the area shared Weninger's views. A letter from the public-relations officer for the Presbytery of San Francisco highlighted that, even though his denomination had pledged its support for the crusade, "that said action was not by any means unanimous."[34]

The ecumenical core of Graham's revival meetings enraged Protestant fundamentalists, and his uncritical endorsement of the American way of life was questioned by mainline Protestants, Catholics, and Jews alike. The camp of his critics was as ecumenical as Graham's audiences. Stern fundamentalists found themselves on the same side as left-wing Protestant intellectuals and concerned Catholics. Among his most outspoken critics were the Protestant fundamentalists who occupied the right fringe of the American religious spectrum. Their criticism, in particular, provides us with an opportunity to assess Graham's liberalism.

Jason Stevens has pointed out that Graham's revival work was initially misinterpreted by liberal intellectuals, such as William McLaughlin, as an ultraconservative response to the liberal consensus.[35] This was a view certainly not shared by precisely those ultraconservatives. The conflict between Graham and the Protestant fundamentalist milieu dated back to the exchange of letters with R. T. Ketcham. It peaked during the 1957 New York crusade when Graham invited well-known liberal Protestant ministers to join his crusade team. These included John Sutherland Bonnell, a theologically moderate preacher at Fifth Avenue Presbyterian Church; Henry Van Dusen, president of the liberal Union Theological Seminary; and Norman Vincent Peale, proponent of a therapeutic faith. The Protestant Council of New York, which represented the full range of Protestant life in the city, sponsored the crusade.

The religious consensus and ecumenical orientation of the Billy Graham crusades provoked an uproar among Protestant fundamentalists. Three leading fundamentalists—James E. Bennet, a Christian attorney based in New York; Carl McIntire, one of the founders of the fundamentalist American Council of Churches in 1941; and Bob Jones, president of the strictly fundamentalist Bob Jones University—publicly challenged Graham's mission.[36] In this debate, the term "liberal" carried its own meaning and referred to a modernist theology that endorsed ecumenism and questioned the significance of biblical literacy.[37] Bob Jones made that clear when he distanced himself from Graham with the words: "We are still religious fundamentalists not religious liberals."[38] At a time when terminology became more blurred in the neo-evangelical milieu, its conservative fringe clearly knew how to define themselves.

In particular, Graham's cooperation with mainline Protestant churches, Jews, and Catholics was considered unbiblical among fundamentalists. Graham's approach to send enquirers not exclusively to fundamentalist churches but to a church of their choice made the *Christian Beacon* fume: "This is the pattern to which evangelicals have been taking such strong exception. Graham's converts are turned back to the Roman Catholics, Graham's converts are turned back to the modernists, Graham's converts are sent, without instruction or warning, to the church of their choice."[39] Even in the consensual world of the 1950s, for Protestant fundamentalists there was only one true faith, and "Protestants who truly rejoice in the grace of God can never approve of turning converts over to the Roman Catholic Church."[40]

The other aspect of the fundamentalist critique aimed at Graham's explanation for why he cooperated with mainline Protestants. In the best American business rhetoric, Graham clarified publicly that only broad ecumenical support would allow him to raise the $900,000 of the originally estimated crusade budget. The embrace of such a secular logic was hard to bear for Protestant fundamentalists. James Bennet observed in the

Christian Beacon: "He apparently trusts more in the money and influence of unbelievers than he does in the power, love, and mercy of our Lord."[41] With this line of argument, fundamentalist Protestants positioned themselves outside the logic of the liberal economic and cultural mainstream. This had become evident in 1951, when R. T. Ketcham, referring back to the Los Angeles crusade, asked Graham: "Are you aware, Billy, of the tremendous problem you are posing when you . . . constantly present Hollywood as being populated by a large number of fine Christian actors and actresses? Through the years hundreds of us pastors . . . have showed that the movie and the Christian life are incompatible."[42] Fundamentalist Protestants had always lived as part of American society, culture, and politics, but the question for them was still to what degree they were willing to embrace this triad.

It is striking that neither the patriotic atmosphere at Graham's revival meetings nor their endorsement by politicians and the U.S. government featured in the critique published by Protestant fundamentalists. For them Graham's work was not a question of national spiritual restoration but was only discussed as a challenge to the purity of Protestant faith. Fundamentalists also did not acknowledge Graham's anticommunist rhetoric, which would have provided the two sides with common ground. Instead, they complained about the political unreliability of liberal Protestants. As an editorial in the *Christian Beacon* explained, "modernism with its Social Gospel has accepted Marxist principles and thus has greatly aided communism."[43] Modernist ministers were the people with whom Graham cooperated.

The fundamentalist criticisms of Graham highlighted the deepening demarcation line between inclusive neo-evangelicals and persistently exclusive fundamentalists who aimed to protect the fundamentalist milieu from any liberalizing tendencies. But this line had become blurred. Despite these attacks on Graham from the right fringe of the fundamentalist wing, the conservative and fundamentalist periodical *Moody Monthly* reported very favorably about the crusades, dating back to a January 1950 article by Dorothy C. Haskin on the Los Angeles crusade.[44] Many fundamentalists like her seemingly hoped that Graham's revival could win over mainline Protestants, Catholics, and the unchurched to a conservative Protestant faith.[45]

That Graham was the focus of the ongoing process of redefining identities and demarcation lines in the U.S. religious landscape became obvious when the mainline journal *Christian Century* labeled his crusade in New York City "Fundamentalist Revival."[46] The highly critical article warned of the growing influence of conservative evangelicalism, with its potential to set back theological debates and liberalization tendencies in religion by half a century. The journal complained about the compliancy of many mainline churches in this project, which "cooperate because they lack the courage to stand up against the powerful coercions of conformity applied in behalf of religion."[47] As much as Graham attracted mainline Protestants to his revival meetings, he also enraged the theologically liberal and socially and politically active wing of American Protestantism. Many mainline Protestants did not see Graham's crusades as a force in liberalizing Protestantism; they saw him instead as the spearhead of a rising theological, social, and political conservatism.

This was, however, only one aspect of the vocal critique raised in the mainline Protestant milieu. Others saw in Graham less the rising star of a new conservatism than the proponent of a vague, nationalistic, self-affirming religiosity stripped of uncomfortable religious realities such as the pain of conversion. Their critique was embedded in broader theological and sociological debates about the future of religious life in the United States. James Hudnut-Beumler captures the tension between the wave of revivalism stirred by Graham and others and the rise of a so-called culture of religion: "Religion in the decade of the 1950s was at its peak of popularity, and the religious revival was celebrated far and wide for filling the houses of worship. . . . Yet to its experts, religion had never been at greater peril, or less faithfully observed."[48]

Indeed, contemporaries such as the leading Protestant intellectual Reinhold Niebuhr complained in an editorial for *Christianity and Crisis* that "the 'unknown' in America seems to be faith itself. Our politicians are always admonishing the people to have 'faith.' Sometimes they seem to imply that faith is itself redemptive."[49] Accordingly, Niebuhr called Graham's religious offer "a bargain" in an article he published in *Look* during the New York crusade. The strong patriotic and confident core of Graham's crusades troubled mainline Protestants as well. An article in the *Christian Century* pointed out that Graham's religiosity could easily be mistaken for mere patriotism: "The presence of the vice-president of the United States was a coup, too, suggesting as it did the endorsement of the crusade by the American government. But the context suggested the other possibility: the crusade was endorsing that cool nationalism which now stands among the world's religions as 'Americanism.'"[50] In questioning the religious authenticity of Graham's revival work, these liberal critics joined the ranks of their fundamentalist brethren.

Graham indeed provided a national faith for the confident nation of the liberal consensus, which explains his attractiveness for Protestants, Catholics, and Jews. It was publicly known that lay Catholics and even priests, Jews and even their rabbis attended the Graham crusades out of curiosity, patriotism, or to restore their own faith. The support for Graham and his critique in Catholic and Jewish circles mirrors the core features of the debate in the Protestant milieu. In the way these religious groups discussed the Graham campaigns, they found allies in the fundamentalist and mainline Protestant milieu and joined the ecumenical choirs of Graham critics and Graham supporters.

The Catholic periodical *Commonweal* under its editor John Cogley restrained itself from association with Graham's critics. Cogley saw several flaws in Graham's revival work, but he praised the young preacher's genuine religious intentions.[51] Cogley's predominantly positive assessment of Graham's crusade in New York was predated by other supportive Catholic assessments, such as those published during the Washington crusade in 1952.[52] The forces of liberalization that had split the evangelical milieu were clearly getting a hold of the Catholic Church in the decade before Vatican II. There were, however, other voices that sounded much more like Graham's critics on the fundamentalist wing. Rev. John E. Kelly, information director of the National Catholic Welfare Conference, echoed the *Christian Beacon*'s critique on Graham's ecumenical approach: "To a Catholic there is no such thing as 'the church of your choice.' . . . You choose the church that Christ has set up as the one true church."[53] Kelly considered the liberalism of Graham's ecumenical offer as much a threat as the Protestant fundamentalist milieu did.

Meanwhile, some New York rabbis sided with the mainline critics and supporters of Graham's crusades. Rabbi Dr. William F. Rosenblum at Temple Israel acknowledged the civil religious relevance of the crusades. He explained that if the revival meetings at Madison Square Garden inspired more Protestants to live according to the Ten Commandments, and if Catholics and Jews did the same, then "New York will soon become the moral capital of the world."[54] He went on to say, however, that as a "liberal" he disagreed with some of Graham's biblical views and distanced himself from what he saw as Graham's religious conservatism. For Rabbi Dr. Louis C. Gerstein, the main problem was not Graham's conservatism but his uncritical embrace of U.S. consumer culture, which had left an imprint on Graham's revival style. Echoing the concerns of cultural critiques such as Niebuhr's, he told the *New York Times*: "I am critical of the slick, smooth, high-pressured salesmanship in selling religion, in technique hardly different from the approach one might use in selling toothpaste or hair dressing."[55] In the words of these critics, Graham's patriotism and his uncritical embrace and reflection of American consumer culture become even more evident.

On the one hand, Graham's critics and supporters clearly show the divisions within the consensual atmosphere of the 1950s religious landscape. In particular, Graham's joining in the celebration of America's moral and economic superiority stirred as much concern as his theological liberalism did. On the other hand, in the debates about Graham's crusades the liberal components of his religious offer became more pronounced. Graham's rise was based on his ability to incorporate components of the societal liberal consensus to enhance his own conservative position. In the joint critique on Graham that evolved on the conservative wing of the Protestant and Catholic milieu, we see the formation of a new religious alliance.

Conclusion

In the political and social climate that Godfrey Hodgson identified as dominated by "the ideology of the liberal consensus," significant transformations took place in the American religious landscape. During the 1950s revival, spearheaded by Billy Graham, U.S. evangelicalism became more inclusive and ecumenical and entered the American cultural mainstream. The communist threat allowed for a consensus in faith to emerge. Religious divisions seemed to become increasingly less important than national unity. This new evangelicalism featured a blatant faith in American society and its possible moral perfection and an undisguised worship of suburban consumerism. Graham's sermons—with their strong anticommunist subtext—and his celebration of the American way of life during his crusades fit perfectly into the 1950s cultural atmosphere of consensus.

In this consensus atmosphere, traditional religious differences became blurred, and Catholics as well as Jews attended the crusades and accepted their function regarding general moral restoration. The communist threat allowed for an increased acceptance of religious pluralism that many contemporaries interpreted as a form of liberalization and secularization of religious life in the United States. Many, in particular mainline Protestant critics such as Reinhold Niebuhr, warned that Graham's offer could be easily mistaken for a civil religious celebration of the American way of life. According to this argument, America saw the arrival of a more liberal, secular God. Therefore, conservative Catholics, orthodox Jews, and Protestant fundamentalists joined this chorus of critics for different reasons: they worried about the future authenticity of their faith traditions in the consensus religious melting pot that Graham seemed to shape.

However, the strong interplay between the liberal consensus and Graham's rise to national and international fame is only one part of the story. Many contemporary critics pointed out that although thousands attended Graham's crusades, thousands of others did not. A key in understanding the success of Graham's ministry is the voices of his critics. While fundamentalists and theological conservatives labeled him a "liberal," liberal Protestants, Catholics, and Jews feared his conservatism and fundamentalism. Graham was both—liberal and modern as well as conservative and traditional—and that explains the attractiveness of his religious offer. His critics defined this particular space Graham had carved out in the religious landscape much more clearly than his supporters ever could. Graham blurred traditional identities, and it is not surprising that the camp of his critics was as ecumenical as the audiences at his revival meetings.

Graham's revival work can easily be interpreted as the religious version of the intellectual and political liberal consensus. At the same time, Graham's rise has to be understood as the reawakening of religious conservatism and the beginning of the Religious Right. Graham was "liberal" compared to his critics on the right such as Bob Jones and Carl McIntire, but he was still a conservative Christian with a clear position on questions of racial integration and gender rights. To include the voices of his critics in the analysis of the Graham ministry sharpens our understanding of the shifts between the liberal and the conservative and the complexity of the U.S. religious landscape in the 1950s.

If we use the concept of the liberal consensus to analyze the evangelical milieu of the 1950s, we have to acknowledge that the formation of the Religious Right took part in the interplay between the liberal and the conservative, between the religious and the secular: only considering both sides of the coin makes the story complete. By appropriating elements of the liberal consensus, such as anticommunism, patriotism, and consumerism, neo-evangelicals like Billy Graham were able to move conservative evangelicalism further into the political and religious mainstream and to lay the groundwork for the rise of the Religious Right. Graham successfully incorporated theological liberalization processes in the religious landscape into his ministry, but he did so to fulfill his own conservative goals.

Notes

1. "40,000 Hear Billy Graham's Sermon in Drizzle at Capitol," *Chicago Daily Tribune*, February 4, 1952, 1. See also "An Evangelistic Meeting on the Steps of the Capitol," *New York Times*, February 4, 1952, 4; "Billy Graham Preaches to Thousands with Capitol Steps as His Pulpit," *Los Angeles Times*, February 4, 1952, 5; for a striking image of the meeting, see also "Washington Crusade Extended," *Youth for Christ Magazine*, March 1952, 64–70.

2. Godfrey Hodgson, *America in Our Time: From World War II to Nixon—What Happened and Why* (1976; reprint, Princeton: Princeton University Press, 2005), 75. His concept of the liberal consensus was recently forcefully endorsed in Jennifer A. Delton, *Rethinking the 1950s: How Anticommunism and the Cold War Made America Liberal* (Cambridge: Cambridge University Press, 2014).

3. Will Herberg, *Protestant-Catholic-Jew: An Essay in American Religious Sociology* (Garden City, NY: Doubleday 1955).

4. Jason W. Stevens, *God-Fearing and Free: A Spiritual History of America's Cold War* (Cambridge: Harvard University Press, 2010), 29–83.

5. Jonathan P. Herzog, *The Spiritual-Industrial Complex: America's Religious Battle against Communism in the Early Cold War* (New York: Oxford University Press, 2011); for an earlier interpretation of America's religious Cold War, see Stephen Whitfield, *The Culture of the Cold War*, 2nd ed. (Baltimore: Johns Hopkins University Press, 1996), 77–100.

6. Herzog, *Spiritual-Industrial Complex*, 173–79.

7. James Hudnut-Beumler, *Looking for God in the Suburbs: The Religion of the American Dream and Its Critics, 1945–1965* (New Brunswick, NJ: Rutgers University Press, 1994).

8. Grant Wacker, *America's Pastor: Billy Graham and the Shaping of a Nation* (Cambridge: Harvard University Press, 2014). Andrew Finstuen, *Original Sin and Everyday Protestants: The Theology of Reinhold Niebuhr, Billy Graham, and Paul Tillich in the Age of Anxiety* (Chapel Hill: University of North Carolina Press, 2009), clearly shows how a focus on the critique of Graham contributes to a better understanding of his role in the religious atmosphere of the 1950s.

9. For "myth of consensus" see Andrew Preston, *Sword of the Spirit, Shield of Faith: Religion in American War and Diplomacy* (New York: Knopf, 2012), 475–95. Preston points out that the focus on a Cold War consensus in the field of religion holds true in parts but that it brushes over significant differences in religious thinking regarding war and foreign policy. Other recent studies have highlighted the plurality even of the evangelical milieu itself: Axel Schaefer, ed., *Countercultural Conservatives: American Evangelicalism from Postwar Revival to the New Christian Right* (Madison: University of Wisconsin Press, 2011); David R. Swartz, *Moral Minority: The Evangelical Left in an Age of Conservatism* (Philadelphia: University of Pennsylvania Press, 2012); Brantley W. Gasaway, *Progressive Evangelicals and the Pursuit of Social Justice* (Chapel Hill: University of North Carolina Press, 2014).

10. On Graham's revival work see Wacker, *America's Pastor*; David Aikman, *Billy Graham: His Life and Influence* (Nashville: Thomas Nelson, 2007); and William Martin, *A Prophet with Honor: The Billy Graham Story* (New York: Morrow, 1991).

11. For the broader transformation of fundamentalism into neo-evangelicalism see Matthew A. Sutton, *American Apocalypse: A History of Modern Evangelicalism* (Cambridge: Belknap Press of Harvard University Press, 2014); Joel Carpenter, *Revive Us Again: The Reawakening of American Fundamentalism* (New York: Oxford University Press, 1999); Schaefer, *Countercultural Conservatives*; and Garth M. Rosell, *The Surprising Work of God: Harold John Ockenga, Billy Graham, and the Rebirth of Evangelicalism* (Grand Rapids, MI: Baker Academic, 2008).

12. Wacker, *America's Pastor*, 2.

13. The interview is reprinted as "Billy Graham Answers!" in *Moody Monthly*, February 1951, 374–75, 396 (quotation on 374).

14. Billy Graham Evangelist Association, *The Story of the Billy Graham Evangelistic Campaigns* (Wheaton, IL: Von Kampen Press, 1950), 124. For the tradition of interpreting communism as a religious challenge, see Herzog, *Spiritual-Industrial Complex*, 39–71.

15. For an introduction to the atmosphere at the revival meetings, see Curtis Mitchell, *God in the Garden: The Amazing Story of Billy Graham's First New York Crusade* (1957; Charlotte, NC: Billy Graham Evangelistic Association, 2005).

16. For the image of Nixon and Graham joined in prayer, see *New York Times*, July 21, 1957, 1 and 48.

17. Graham's international ministry is still under-researched. For a contemporary account see John Pollock, *Billy Graham: Evangelist to the World: An Authorized Biography of the Decisive Years* (New York: Harper & Row, 1979). For the broader context of evangelical activism abroad during the Cold War, see William Inboden, *Religion and American Foreign Policy, 1945–1960: The Soul of Containment* (New York: Cambridge University Press, 2008); Sarah Ruble, *The Gospel of Freedom and Power: Protestant Missionaries in American Culture after World War II* (Chapel Hill: University of North Carolina Press, 2015), 55–90; Andrew Preston, "Evangelical Internationalism: A Conservative Worldview for the Age of Globalization," in Laura Jane Gifford and Daniel K. Williams, eds., *The Right Side of the Sixties: Reexamining Conservatism's Decade of Transformation* (New York: Palgrave Macmillan, 2012), 221–40.

18. Billy Graham, "The Price of Freedom: A Message for Memorial Day," reprinted in several local and regional newspapers, including *Yonkers Times*, May 29, 1957, folder 21, box 2, collection 1, Billy Graham Center Archives [hereafter BGCA], Wheaton College, Wheaton, Illinois.

19. Hodgson, *America in Our Time*, 75.

20. Quoted in Mitchell, *God in the Garden*, 180.

21. Beavan to Ketcham, November 6, 1950, reprinted as part of Graham-Ketcham Correspondence, 1, folder 21, box 11, collection 318, BGCA.

22. Steven P. Miller, *Billy Graham and the Rise of the Republican South* (Philadelphia: University of Pennsylvania Press, 2009); Randall J. Stephens, "'It Has to Come from the Hearts of the People': Evangelicals, Fundamentalists, Race, and the 1964 Civil Rights Act," *Journal of American Studies* 50, no. 3 (August 2016): 559–85.

23. This made Graham a conservative in an evangelical world that rapidly changed its

stand on its relationship to state and government, as shown in Axel Schaefer, *Piety and Public Funding: Evangelicals and the State in Modern America* (Philadelphia: University of Pennsylvania Press, 2012).

24. Sutton, *American Apocalypse*, 322 (on gender politics, 332–33). Steven Miller's verdict regarding Graham's support of the civil rights cause is slightly more favorable. Miller points out that Graham refused to preach in front of segregated audiences as early as 1953 and that he openly advocated racial tolerance. Miller, *Billy Graham*, 13–38. More critical is Michael G. Long, *Billy Graham and the Beloved Community: America's Evangelist and the Dream of Martin Luther King, Jr.* (New York: Palgrave Macmillan, 2006).

25. On the attractiveness of neo-evangelicalism for the white suburban middle class, see Darren Dochuk, *From Bible Belt to Sunbelt: Plain-folk Religion, Grassroots Politics, and the Rise of Evangelical Conservatism* (New York: Knopf, 2011); Bethany Moreton, *To Serve God and Wal-Mart: The Making of Christian Free Enterprise* (Cambridge: Harvard University Press, 2009).

26. This is explored further in Uta Balbier, "'God's Own Consumers': Billy Graham, Mass Evangelism, and Consumption in the United States in the 1950s," in Hartmut Berghoff and Uwe Spiekermann, eds., *Decoding Consumer Societies* (New York: Palgrave Macmillan, 2011), 195–209.

27. Kurt Lang and Gladys Lang, "Decisions for Christ: Billy Graham in New York," in Maurice R. Stein, Arthur J. Vidich, and David M. White, eds., *Identity and Anxiety. Survival of the Person in Mass Society* (New York: Free Press, 1960), 415–27.

28. Robert Wuthnow, *The Restructuring of American Religion: Society and Faith since World War II* (Princeton: Princeton University Press, 1988), 17. See also Hudnut-Beumler, *Looking for God*, 29–84.

29. Wuthnow, *Restructuring of American Religion*, 140–45.

30. Hudnut-Beumler, *Looking for God*, 31; "Religious Revival Runs at Flood Tide," *Washington Post*, May 14, 1952, 10.

31. Martin, *A Prophet with Honor*, 106.

32. "Billy Graham Answers!" 375.

33. "The Graham Debate," *Christian Beacon*, February 28, 1957, 1 and 8 (quotation on 1).

34. Letters to the Editor by Barrington Baptist David L. Madeira and Louis A Petersen, United Presbyterian Church, U.S.A., *Christianity Today*, June 23, 1958, 27.

35. Stevens, *God-Fearing and Free*, 64–68, referring to William McLoughlin, *Billy Graham: Revivalist in a Secular Age* (New York: Ronald Press, 1959).

36. Compared to recent studies on the history of neo-evangelicalism, the fundamentalist milieu in the twentieth century has received less academic attention. This has now changed, however, with the publication of Markku Ruotsila, *Fighting Fundamentalist: Carl McIntire and the Politicization of American Fundamentalism* (New York: Oxford University Press, 2015). See also Markku Ruotsila, "Carl McIntire and the Fundamentalist Origins of the Christian Right," *Church History* 81 (2012): 378–407; with an interesting focus on right-wing broadcasting, see Heather Hendershot, "God's Angriest Man: Carl McIntire, Cold War Fundamentalism, and Right-Wing Broadcasting," *American Quarterly* 59 (2007): 373–96; on Bob Jones's fundamentalist legacy, see Mark Taylor Dalhouse, *An Island in the Lake of Fire: Bob Jones University, Fundamentalism, and the Separatist Movement* (Athens: University of Georgia Press, 1996).

37. William R. Hutchison, *The Modernist Impulse in American Protestantism* (Cambridge: Harvard University Press, 1976).

38. "Dr. Bob Jones Makes Statement on Billy Graham," *Christian Beacon*, April 11, 1957, 1.

39. "Graham's Catholic Converts," *Christian Beacon*, May 23, 1957, 5.

40. Ibid.

41. "Bennet Answers Criticism of 'Extreme Fundamentalists' by Christianity Today Editor," *Christian Beacon*, March 21, 1957, 2, 4 (quotation on 2).

42. Ketcham to Graham, November 6, 1951, reprinted as part of Graham-Ketcham Correspondence, p. 12, folder 21, box 11, collection 318, BGCA.

43. "This Issue of Christian Beacon," *Christian Beacon*, March 28, 1957, 8.

44. Dorothy C. Haskin, "Spiritual Awakening in California," *Moody Monthly*, January 1950, 328–29.

45. Ralph Lord Roy, "Special Report: Billy Graham in New York," *Christianity and Crisis*, May 27, 1957, 71–72 (quotation on 71).

46. "Fundamentalist Revival," *Christian Century*, June 19, 1957, 749–51.

47. Ibid., 750.

48. Hudnut-Beumler, *Looking for God*, 77.

49. Reinhold Niebuhr, "Religiosity and the Christian Faith," *Christianity and Crisis*, January 24, 1955, 1–2 (quotation on 1).

50. "The Long Anticlimax," *Christian Century*, August 7, 1957, 933.

51. John Cogley, "Billy Graham at the Garden," *Commonweal*, June 21, 1957, 302.

52. "Catholic Paper Lauds Dr. Graham," *Washington Post*, February 3, 1952, M13.

53. "Priest Explains Ban on Revival Meetings," *World-Telegram and Sun*, May 31, 1957, folder 21, box 2, collection 1, BGCA

54. "Rabbis Commend, Criticize Graham," *New York Times*, May 19, 1957, 53.

55. Ibid.

13

Gender in an Era of Liberal Consensus

HELEN LAVILLE

It would be fair to say that gender is not a central concern of Godfrey Hodgson's account of the era of liberal consensus. References to women throughout the book are sparse at best. Women appear more as bit players providing color and detail, rather than as central characters: Julie Andrews was playing in *Camelot* at the Majestic Theatre in January 1961; Jacqueline Kennedy was helped down the steps of Air Force One, her suit still smeared with the blood of her assassinated husband; and a reporter, waiting in the "lovely home . . . in one of Washington's nicest suburbs" of the political aide and later Watergate co-conspirator Jeb Stuart Magruder, was entertained by "his pretty young wife, playing with her babies. She made her guest welcome, her legs crossed at the ankle, until her husband got home from the office."[1] In our time, Hodgson narrates without question, women's place was in the domestic sphere, not the public realm of politics, liberal or otherwise. "Betty Friedan's upper-middle-class housewives," Hodgson asserts in his one-sentence reference to women and gender in the age of liberal consensus, "taking advantage of their new economic security, obeyed the feminine mystique by having big families."[2] The strong gendered division between the public and private spheres that existed during the era of liberal consensus, rather than being incidental or peripheral to the maxims that Hodgson argued underlay the establishment of American liberal consensus, was, in fact, central to them. The importance of gender roles in the period of liberal consensus was not confined to the individual life choices of one privileged group of women but rather lay at the heart of the organization of American life in the period between 1945 and 1960. Notwithstanding the paucity of references to gender throughout Hodgson's work, the promotion of the masculinity of the public sphere and the feminization of the private sphere was central to the development of the liberal consensus. An unquestioning acceptance of conservative understandings of gender roles was vital to the construction of the economic and ideological maxims that underlay liberal consensus. The importance of these gendered roles to the liberal consensus goes some way to explaining why the withdrawal of upper-middle-class women into their homes has had such a stranglehold on our historical imagination of the period.

The much vaunted—and arguably much overstated—withdrawal of American women to the home served as an important symbol of the strongly gendered nature of the division between public and private spheres. As such, it lay at the heart of the ideology of liberal consensus. However, it was not an accurate reflection of the experience of American women in the period of liberal consensus. Historians of both African American women and working-class women have pointed out that the feminine mystique was either not accessible or not sought-after for large numbers of American women. Even among the select group of upper-middle-class women referenced by Hodgson, "obedience" to the feminine mystique was limited. As historians such as Susan Ware have ably demonstrated, the domestic ideals of the feminine mystique were not unique to this period. Moreover, as Ware demonstrates, "many women managed to lead active and interesting lives, even at its height."[3] While the inaccuracy of the model of domestic contentment as the norm for American women has become conventional wisdom among historians, the way in which women articulated a public role in the era before the rise of second-wave feminism in the mid-1960s has been underexplored. As the historian Susan Hartman has argued, the extraordinary strength of the "second wave" metaphor of American feminism has gained traction by largely ignoring the extent to which American women in the 1950s articulated their own challenge to the seemingly ubiquitous gender ideology of that period. In particular, the failure of most American women in the period before the mid-1960s to identify as feminists or to engage with gender politics has meant that their promotion of women's public role has been under-theorized. "The groundwork of 1960s protest," Hartman argues, "was constructed by women written out of the definition of feminism both by their own reluctance to wear the label and by new feminists' unawareness of what had immediately preceded their awakening."[4]

The majority of American women avoided a direct challenge to both the conservative gender ideology and the mapping of these gender roles onto the private and public sphere. This did not, however, mean that they acceded to a withdrawal to the home. On the contrary, many American women in the period of liberal consensus recognized the need to increase the number of American women in public life and to put forward a range of arguments that promoted the role of women in the public sphere. Crucially, American women argued that the lessons of World War II and the needs of the emerging Cold War—the very factors which according to Hodgson fueled the rise of the liberal consensus—demanded, not the retreat of women to the domestic sphere, but rather the increased participation of American women in public life. In the decades before the emergence of second-wave feminism in the mid-1960s, American women consistently warned against the consequences of an entirely masculine public sphere. While actively—sometimes passionately—spurning an identification with feminism, upper-middle-class American women, rather than meekly "obeying" the dictates of the feminine mystique, worked through their voluntary associations and through mainstream political parties to construct and promote ways in which women could carve out public roles for themselves within the political world. Their arguments were not predicated on a feminist identification and the rights and entitlements of American women, but rather on the responsibilities and duties of women to take a role in public life, accompanied by dire warnings about the consequences for the nation of an entirely masculine public sphere. Focusing not on the rights of American women but on their responsibilities to their nation, these women consistently argued that the masculinizing of the public sphere carried with it two significant dangers: first, it threatened the stability of liberal consensus by making the nation vulnerable to political extremism, and second, it undermined the ability and capacity of the United States to triumph in the Cold War. Women who themselves had sought elected office, women who contributed to mainstream political party organization, and women in sex-segregated women's voluntary associations all articulated arguments that sought to promote the presence of women in politics and employment. That they worked along rather than against the grain of liberal consensus should not obscure the significance of their efforts.

The strength of the gendering of the private/public sphere in the postwar period undoubtedly drew from a nostalgic vision of the home that served as a national comfort blanket throughout the disruptions and insecurities of World War II. An editorial in *Life* magazine in 1945 explained, "The trials and separations of war have made real to millions of Americans the beauties and contentment of home. As a sentimental notion the home today is a great success."[5] Beyond its emotional value as a "sentimental notion," however, celebration of the comforts of the prosperous American home, effortlessly managed by a contented housewife, had a vital economic value in postwar America. The economic abundance that Hodgson asserted Americans relied on to eradicate social tensions and class conflict depended on the masculinization of the public world of work and the femininization of the domestic sphere of mass consumption. Remasculinizing the world of work after the significant increase of women in the workplace during World War II, together with the feminization of the home as a sphere of consumption, were widely believed to be two sides of the coin that would assure the United States of prosperity. True, propaganda campaigns during World War II praised American women's willingness to take up roles in traditionally masculine fields of work. Rosie the Riveter donned unflattering overalls and took her place on the factory floor in the interests of winning the war. Celebrations of women's place in the workforce, however, took pains to explain that disruption to the gendered segregation of the factory floor was for the duration of the hostilities only. Newsreel footage of women in industrial jobs reassured viewers: "My job belongs to some solider," explained one woman worker. "When he comes back he can have it."[6] "There is little doubt," the War Production Board noted, "that women will be required to leave their jobs at the end of the war to permit the return of men to their jobs once they are released from the armed forces."[7] Pressures were brought to bear on women who hoped—and needed—to keep their wartime job.[8] Management and unions, fearful that reconversion and an end to the war-fueled production demand would result in the return of unemployment figures akin to the Depression years, were determined to oust women from the workplace and to remasculinize the world of work. "When management began rehiring workers in the reconversion period," Karen Tucker Anderson explains, "it reinstituted most pre-war discriminatory policies regarding women . . . a practice facilitated by union acquiescence."[9]

The economic model that emerged in the United States after World War II depended on the remasculinization of work to deliver abundance through the full employment of American men. However, it also depended on the mapping of strict gender divisions onto the domestic home as the sphere of consumption. The ability of American production to adapt itself from the needs of war to the needs of mass consumption and domesticity had dominated the advertising space of American magazines during the war. Domestic goods companies explicitly connected the desire for the end of the war, the blissful return of reunited couples to the domestic setting, and the provision of new products, improved beyond imagination by the technological and production advances gained as a result of the demands of wartime production. Postwar mass domestic consumption was thus explicitly harnessed to a yearning for peace, domestic retreat, traditional gender roles, and an end to the sacrifices, separations, and hardships of wartime. Washing-machine manufacturer Maytag promised American women, "You've waited a long, long time for a new washer. But there'll come a day when Uncle Sam will say 'Go ahead' . . . and then we can start making those handsome new 'post-war' Maytags we have planned for you."[10] Kelvinator advertisements waxed lyrical about the return to postwar domesticity, with its customer dreamily imagining the return of her soldier husband: "When you come home to stay . . . We'll live in a kingdom all our own . . . a kingdom just big enough for three . . . with a picket fence for boundary." This kingdom might be only big enough for three, but it still had space for a suitable number of electrical appliances. It was implicit in the rosy images of postwar homemaking that wartime sacrifices and separations would reap their reward not only in the triumph of democracy over totalitarianism but also in the better quality of domestic goods made possible by wartime advances. "Kelvinator will build more and finer electrical appliances than we have ever built before. It means refrigerators, electric ranges, home freezers and electric water heaters to make the kitchens of American the truly enchanted places they can be. It means that the new developments, the scientific advances made in the war will be incorporated into these appliances as rapidly as possible to make them . . . the more useful part of the home you want—when peace comes. That will be our part in the building of a greater, a happier nation."[11]

Women's housewifely role as the consumer of domestic goods was central to the mass consumption that drove American postwar affluence. The postwar consumer's republic tied together the promise of mass affluence for Americans, traditional gender roles, and limitless domestic consumption. The central importance of consumer demand to American economic success, asserted by Vice President Richard Nixon in the famous kitchen debate at the American exhibition in Moscow in 1959, rested on a celebration of feminine domestic consumption. "In America," Nixon explained, "we like to make life easier for women."[12] This ease was secured by the availability of a range of affordable, technologically advanced domestic products that would make household chores less physically demanding and time-consuming. Gendered divisions that promoted women's roles as housewives in the all-American kitchen were thus a vital component of the economic maxims of abundance which underpinned the emergence of a liberal consensus.

The need to "remasculinize" the public sphere and to put women back in the home reflected not only economic needs but also the strong connection between stable gender roles and American ideology. Attesting to this in a letter to President Dwight Eisenhower in 1955, Boeing Company vice president J. Earl Schaefer declared, "It has always been our policy to encourage women to stay in the home . . . [W]e all should work closely together in an effort to get our women back in the home where they, and they more than anyone else, can make it the shrine it should be and the solid foundation it has been for building real Americanism."[13] The strong alignment between women and the domestic sphere served multiple ideological functions in the era of liberal consensus. First, as Elaine Tyler May and, more recently, Laura McEnaney have argued, strong gender roles provided reassurance that the physical and psychological refuge of the American home could withstand the communist threat, even in the event of nuclear attack.[14] "The security of the family is threatened by the greatest crisis ever to face it," explained Katherine Howard, deputy administrator of the Federal Civil Defense Administration from 1953 to 1954. "We look to women for support and cooperation in finding the solution."[15] "It is in the hands of the American housewife and mother," she told the Ladies Auxiliary to the Veterans of Foreign Wars in 1953, "that the defense of our home front must lie."[16] Second, if strong female domestic roles were vital in defending American homes from a physical attack, strong masculine gender roles were essential in ensuring that the political will and determination of Americans to fight the communist threat did not crumble from within. Examples of the connections between deviation from traditional gender roles and accusations of political deviancy—specifically, being either communist or soft on communism—are myriad. Historians have demonstrated the strong association between the anticommunist worldview that was at the heart of liberal consensus, and the defense of strong gender roles. Kyle Cuordileone and Robert Dean, for example, have provided detailed accounts of the connections between anticommunist ideology and conservative conceptions of gender roles.[17] Strong, or "hard," masculinity was vital to the liberal consensus in providing the vitality and force of will necessary to fight the communist challenge.

The media were an important agency in policing the gender identity of the public and private spheres. Press coverage of the few women who did enter the public world of politics emphasized how they were able to retain their femininity. Newspaper accounts of Dorothy McCullough Lee's appointment to the Subversive Activities Board in 1956, for example, reassured readers that her political work had not damaged her womanliness. The *New York Daily News* described Lee—who had served as the first female mayor of Portland, Oregon, between 1949 and 1953—as the "Top Gal" of the executive branch. *Washington Post* reports on her appointment described her as "soft spoken" and "attractive."[18] One report even detailed that the "top gal" was "an attractive woman of 55 with gray hair and blue eyes who stands five feet six and weighs 115 pounds."[19] One article on her appointment—titled "I Can Also Cook, Admits Mrs. Lee"—noted, "she is a soft-spoken self-assured career woman with 'quite a domestic streak' who loves to sew and cook in her home."[20] Media coverage of other women in the public sphere was of similar tenor. An NBC report on the record number of female delegates from Dixie at a Democratic convention in 1954 noted, "Southern male delegates insist that their women haven't lost any of their femininity by getting into politics." This broadcast exhorted women viewers to "get out your fan and don your prettiest hat and look up the headquarters of the party you're interested in right in your ward, and get to work. It seems it's a woman's job after all, and you can still be a lady!"[21]

Overall, the press tended to portray women as an incongruous presence in public life. *Life* magazine titled its two articles about their role in local government in New Mexico and Virginia "Petticoat Rule in New Mexico" and "Petticoat Rule Scores Again."[22] Alongside this focus on feminine qualities, journalists emphasized that the entry of women into the public sphere did not reflect a resurgence of feminism. Dorothy McCullough Lee, one reporter informed readers, "would like to see many more women run for public office," but was at pains to explain, she "is decidedly not a feminist."[23] The women at the 1956 Democratic convention "wore real pretty dresses in sheer cotton in becoming colors and styles. Yes, they were feminine as against being feminist.'[24] As historian Joanne Meyerowitz has commented, "In their opening paragraphs numerous authors described their successful subjects as pretty, motherly, shapely, happily married, petite, charming, or soft voiced." This dogged focus on femininity, she suggests, "seems to have cloaked a submerged fear of lesbian, mannish, or man-hating women."[25] The consequence of the remasculinization of the public sphere was that women who sought to gain a place there risked being labeled "subversive" of either gender or political norms. Recent historiography on women activists in the period has lent credence to the suggestion that women who stepped into the public realm were subject to accusations of being either political deviants or sexual misfits.[26]

The pitifully low number of American women serving in elected positions at state and federal levels in this period would seem to testify to women's retreat to the domestic sphere in response to this media pressure.[27] In 1951 there were only eight women in the House of Representatives, and one woman (Margaret Chase Smith of Maine, a Republican) in the Senate. Yet these low numbers did not reflect American women's approval of or "obedience" to the feminine mystique. On the contrary, American women viewed the low number of women in public life as a dangerous problem rather than an appropriate reflection of the importance of strong gender roles to liberal consensus. Those women who had themselves sought public office recognized the need to persuade more women to join their ranks. Olive Remington Goldman, who ran unsuccessfully for congressional office in Illinois in 1946 and 1948, insisted, "No social order can function properly in which the largest single division of the population contributes, as women do in the US today, less than 5% of the highest legislative body."[28] Significantly, however, American female politicians argued that the low number of women in public life was the result, not of structural failings in the American system, but of women's timidity and lack of confidence. Rather than campaigning to challenge the sexism of mainstream politics or the media or the force of the feminine mystique and the masculinization of the public sphere, American women in politics urged their female colleagues to toughen up in response to the harsh demands of public life. Dorothy McCullough Lee exemplifies this approach. Lee insisted that the underrepresentation of women in political life did not reflect a lack of interest in politics or a preference for the domestic sphere. "The fear of defeat," she declared, "is the greatest single factor keeping women from running for public office."[29] Noting that "women in other countries who have won their rights more recently are taking more leadership in government and public life than are women in this country," Lee asserted, "We have to stop thinking of it as a man's world in which women are struggling to assume their place in fields other than those allocated to them."[30] "Women," she pronounced, "must realize how greatly we are needed [and] then get over our fears of defeat and criticism and our timidity and our sensitive feelings. They are luxuries we can no longer afford."[31]

Within both the Republican Party and the Democratic Party, influential women activists made the same argument, insisting that American women should not expect special treatment in order to facilitate their entry into the difficult world of mainstream politics. Post-suffrage activism within mainstream parties had initially imagined that women would constitute gender-specific groups both as voters and as political actors. Both the Republican and Democratic Parties had quickly established separate divisions, which party leaders hoped would demonstrate their commitment to women as politicians and voters. The integration of these divisions into the mainstream party organization in 1952 (on the Republican side) and 1953 (on the Democratic side) reflected the prevailing view of both male and female party activists that the existing American political framework offered sufficient opportunities regardless of sex, and that singling out women for special treatment or notice was unnecessary. While some party women had misgivings about the high-handed manner in which this reorganization was managed, many agreed that integration reflected the need for American women to contribute to political life as citizens rather than as women per se.[32] Recognizing the significant contribution of women at the grassroots level, influential women within both parties argued that women needed to reconcile themselves to the rough-and-tumble of political life if this grassroots activism was to contribute to an increase in the number of women in more visible political positions. India Edwards, executive director of the Women's Division of the Democratic Party between 1948 and 1953 and close adviser to Harry Truman, was robust in her analysis of women and politics. Speaking to the Young Democratic Club at Barnard College in 1956, Edwards explained, "The female politician must cultivate a skin like a rhinoceros so that she will not be hurt by the frequent abuses of political life. . . . Women must make men realize that they want to be accepted on the same basis of fair play and ability that men seek in male politicians."[33]

Despite the insistence of some American women that the low numbers of women in American public life required individual resolve rather than structural redress, the strong masculinization of the political world proved daunting. The perhaps understandable unwillingness on the part of many American women to subject themselves to the "abuses" of the public sphere, coupled with their strong desire to exercise some form of public engagement, contributed to a significant increase in the membership of women's associations.

For the majority of their members, women's voluntary associations in the period 1945–60 offered an attractive form of activism that served as an alternative to engagement with mainstream politics and facilitated the activism of American women without challenging the gendered structure of liberal consensus. Membership in these associations steadily increased throughout the 1950s and early 1960s as women recognized in these sex-segregated groups the opportunity to benefit from a supportive female network, to gain skills and confidence, and to wield the considerable influence accorded to these associations as the de facto national representatives of American women. Membership in the League of Women Voters (LWV) grew by 44 percent between 1950 and 1958, while membership in the American Association of University Women (AAUW) increased from 112,746 in 1950 to 170,000 in 1966.[34] While these figures do not constitute a mass movement, they do represent the continued relevance of women's voluntary associations in shaping the public activism of educated and influential women in America. Women's associations, by "domesticating" female activism, offered a way for women to move outside, but not too far outside, their domestic roles. A LWV survey suggested that "its members were quite fulfilled by combining familial roles with participation in local and community affairs."[35] "Groups such as the LWV and the PTA [Parent Teacher Association]," historian Susan Ware concludes, "created public roles for women denied access to the usual sources of power. And they made these roles available on the local level, where women could most easily make political contributions without necessitating drastic changes in their familial arrangements."[36] American women's associations were reluctant to challenge the primacy of women's role as homemaker, and their efforts to promote women's visibility in the public world were often represented as an effort to expand that role rather than a rejection of it. Like their nineteenth-century counterparts, American women's associations in the 1950s did not seek to challenge conservative gender roles and the strong sense of separate sphere ideology with which their culture was imbued, but rather sought to stretch and extend the boundaries of the home in order to promote women's public activism. Such promotion was carefully aligned with a strong approval of women's domestic role and the significant contribution made by homemakers to their nation.

For some observers, the existence of a strong and vibrant "separate sphere" of single-sex voluntary association in the United States was a contributing factor to the low numbers of American women in political life. In Dorothy McCullough Lee's opinion, "Too many women have permitted themselves to become victims of their fears and inhibitions . . . [W]e have not induced enough women who are leadership material *to step out of the security of their organizations* [emphasis added] and, as individuals to give their talents to the government."[37] At a time when gender conservatism restricted opportunities to enter the public world, women's associations offered a less demanding road to public activism for women. LWV president Percy Maxim Lee noted that while the vibrant voluntary sector was a benefit in American society, it did have an impact on women's entry into mainstream politics. "Invariably foreigners who visit the US and are interested in government," she commented, "ask why there aren't more women in public office." Lee argued, "our unique system of voluntary associations takes out of the hands of government many enterprises of a public character. . . . I believe that this multitude of voluntary associations constitutes a tremendously important safeguard in American life. . . . [T]hey do, however, in a very real sense keep out of politics many worthy people."[38] Acknowledging the need to increase the number of American women in public life, some women's associations did seek to push their members to move beyond their associational comfort zone. The Federation of Business and Professional Women, for example, abandoned its previously strict policy of nonpartisanship in 1946, so that its members could engage directly with party politics.[39]

Efforts on the part of American women's associations to encourage their members to think beyond their private role in the home consistently warned about the danger such a retreat would pose to the security and political stability of the nation. Rather than challenging or opposing the central tenets of the liberal consensus, women's associations thus appealed to the same Cold War imperatives that served to promote women's role in the private domestic sphere in order to promote women's entry into the public sphere of politics. The atomic threat, which was so frequently linked to the domestic roles of women as housewives and mothers, was seized upon by American women as a motivation for women to take a more prominent role in public life. The threat to the home front from atomic warfare was so great that American women argued it demanded that women bring their particular interest and skill in peace and negotiation into the public realm. Anthropologist Margaret Mead informed readers of the LWV journal, *Women's Day*, that male policymakers depended on the fear and passivity of homemakers in the face of the atomic threat, arguing, "the day the polls show that people aren't thinking about atomic power any more, that they are either too satisfied or too frightened even to talk about it, then the men who govern the country will start to relax."[40]

Efforts to increase the extent of American women's participation in public life also drew from a hitherto overlooked source: the strong correlation that American women activists recognized between fascist politics and the enforcement of gendered divisions of the public/private sphere. The influence of fascism on women activists across the world has been largely overlooked in favor of a focus on the impact of emerging Cold War tensions and divisions. In the aftermath of World War II, however, members of American associations, like their counterparts in other nations, were quick to recognize the gendered politics of fascism and urged women's greater participation in the public sphere as part of their responsibility in fighting for a truly democratic body politic. Drawing from the recent example of women in Germany and Italy, members of American women's associations argued that women had a special interest in promoting democracy and a responsibility to take an active role in political life. Freda Kirchwey, editor of *The Nation*, told members of the AAUW, "Generally speaking I don't like to speak generally about women," but "for special reasons of their own women should develop a fanatic attachment to the institutions and vital concepts of democracy. . . . Men of all professions can, if they accept its tenets, function somehow under tyranny. Women can function too, but only within the limits assigned to them. In other words, they can bear children."[41] In its celebration of the one hundredth anniversary of the Seneca Falls Declaration, the *Independent Woman*, the journal of the National Federation of Business and Professional Women, reminded its readers, "It was basic political philosophy in Hitler's Germany that woman's place was in any kind of home the state permitted her to have. . . . Are we going to let ourselves be pushed out of politics as the German women were?"[42]

Campaigns by American women to ensure that the conceptual masculinization of the public sphere of politics did not result in the exclusion of women from political life thus utilized the tenets of liberal consensus. In their efforts to promote American women's political role, American women politicians and members of women's associations referenced both the capacity of the existing American political system for inclusivity irrespective of gender and the need to defend the nation against extremism. Efforts to undermine the masculinization of the public world of work similarly used the tenets of liberal consensus to build a case against the exclusion of women. While the remasculinization of the workplace and the promotion of female consumption might have been an important part of the creation of the limitless abundance that would secure social harmony in the United States and would demonstrate the nation's superiority over the Soviet Union, some areas of work demanded the participation of women. Women's efforts to penetrate traditionally male spheres were justified by the Cold War imperative of defeat over the Soviet Union. Judge Lucy Somerville explained that the demands of the Cold War, like the military imperatives of World War II, required that women play their part. "Preparation for such a struggle," she explained, "demands that *all,* not part of the Nation's resources be mobilized. . . . From now on any war will mean total war and plans should be underway now for the utilization of women and men in case of war."[43] The Federation of Business and Professional Women's Clubs campaigned in the early 1950s to extend the draft to include eligible women, arguing that "the necessity and desirability of long-range planning for national security" meant that women, alongside men, should be prepared to serve their country. The federation explained, "the services of women as well as those of men are essential to the national security."[44]

A final, specific challenge to the masculinization of the workplace targeted the near monopoly held by men in the fields of engineering and science, as American women argued that women's efforts in skilled science and technology jobs could be crucial to U.S. success against the Soviet Union. In 1948, the *Journal of the American Association of University Women* warned that the substantial postwar U.S. technological and industrial superiority, on which the nation's status as the world's only superpower rested, was at risk if American women were not encouraged to take up jobs in emerging engineering industries. "The handwriting on the wall warns that Russia may surpass the U.S. industrially in the next few decades, if her people continue to develop at the rate of these past years and the U.S. continues to utilize only a small part of its latent power," the AAUW argued. "If industry of this country is to maintain its position of leadership, we shall need to make use of all our ability and ingenuity. With the abilities of both men and women released we women may need to make our maximum contribution in useful work and help democracy to retain its place in the sun."[45]

The failure of American women to challenge the gendered assumptions that lay at the heart of liberal consensus should not be interpreted as a slavish "obedience" to the feminine mystique. On the contrary, many American women feared the consequences of a masculinized public sphere, warning that such an imbalance might prove damaging to American democracy and security. The central role of gender in constructing the framework for liberal consensus, however, meant that few women were prepared to challenge the structural nature of the sexism that policed the boundaries between the private and public spheres. To critique the strong gender roles that underpinned the liberal consensus could all too quickly be interpreted as a critique of the liberal consensus itself. As one woman wrote to Betty Friedan, "I am not advocating that women become communist sympathizers, but

I am expecting progressive women will be so labeled."[46] The importance of gender as one of the building blocks of liberal consensus meant that few American women had the courage to identify gender roles and structural sexism as a problem in American life. While recognizing the need to oppose the effective masculinization of public life, American women sought to articulate this opposition in ways that stressed their loyalty and service to liberal consensus. "We must crash through that psychological barrier around the 'man's world idea' and range ourselves confidently beside the best that men have to offer," explained Dorothy McCullough Lee. "Then truly, our arsenal of democracy will present a formidable defense against any attempt to disrupt our way of life."[47] In articulating the desire and responsibility of American women for a public role in terms that stressed their role as engaged citizens, these women effectively concurred with prevailing ideologies regarding the stability and fairness of the existing political system and its ability to secure rights and representation for all American citizens. Encouraging American women to practice these rights was not presented as a critique or criticism of liberal consensus, but as much-needed support.

Notes

1. Godfrey Hodgson, *America in Our Time* (Garden City, NY: Doubleday, 1976), 496.

2. Ibid., 315.

3. Susan Ware, "American Women in the 1950s: Nonpartisan Politics and Women's Politicization," in Louise A. Tilly and Patricia Gurin, eds., *Women, Politics, and Change* (New York: Russell Sage Foundation, 1990), 290.

4. Susan M. Hartman, foreword, in Kathleen A. Laughlin and Jacqueline L. Castledine, eds., *Breaking the Wave: Women, Their Organizations, and Feminism, 1945–1985* (London: Routledge, 2011), xii.

5. Editorial, *Life*, January 22, 1945, 63.

6. *The Life and Times of Rosie the Riveter* (Video: Connie Field, Clarity Education Productions, 1980).

7. Quoted in Sherrie A. Kossudji and Laura J. Dresser, "Working Class Rosies: Women Industrial Workers during World War II," *Journal of Economic History* 52 (1992): 431–46 (quotation on 432).

8. See, e.g., Shelia Tobias and Lisa Anderson, *What Really Happened to Rosie the Riveter: Demobilization and the Female Labor Force 1944–1947* (New York: MSS Modular Publications, 1974); Amy Kesselman, *Fleeting Opportunities: Women Shipyard Workers in Portland and Vancouver during World War II and Reconversion* (Albany: State University of New York Press, 1990); Ruth Milkman, "Rosie the Riveter Revisited: Management's Post-war Purge of Women Automobile Workers," in Nelson Lichtenstein and Stephen Meyer, eds., *On the Line: Essays on the History of Autoworkers* (Urbana: University of

Illinois Press, 1989), 129–52; Ruth Milkman, *Gender at Work: The Dynamics of Job Segregation during World War II* (Urbana: University of Illinois Press, 1987)

9. Karen Tucker Anderson, "Last Hired First Fired: Black Women Workers during World War II," *Journal of American History* 69 (1982): 82–97, 95.

10. Advertisement for Maytag washer, *Life*, January 15, 1945, 79.

11. Advertisement for Kelvinator electrical appliances, *Life*, January 22, 1945, facing page 1.

12. See Karol Ann Marling, *As Seen on TV: The Visual Culture of Everyday Life* (Cambridge: Harvard University Press, 1994).

13. Schaefer to Eisenhower, November 22, 1955, "Women" file, box 852, Official File, Central Files, Eisenhower Presidential Library, Abilene, Kansas.

14. See Elaine Tyler May, *Homeward Bound: American Families in the Cold War Era* (New York: Basic Books, 1990); Laura McEnaney, *Civil Defense Begins at Home: Militarization Meets Everyday Life in the Fifties* (Princeton: Princeton University Press, 1990).

15. Katherine Howard, "Home Preparedness—Cornerstone of National Defense," address to Regional Civil Defense Council, box 1, Katherine Graham Howard Papers, Schlesinger Library, Radcliffe College, Cambridge, Massachusetts.

16. Katherine Howard, "The Land of the Free," address to the Ladies Auxiliary to the Veterans of Foreign Wars, Milwaukee, Wisconsin, August 5, 1953, box 1, Howard Papers.

17. Kate Weigand, "The Red Menace, the Feminine Mystique and the Ohio Un-American Activities Commission: Gender and Anti-communism in Ohio 1951–1954," *Journal of Women's History* 3 (1992): 71–94; Wendy Kozol, "'Good Americans': Nationalism and Domesticity in *Life*," in John Bodnar, ed., *Bonds of Affection: Americans Define their Patriotism* (Princeton: Princeton University Press, 1996); Robert Corber, *Homosexuality in Cold War America: Resistance and the Crisis of Masculinity* (Durham: Duke University Press, 1997); May, *Homeward Bound;* Robert Dean, *Imperial Brotherhood: Culture, Politics and the Cold War* (Amherst: University of Massachusetts Press, 2003); Alan Nadel, *Containment Culture: American Narratives, Postmodernism and the Atomic Age* (Durham: Duke University Press, 1995); K. A. Cuordileone, "'Politics in an Age of Anxiety': Cold War Political Culture and Crisis in American Masculinity 1949–1966," *Journal of American History* 87 (2000): 515–45.

18. *New York Daily News*, March 23, 1957; Elizabeth Shelton, "I Can Also Cook, Admits Mrs. Lee," *Washington Post*, September 1, 1956.

19. "Lawyer from the West," *New York Times*, September 1, 1956.

20. Shelton, "I Can Also Cook."

21. Transcript of NBC Broadcast from Chicago Democratic Convention, broadcast July 23, 1954, file 174, box 6, Martha R. Ragland Papers, Schlesinger Library.

22. "Petticoat Rule in New Mexico," *Life*, May 29, 1950, 25; "Petticoat Rule Scores Again," *Life*, September 18, 1950, 49.

23. Shelton, "I Can Also Cook"; "Lawyer from the West"; Eileen Summers, "Feminine Official Is No Feminist," *Washington Post*, April 28, 1957.

24. Summers, "Feminine Official Is No Feminist."

25. Joanne Meyerowitz, "Beyond the Feminine Mystique: A Reassessment of Postwar Mass Culture, 1946–1958," *Journal of American History* 79 (1993): 1455–82 (quotation on 1460).

26. See, e.g., Landon R. Y. Storrs, "Red Scare Politics and the Suppression of Popular Feminism: The Loyalty Investigation of Mary Dublin Keyserling," *Journal of American History* 90 (2003): 491–524; Landon R. Y. Storrs, "Left Feminism, the Consumer Movement, and Red Scare Politics in the United States, 1935–1960," *Journal of Women's History* 18 (2006): 46–67.

27. See Emmy E. Werner, "Women in Congress: 1917–1964," *Western Political Quarterly* 19 (1966): 16–30; and Emmy E. Werner, "Women in the State Legislatures," *Western Political Quarterly* 21 (1968): 40–50.

28. Olive Remington Goldman, "The Inexperienced Politician—Some Advantages and Handicaps of a Woman Candidate," *Journal of the AAUW* 41, no. 1 (Fall 1947): 19.

29. Quoted in "Women Told How to Run for Office," *New York Herald Tribune*, February 2, 1957.

30. "Chides Women for Failure to Use Rights, Privileges," *Washington Post and Times Herald*, July 18, 1958; Dorothy McCullough Lee, speech to National Municipal League, Kansas City (November 1954), file 168, Dorothy McCullough Lee Papers, Schlesinger Library, Radcliffe College, Cambridge, Massachusetts.

31. Dorothy McCullough Lee, speech to the American Legion Ladies Auxiliary, 1954, file 168, Dorothy McCullough Lee Papers. For a case study in the difficulties faced by women in electoral competitions see Greg Mitchell, *Tricky Dick and the Pink Lady: Richard Nixon vs. Helen Gahagan Douglas—Sexual Politics and the Red Scare, 1950* (New York: Random House, 1998).

32. See Kimberly Brodkin, "'We are neither male nor female Democrats': Gender Differences and Women's Integration within the Democratic Party," *Journal of Women's History* 19 (2007): 111–37.

33. "India Edwards Speaks Out on Female Political Role," *Columbia Spectator*, January 10, 1956.

34. Susan Levine, *Degrees of Equality: The American Association of University Women and the Challenge of Twentieth-Century Feminism* (Philadelphia: Temple University Press, 1995), 104; Eugenia Kaledin, *Mothers and More: American Women in the 1950s* (Boston: Twayne, 1984), 33.

35. Ware, "American Women in the 1950s," 290.

36. Ibid., 291.

37. Dorothy McCullough Lee, "Women: Their Interest in Public Affairs," speech, August 13, 1959, file 169, Dorothy McCullough Lee Papers.

38. Percy Maxim Lee, "Is It a Man's World?" speech to College Club of Hartford, Connecticut, February 12, 1953, file 12, box 1, Percy Maxim Lee Papers, Schlesinger Library, Radcliffe College, Cambridge, Massachusetts.

39. Kathleen A. Laughlin, "Civic Feminists: The Politics of the Minnesota Federation of the Business and Professional Women's Clubs, 1942–1965," in Laughlin and Castledine, *Breaking the Wave*, 17. Lena Phillips, the federation's founder, took advantage of this change in policy to run (unsuccessfully) for lieutenant governor of Connecticut on Henry Wallace's Progressive Party ticket.

40. Margaret Mead, "There's One Thing We Can Do about Atomic Energy," *Women's Day*, April 1946, 20.

41. Freda Kirchwey, "Democracy, Indivisible," *Journal of the AAUW* 39, no. 1 (Fall 1945): 4.

42. Mary Donlon, "Our Next Hundred Years," *Independent Woman,* July 1948, 195.

43. Press release, November 5, 1948, ref 00508, series III, American Association of University Women: Archives, 1881–1976 (microfilm).

44. "Our Stand on Registration and the Draft of Women," *Independent Woman,* September 1951, 295.

45. Alice L. Goff, "Women CAN be Engineers," *Journal of the AAUW* 41, no. 2 (Winter 1948): 76.

46. Quoted in May, *Homeward Bound*, 213.

47. Dorothy McCullough Lee, speech to the National Municipal League, Kansas City, Missouri, November 9, 1954, file 168, Dorothy McCullough Lee Papers.

14

Memories of the Movement

Civil Rights, the Liberal Consensus, and the March on Washington Twenty Years Later

GEORGE LEWIS

Identifying and categorizing the relationship between the historical realities of the civil rights movement and the explanatory model provided by the idea of a liberal consensus is far from simple. In one sense, for example, it is clear that the leading proponents of the movement viewed that relationship very differently from the leading progenitors of the model. Historians have come to different conclusions still, and so indeed have those who have sought to commemorate the movement subsequent to its demise. Despite—or perhaps because of—those apparent disparities, analyzing the positioning of the civil rights movement within the liberal consensus model is both historically and intellectually rewarding, for it not only offers a significant critique and then partial reassessment of the efficacy of the very idea of a liberal consensus, but also reveals much about the process of commemoration and the development of discourses of race and racism in recent U.S. history.

Viewed through one particular lens, it is clear that the jagged contours of the civil rights movement were never held to have sat easily within the smooth surfaces of the liberal consensus model. Even as that model's foremost contemporary proponents proclaimed it to be the most accurate means of describing and understanding the postwar United States, developing the consensus view that capitalism would work positively for society and bring progressive change in its wake, issues of race remained conspicuous by their absence. Thus, for example, Arthur Schlesinger Jr. not only glossed over issues of race and rights in his pivotal 1949 work, *The Vital Center*, but continued to do so in a 1962 edition which he had revised and developed while holding a roving brief within the Kennedy White House.[1] Schlesinger's fellow white liberal intellectuals were similarly unprepared to accommodate growing civil rights activism and protest within their explanatory frameworks for the 1950s and 1960s. As Walter A. Jackson has shown, liberalism's intellectual advocates were unresponsive to the questions that aspiring civil rights activists were posing; any discussion of the burgeoning civil rights movement in which they did deign to indulge was lent "an air of unreality" born of their collective "lack of comprehension" of that movement's aims, philosophies, goals, and drivers.[2]

When Godfrey Hodgson published his original "liberal consensus" thesis in 1976, he chose neither to ignore the postwar era's increasingly vocal campaigns for an end to institutionalized racial inequality nor to sublimate issues of race behind broader critiques of the economic backwardness of the South. Instead, he openly acknowledged that civil rights provided his theory with its singular blind spot: such activism did not fit within the bounds of the original liberal consensus thesis, and Hodgson was quick to admit to it. "The discrediting of any intellectual thesis usually begins with the discovery that it does not predict all the observable data," he wrote. "The first discovery the civil rights movement made was that the liberal account of American society simply did not predict what would happen in the Mississippi Delta or the Alabama Black Belt or southwestern Georgia. . . . A second discovery went further. It wasn't only local institutions that didn't fit the theory; national institutions didn't either, when they had to confront the reality of the Deep South."[3]

On particular points as well as generalities, the rough edges of the observable truth would simply not conform to the beautiful symmetry of an imposed academic pattern. In response to the notion that capitalism would inevitably bring positive, progressive societal change, Hodgson detected that some of the movement's key intellectuals and theorists rebuffed capitalism to find more comfort in the possibilities of a socialist future. As historians have recently returned to argue, such critiques positing economic injustice as an integral part of U.S. racial inequality were not simply confined to the margins of movement activity, but, as the confirmed leftists A. Philip Randolph and Bayard Rustin vividly displayed, came from as central a position as the organizing tents of the 1963 March on Washington. Similarly, a majority of American universities may well have stood as bastions of intellectual liberalism, but anti-desegregation riots at the University of Mississippi were populated as much by local students as by segregationist interlopers, forcing liberal voices such as faculty member James W.

Silver to resign and flee, and George Wallace's "Stand in the Schoolhouse Door" was such an integral part of the fabric of the University of Alabama that it was not until fifty years after the event, in 2013, that a concerted attempt to critique its memorialization had begun in earnest. In portentous terms, then, civil rights activists, and in particular northern white liberal volunteers, were left to discover "an appalling alternative explanation" to that offered by the liberal consensus: "that southern police, southern jails, southern institutions and southern racism might be not medieval extravagancies doomed to be reformed by the march of progress but mere variants of American police, American jails, American institutions and American racism."[4]

Recent historiographical shifts have accentuated rather than diminished the gap between the theory of the liberal consensus model and the historical reality that it purports to explain. Since Hodgson's thesis first appeared, historians have used a series of seminal texts to alter the prevailing view of civil rights activism to such an extent that any idea of a single narrative of consensus has long been replaced by balkanized narratives of geographical, institutional, temporal, and tactical division. To give but a few examples, William Chafe's *Civilities and Civil Rights* has pioneered the local case study approach that continues to dominate current historiographical thinking; Mary Dudziak has convinced many of the existence of a Cold War "imperative" for top-down civil rights change; J. Mills Thornton's *Dividing Lines* has suggested that 750 pages of fine-toothed research are necessary to do justice to the arcane complexities of civil rights organization and mobilization at the municipal level in a single state; an array of scholars have elucidated on the continuities that linked support for Jim Crow to the emergence of "new" conservatism in the late 1960s, 1970s, and 1980s; and robust critiques of the "declensionist" narrative of the end of the movement and the subsequent rise of a separate—and separatist—Black Power movement have been roundly accepted.[5]

In such a context, those seeking to revisit Hodgson's consensus model could be forgiven a certain degree of pessimism: in an era in which the historiographical trend has been to highlight a "long" civil rights movement and continuities in African American resistance to racism, his account of the movement accelerates from its purported origins to Rosa Parks's refusal to move on a Montgomery bus in precisely fifty words.[6] What remains striking, then, is just how accurate a view of the movement Hodgson went on to present, for in many parts his sophisticated take on movement dynamics foreshadowed later historiographical revisions. There is, for example, a realization missing in later fatuous and hagiographical accounts of Martin Luther King Jr. that, although he had become well known after the Montgomery Bus Boycott, King had, in Hodgson's words, "actually *done* very little" between the boycott and the sit-ins, along with an awareness that King was not a fully paid-up Gandhian disciple during the boycott, but that he was moved to learn about the details of Gandhi's work thereafter. In terms of movement organization, too, Hodgson was quick to note that unity was often an external facade that belied considerable internal division, both philosophical and tactical, and he brought similar insights to his analysis of movement organizations. Although the Southern Christian Leadership Conference (SCLC) managed to succeed in uniting lower- and middle-class black constituencies, it was "slow moving," while the National Association for the Advancement of Colored People (NAACP) was a lethargic behemoth that, in Hodgson's memorable prose, had worked for half a century for a new day, but "now it was dawning . . . was finding it hard to get out of bed." It also remains a measure of the continuing intellectual rigor of the mind that brought us the liberal consensus model that, when a new paperback edition to *America in Our Time* appeared in 2005, it was Hodgson himself who issued a corrective to the missing links between segregationist resistance and national conservatism.[7]

It needs no more than a brief knowledge of Hodgson's life, career, and working methods to understand why his insights on the civil rights movement remain so sharp. He often demonstrated a prescience and timeliness that led him to the epicenter of developing movement activity before it had fully formed, and as a result was able to interview more of the participants, organizers, and tacticians than most revisionist works combined. Thus, for example, he notes that not only was he present at the Freedom School in Oxford, Mississippi, in 1964 but that he met and interviewed Bob Moses there, that he covered the Atlantic City Convention where he interviewed Joseph L. Rauh Jr., that he happened to be staying with a friend in Montgomery when the bus boycott developed and was able to meet King, that he was at the Selma demonstrations, and that when the issue of Student Nonviolent Coordinating Committee (SNCC) volunteers carrying guns came to the fore, he was able to settle down to a "long, tape-recorded interview" with Stokely Carmichael. Elsewhere, a selection of his other interviewees includes Willie Ricks and Floyd McKissick on Black Power, Ezell Blair Jr. on the genesis of the sit-ins, George Wallace on massive resistance, Ella Baker on SCLC and SNCC, Bayard Rustin on tactical organization, and Julian Bond on radical politics.[8] It was the substantial insights that Hodgson gained from such encounters, allied to his own journalistic sense of realism, that led him to view the relationship between civil rights activism and the liberal consensus in a way that was signally different from the analysis of the liberal intellectuals of the 1950s and 1960s.

Given the clarity of the fact that, from the inception of the "liberal consensus" thesis, African American rights were not bound by it and the civil rights movement was not held to have operated within it, a central question needs to be addressed: why is it, then, that historical commemoration and iterations of public memory have actively chosen to do just the opposite, and have instead sought to represent the civil rights movement as part of that consensus? The process of revising the evidence of the historical record, and of canonizing the movement not as the exception to prove the liberal consensus rule but as a clear reflection of the consensus in action, took place swiftly and predated even the campaign to have Martin Luther King Jr.'s birthday celebrated as a national holiday. Indeed, it was largely in place by the time of a 1983 event that was designed primarily to commemorate but also to gain capital from the 1963 March on Washington. The "March Twenty Years Later" was held on August 27, 1983, and witnessed a larger crowd descend on the Mall in the nation's capital than that which had attended the original 1963 event. It received massive media coverage, with live television footage on the Cable News Network starting at 8 a.m., a parallel three-hour C-SPAN tribute to Martin Luther King Jr., some stations "cutting in" for live coverage throughout the day, and others, such as WDCA-Channel 20, showing a "highlights" package in a primetime evening slot.[9] SCLC member, District of Columbia congressman, chair of the Congressional Black Caucus, and part-organizer of the original 1963 March Walter E. Fauntroy served as the event's national director in front of a stellar cast of activists and celebrities, the majority of whom had either participated in or at the very least attended the original march, including Coretta Scott King, Joseph Lowery, John Lewis, Bill Cosby, Dick Gregory, Harry Belafonte, Julian Bond, Andrew Young, and Jesse Jackson, but others who were new to the roster were also included, such as Gloria Steinem.

The March Twenty Years Later carries a historical significance that belies its current omission from both the rich historical record and popular memory of civil rights activists and activism. It has, for example, thus far evaded the lens of those historians who have begun to extend analysis of the civil rights movement of the King era to incorporate the messy strands of late-1970s and 1980s protest and politics, when the boundaries and coalitions familiar from the 1950s and 1960s continued to fray and snap.[10]

Similarly, if less easily comprehensible, it is also missing from the autobiographies that have been written by, or at least ghosted on behalf of, many of those who were tasked with organizing or speaking at the anniversary event, including Ralph Abernathy, James Farmer, John Lewis, and at least two of Dick Gregory's, in which the comedian and activist skips from the original 1963 march to Louis Farrakhan's "Million Man March" of October 1995.[11] The importance of offering a corrective to those parallel omissions by ensuring that the March Twenty Years Later finds its place in both history and memory is not drawn from the need to offer a quantitative, event-by-event reconstruction of all civil rights protest. Rather, it rests on the qualitative difference that an analysis of the March Twenty Years Later can bring to ongoing discussions of the veracity, durability, and utility of the liberal consensus model, and also to the ways in which the event affects the most pressing debates surrounding the shape and character of the civil rights movement itself.

Historians of the civil rights movement have often had a complex relationship with the subjects of their studies, not least because, in stark comparison to so many other historical fields, many of those subjects are still active and often vociferous commentators on issues of race and rights. The particular complication generated by analyses of race and the liberal consensus is that a significant number of the movement's veterans, whether organizers, activists, or tacticians, have sought to represent the movement's relationship to the liberal consensus in a way that directly contradicts historians' understanding of that same model, including Hodgson's itself. Many of those involved in the March Twenty Years Later used the event to construct and propagate the view that the original 1963 March on Washington, and the particular phase of movement activity that they were seeking to commemorate more widely, was and always had been operating from deep within a liberal consensus model.

Given the roll call of those taking part in 1983, it would have been far easier to emphasize difference and divergence over consensus, for they formed a disparate group of unlikely bedfellows in what was a magnification of the differences that had beset elements of the original 1963 event. If, in 1963, an outward display of unity had masked significant inner differences between, for example, the increasingly mainstream methods of change espoused by King's SCLC and the capital's Catholic prelate, Archbishop Patrick O'Boyle, on the one hand, and SNCC's more radical John Lewis and the Congress of Racial Equality's James Farmer on the other, those differences were minor indeed compared to the coalition that assembled in 1983. Then, rather than marching for jobs and freedom, the commemorative event was officially a mobilization for "jobs, peace and freedom," which added deep-seated complications to its organizational focus and another tier of activists and protest groups to already fractious originals.

Thus, alongside returning stalwarts such as the NAACP and SCLC, representations were made by groups campaigning for nuclear disarmament, non-intervention in Latin America, opposition to loans to South Africa, greater rights and jobs for union members, an end to the death penalty, greater women's rights, gay rights, black fraternities, ecological rights, the "Gray Panthers," the Nation of Islam, and the remnants of Malcolm X's followers. Indeed, there were so many speakers due to speak from so many causes that Rustin declined to attend in 1983, citing the gravitational shift away from what he saw as the original agenda of the 1963 march.[12] The only significant reduction in representation came from Jewish groups, a number of which, disgruntled by the presence of others advocating dialogue with the Palestine Liberation Organization, cited the fact that the 1983 march was taking place on the Jewish Sabbath as a rationale for withdrawal: the 1963 march, by contrast, had taken place on a Wednesday.[13]

In a practical sense, the cornucopia of rights groups, speakers, and supporters at the March Twenty Years Later were also united not by the idea of putting unprecedented pressure on the sitting presidential administration, as had been the case in 1963 when Kennedy was the incumbent, but by outright opposition to the Reagan administration in general, and a willingness to obstruct his mooted return to the White House in 1984 in particular. That was certainly true of Jesse Jackson, whose participation was clearly for parallel purposes: to seek to further associations in the public mind between himself and King, both in terms of what King had achieved and stood for as an individual and in terms of his status as the primary leader of black America; and to use the 1983 march as a springboard for his own presidential campaign. The extent of Jackson's personal ambition was clear. The number of individuals clamoring to speak at the 1983 march was so great that organizers had to insist on a five-minute maximum at the podium, after which the public-address system would be unceremoniously turned off. Had such scheduling been in effect in 1963, it would have left King just short of his "Valley of Despair" rhetoric and yet to embark on his "Dream" codicil.

Twenty years later, in 1983, only one of the more than fifty speakers to address the rally was sufficiently bullish and suffused with his own sense of self-importance to demand longer at the microphone, and that was

Jackson. In the context of his potential tilt at the upcoming Democratic primaries, the day's organizers eventually met his demands, and Jackson used his ten-minute slot as a figurative means of elevating himself above his fellow speakers, as well as a more concrete opportunity to broadcast his developing campaign platform to a ready-made national audience. Throughout his ten minutes, he pointedly repeated the phrases that he had honed earlier that summer, when he had begun to generate political momentum with a swing through six southern states.[14] There was a clear and significant change of emphasis in his remarks and his demeanor. Gone was the idea of Jackson as but one of a number of political figures attempting to represent the African American community, replaced by the sense of a single individual intent upon harnessing black support to build a national coalition. Here was a base of support that was just as broad as that professed by the original proponents of the liberal consensus, as articulated by a politician with a particular interest in viewing previous iterations of the movement as unified. With its mix of representatives from Catholicism, Judaism, African American communities, organized labor, and white liberalism, it was also a prototype of the "rainbow coalition" concept that Jackson placed at the heart of his presidential quest. The vibrant dashikis that had undergirded Jackson's public appearances in the 1970s had also disappeared, replaced by the faux military fatigues of a revolutionary general: Jesse really was declaring war on Reagan's America.

The day's true coherence was drawn from its symbolism. In particular, it became clear that its organizers had consciously decided to represent the 1963 March on Washington as the high point of what Rustin referred to as the "classical" movement that had begun in the mid-1950s, and which, to all intents and purposes, culminated in the 1963 march—a version, in other words, of that which is now referred to as either the "master narrative" or "grand narrative" of the movement.[15] The successful construction of that narrative was predicated upon ideas of unity and consensus among its participants and, equally importantly here, among those in the legislative halls of power. Within that schema, the 1963 March on Washington was held to have been not the pivotal point of pressure that kept a reluctant White House interested in the idea of civil rights legislation, but a single symbolic representation of all of the civil rights activism and pressure of the postwar period, while the Civil and Voting Rights Acts that postdated it were viewed as its direct corollaries. The March on Washington, then, was a celebration of what could be achieved by those working within an American political system that wanted to facilitate the processes of racial change; it was in no way a product of the bloody battles and skirmishes that had been fought as a result of Hodgson's "appalling alternative explanation" that endemic racism was itself part of Americanism.

The public-relations opportunity that Kennedy had engineered for the end of the 1963 march, in other words, when its many leaders were pictured with him in the White House, had been successful: the civil rights movement worked within the Oval Office both literally and figuratively, to effect democratic change hand-in-hand with politicians who were delighted to be involved. Looking back twenty years later on that day on the Mall in 1963, the *Washington Post* recalled that it "today stands as a symbol of the democratic process at work."[16] Even Reagan tried to get in on the act, releasing a statement from his ranch in California noting that the 1963 march espoused values that "are shared by all of us," by which he meant a more just and free society, as well, of course, as a "more abundant" one.[17] That is less surprising in light of the fact that two of the individuals closely associated with the 1963 march, James Farmer and Ralph Abernathy, were not only significant figures in the 1983 event but had also followed their roles in the "classical" movement by either serving in or advising Republican presidential administrations.

Most noticeably, the 1983 version of the civil rights movement of the 1950s and 1960s was one in which the system was still held to work, one through which change would come organically via the constitutional institutions and processes at the heart of the United States, one in which a deceptively simple movement, united by the leadership of a single man, Martin Luther King Jr., worked and was allowed to work within the understood fabric of Americanism, and, finally, one that saw increasing economic development and American capitalism as part of a ready-made panacea for racial ills. Thus, when the *New York Times* editorialized on the differences between the 1963 and 1983 marches, it was the 1963 version that had "more cohesion and more sense of purpose," and, equally importantly, "a collective consciousness [that] was shaped and given definition by Dr. King's speech"—even if such comparisons went against the advice of Dick Gregory, who had preceded Jesse Jackson's tilt at the presidency by running as a write-in candidate in 1968. "Don't go comparing this march to the one 20 years ago," Gregory yelled out to the crowd at the 1983 march, before doing just that. "When we came here 20 years ago, most of us were scared. We're not scared today. When we came here 20 years ago, we came to ask the folks to take care of our business," he continued, rich in the myth that, in 1963, the movement merely had to come with a polite request to the Kennedy White House for civil rights change to be granted. "We're here to take care of our own business today," he concluded, for there was no longer the political will to be so accommodating.[18]

Indeed, the idea that fear among those participating in the original 1963 march was both pervasive and—by 1983—forgotten is symptomatic of the way in which a cleaner, more useful, and more joyful version of the original day had so swiftly been created. Duncan Howlett, for example, who was serving as associate pastor to James Reeb when he was clubbed to death in Selma, Alabama, remembered the original March on Washington as "one of my most joyous days. . . . You don't understand the euphoria," he explained, "until you first grasp the anxiety that existed throughout American society and in Washington over the gathering of a quarter of a million people on this explosive issue."[19] That potential explosion had never taken place, and, it followed, fears had been assuaged on the basis that the march had not been a threat because there was a national will to work with its leaders. The *reductio ad absurdum* came from Benjamin Hooks, who by 1983 was chair of the NAACP, and who looked back on the original march as a day on which those present had had to do little more than sing "We Shall Overcome" to bend the White House to their collective will.[20] Even such usually thoughtful and objective commentators as M. Carl Holman, Patt Derian, and Harry Ashmore bought in to the "Twenty Years Later" mythologizing. Brought together specifically to discuss the 1983 march and to reminisce about 1963, they unanimously recalled King as the day's central, totemic figure in what Holman labeled a "kind of a highwater mark event." It was, Derian recalled, "the first time that anybody had ever promised black southerners anything."[21]

The King-centric focus that pervaded an event that was avowedly a memorialization of a day-long march during which the Atlanta pastor spoke for a little over ten minutes is, of course, another example of the distorting effects of both history and memory. Given the extent to which King was represented, the surprise is that the day's event was not named after him directly. The 1983 stage was adorned with a giant banner proclaiming that "We Still Have a Dream," and one of the 1983 comperes, Bill Cosby, wore a King T-shirt that reflected his personal attachment to the leader which resurfaced in other aspects of his entertainment work, not least his eponymous, multi-award-winning television show, where, four days before the first observance of King's birthday as a national holiday on September 26,

1985, an episode was aired in which his fictional family ended a feud and returned to its own state of consensus because of a chance encounter with the "I Have a Dream" speech on the household's television set.[22]

As is now clear in the historical record, many of King's closest advisers believed him to have failed to make the most of the magnitude of the opportunity afforded to him: much of the original 1963 audience missed King's speech because they had already begun the journey homeward, and as *Washington Post* journalist Haynes Johnson recalled, his own paper's final edition failed to print any part of King's text, and neither "did its lead story," printed on two full pages, "quote a single word he said." When that leader listed the names of all those who spoke at the bottom of the page and concluded with the last name, "the Rev. Dr. Martin Luther King Jr. of the Southern Christian Leadership Conference," it was the first mention of his name in that day's paper. In a story on an adjoining page, halfway down, his name appeared again. It was noted that "he had used the refrain 'I have a dream' in his remarks about brotherhood."[23] By 1983, not only did the day's message and oratory center firmly on King, but so too did many of the participants, not least fourteen-year-old Martin Luther King Williams, and others who explained their participation as a bid "to rekindle the spirit" of King. Coretta Scott King, whose pronouncements on her slain husband should make all advocates of careful balance a little nervous, chose to remember the 1963 march similarly, anthropomorphizing a day of protest, speeches, and performance into a vision of a single "young American"—her husband—which "kindled the aspirations of the best of our nation."[24]

The decision to recast the 1963 march as the high point of a movement that operated cleanly and clearly within the liberal consensus model was keenly observable in the representation of the classical movement's economic aims. The chosen view from 1983 was of a 1963 movement that thought in terms of greater job opportunities for all Americans leading inexorably to the attainment of the American dream, not the more critical economic critiques that saw King's later years tarred by those in the political mainstream as dangerously radical. The view from the Reagan-era participants in the 1983 march was that by 1963 liberalism had allowed real economic gains to be made in the wake of the movement, only for growing conservatism to roll them back in the decades that followed as the consensus broke. Thus, for example, the cornucopia of speeches and rhetoric that formed the events of August 27, 1963, was boiled down to the repeated refrain of King's "Dream": absent were 1963's radical calls for a return to "revolution" from the then twenty-three-year-old John Lewis; gone, too, were any references to the less-well-known passages of King's speech, in which he had presaged the passages of his "Dream" with a critique of the liberal consensus theory, by devising the metaphor of African Americans living "on a lonely island of poverty in the midst of a vast ocean of material prosperity," and African Americans who had, as a result, come to Washington to "cash a check" because they "refuse to believe that the bank of justice is bankrupt."[25]

The "bad check" motif played directly into a central tenet of the liberal consensus model, which held that positive and progressive change would come to African Americans, and indeed to all disadvantaged Americans, via the capitalism-driven economic growth central to the liberal consensus model and from an active polity that included all aspects of society. Schlesinger, for example, lit upon the United States' "mixed economy" response to Soviet communism as the defining element of American liberalism when revisiting his *Vital Center* in the year prior to the 1963 march, while his fellow liberal intellectuals continued to adhere to a gradualist approach that cast the South's problems as primarily economic and only secondarily racial.[26] The importance of such an economically centered approach was still visible in 1983, not least in the shape of union participation: more than thirty major labor unions offered the marchers support at the national level, local unions from over three hundred U.S. cities contributed financial support, and, while elements of the 1963 march had openly attacked the AFL-CIO for being insufficiently supportive of African American labor rights, and indeed of contributing to the problem besetting African American economic equality through a continued lack of genuine desegregation of unions and union opportunities, by 1983 the AFL-CIO had become a central organizing hub of the march due to rising black unionization trends and increased unemployment. Of the four thousand buses that were booked to ferry participants to Washington in 1983, the vast majority were chartered by unions. As those unions were wont to argue, opposition was no longer in the gothic form of "Bull" Connor but in "lifeless statistics": black unemployment ran at 17.9 percent in comparison to 9.5 percent for white Americans, and black median family income was half that of its white equivalent.[27]

Understanding why, precisely, the March on Washington was memorialized as part of the liberal consensus model, when many of the disparate parts of the movement that it sought to represent had rejected liberalism and had never operated within the liberal consensus model, is not easy. At least a partial explanation lies with the certainties that such modeling provided for those veterans of the civil rights struggle who, by the 1980s, were finding it progressively more difficult to understand the new environment in which they were being forced to operate.

The increasingly fragmented nature of the coalition that came together to organize the March Twenty Years Later reflected wider changes in racial protest and policies that had taken place by the Reagan era. The singular, issue-driven clarity that had characterized and united a previous generation of activists had been replaced by a broadening of the lens and a resultant loss of focus, as characterized by the response from the totemic publications of black consciousness. The NAACP, for example, dedicated the edition of *The Crisis* magazine that directly preceded the 1983 march not to memorializing King or advertising the upcoming event but to a celebration of "the black woman," while the equivalent edition of *Ebony* carried not an in-depth report on the day's commemoration and aims but a special issue dedicated to "The Crisis of the Black Male." Gone were the days in which issues of gender were consciously sublimated by activists in the name of preserving a unified front in a single-issue campaign.[28]

At least with its September issue, *Ebony* paid homage to the idea of forging consensus out of previous separation, albeit circuitously. It featured an interview between Charles L. Sanders and Alabama governor George Corley Wallace, who, little more than two months before King stood at the feet of the Lincoln Memorial to deliver his "I Have a Dream" speech, had stood in the schoolhouse door at the University of Alabama to block the institution's desegregation. It was such a brazen act of defiance that Wallace swiftly became a national and international symbol of unrepentant white supremacy. By 1983, however, Wallace, too, was trying to reevaluate the past and had reinvented himself as a politician of racial consensus. The *Ebony* interview came replete with images of "some blacks" appointed by Wallace, although Sanders would doubtless have wanted to emphasize the former of those two words and Wallace the latter. As part of a concerted attempt at a political transformation that was so radical as to reimagine the arch-segregationist Wallace as a key component of the consensus model, the governor had instructed one of his African American aides, Dolores Pickett, to campaign on his behalf in November 1982 with the slogan "Forgiveness is in our Christian upbringing; it's something that Martin Luther King taught us."[29]

It is also of particular importance here that many of those actively involved in the March Twenty Years Later, and in particular in the formulation of a memory of the 1963 march as a celebration of liberalism and its possibilities, had also been actively involved in the 1963 march. Certainly, in some cases, youthful radicalism looked very different when viewed through the cataracts of older age and a more conservative hindsight. James Farmer, of course, had thrown down the gauntlet to King at the 1963 March on Washington by preferring to remain in jail in Louisiana as a matter of principle, when he could have posted bail in time to have allowed him to take up a slated speaker's position on the march's podium. In 1963, then, Farmer had made a conscious and very public declaration of his ideological attachment to nonviolent direct action and the importance of grassroots activism. By 1983, however, Farmer's recollections suggested a rather different ideological take: "In the early '60s we were very popular people—no one would think of having a cocktail party without one of us there," was his inexplicable recollection to one journalist.[30]

Elsewhere, the particular political pathways that certain activists had followed since the 1960s inevitably altered the way in which they chose to recall the past. King's former confidant and SCLC stalwart Ralph Abernathy, for example, defected from lifelong Democratic Party allegiance to an open endorsement of Reagan's candidacy in 1980. Abernathy's rationale offers another glimpse of the complexity of the terrain, for he sided with Reagan precisely because he believed the former California governor to be closer to the ideals of liberalism than his Democratic Party foes. Reagan would boost the economy and return the United States to a working capitalism, Abernathy believed, and that in turn would lead to government-supported free-enterprise programs that would be used to improve society. For Abernathy, this positioned Reagan closer to the ideals of liberalism.[31] Having received a preelection pledge of backing for his putative Foundation for Economic Enterprises Development in return for his visible support, however, Abernathy found that he could not contact Reagan—or indeed anyone remotely close to him—after his electoral victory, and he returned in 1984 to the safer waters of Jesse Jackson's primary run.

Part of the answer, too, doubtless lies in sections of the population wanting to believe that the United States was capable of a period as apparently virtuous as that delineated by the liberal consensus. Here, there are close similarities with the desire to believe in an Obama-centered "post-racial" nation.[32] Such a scenario allows King to be remembered as a mainstream figure with whom the whole nation could empathize rather than as the radical critic of U.S. economic and military policies that he became, and also largely erases any memory of the role of more complex figures, such as the brooding presence of Malcolm X, who frequented the hotel lobbies of Washington in the days leading up to the March, despite Elijah Muhammad's embargo on the event for Nation of Islam supporters and Malcolm's own depiction of the "Farce on Washington" as little more than a "one-day 'integrated' picnic."[33] As Julian Bond noted on the fortieth anniversary of the 1963 march, when he was serving as chair of the NAACP, "For many white people, the laws that were passed in the 1960s took care of everything. For them, they just shrug their shoulders and say 'What's the problem? I don't get it.'"[34] That also reflects a willingness to believe in the structural architecture of participatory liberal democracy, especially from within the context of a presidential administration that appeared so willing to ignore demands to intervene directly on behalf of African Americans: Reagan, of course, not only famously failed to recognize his one black cabinet member but also met the Congressional Black Caucus only once during his two terms of office.

Finally, the issues surrounding the portrayal of the civil rights movement and the 1963 march have been influenced by, and in turn must have an influence upon, the ways in which historians have sought to portray that period of protest. In general terms, it represents a desire to bring the civil rights movement back within easy comprehension. It is certainly true that the earliest histories of the classical phase of the movement so distorted its contours and flattened its complexities as to leave a leader-focused, top-down history that was so alien to many of those activists who had themselves taken part that they could not reconcile it with their own experiences and recollections. Equally, however, the historiographical correctives that have since been issued have added such dense complexity and fragmentation that the very concept of a single civil rights movement that bound its participants into one identifiable movement is in danger of being lost. Historians have offered compelling analyses of the ways in which activism took on different forms for different people in different places at different times, and continue to offer exhortations for ever-greater layers of complexity, alongside equally compelling arguments for why further case studies, other voices, and wider perspectives must not be forgotten. What they have not been able to do, however, is to offer a solution for how that great mass of material should—or, indeed, could—be reworked into a single, essential historical narrative.[35] For those wishing to remember the movement publicly in 1983, and to use its capital for their own advantage, it was critical to have a workable, usable, and above all easily disseminated description and definition of what that movement had been. Here, the liberal consensus model remained crucial.

In more specific terms, the way in which the veterans of the 1963 march chose to remember that event, and the movement of which it formed such a signal part, offers an informative commentary on one of the most urgent historiographical debates in the field. Hodgson may have unnecessarily compressed the timespan of the civil rights movement's origins, but others have more recently attempted to elongate it beyond useful boundaries. Most notably, those who have been termed the "UNC School" of historians have driven a debate in which they argue for the reconceptualization of civil rights as a "long" movement with its origins decades before the 1963 March on Washington. Such a view necessarily brings with it a sharp critique of the way in which a selective, top-down "master" narrative of that struggle, revolving around King at its centripetal core, has come to dominate public consciousness and discourse as well as a number of historical analyses. Led by Jacqueline Dowd Hall, they have argued that broad acceptance of the idea of the movement running from "Montgomery to Memphis," but with a significant pause in Washington, DC, in the summer of 1963 for King's "I Have a Dream" speech, has produced a "narrative breach" and skewed the true history of activists and activism. From this critical perspective, it has led to the memorializing and commemoration of a national movement as one that was merely southern, and to the compression of a movement that was equally centered around jobs, opportunity, race, and rights into one remembered as having had little more than a "limited, noneconomic objective."[36]

As the detail of the March Twenty Years Later has shown, though, such an analysis once again returns the movement's activists and participants to a view of a movement that they do not themselves recognize, or at least which they themselves do not choose to recollect. That is especially true of the critique that Hall offers of the way in which the movement's putative economic work has been judged. In the prism through which the UNC School has sought to review the movement and its memory, "the struggle for economic justice," to quote Hall, "has been erased altogether."[37] That was certainly not the case in the commemoration and memorialization presented by the organizers and speakers of the 1983 march, for whom economics, and in particular union solidarity, remained central.[38] Finally, in seeking to explain the disjunction between the movement's complexities and memory's distortions and simplifications, Hall has pointed to the political role played by the New Right and has argued that many of those distortions were not due to an organic process but were actively "germinated in well-funded right-wing think tanks."[39] With the March Twenty Years

Later, however, that was clearly not the case, for it was the participants themselves who were responsible for recasting the civil rights movement in general and the 1963 March on Washington in particular as products of a liberal consensus.

Notes

1. See the introduction in Arthur M. Schlesinger Jr., *The Vital Center: The Politics of Freedom* (Cambridge, MA: Riverside Press, 1962), ix–xvii. Although not part of the official subtitle, the cover of Schlesinger's book includes "Our Purposes and Perils on the Tightrope of American Liberalism."

2. Walter A. Jackson, "White Liberal Intellectuals, Civil Rights and Gradualism, 1954–1960," in Brian Ward and Tony Badger, eds., *The Making of Martin Luther King and the Civil Rights Movement* (Basingstoke: Macmillan, 1996), 96, 98.

3. Godfrey Hodgson, *America in Our Time* (Garden City, NY: Doubleday, 1976), 182–83.

4. Ibid., 182–83, 189–90 (quotations on 183). "And so," Hodgson concluded, "the civil rights movement had two faces: a public face of victory and a private face of disillusionment" (184); see also William P. Jones, *The March on Washington: Jobs, Freedom, and the Forgotten History of Civil Rights* (New York: Norton, 2013); James W. Silver, *Mississippi: The Closed Society* (New York: Harcourt, Brace & World, 1963); and for a filmic interrogation local memory and the School House Door incident, see Sarah Melton, "A Sleight of History: University of Alabama's Foster Auditorium," *Southern Spaces,* October 2009, available at http://www.southernspaces.org/2009/sleight-history-university-alabamas-foster-auditorium (accessed August 15, 2016).

5. For examples of those historiographical shifts, see Jacqueline Dowd Hall, "The Long Civil Rights Movement and the Political Uses of the Past," *Journal of American History* 91 (March 2005): 1233–63; William H. Chafe, *Civilities and Civil Rights: Greensboro, North Carolina, and the Black Freedom Struggle* (New York: Oxford University Press, 1980); Mary L. Dudziak, "Desegregation as a Cold War Imperative," *Stanford Law Review* 41 (November 1988): 61–120; J. Mills Thornton III, *Dividing Lines: Municipal Politics and the Struggle for Civil Rights in Montgomery, Birmingham, and Selma* (Tuscaloosa: University of Alabama Press, 2002); Lisa McGirr, *Suburban Warriors: The Origins of the New Right* (Princeton: Princeton University Press, 2002); Joseph Crespino, *In Search of Another Country: Mississippi and the Conservative Counterrevolution* (Princeton: Princeton University Press, 2007); and Peniel E. Joseph, introduction to Joseph, ed., *The Black Power Movement: Rethinking the Civil Rights–Black Power Era* (New York: Routledge, 2006), 1–26.

6. Hodgson, *America in Our Time,* 184; Hall, "Long Civil Rights Movement."

7. Hodgson, *America in Our Time,* esp. 184 and 186; afterword in Godfrey Hodgson, *America in Our Time: From World War II to Nixon—What Happened and Why* (Princeton: Princeton University Press, 2005), 537–61.

8. See Hodgson's endnotes to the original edition of *America in Our Time* for details of his oral histories and interviews. He also had full access to contemporary news film footage of direct-action protests for an independent television documentary that he was charged with making.

9. "The TV Column," *Washington Post*, August 27, 1983, C8.

10. That extended view has already led to some impressive studies, notably Stephen Tuck, *We Ain't What We Ought to Be: The Black Freedom Struggle from Emancipation to Obama* (Cambridge: Belknap Press, 2010); and Adam Fairclough, *Better Day Coming: Blacks and Equality, 1890–2000* (London: Penguin, 2001).

11. Ralph David Abernathy, *And the Walls Came Tumbling Down: An Autobiography* (New York: Harper & Row, 1989); James Farmer, *Lay Bare the Heart: An Autobiography of the Civil Rights Movement*, with a new preface (Fort Worth: Texas Christian University Press, 1998); John Lewis with Michael D'Orso, *Walking with the Wind: A Memoir of the Movement* (San Diego: Harcourt, Brace, 1998); Dick Gregory with Robert Lipsyte, *Nigger: An Autobiography* (London: George Allen & Unwin, 1965); and Dick Gregory with Sheila P. Moses, *Callus on My Soul: A Memoir* (Atlanta: Longstreet Press, 2000), 79.

12. "Jobs, Peace, Freedom Demonstration to Mark King's '63 Rally," *Los Angeles Times*, August 13, 1983, A10.

13. For a list of those represented, see, e.g., "Over 20 Years, the Mood Has Changed Markedly," *New York Times*, August 28, 1983, A28; and "Veterans of '63 Reunited in Joy, Sorrow, Nostalgia," *Washington Post*, August 28, 1983, A19. For the decision of certain Jewish groups to stay away, see "Religion Supplement" to *Washington Post*, August 6, 1983, esp. B6; and for opposition to South African loans, see "The Movement's Unfinished Business Is a Tough Agenda," *New York Times*, August 28, 1983, E5.

14. "Reagan Assailed at Rally of 250,000," *Los Angeles Times*, August 28, 1983, A1; Fay S. Joyce, "Fiery Jesse Jackson Attracting Politicians' Praise and Criticism," *New York Times*, June 27, 1983, A10; Howell Raines, "Pressure on Jackson," *New York Times*, June 22, 1983, A21; Marshall Frady, *Jesse: The Life and Pilgrimage of Jesse Jackson* (New York: Simon & Schuster, 1996), 306.

15. The "master narrative" or "grand narrative" of the civil rights movement, constructed by some historians, begins with either the *Brown* decision of 1954 or the Montgomery Bus Boycott of 1955–56. The March on Washington was the penultimate event before the climactic legislative and grassroots developments of 1964–65. Kathryn L. Nasstrom urges the use of the "grand" rather than "master" descriptor "to avoid the gendered and racialized connotations of the word *master*." See Nasstrom, "Between Memory and History: Autobiographies of the Civil Rights Movement and the Writing of Civil Rights History," *Journal of Southern History* 74 (May 2008): 325–64, esp. 329.

16. "Day That Altered a Nation," *Washington Post*, August 27, 1983, A11, A14.

17. Reagan quoted in "Reagan Assailed at Rally of 250,000."

18. "Over 20 Years, the Mood Has Changed Markedly," *New York Times*, August 28, 1983, A28. Gregory's speech can be seen on the newsreel footage of the "March Twenty Years Later," which is available on *Martin Luther King: I Have a Dream* (DVD, MPI, 2005).

19. "Duncan Howlett: Minister's Washington Pulpit Focused on Civil Rights Issue," *Washington Post*, August 27, 1983, A13.

20. For an excerpt of Hook's 1983 speech, see "Excerpts of Speeches," *Washington Post*, August 28, 1983, A20. Excerpts of his speech also made the newsreel footage of the "March Twenty Years Later."

21. "The Movement's Unfinished Business Is a Tough Agenda." Holman was president of the National Urban Coalition and a previous community leader in Atlanta. Derian

had served as President Carter's assistant secretary for human rights. Ashmore provided a leading voice of southern moderation throughout much of the classical phase of civil rights activity, serving as editor of the *Arkansas Gazette* from 1947 to 1959.

22. "Vanessa's Bad Grade," *The Cosby Show*, series 2, episode 14.

23. Haynes Johnson, "Amid the Hoopla and Hype, Let's Not Forget What King Said," *Washington Post*, August 21, 1983, A3.

24. "DC: From Protest to Power," *Washington Post*, August 27, 1983, A14.

25. "Text of the Speech Dr. King Delivered 20 Years Ago Today," *New York Times*, August 28, 1983, A28.

26. See introduction in Schlesinger, *The Vital Center*; and Jackson, "White Liberal Intellectuals," esp. 97.

27. "Labor Unions Get in Step for March on DC," *Washington Post*, August 7, 1983; see also *Los Angeles Times*, August 27, 1983. For an analysis of the machinations that led to the AFL-CIO's position as the "one major liberal body that rebuffed Randolph's request for support" in 1963, see Jones, *The March on Washington*, esp. chapter 5 (quotation on 171).

28. *The Crisis*, June/July 1983; *Ebony*, August 1983. For conscious—and unconscious—sublimations of gender in the Movement, see Anne Standley, "The Role of Black Women in the Civil Rights Movement," in Vicki L. Crawford, Jacqueline Anne Rouse, and Barbara Woods, eds., *Women in the Civil Rights Movement: Trailblazers and Torchbearers, 1941–1965* (Bloomington: Indiana University Press, 1993), 181–202.

29. Charles L. Sanders, "Has Governor George Wallace Really Changed?" *Ebony*, September 1983, 44–46, 48, 50.

30. "SCLC Vows to 'Change Nation Around,'" *Washington Post*, August 25, 1983, A12.

31. In his memoir, *And the Walls Came Tumbling Down*, Abernathy recalled endorsing Reagan because he "advocated and initiated job-training programs to remove [black] people from welfare" (590).

32. The idea of Obama as a "post-racial" candidate began to gather momentum after his speech to the Democratic National Convention in 2004 and continued apace after his 2008 election. For C-SPAN's coverage of the former, see http://www.c-span.org/video/?182718-3/watch-president-obamas-2004-dnc-convention-keynote-address (accessed August 15, 2016); for commentary on the latter, see Michael Eric Dyson, "Race, Post Race," *Los Angeles Times*, November 5, 2008, available at http://www.latimes.com/opinion/la-oe-dyson5-2008nov05-story.html (accessed August 15, 2016).

33. Malcolm X with Alex Haley, *The Autobiography of Malcolm X* (London: Penguin, 1965), 385, 388; Charles Euchner, *Nobody Turn Me Around: A People's History of the March on Washington* (Boston: Beacon Press, 2010), 54.

34. "Old Dream and New Issues 40 Years after Rights March," *New York Times*, August 24, 2003, 1, 22.

35. Emilye Crosby, e.g., argues for the need to include local narratives and bottom-up case studies in a bid to expose what she terms the popular "sugar coated," top-down narrative that predominates in movement histories. While her critique is entirely defensible, she does not offer any suggestions of how such a multi-stranded approach might be brought together into a single unifying framework. See "Introduction: The Politics of Writing and Teaching Movement History," in Crosby, ed., *Civil Rights History from the Ground Up:*

Local Struggles, A National Movement (Athens: University of Georgia Press, 2011), 1–39 (esp. 7).

36. Hall, "Long Civil Rights Movement," esp. 1234, 1238.

37. Ibid., 1258.

38. A *New York Times* article, "Old Dream and New Issues 40 Years after Rights March," published on the fortieth anniversary of the 1963 march, clearly recognized those initial 1963 economic goals, noting that "the liberal economic agenda championed by Randolph, Rustin and King remains stalled in the eyes of many."

39. Hall, "Long Civil Rights Movement," 1238.

Contributors

Editors

Robert Mason is professor of twentieth-century U.S. history at the University of Edinburgh. He has published widely on the modern Republican Party. In addition to journal articles and book chapters, he has written two monographs in this field: *Richard Nixon and the Quest for a New Majority* and *The Republican Party and American Politics from Hoover to Reagan*. With Iwan Morgan, he also coedited *Seeking a New Majority: The Republican Party and American Politics, 1960–1980*.

Iwan Morgan is professor of U.S. studies and Commonwealth Fund Professor of American History in the Institute of the Americas, University College London. He also holds an honorary fellowship at Oxford University's Rothermere American Institute. He was chair of the executive committee of the Historians of the Twentieth Century United States from 2007 to 2013. He has published in various fields of political, economic, and film history, including three books on fiscal policy: *Eisenhower versus "The Spenders": The Eisenhower Administration, the Democrats and the Budget, 1953–60*; *Deficit Government: Taxation and Spending in Modern America*; and *The Age of Deficits: Presidents and Unbalanced Budgets from Jimmy Carter to George W. Bush*, winner of the American Politics Group Richard E. Neustadt Prize for 2010. His most recent publication is a biography of America's fortieth president, *Reagan: American Icon*.

Contributors

Uta A. Balbier is senior lecturer in American history at King's College London. She was previously a research fellow at the German Historical Institute in Washington, DC. She has published widely in German sports history, her initial field of interest, but now focuses on U.S. and transnational history. In addition to her published journal articles and book chapters, she is presently completing a monograph on Billy Graham's revival campaigns in the United States and Europe in the 1950s and 1960s.

Jonathan Bell is professor of American history and director of the Institute of the Americas at University College London. He is chair of the executive committee of the Historians of the Twentieth Century United States. His research focuses on the relationship between political ideas and social change. In addition to numerous scholarly articles and book chapters in this field, he has published *The Liberal State on Trial: The Cold War and American Politics in the Truman Era*; *California Crucible: The Forging of Modern American Liberalism*; and *Making Sense of American Liberalism* (coedited with Tim Stanley).

Gary Gerstle was formerly John G. Stahlan Professor of American History and professor of political science at Vanderbilt University and is currently Paul Mellon Professor of American History at the University of Cambridge. His publications include *Working-Class Americanism: The Politics of Labor in a Textile City, 1914–1960*; *The Rise and Fall of the New Deal Order, 1930–1980* (coedited with Steve Fraser); and *American Crucible: Race and Nation in the Twentieth Century*, winner of the Theodore Saloutos Book Award for outstanding work on immigration and ethnicity. His latest book is *Liberty and Coercion: The Paradox of American Government from the Founding to the Present*. He is also editor of the Princeton University Press series Politics and Society in Twentieth Century America.

Alex Goodall is senior lecturer in international history at University College London. His research focuses on both the United States and Latin America in examining the political and intellectual history of communism and anticommunism and other revolutionary and counterrevolutionary movements in the modern Americas, considered in both a national and transnational perspective. In addition to numerous scholarly articles and book chapters in this field, he has published *Loyalty and Liberty: American Countersubversion from World War I to the McCarthy Era*. He is presently completing a coauthored volume on the history of "Open Door" American foreign policy.

Michael Heale is research and teaching fellow at Oxford University's Rothermere American Institute. He spent the greater part of his career at the University of Lancaster, where he is now Emeritus Professor of American History. His research interests have embraced early-nineteenth-century U.S. history (social reform and the Jacksonian era), the British historiography of America, American anticommunism, the Reagan administration, and (currently) late-twentieth-century U.S. political history, particularly the interaction between domestic politics and globalization. His major publications include *The Presidential Quest: Candidates and Images in American Political Culture, 1787–1852*; *American Anticommunism: Combating the Enemy Within, 1850–1970*; *McCarthy's Americans: Red Scare Politics in State and Nation, 1935–1965*; and *Twentieth Century America: Power and Politics in the United States, 1900–2000*.

Godfrey Hodgson was formerly director of the Reuters Foundation Programme at Oxford University, and before that the *Observer*'s correspondent in the United States and foreign editor of the *Independent*. A prolific and influential author and commentator, he is the author of *America in Our Time* (1976; reissued in 2005), the study that principally advanced the idea of the "liberal consensus." His most recent book is *JFK and LBJ: The Last Two Great Presidents*. His earlier books include *The World Turned Right Side Up: A History of the Conservative Ascendancy in America*; *The Gentleman from New York: Senator Daniel Patrick Moynihan*; *More Equal Than Others: America from Nixon to the New Century*; *A Great and Godly Adventure: The Pilgrims and the Myth of the First Thanksgiving*; and *The Myth of American Exceptionalism*.

Helen Laville is professor and Pro-Vice-Chancellor for Education at Manchester Metropolitan University. Her research focuses on women's history, particularly in the Cold War era. She has published numerous scholarly articles, book chapters, and a monograph, *Cold War Women: America's Women's Organization in the Cold War*, which was shortlisted for the Gladstone Prize. She is currently doing research on the internationalization of women's rights and on women's role in the implementation of civil rights in the United States.

George Lewis is reader in American studies and director of the American Studies Centre at the University of Leicester. He is a former member of the British Association for American Studies executive committee. His research has focused on the white South's reaction to the civil rights movement. In addition to numerous articles and book chapters, he has published *The White South and the Red Menace: Segregationists, Anticommunism and Massive Resistance, 1945–1965* and *Massive Resistance: The White Response to the Civil Rights Movement*. He is currently the recipient of a major British Academy research development grant for his project *Americanism and Un-Americanism*.

Andrew Preston is professor of American history at the University of Cambridge, where he is a member of Clare College. He is a former coeditor of *The Historical Journal*, a member of the *Diplomatic History* editorial board, and serves on the executive council of the Society for Historians of American Foreign Relations. His publications include *The War Council: McGeorge Bundy, the National Security Council, and Vietnam*; *Nixon in the World: U.S. Foreign Relations, 1969–1997* (coedited with Frederik Logevall); and *Sword of the Sprit, Shield of Faith: Religion in American War and Diplomacy*, winner of the Charles Taylor Prize for Literary Non-fiction, which recognizes excellence in Canadian non-fiction writing, the British Association for American Studies book prize, and the American Politics Group's Richard E. Neustadt book prize.

Elizabeth Tandy Shermer is assistant professor of history at Loyola University Chicago and was previously postdoctoral fellow at Clare College, University of Cambridge. Her research focuses on twentieth-century American political and urban history. In addition to numerous scholarly articles and book chapters, her publications include *The Right and Labor in America: Politics, Ideology, and Imagination* (coedited with Nelson Lichtenstein); *Barry Goldwater and the Remaking of the American Political Landscape*; and *Sunbelt Capitalism: Phoenix and the Transformation of American Politics.*

David Stebenne is professor of history and law at Ohio State University. He is a member of the Maryland bar. The recipient of numerous grants and fellowships, he has wide-ranging interests in political, legal, and urban history, in which he has published numerous articles and book chapters. He has also written three books: *Arthur J. Goldberg: New Deal Liberal*; *Modern Republican: Arthur Larson and the Eisenhower Years*, winner of the Ohio Academy of History 2007 publication award and a finalist for *ForeWord* magazine's book of the year; and *New City upon a Hill: A History of Columbia, Maryland* (coauthored with Joseph R. Mitchell). He is presently writing a political and legal history of the United States from the 1930s through the 1960s.

Wendy L. Wall is associate professor of history at Binghamton University, State University of New York. Her research focuses on political culture and the construction of American identity. Her publications include *Inventing the "American Way": The Politics of Consensus from the New Deal to the Civil Rights Movement*, which was co-winner of the Organization of American Historians' 2008 Ellis Hawley Prize, winner of the Phi Alpha Theta Best First Book Award, 2008, and a CHOICE Outstanding Academic Title, 2009. She is presently engaged in two book projects: a history of the Immigration Act of 1965, and an examination of the promotion and permutations of civil religion from FDR to Ronald Reagan.

Index

www.ingramcontent.com/pod-product-compliance
Lightning Source LLC
Chambersburg PA
CBHW020829270326
41928CB00006B/473
* 9 7 8 0 8 1 3 0 6 4 4 4 4 *